MUSLIM DEMOCRATIC PARTIES
IN THE MIDDLE EAST

INDIANA SERIES IN MIDDLE EAST STUDIES
Mark Tessler, *general editor*

MUSLIM DEMOCRATIC PARTIES IN THE MIDDLE EAST
Economy and Politics of Islamist Moderation

A.Kadir Yildirim

Indiana University Press

Bloomington and Indianapolis

This book is a publication of

Indiana University Press
Office of Scholarly Publishing
Herman B Wells Library 350
1320 East 10th Street
Bloomington, Indiana 47405 USA

iupress.indiana.edu

© 2016 by A. Kadir Yildirim

All rights reserved

No part of this book may be reproduced or utilized in any form or by any means, electronic or mechanical, including photocopying and recording, or by any information storage and retrieval system, without permission in writing from the publisher. The Association of American University Presses' Resolution on Permissions constitutes the only exception to this prohibition.

The paper used in this publication meets the minimum requirements of the American National Standard for Information Sciences—Permanence of Paper for Printed Library Materials, ANSI Z39.48-1992.

Manufactured in the United States of America

Cataloging information is available from the Library of Congress.

ISBN 978-0-253-02281-3 (cloth)
ISBN 978-0-253-02309-4 (paperback)
ISBN 978-0-253-02329-2 (ebook)

1 2 3 4 5 21 20 19 18 17 16

Contents

Acknowledgments … *vii*
Abbreviations … *ix*

Introduction: Muslim Democratic Parties … *1*

1 A Social Theory of Muslim Democratic Parties … *20*

2 Modeling Economic Liberalization in a Comparative Perspective … *41*

3 From the Periphery to the Center: Competitive Liberalization in Turkey … *73*

4 Stuck in the Periphery: Crony Liberalization in Egypt … *128*

5 Pathways from the Periphery: Competitive Liberalization in Morocco … *183*

Conclusion … *230*

Appendix: List of Interviews … *235*
Notes … *239*
Bibliography … *257*
Index … *275*

Acknowledgments

THIS BOOK IS the product of many years of study and research, including my study at the Ohio State University. It could not have been possible without the support and guidance of many individuals. During the six years I spent at Ohio State, Sarah Brooks, Marcus Kurtz, Irfan Nooruddin, and Amaney Jamal were all excellent mentors. Sarah, my advisor throughout my time at Ohio State, thoroughly engaged with my project during the many days she spent reviewing my work at different stages of the project. Her constructive criticism and guidance have been vital. Sarah continually probed the causal mechanisms and the methodology, and hence was most helpful with her feedback. Most importantly, however, Sarah showed an unwavering support for me and the project throughout the entire process, thereby setting a great example on how to be an advisor. Marcus always challenged me with questions to probe further into my thinking in order to make deeper connections between various parts of the project. He also underscored the importance of a comparative perspective in analyzing the politics of economic liberalization. Marcus's push for a comparative approach led my work to be a contribution to the broader political science literature instead of being only an area study. Irfan emphasized the "big picture" and has consistently pointed out the potential implications of distinct elements of the theory. By questioning my assumptions, he pushed me to be more clear, concise, and explicit about my theory. Last but not least, Amaney Jamal of Princeton University was a great resource for improving the substantive elements of the project as well as ensuring that the framework was commensurate with the scope of the research. If this project is a contribution to social scientific research, it is due to the privilege I enjoyed in working with my advisors. All of them are inspirational examples of truly great scholars. Sarah, Amaney, Marcus, and Irfan deserve all credit and praise for overseeing the materialization of this book.

I am also indebted to many friends and colleagues who have contributed to the development of this project at different stages by reading, offering feedback, and/or engaging in stimulating intellectual conversations. I am grateful to Azzedine Azzimani, Quintin Beazer, Eva Bellin, Nathan Brown, Soundarya Chidambaram, Dino Christenson, Vefa Erginbas, Andrea Haupt, Douglas Jones, Ramazan Kilinc, Ahmet Kuru, Marie Lawrence, Jennifer Nowlin, Jennifer Regan, Yusuf Sarfati, Emily Secen, and Sarah W. Sokhey.

Many individuals in Egypt, Morocco, and Turkey were helpful in my field research. In Egypt, I received help from Durmus Dogan, Osama Farid, Ebtisam

Hussein, Cumali Onal, and Amal Wahab in establishing contacts; I also enjoyed our conversations on Egyptian political and social life. In Morocco, several individuals facilitated my fieldwork and put me in contact with officials and business owners. For this, I thank Azzedine Azzimani, Driss Bouanou, and Orhan Coskun for their help. The fieldwork in Turkey was efficient and effective due to MUSIAD officials in various cities who were kind enough to schedule appointments with their members. I also thank the following individuals who made it possible for me to conduct interviews with politicians and business owners: Kemal Baskaya, Ekrem Gurel, and Serif Soydan.

The financial support I received from various institutions made the fieldwork and writing of this book feasible. I thank the Department of Political Science at the Ohio State University for its support during my study there. The department also offered research grants for fieldwork. The Graduate School, the Mershon Center, and the Office of International Affairs at Ohio State supported the project with various grants for fieldwork. I also acknowledge the Foreign Language Enhancement Program (FLEP) Fellowship for providing me with a chance to improve my Arabic. I thank the Baker Institute for Public Policy at Rice University and its director Ambassador Edward Djerejian for their support in completing this book.

I also want to acknowledge Indiana University Press's editorial team for their help throughout the review and publication phases of this book, making it a very smooth and easy process. Mark Tessler, Rebecca Tolen, Dee Mortensen, Sarah Jacobi, Mollie Ables, and John Rogers have been tremendously helpful and knowledgeable. The feedback from two anonymous reviewers was quite instrumental in revising the manuscript; I am most grateful for their critical readings of the argument and the evidence.

Last but not least, I am grateful to members of my family. My wife, Hatice, showed wholehearted support through the completion of this project, at times of ebb and flow. Without her support, I could not be successful. Our children, Emine Beyza, Mirza Enes, and Tarik Emre, put up with a father who had seemingly endless studying to do. Many other individuals in everyday life, including brief acquaintances, have showed their support for this project, and I thank them all for their support. Any mistakes are due to me.

Abbreviations

EC	European Community
EU	European Union
FDI	foreign direct investment
FTA	free trade agreement
ISI	Import Substitution Industrialization
MDP	Muslim democratic party
SME	small and medium enterprise
SOE	state-owned enterprise

Egypt

EBA	Egyptian Businessmen's Association
ERSAP	Economic Reform and Structural Adjustment Program
LE	Egyptian pound
MB	Muslim Brotherhood
NDP	National Democratic Party
WP	Wasat Party

Morocco

AMITH	Textile and Apparel Manufacturers' Association
AWI	Al-Adl wal-Ihsan
CGEM	Moroccan Confederation of Businesses
CMPE	Moroccan Export Promotion Center
MPDC	Mouvement Populaire Démocratique et Constitutionnel
MUR	Movement of Unity and Reform
ONA	Omnium Nord Africain
PJD	Party for Justice and Development

Turkey

AKP	Justice and Development Party
CHP	Republican People's Party
DP	Democrat Party
DTP	Demokratik Toplum Partisi
FP	Felicity Party
MNP	National Order Party

MSP	National Salvation Party
MUSIAD	Independent Industrialists and Businessmen's Association
NOM	National Outlook Movement
TOBB	Union of Chambers and Commodity Exchanges of Turkey
TUSIAD	Turkish Industrialists and Businessmen's Association
VP	Virtue Party
WP	Welfare Party

MUSLIM DEMOCRATIC PARTIES
IN THE MIDDLE EAST

Introduction
Muslim Democratic Parties

IN THE WAKE of the Arab Spring, few questions seem as pertinent as the role of Islamist parties in the Middle East, in light of looming possibilities for democracy. Sharing in a desire to Islamize state and society, Islamist parties were once marked by a monolithic antidemocratic stance and a collective desire to oppose existing regimes. As of late, however, they are facing a formidable challenge from a different quarter, with the emergence of a qualitatively different and more moderate Islamic political party. These parties, generally known as Muslim democratic parties (MDPs), have materialized in several countries across the region. Turkey's Justice and Development Party (AKP), Morocco's Party for Justice and Development (PJD) and Egypt's Wasat Party (WP) all serve as clear examples of this phenomenon.

Analogous in many ways to Christian democratic parties in Europe (Kalyvas 1996; Altinordu 2010), MDPs adhere to a secular political regime, have a normative commitment to the rules of a democratic political system, and desire the democratic political representation of a religious identity (Stacher 2002; Wickham 2004; Nasr 2005; Heper 2009; Wegner and Pellicer 2009; Yavuz 2009; Gümüşçü 2010; Yildirim 2015b). Although Islamist parties have existed in the Middle East for some time, MDPs have only emerged recently in a select few countries and are viable competitors for political power in fewer still. As an example, since its inception in 1995, the Egyptian WP has yet to obtain a sizeable following, remaining largely marginal under the shadow of the robust and popular Muslim Brotherhood (Ikhwan Al-Muslimin). Nevertheless, it should be noted that MDPs do not uniformly experience poor performance. In Turkey, the AKP has managed to win successive landslide electoral victories since 2002 against both secular and Islamist parties. These contrasting trends raise two interrelated questions: What explains the emergence of MDPs recently, and why have these parties been successful in some cases but not in others?

The case of Islamist parties, that is, whether they moderate and how successful they become in this moderation, presents itself as an important issue for both theoretical and empirical reasons. As the dust of the Arab Spring settles in most countries of the region, the role of Islamist parties in this transitional and post-transitional period asserts itself as potentially the most critical issue to tackle en route to democracy. The issue is a monumental one. On one hand, Islamist parties have emerged as the best-organized and most popular political group following revolutions in several Arab countries. Such strong showing reinforces suspicions about Islamists' strength before the Arab Spring. On the other hand, Islamist ideology is regarded as being inimical to any hopes of democracy sprouting. This sentiment is perhaps best illustrated by the phrase "one man, one vote, one time," a phrase coined by American diplomat Edward Djerejian to represent the seeming threat that political Islam poses to democracy. As opposition demonstrations against the Mubarak regime brewed in Egypt in 2010, an early source of concern was the role to be assumed by the Muslim Brotherhood in the post-transition government as the bastion of conservative Islamist ideology in the Middle East and beyond (El Sherif 2011; Brown 2012a; Farag 2012; Al-Awadi 2013; Pioppi 2013; Roy 2012). The slow and inconsistent support for the opposition demonstrations attests to the hesitancy of the American and European governments to a regime change in favor of an Islamist government (Phillips 2012; Keiswetter 2012; Byman 2013; Metawe 2013). Regardless of whether Islamists would indeed undermine the democratic process, the perception by secular groups that it will implies that deep divisions and conflict are brewing, with possible ramifications over the course of democracy in these countries. Thus a moderate Islamic party might alter the dynamics of this conflict by alleviating some of the concerns of secularists.

Theoretically, the success of such moderate parties, that is, MDPs, reveals much information about the social origins of democratization in the Muslim world. The growing success of such parties in countries like Turkey, Morocco, and Tunisia bears witness to potential channels of increasing democratization in Muslim-majority countries, especially in light of concerns with Islamist parties' popularity. The rise of a viable democratic regime hinges on a strong social commitment, which is conditional on the support of conservative constituency in such countries. Likewise, an examination of the path of Islamist moderation will tell us plenty about an analogy to Christian democratic parties of Europe and elsewhere.

The analysis of MDPs also carries implications for related issues. First and foremost, the analysis I present provides a socioeconomic basis for answering questions about the compatibility of Islam and democracy, and it offers an explanation that relies on something other than cultural generalities: I emphasize the political-economic dynamics. This empirically testable model for the Islam-democracy relationship contrasts with the conventional essentialist arguments (Lewis 2002; Huntington 1993), and moreover suggests that the democratic political incorporation of religion in the Muslim world may share important similarities with the incorporation of confessional politics in early twentieth-century Europe.

Second, when considering the future state of political and economic development in the Middle East, it is of great importance to understand the dynamics of economic liberalization in the region. Whether Islamist parties or MDPS become the choice of the Islamic constituency is, essentially, a choice between ideological rigidity and pragmatism. This competition over the parameters of an Islamic doctrine can potentially result in higher levels of both democracy and prosperity. Hence it is crucial to probe the mechanisms that allow for pragmatism and moderation to transpire.

Finally, MDPS may play a vital role in curbing the influence of antisystem Islamist parties in Muslim-majority countries, and in so doing, may stabilize democratic politics. Indeed, by addressing the legitimate economic and social demands of the Muslim electorate, MDPS may deal a serious blow to the hegemony of Islamist parties. Such a transformation in the political sphere could potentially reduce polarization and strengthen democracy in the Middle East.

I approach the question of how and when MDPS arise from a socioeconomic perspective, theorizing that changes in the preferences and strength of key constituents of Islamist parties, such as small and medium enterprise (SME) owners, underpin the emergence and success of MDPS as a viable political force. The political aspect of economic liberalization constitutes the key component of my theory. Specifically, I demonstrate that preexisting social cleavages interact with the liberalization process to create a cross-class coalition in support of MDPS in some countries, but not others. To this end, I distinguish two types of economic liberalization: *competitive liberalization* and *crony liberalization*. The rise of MDPS (i.e., moderate Islamist politics) enters the realm of possibility when the implementation of economic liberalization brings the statist and authoritarian status quo ante to an end; the latter is a situation where the Islamic constituency (or peripheral socioeconomic groups composed of small businesses [SMES] and masses) were excluded from meaningful participation in political and economic power, a common occurrence throughout the Middle East in the post–World War I era.

In particular, I argue that the way in which a country liberalizes its economy shapes the social foundations of Islamic party politics. MDPS emerge and find societal support when small businesses are afforded the opportunity to compete economically—a feature of *competitive liberalization*—and when masses experience an improved income. In contrast, when economic liberalization's reach remains limited due to both its uncompetitive character and the perpetuation of a preliberalization economic structure, societal support for the moderate policies of MDPS fails to materialize, leaving Islamist parties' societal support base intact. I call this process *crony liberalization*. Although it is often said that economic liberalization will "moderate" conservative Islamist parties (Nasr 2005, 2009), little is known about the mechanisms through which this moderation is achieved or when such outcomes are likely. Indeed, the evidence is clear that economic liberalization can also drive polarization, as is observed in many cases of such liberalizations in the developing world.

Identifying the actors, preferences, and political contexts in which this moderation effect of economic liberalization is likely to materialize will address a significant gap in the scholarly literature on democratization in the Middle East and in the broader Muslim world. Specifically, this book offers one of the first systematic analyses of the development of political party systems in the Middle East by integrating social cleavages and the economic liberalization process into such an understanding.

Muslim Democracy

What sets MDPs apart from Islamist parties? In other words, what makes MDPs more moderate than conventional Islamist parties? The notion of Muslim democracy is recent, and a clear and concise definition of it has yet to be established.[1] Vali Nasr's attempt, based on the method used by MDPs and not their policy platforms, appears to be the most lucid definition thus far. Specifically, Nasr emphasizes the "democratic" aspect of this concept. Muslim democrats, for Nasr, commit to the democratic regime and will not defect to an Islamic state once they obtain power through democratic means. For Nasr, policy platforms of such parties do not carry much weight because they are pragmatic, and each party will emphasize issues salient in their own society at that point in time (Nasr 2005). Even though Nasr's definition emphasizes a critical aspect of MDPs, that is, their methodical adherence to democracy, it overlooks the relevance of the "Muslim" part, which implies a "Muslim" political platform. Following Kalyvas's definition of Christian Democratic parties, I argue that MDPs do stand for a distinct policy platform and that they are not as malleable with respect to the policy component of their ideology as Nasr claims. Three policy areas in particular stand out in party platforms, reflecting the policy preferences of their key constituencies: Islam, a liberal economy, and social policies. Table I.1 classifies MDPs vis-à-vis other Islamist groups for a concise typology of Islam in politics.

MDPs harness Islam most significantly for the "Muslim" content of their platforms. They promote conservative moral values, consistent with their emphasis on Islam as the main source of society's value structure. The focus on conservative social values goes hand-in-hand with their adherence to universal human rights and individual liberties. Without the latter emphasis, MDPs could not meaningfully distinguish themselves from conventional Islamist discourse. The use of "Muslim" instead of "Islam" in categorizing such parties is a clear indication of the absence of a claim to represent Islam as such, which political Islam typically does. Crucially, this social conceptualization of Islam, rather than a political one, caters to the changing preferences of SME owners (Dagi 2006).

A liberal market economy with a regulatory role for the state marks the basic economic framework embraced by MDPs. Because the support they enjoy from

Table I.1 Typology of Islamic Groups and Parties

	Radical/Revolutionary	Reformist	Liberal/Moderate
Islam Goal	Political Islam Islamization of State and Society	Political Islam Islamization of State and Society	Social Islam Promotion of Muslim Values
Violence	Permissible	Nonviolent	Nonviolent
Democracy	Opponent	Instrumental	Committed
Economy	No Significant Position	Nationalist and Protectionist	Pro–Liberal Economy
EXAMPLE	Al-Gama'a Al-Islamiyya	Muslim Brotherhood	Party for Justice and Development
	Islamist Ideology		**Muslim Democrat**

their key constituents, and thus indeed their very existence, depends on this liberal conception of the economy, they endorse a free market economy with limited state intervention.[2]

Lastly, MDPs opt for higher levels of spending on social policies such as health care, education, and social protection, which accompany their emphasis on an open economy. In this way, they would be very similar to Social Democratic parties. MDPs' emphasis on social safety nets, despite their liberal economic stance, stems from two sources. First, a Muslim democratic platform addresses a cross-class coalition resting on both lower socioeconomic classes and peripheral businesses (SMEs). The emphasis on social safety nets provides an effective mechanism for MDPs to reconcile a potential conflict between the interests of these two key constituents. While liberal economic policies ensure the chance for small and medium businesses to compete in a free market, generous social policies address the potential discontentment with such liberal policies on the part of lower-income citizens and compensate for such market-induced dislocations. Second, pro-poor policies have always figured greatly among Islamic parties; as such, MDPs' emphasis falls in line with this history (Clark 2004a; Zubaida 2000). Essentially, running on an Islamic platform commits these parties to social policies that benefit the impoverished. This focus on social protection and redistribution is distinct from pursuing a strictly liberal economy. However, the former does not impede the latter. In this sense, MDPs' position on the economy and social policy is very similar to that of Christian democracy.[3]

Table I.1 offers a brief summary of a Muslim democratic platform contrasted with political Islam. A Muslim democratic discourse differs from an Islamist ideology, essentially, on four key grounds. Muslim democracy does not advocate for the Islamization of state or society—a key element of Islamist discourse (Hallaq 2012). Instead, Muslim democrats adhere to a social understanding of Islam simply because they desire to nurture Muslim values in society, which is distinct from an effort to impose Islam on others. Concerning democracy, Muslim democracy adheres both to procedural elements of democracy, that is, elections and alternation of power, and to democratic principles such as the protection of minority rights and individual liberties, unlike Islamists who are more reserved on this issue. Muslim democrats also endorse a liberal economic discourse, advocating integration into the global economy; political Islam, conversely, is usually characterized by nationalist and state-centered economic discourse. In regard to violence, Muslim democracy differs only from the radical fringe of Islamism—the only form of Islamism that condones violence. Muslim democracy, like reformist Islamists (the Muslim Brotherhood of Egypt, for example, until 2015) does not, by any means, endorse the use of violence.[4]

Before I proceed, let me clarify a distinction in terminology. In this book, I use the notion of "Islamic party" to refer to both Muslim democratic and Islamist parties as an encompassing term. The use of this term is akin to the idea of "religiously oriented party" as introduced by Ozzano, irrespective of the distinct category into which each party falls under Ozzano's typology. Ozzano defines "religiously oriented parties" as "political parties focusing significant sections of their manifestos on 'religious values,' explicitly appealing to religious constituencies, and/or including significant religious factions" (2013, 810). In Ozzano's typology, MDPs largely fall under the "conservative" category, whereas Islamist parties fit under the "fundamentalist" type.

Explaining the Rise of Muslim Democratic Parties

MDPs have arisen fairly recently; thus the literature discussing these parties is overwhelmingly thin, limited largely to isolated case studies of the Justice and Development Party in Turkey (Yavuz, 2006; Özbudun 2006; Cizre 2009), the WP in Egypt (Wickham 2004; Stacher 2002), or the Party of Justice and Development in Morocco (Willis 2004; Wegner and Pellicer 2009; Wegner 2011). As valuable as such single case studies are, this narrow focus constrains our ability to draw inferences and theorize about these parties' origins and support bases.[5] The broader scholarly literature on Islamist parties offers a number of explanations about the moderation of Islamist parties and ideologies, although little discussion about the success of moderation exists (Karakaya and Yildirim 2013).

State strategy stands out as one of the most common explanations for why Islamist parties moderate. Specifically, the inclusion-moderation hypothesis suggests that state policies that are accommodating and inclusive are more likely to resonate among Islamists, moving them toward a more moderate discourse. Conversely, repressive and exclusionary policies tend to lead to increased radicalism on the part of Islamists (Chhibber 1996; R. Brooks 2002; Schwedler 2006, 2011; Wickham 2004). This reasoning is analogous to the integration of European socialist and communist parties into democratic politics in the early twentieth century and post–World War II period (Herzog 2006; Berman 2008). Others maintain, however, that state strategy—that is, repression—drives Islamist moderation (Willis 2004; Somer 2007; Cizre 2009; Cavatorta and Merone 2013), although recent indications of the Muslim Brotherhood's inclination toward violent retribution undermine this theory (Brown and Dunne 2015; Fahmi 2015). Carrie Wickham applies the inclusion-moderation argument, along with other factors, to the emergence of the Muslim democratic WP in Egypt (2004). Jillian Schwedler presents a variant of the inclusion-moderation hypothesis in her analysis of the Islamist parties in Jordan and Yemen (2006). While such studies have tremendously advanced our understanding of Islamist politics, they fail to account for the reasons why Islamist groups moderate when political institutions remain unchanged. In other words, state strategies do not correspond to Islamist parties' ideological moderation in many cases; in others, state strategies result in contradictory outcomes. A case in point is the emergence and eventual success of the Justice and Development Party in Turkey in the face of increased exclusion in the post-1997 period, not inclusion.

The Turkish experience runs contrary to the inclusion-moderation hypothesis in another way as well. The Islamist party—the Welfare Party (1983–98)—faced severe constraints on participation in the democratic regime and experienced several bans over the course of a decade, effectively excluding them from the system. Nonetheless, in the political discourse of the party, stability rather than radicalization was observed during this time period. Likewise, in the face of state repression and persecution that was, at times, even severe, the political discourse of the Egyptian Muslim Brotherhood remained unchanged over the last several decades, never displaying signs of radicalization. As a result, the WP's break from the Muslim Brotherhood seems unrelated to strategies pursued by the state.

Most recently, Shadi Hamid (2014) offers a compelling critique of both the inclusion-moderation and exclusion-moderation arguments. Hamid maintains that while many Islamist actors went through a phase of moderation, many of these actors swerved back to their original conservative positions as political structures opened up to include them in the system. What is notable in Hamid's analysis is that the entire process rests on the existence of a conservative society, which allows Islamists to pursue their goal of Islamization of the state and society to fulfill the demands of the "popular will." Put differently, the conservatism in Islamist discourse is merely a reflection of the society's preferences, an observation I found to be true in my own fieldwork for this book, a tactical moderation rather than an ideological one (Karakaya and Yildirim 2013). Likewise, in their analysis of Tunisian Ennahda, Cavatorta and Merone (2013) find that "the strong rejection the party faced in large sectors of Tunisian society" was a key factor in facilitating the party's eventual moderation.

The social learning argument takes the interaction of Islamist leaders with people from "other" beliefs and ideologies as the key explanatory factor. As the level of interaction increases, prompting Islamist leaders to take more responsibility and serve "others," Islamist leaders become more likely to be accommodative and tolerant of others and eventually moderate (Cavatorta 2006; Wickham 2004). As Wickham explains, the leadership of the WP in Egypt became responsible for serving members of professional associations during the 1990s with no regard for their ideological commitment. The middle-aged leadership of the Muslim Brotherhood during this period ultimately realized that political engagement required acceptance of the give-and-take nature of politics, the centrality of compromise. To this end, moderation on a number of policy positions was inevitable. Unable to uncover an environment for such a change within the Brotherhood, several individuals established the WP. The leadership of the WP consisted of (prior to their departure from the party) high-ranking officials from the Muslim Brotherhood, the dominant opposition political group in Egypt. And according to Wickham's account, they experienced social learning during their service in the professional associations in Egypt, which served as the major political outlets in the absence of democratic politics. The new and moderate WP's establishment, however, did not resonate with the society; the Muslim Brotherhood still retained its popular support. The social learning argument falls short in one key aspect. While leaders of Islamist groups certainly play a role in the moderation process, the Islamic constituency is entirely absent. Even if Islamist leaders moderate as a result of social learning, how do they convey the message of moderation to their societal base and make sure their constituents also embrace these shifts?

The middle-class explanation is the closest one to a social account of Islamist moderation. Typically, the analogue to this hypothesis is Barrington Moore's seminal work on the origins of democracy in the Western world (Moore 1966). The emphasis on the middle class as a social actor correlates with the moderation and democratic disposition of the country in general (Lipset 1994; Salame 1994; Gülalp 2001; Langohr 2002; Gümüşçü 2005; Nasr 2005; Demiralp 2009; Sokhey and Yildirim 2012). The assumption that the middle class has, homogenously, the same interests and influence is a major shortcoming of this explanation.

The middle class can largely be divided into two groups, the first of which consists of professionals such as lawyers, teachers, academicians, and doctors. By its very nature, this group is not "anchored" in the capitalist relations of production; hence it does not have an intrinsic interest in a liberal system. The expansion of the middle class has, at best, a tangential relationship with moderation, in respect to this first group, because this group has only an ideological affinity to moderation, democracy, and liberalization, not a vested interest in these concepts (Gülalp 2001; Langohr 2002). In other words, this group respects moderation, democracy, and liberalization simply because it views them as beneficial to the greater welfare of the society, not because it is in the group's self-interest to support such values. The second group comprises small and medium-sized business owners, individuals who potentially have a more personal relationship to a liberal order. Economic liberalization, political stability, and moderate political discourse relate closely to the business owners' political preferences. Contrasted with the first group, this second group does have a vested interest in these issues. The connection of the middle class to the global economy is the critical criterion with which to evaluate the impact of the middle class on moderation. The absence of a clear distinction between professionals and business owners will lead to an underspecified model of if, why, and how moderation will follow the middle class's lead. As important as the middle class explanation may be, it falls short of disentangling heterogeneous components of the middle class, particularly by failing to explain how or why distinct elements of the middle class relate to moderation and to a more democratic platform.

An alternative and more convincing explanation for the moderation of Islamist parties points to economic liberalization (Zakaria 2004; Ateş 2005). According to Zakaria, economic liberalization should take priority in reform efforts in the Middle East due to its potential to create a business group with "a stake in openness, in rules, and in stability" (Zakaria 2004, 16). This new socioeconomic group has a vested interest in a liberal economic system due to its integration into the global economy. In a certain way, global integration will provide reformers with an anchor to ensure that no reversion occurs in liberalization. Although this line of reasoning is plausible in its general contours, I find it underspecified in two interrelated respects, both of which deal with the character of the new business groups. First, the size and strength of the new business groups are critical to the success of the liberal model. They define the relationship or conflict between the new groups and the existing privileged business elite, usually under the tutelage of the state in a sheltered economy. Second, the liberalization model is silent on the role of the Islamic constituency in this process of moderation, although it is the largest social group in the region. The role of the Islamic constituency is critical to defining the shape of the social conflict between the old and the new business groups. This study will build on the liberalization thesis by offering a causal mechanism to explain this link and by analyzing it empirically.

To a lesser extent, there is an emerging literature on how Islamists perform in elections. Garcia-Rivero and Kotzé (2007), for example, find that a certain kind of constituency (religious and antidemocratic) lends more electoral support for

Islamic parties in the Middle East, reinforcing the idea that there is a distinct Islamic constituency. Complementing this finding, Gidengil and Karakoc (2014) find that in addition to religiosity, AKP's performance in social service provision, the economy, and democracy were critical factors to bolster the party's successive electoral success. In a different approach, Kurzman and Naqvi (2010) analyze electoral data in the Muslim world and find that Islamic parties, unlike the common expectation, do not perform particularly well in free and fair elections, while Wegner (2011) finds that PJD's relationship with a "powerful social movement" underlies its electoral success.

I propose an alternative social theory to explain the rise and empowerment of MDPs in the Middle East. My point of departure is that Islamic political parties, as in any other modern political system, strive to reflect the preferences and interests of the constituency they aspire to represent. I argue that changes in the socioeconomic structure enable MDPs to emerge and challenge the dominance of conservative Islamist parties. The distinction I make between two types of economic liberalization becomes crucial at this point, which rests on the levels of integration into the global economy and of domestic competition and business concentration. *Competitive economic liberalization* facilitates the integration of peripheral groups into the global economy, which in turn leads to the transformation of their political and economic preferences. MDPs, in this context, benefit from the change in the political preferences of the peripheral groups, where Islamist parties' platforms become untenable in the face of changing economic and social structure. By contrast, the process of *crony liberalization* perpetuates the more archaic forms of state-business relations that reinforce the preliberalization social structure, leaving the peripheral groups at the margins of political and economic power. Hence we do not observe changes in the political preferences of the periphery in the crony liberalization context that would facilitate the rise of MDPs. Islamist parties under these circumstances are better able to address the interests of peripheral groups and thus remain strong. Even if MDPs do emerge in a crony liberalization context, they face considerable obstacles in establishing themselves as a strong challenger to Islamist parties. The model I propose to explain this dynamic thus places its central focus on the distribution of socioeconomic power in Muslim-majority societies and its reflection in the political space.

A key question here is the following: why did MDPs suddenly develop a commitment to democracy and a liberal economy? I answer this question in greater detail in chapter 1 where I offer a historical overview of the dynamics of such a transformation. Briefly stated, MDPs merely represent the shift in the preferences of peripheral, that is, Islamic, constituencies. A competitively liberal economy enables peripheral constituencies to materially benefit from the new open economy while simultaneously embracing democracy as a mechanism to ensure continued political stability and to avoid radical, antisystem discourses, thereby reducing economic risks. In other words, this transformation is a purely interest-driven process. By contrast, when the economic conditions fail to improve for peripheral constituencies, such groups do not have an incentive to embrace more open political and economic structures.

With this analysis, my goal is not to merely compare levels of electoral support of Islamist and MDPs. This would depend not only on core constituencies of such parties but also on contextual factors that directly influence electoral outcomes. That is beyond the scope of the analysis presented here. Rather, the goal is to gauge *relative* societal support for MDPs and Islamist parties among the peripheral groups that constitute the core support base for Islamic parties and to evaluate the extent of the social change as a result of liberalization. Accordingly, I bring evidence to evaluate my theory by examining the relative electoral support levels for Islamist and MDPs, rather than absolute levels only. Because both types of parties speak to the same social groups, their relative strength should inform us of how the social base reacts to the distinct platforms of the two parties as direct competitors in the electoral market. To this end, I compare electoral support for Islamist and MDPs in recent legislative elections.

Research Methodology

I test my theory in a three-country, longitudinal, and structured comparison of Egypt, Morocco, and Turkey. These countries were selected in order to maximize the variation I observe on my key causal variables while holding other factors constant, such as structure of social cleavages, level of economic development at the time of initial economic liberalization reforms, and economic ideology prior to liberalization. Despite some limitations (Geddes 1990; King, Keohane, and Verba 1994), one distinct advantage of the most similar systems design (Przeworski and Teune 1970; Lijphart 1975) is that it allows me to eliminate "irrelevant systemic factors" and focus at the subsystem level (Anckar 2008; Gisselquist 2014). In Egypt, I analyze the Muslim Brotherhood (Ikhwan al-Muslimin) and the WP (Hizb al-Wasat) as cases of Islamist and MDPs, respectively. In Morocco, the Party for Justice and Development (Hizb al-Adalah wa Tanmiyya) represents the Muslim democratic platform, whereas Justice and Charity (Al-Adl wal-Ihsan) is the main Islamist opposition. Finally, in Turkey, the Justice and Development Party (Adalet ve Kalkinma Partisi) is the Muslim democratic case, which I compare with the Islamist Felicity Party (Saadet Partisi). On a broader level, the selection of these three countries ensures that similar social cleavages exist in all cases. From a historical perspective, all three countries underwent a similar process of secular-religious social conflict *and* the growth of a big business class nurtured by the state in contradiction to an impoverished rest of the society. A similar structure of social cleavages is critical to testing whether

Table I.2 Country Scores on Key Variables

	Democracy	Economic Liberalization	Islamist Party	Muslim Democratic Party
Egypt	limited liberalization	crony	strong	weak
Morocco	limited liberalization	semicompetitive	medium	medium
Turkey	democracy	competitive	weak	strong

economic liberalization has a (dis)similar impact on Islamic constituency and Islamist parties.

In terms of the main variable of interest, that is, economic liberalization, the three cases represent different categories along the continuum of competitive and crony liberalization (Table I.2). Turkey represents the competitive liberalization model, whereas Egypt is a case of a highly politicized economy that is emblematic of crony liberalization. Morocco, a semicompetitive economy, represents a middle case with features from both competitive and crony models of liberalization.

With regard to the outcome of interest, the three cases also offer wide variation in the popular support that each MDP enjoys. The Turkish and Moroccan MDPs, the Justice and Development Party and the Party for Justice and Development, enjoy greater societal support compared with their Islamist counterparts, the Felicity Party and Al-Adl Wal-Ihsan. In contrast, the Egyptian MDP, the WP, remains largely marginal relative to the Islamist Muslim Brotherhood. Despite the similarities in key factors, one critical variable remains to be accounted for, namely, the level of democratic governance. Although Egypt and Turkey offer variation in both their dependent and independent variables and allow me to establish a causal relationship, the contrast between Turkey and Egypt in terms of popular support for MDPs may be said to result from the difference in the degree of their democratic governance. In other words, perhaps the fact that Egypt lacks a democratic form of governance at the country level explains the diverging paths of Islamic parties in Turkey and Egypt.

This question can be addressed with the help of a third case that features a similar level of democratic governance to Egypt or Turkey but differs in terms of the outcome of interest (electoral success of Muslim democracy). The Moroccan case provides just that. Because Morocco and Egypt have similar levels of political openness but varying levels of support for MDPs, Morocco provides an ideal case in which to assess the impact of the level of democratic governance as an alternative causal factor. The Moroccan case, therefore, will be instrumental in testing the impact of democracy on the rise of MDPs. Egypt and Morocco are similar in terms of how they are scored by different quantitative indices of democratization. For example, Freedom House scores Egypt 8 out of 40 while Morocco is rated 15 out of 40 points in terms of political rights in 2015. Likewise, the Polity IV dataset assigns Egypt scores between (−2) and (−6), while Morocco's score ranges between (−4) and (−8) in the post-1980 period.[6] One could point out the different natures of the authoritarian regimes that are in place in Egypt (dictatorship) and Morocco (monarchy). While the differences in the nature of nondemocratic governance must be acknowledged (Lust-Okar 2004), such differences in authoritarianism cannot explain the dissimilar trajectories of Islamist moderation and the level of Islamist parties' electoral success. While the differences in the nature of political regimes are long-standing, moderate Islamic parties have only recently emerged and therefore do not correlate with differences in regime types.

Another concern with the selection of cases might relate to whether the distinction between Islamist parties (Party for Justice and Development, Felicity Party) and Islamist movements or groups (Justice and Charity, Muslim Brotherhood) matters for the goals of the research in this book. On one hand, the distinction between an Islamist party and an Islamist group is largely an inconsequential one that merely changes the form of participation rather than the underlying dynamics of ideology and policy-making. That is, Islamist groups, unable to run as a party and to field candidates as members of that party, might decide to run as independents just as the Muslim Brotherhood did in Egypt for several elections (Table I.3). On the other hand, the distinction between an Islamist party and an Islamist group/movement might be a reflection of the ideological separation between the two (therefore in support of the argument developed in this book). Conventional Islamist movements tend to maintain institutional affiliation between the political and nonpolitical components of the movement, with the ensuing subservience of the political group (which might operate as a political party) to the nonpolitical. By contrast, moderating Islamist parties such as the MDPs establish institutional separation between the political and nonpolitical components, maintaining autonomy of the former.

The empirical analysis here is based on my field research in all three countries between August 2008 and December 2009. The fieldwork entailed more than 100 open-ended interviews with politicians, business owners, business association representatives, journalists, and experts. In Egypt, I conducted interviews with officials from the Muslim Brotherhood, the WP, and business owners. In Morocco, I interviewed officials from the Party for Justice and Development, Al-Adl wal-Ihsan, and business owners. Similarly, in Turkey I conducted interviews with politicians from the Justice and Development Party, the Felicity Party, and

Table I.3 Party Support Levels in Parliamentary Elections

	Islamist Party	MDP
Egypt	Muslim Brotherhood 20% of seats in 2005 37% of votes (46% of seats) in 2011–12	Wasat Party 3.7% of votes in 2011–12
Morocco	Justice and Charity Does not compete in formal politics Strong popular support	Party for Justice and Development 22.8% of votes in 2011 (first party) 11% of votes in 2007 (first party) 13% of votes in 2002 (third party)
Turkey	National Outlook Movement 1.2% of votes in 2011 2.5% of votes in 2007 2.5% of votes in 2002	Justice and Development Party 50% of votes in 2011 (first party) 47% of votes in 2007 (first party) 34% of votes in 2002 (first party)

business owners. As for business associations, I conducted interviews with MUSIAD (Independent Industrialists' and Businessmen's Association) in Turkey, EBA (Egyptian Businessmen's Association) in Egypt, and AMITH (Textile and Apparel Manufacturers' Association) and CGEM (Moroccan Confederation of Businesses) in Morocco. In addition to secondary sources, the book draws on various primary documents, including party publications, to determine party platforms. Among such publications are booklets, election manifestos, party programs, and position statements of the political parties and movements under analysis.

With respect to politicians, I employed the snowball sampling method. After I established initial contacts with politicians from different parties, I sought out other officials who could address questions regarding the party and its policies. In this, however, I paid particular attention in drawing a wide range of representation from the party in terms of both level of representation within the party (members of parliament, party administration, and local offices) and the personal backgrounds of party members (region, ideological orientation, and gender).

As for business owners, in different countries, the sampling was constrained by various factors. In Turkey, my goal was to conduct interviews with members of MUSIAD, the business association representing small and medium businesses in Turkey. Therefore I established contacts with local offices of MUSIAD in order to meet with their membership at the local level in various cities. In Egypt, the issue of meeting with business owners was more intricate. In the first place, there are no business associations representing small and medium businesses in Egypt, which is the main focus in this project. Second, the level of sensitivity in discussing political issues is substantially high among business owners, especially so among those of smaller businesses. Given these constraints, I was nonetheless able to meet with small business owners through the contacts I established in the field. In addition, I conducted interviews with big business owners from the EBA on the assumption that the differences in the preferences of small and big business in Egypt should provide evidence on the benefits and drawbacks of the Egyptian liberalization process. If, indeed, crony liberalization favors a certain group of business owners over the rest, interviews should make such differences evident, as losers and winners of the liberalization reforms would react to the reforms differently. In Morocco, the sample of business owners was randomly selected from both AMITH and CGEM on one condition: contacts were established with only those businesses that could be considered SMEs.

Organization

Chapter 1 develops the social theory of the rise of MDPs by first analyzing social cleavages in the Middle East. Through analysis of the preliberalization status quo, I identify the preferences of peripheral Islamic groups that readily follow from the exclusion of these groups from the economy and politics in this period (until the early 1980s). Liberalization reforms undertaken between the mid-1970s and the early 2000s have had a decisive impact on the role played by peripheral Islamic groups in the postliberalization structure and on their political preferences. The last part of the chapter identifies two categorical responses to impending liberalization reforms by the Islamic constituency, contingent on the kind of economic liberalization implemented. Briefly stated, I detail two hypotheses. First, if there is competitive liberalization, I expect to observe changes in the preferences of peripheral businesses—small and medium business owners—and peripheral masses, for a more democratic political system, liberal economy, and a social/moderate version of Islam. In this context MDPs are more likely to rise and prosper electorally. Alternatively, if there is crony liberalization, I expect to observe no change in the political and economic preferences of SMEs. In this case, I expect to see Islamist parties remaining the major political representative of the peripheral groups.

To make sense of highly politicized liberalization reforms and their impact on political and social processes—Islamist moderation, in this case—I offer a comparative analysis of economic liberalization models in three cases in chapter 2: Egypt, Morocco, and Turkey. Building on the typology created in chapter 1, I analyze each country's economic reform process from the 1980s onward in order to categorize them accordingly. In doing this, I first analyze various observable implications of economic liberalization processes to identify each case as competitive versus crony liberalization. I focus on two parts of liberalization: (1) integration into the global economy and (2) domestic economic liberalization. This analysis is crucial to observing the economy-wide implications of peripheral businesses' size and power, which constitutes the backbone of my theory in explaining MDPs' rise and success. The second half of the chapter presents a thorough discussion of economic liberalization processes in Egypt, Morocco, and Turkey. More specifically, I discuss the state's role in the economy, trade liberalization, financial liberalization, and privatization in each case. The analysis in chapter 2 makes it clear that Turkish economic liberalization, a case of competitive liberalization, offered greater opportunities for SMEs to integrate to the global economy, whereas the Egyptian economic liberalization, crony liberalization, prevented potential participation of SMEs in a liberalizing economy. Morocco falls in between Egypt and Morocco; therefore, I categorize it as a case of semicompetitive liberalization.

The following three chapters in the book are case studies of Turkey, Egypt, and Morocco. The primary focus of the book is explaining how the economic liberalization process has impacted the moderation or the democratization of Islamist parties and their success in some cases but not others. The time period chosen for analysis (1970s–late 2000s) thus reflects analytical concerns with the variation of the dependent and independent variables during this timeframe as part of the analytical narrative. Hence the discussions in these chapters are not meant to provide a complete historical account of political developments in the three countries. As such, a thorough discussion of the recent developments in Egypt, Morocco, and Turkey (such as the Muslim Brotherhood and the Moroccan Justice and Development Party's ascension to government and the AKP's authoritarian turn) relates indirectly to the goal of this book and is beyond its scope. Nonetheless, they are critical developments and they deserve discussion insofar as they offer critical tests of the theory presented in this book. Therefore, at the end of each chapter, I provide a brief overview of recent political developments and explain whether and how they fit within the theoretical framework I provide.

In chapter 3, I show that the deeply rooted economic liberalization process in Turkey in the aftermath of 1980, a case of competitive liberalization, led to a profound social transformation in the Turkish Islamic periphery and has redefined the course of Islamic politics. I analyze the relationship between the transformation of the Turkish periphery and the rise of the AKP as a successful MDP, and bring empirical evidence to demonstrate the relationship between the two processes. The extensive economic liberalization reforms undertaken by Turgut Özal opened up many opportunities for the peripheral small and medium enterprises in the Turkish and global economy. Such new economic opportunities enabled peripheral business owners to operate under conditions close to a liberal market economy. Therefore, politically, peripheral businessmen's political and economic preferences would undergo a major change to reflect their new material interests. Interviews with peripheral business owners show that SME owners developed a strong interest in democracy, a liberal economy, and a nonpoliticized emphasis on Islamic values as a way to ensure predictability, low polarization, and rule of law; such issues were of highest concern to this segment of business owners as they prospered as an economic and political force. Interviews with AKP officials and party publications illustrate that the AKP, as an MDP, duly emphasized Islamic values (rather than political Islam), democratic principles and individual liberties (rather than procedural democracy), and a liberal economy (rather than the nationalist and protectionist economic discourse of Islamists). In addition, the AKP underscored the extension of social protection as compensation for the losers of the liberalization process, that is, peripheral masses, to bring the rest of the periphery on board with its new economically liberal platform. The AKP's new platform seems to have captured the periphery's changing political preferences as the party won three successive parliamentary elections in 2002, 2007, and 2011, whereas the Islamist Felicity Party remained in the margins of the political space in Turkey in the aftermath of the AKP's emergence. The Turkish case shows the relationship between the transformation of peripheral political preferences and their impact on Islamist political discourse distinctly among the three cases due to the depth of economic liberalization in Turkey. Lastly, developments in recent years are analyzed through the theoretical lens of the book to conclude chapter 3.

Chapter 4 introduces a case of crony liberalization, Egypt, and examines its impact on the moderation of political Islam and the electoral failure of the Egyptian MDP, the WP. Through my analysis of the Egyptian case of crony liberalization, I demonstrate that the economic liberalization policies, in their entirety and as individual policies such as trade liberalization and privatization, pursued by successive Egyptian governments have shaped the course of Islamist politics in Egypt. Egyptian economic reforms, initially framed as *infitah* (open door) and later structural adjustment programs, served to create and reinforce a local class of big business owners with interests directly tied to their connections with the political elite. The distorted nature of economic liberalization, which I call crony liberalization, enabled this group of big business owners to maintain its privileged access to state resources, credit, and the domestic market. This outcome is largely due to the selective and politicized nature of liberalization policies implemented in Egypt, which ensured that the socioeconomic structure created in the postindependence period—that is, the economic and political division between the secular center and the Islamic periphery—remained intact in the postliberalization period. The result of such limited economic competition was to avoid the potentially destabilizing socioeconomic effects of economic liberalization on the dominant political regime. Peripheral businesses—that is, SMEs—were largely among the losers of this process along with the masses, which fostered their overwhelming dissatisfaction with liberalization as evidenced by interviews I conducted. Consequently, even though a small group from among the Islamist Muslim Brotherhood emerged and adopted a moderate Muslim democratic political platform, the WP (Hizb ul-Wasat), they were, for the most part, not successful in representing the Islamic periphery. Instead, the conservative Muslim Brotherhood continued its domination of the Islamic periphery via its Islamist discourse and strong criticism of the political and economic status quo. In the 2005 elections, the Muslim Brotherhood captured one-fifth of the seats in the Egyptian parliament with eighty-eight deputies, whereas the WP remained a marginal party "without a mass base," and the latter party's support does not exceed a couple of percentage points at best. Given the WP's current platform, which fails to address the dissatisfaction of the Muslim periphery, the possibility for the WP to rise electorally is quite limited. Overidentification with crony-style economic liberalization, as it has been implemented in Egypt, has undercut the credibility of the WP's economic program and is one of the key reasons why the party has not been able to muster support from the masses, remaining a marginal player. The parliamentary elections of 2011–12 only reinforce this inference. Chapter 4 concludes by exploring the implications of my argument for the future trajectory of Islamist moderation and the success of an MDP in the event that the Egyptian revolution of 2011 gives rise to true economic and political opening in Egypt.

Chapter 5 is the Moroccan case study. The Moroccan MDP, the Party for Justice and Development (PJD), has been moderately successful in garnering the support of the Islamic periphery vis-à-vis the Islamist al-Adl wal-Ihsan (AWI). This has been largely due to the quality of the Moroccan economic liberalization and its implications for the Muslim peripheral sectors in that country. Moroccan liberalization is far from being a competitive model as in the case of Turkey, yet with the wide array of opportunities offered to smaller businesses and new actors in the economy, it proves to be more competitive than the Egyptian case. This semicompetitive character of the Moroccan economy thus provides a suitable opportunity to observe where the losers and winners of liberalization among the peripheral groups have developed distinct political preferences. In the Turkish and Egyptian cases, the distinct elements of the periphery were unified in their loss or gain as a result of the liberalization process. By contrast, in Morocco, as a result of this clear separation between the losers and winners of the periphery, I observe distinct, and fairly equal in size, societal support bases for Islamist and MDPS. The losers in the periphery (the masses) identify with the Islamist AWI, whereas the relative winners of the periphery (peripheral business owners) have sided with the liberal discourse of the Muslim democratic PJD. The result is a divided peripheral constituency, which has weakened the PJD's electoral strength. The Moroccan case is also valuable for analytical purposes. Specifically, it provides a critical test of an alternative hypothesis, namely, that the rise of MDPs depends on the level of democratic governance in a country. Indeed, the contrast between Turkey and Egypt in terms of popular support for MDPs may be said to have resulted from their difference in degree of democratic governance. However, because Morocco and Egypt have roughly similar levels of political liberalization but varying levels of support for MDPs, Morocco provides an ideal case in which to eliminate the level of democratic governance as an alternative explanation for this observed variation in the rise of MDPs.

Chapter 6 summarizes the theoretical argument of the book and reviews the findings in each of the three empirical chapters. One of the critical implications of the research in this book pertains to the democratizing effect of moderate and democratic Islamic parties. The empirical analysis regarding the MDPs in the case studies was strictly limited to the discourse of such parties rather than their actions in the government or in the opposition. Looking ahead, the role of Islamic parties constitutes one of the most important issues in the post–Arab Spring era.

1 A Social Theory of Muslim Democratic Parties

IN THIS CHAPTER, I introduce a socioeconomic theory of Muslim democratic parties (MDPs) on which the rest of the analysis in this book will rest. The primary goal of this chapter is to identify the actors, preferences, and political contexts in which the moderation effect of economic liberalization is likely to come about as it relates to Islamist parties. I develop my socioeconomic theory of MDPs by building on social cleavages in the Middle East principally between the center—a cluster of secular groups with economic and political power at their disposal—and the periphery—the rest of the society with an Islamic identity but lacking the means to reach political and economic power. Even though social cleavages are an important factor in analyses of political parties, they are largely underutilized in Middle Eastern studies. To this end, I first identify the preliberalization interests and preferences of peripheral Islamic groups, which readily follows from the exclusion of these groups from the economy and politics. This is because Islamist discourse claims to represent the political preferences of peripheral groups.

In the second part of this chapter, I continue discussing economic liberalization as a political process and the leverage that decision makers have in shaping the course of liberalization reforms. In this, I underscore the distinctive forms that economic liberalization may take and discuss two ideal types of economic liberalization models: competitive liberalization and crony liberalization. Competitive liberalization refers to the idea that liberalization reforms offer economic opportunities to those peripheral groups who were excluded from such opportunities in the preliberalization period. Utilizing such opportunities, peripheral businesses (small and medium enterprises [SMEs]) find a chance to grow and enjoy economic benefits. In turn, peripheral businesses experience a transformation in their political preferences to reflect the new socioeconomic conditions offered by competitive economic liberalization. Crony liberalization, on the other hand, is the ideal type that enables members of the center (the political and economic elite) to continue their dominance by choosing which elements of economic liberalization to implement. Such leverage over the course of economic reforms ensures the continuation of the preliberalization political economic structure.

The last part of the chapter identifies two categorical responses to impending liberalization reforms by Islamist parties contingent on the kind of liberalization. Briefly stated, I test two sets of hypotheses. First, if there is competitive liberalization, then I expect to observe changes in the interests and preferences of SMEs toward a more democratic political system, a liberal economy, and a social role for Islam. In this context, MDPs are more likely to rise and prosper electorally due to the overlap between peripheral preferences and their discourse. Alternatively, if there is crony liberalization, then I expect to observe no change in the political and economic preferences of the periphery. In this case, I expect to see Islamist parties remaining the major political representative of the peripheral groups. Overall, MDPs depend on the strength of the competitive economic model.

Social Cleavages

Social cleavages and class conflict are a persistent element of politics in the Middle East. Without integrating social cleavages, we stand to miss a very critical dynamic of Middle Eastern and Islamist politics. Cleavages offer valuable information on sources of social conflict within a society and on the potential for the politicization of issues via political parties. Social cleavages are also important for another reason. They inform us of issues and actors within a given political context with which to analyze dynamics of change in societies that face major transformations such as globalization. The dynamic nature of society and the actors therein require careful analysis of underlying cleavages in order to trace the origins and causes of change.

For the purposes of the analysis here, a social cleavage can be defined as a division in a society between two different groups that hold opposite views on a particular issue. This division is deemed both fundamentally important to the way society is envisioned and critical for the interests of both groups. It may take the form of an identity conflict, as in the case of secularism-religion divisions, or more of an economic one, such as the conflict between business and labor.

The discussion of social cleavages here does not serve to lay out a theory of social cleavages and party structure in the Middle East. By making use of social cleavage structures, I account for the distinctive effects of economic liberalization on Islamist parties, which will be instrumental in explaining the emergence and strengthening of MDPs. Without recourse to social cleavages and socioeconomic conflicts in Middle Eastern societies, our understanding of the changes in the region would be limited at best. This is also in parallel with how democratic development in the West is usually conceived, that is, via social dynamics (Collier and Collier 1991; Deutsch 1961; Luebbert 1987; Moore 1966; Rueschemeyer, Stephens, and Stephens 1992). The parallel between the West and the Middle East in emphasizing social dynamics is critical to moving away from essentialist and culturalist perspectives, which plagued research on the politics of the Middle East for a long time (Haklai 2009).

In their pioneering study, Lipset and Rokkan (1967) present a framework to analyze how social cleavages come into existence, are politicized, and then are projected into the political arena through political parties; why certain cleavages are politicized and others are not; and which events transform the nature of cleavages once social cleavages are stabilized at some point in time. Lipset and Rokkan identify two distinct sources of cleavages, or "fundamental processes of change," to use their terminology, each producing two different social conflicts: the National Revolution and the Industrial Revolution. The National Revolution refers to the creation of nation-states, resulting in (1) a conflict between the dominant culture ("central nation-building culture") and peripheral cultures and (2) a conflict between the central government and the church. The Industrial Revolution, on the other hand, leads to (1) the conflict between industrial entrepreneurs and landed elites and (2) the conflict between owners and workers.

The edited volume by Lipset and Rokkan deals largely with the cleavages and party systems in the western hemisphere, where the origins of cleavages and their politicization take a dramatically different form than the one in the developing world. A major problem in a developing world context is the relative absence of "democratic" politics leading to questions about the viability of political parties as instruments of political representation. One way the absence of democracy might be an issue is the dominance of single-party regimes thwarting political alternatives. Also, if political parties do not necessarily serve as outlets of social conflict, how do people express their preferences, or is there social conflict at all?[1]

As important as these fundamental issues may be, social cleavages present themselves as a pivotal departure point in conceptualizing the structure of political conflict in the Middle East; cleavages are real, and they do shape political parties. So far, as an analytical tool, social cleavages have rarely been used in studies of Middle Eastern politics.[2] In the rest of this chapter, I identify issues that are politicized and processes of change leading to distinct social cleavages, and delineate which social conflicts emerge as a result. An extension of this analysis will illustrate the political representation of cleavages in the Middle Eastern context. To reiterate, the goal of this exercise is not providing a detailed account of political party structure in the region, but rather laying out the "overall makeup" of the emerging cleavages and party systems in the region, to use Herbert Kitschelt's terms, in order to obtain a better understanding of the moderation of Islamist parties (Kitschelt 1992, 14).

The history of the Middle East indicates one possible "fundamental process of change" creating social cleavages, and that is the political independence for the regional countries in the twentieth century. Independence movements prove instrumental for two principal reasons. First, the independence process helps crystallize the coalitions for the emerging nation. Independence movements bring certain issues to the forefront, politicizing them; distinct groups build their coalitions with diverging interests around these issues, leading to the crystallization of cleavages. Second, the moment of independence leads to the freezing of the political system due to the mostly authoritarian and military nature of the emerging regimes (Zielinski 2002). Overall, independence is key to defining the source, nature, and consequences of the cleavages emerging among social groups with implications for the prospective Islamist transformation.

The Ottoman Empire, the dominant political power in the region for several centuries and until modern times, shaped the social structures and state-society relations to the extent that most post-Ottoman nations demonstrate similar social structures and cleavages on which postindependence politics are built. As Özbudun underscores, the state-society relationship is the most important legacy of the shared Ottoman history for the regional countries (Özbudun 1996, 134). State autonomy, implying the state's insulation from the pressure of social groups and societal interests, marks the most commonly identified characteristic of the Middle Eastern countries. In this regard, independence movements and the accompanying crystallization of societal cleavages cannot be evaluated separately from the Ottoman legacy of state autonomy. State autonomy entails a dual structure divided between the military-bureaucratic elite along with their allies in the society and the ruled, or the subjects. The latter consisted of heterogeneous societal elements such as a rural population, small commercial interests, and various ethnic groups. In this dual structure, there were no intermediary institutions for interest representation; in other words, the society was "unincorporated" to the state. This is a reasonable assertion because there were no powerful economic interests to politically represent in the first place.[3] In Carter Findley's terms, "Ottoman reformers did not doubt the desirability of maximizing state power" and had "faith in the rightfulness of the powerful state" (Findley 1996, 159).

The resemblance among post-Ottoman countries is striking despite the temporal difference in achieving independence across cases. The Turkish experience in political and economic modernization under Ataturk's leadership throughout the 1920s and the 1930s was closely followed by Arab experiences such as Bourguiba and Nasser two decades later, as Issawi notes: "In many respects, the Arab countries and Iran followed, one generation behind, in the footsteps of Turkey. Thus the policies of the 1950s and '60s in the Arab lands recall those of Turkey in the 1920s and '30s" (Issawi 1996, 241).[4] Moreover, such resemblance between Turkey and Arab countries demonstrated striking similarity and continuity with the state-society relations in the Ottoman Empire rather than being completely new inventions: "Against the Ottoman backdrop, Ataturk's widely emulated expansion of the state's economic role was not as innovative as sometimes supposed.

Nor were the Middle East's most advanced assertions of the state's economic role, as in Nasser's Egypt, totally divorced from Ottoman antecedent. . . . The distressing clarity with which continuities emerge in the economic history of the last two centuries—once changes in the terms for certain phenomena have been noted—spotlights how difficult it will be for most of the region to achieve high levels of economic development" (Findley 1996, 172).

The road to independence in many ways was a process both unifying and divisive at the same time. Independence was politically unifying because distinct social groups downplayed their differences in background and ideology in an effort to establish a front against a common enemy, that is, the occupying forces as in the case of Turkey or colonial powers as in the cases of Egypt and Morocco. The temporary unification enabled various factions to more forcefully confront colonial powers. However, factions were also clearly separated from each other in critical ways. Most important among such differences were their vision of the character of the prospective nation-state and distribution of power and resources within this new polity. While mostly secular military leadership was taken by the socialist-leftist ideas of their time such as Nasser and Ataturk, Islam constituted one of the main alternatives constraining the ubiquitous reach of secular ideologies. Factions' fundamental difference on ideology also extends to how they view the postindependence political regime and what modernization means. Especially crucial was the secular conceptualization of the modernity for the whole state and society as opposed to an Islamic one. This proto-cleavage on the secularism-religion dimension broadly overlaps with the second dimension, which is the distribution of political-economic power and resources in the society. Though lines were less clearly articulated, still, most secular-minded groups were closer to the epicenter of political and economic power, and most Islamic groups were distant from such centers of power.

Political preferences of distinct social groups follow readily from their socioeconomic interests. Secular groups envisioned a future with an economic structure ensuring continuity in the existing system. Parties with a leftist and revolutionary propensity, emphasizing strong state control over economic activity, were a match made in heaven for seculars. The Islamic constituency, in contrast, viewed parties with an Islamic undertone, Islamist or otherwise, more in line with their political interests.

The immediate aftermath of independence in almost all regional countries saw consolidation of two overlapping proto-cleavages. In most cases, groups with a more secular mindset with direct or indirect military affiliation assumed power in the postindependence period. Their leadership during the independence movement certainly facilitated postindependence ascendance to power. Throughout this period secular groups were able to utilize their proximity to economic and political power to effectively marginalize and exclude other groups from decision-making mechanisms. The control over political power facilitated the control over economic power and helped in "creating a national bourgeoisie which would support the state" (Chaudhry 1994, 6). The social groups that associate themselves more with Islam and less with secularism are also the groups that saw themselves being excluded from obtaining real social, economic, and political power.

One of the best studies on the evolution of social cleavages in the Middle East is that of Serif Mardin (Mardin 1973). The model Mardin offers deals, in essence, with the distribution of socioeconomic power in the Turkish state and society in a historical perspective from the nineteenth century into the twenty-first century and its reflection on the political space. Throughout the modern era, sociopolitical conflict in the Ottoman Empire and the new Turkish state is shaped along the competition between two broad groups: center and periphery. Even though the conceptualization was introduced to analyze Turkish politics, I find it useful for the broader set of Muslim-majority countries in the Middle East as we observe state-society relations and social cleavages being structured along the same lines.

According to this framework, the center of the society is composed of the secular elite commanding the political system and economic power, and it portrays itself as the sole modernizing force in the country. The center, in this formulation, represents the secular elite dominating political and economic centers of power. In a stylized reading of pre-reform political economy, the center is composed of various social elements such as the political elite, bureaucracy, military, big business, and urban middle and upper classes. Secularism stands out as the identifying characteristic of the center, and members of the center make up the relative minority in the society.

The periphery, by contrast, is not a homogenous bloc. Peripheral groups, by contrast, are identified by their marginalization and exclusion from political and economic power. Islam, regardless of cultural, ethnic, or socioeconomic status, defines the contours of the "peripheral" identity. The periphery is left out of the political decision-making mechanism and the economic suzerainty of the state and is on the recipient end of the modernization project, living mostly in the suburbs of major cities and rural areas.[5] Small and medium enterprise (SME) owners, who survive outside the network of state protection and promotion, constitute an important element of the periphery. The conflict between the center and the periphery, in this regard, revolves around two cleavages: secularism-religion and socioeconomic power. Even though the two dimensions are analytically distinct, when projected onto the political space, they create a "unidimensional competitive space" as a result of "elective affinities" afforded by the overlap between the two dimensions (Kitschelt 1992, 14).

The unique and close relationship between the state and big business in the Middle East, an important relationship for analytical purposes in this study, resembles the model laid out by Peter Evans as "embedded autonomy" (Evans 1995). Embedded autonomy, which Evans sees critical to the development prospects in the developing world, aims to limit the undue influence state officials and business might have on each other. The state does have a certain level of independence from business interests ensuring the observance of developmental goals, whereas state bureaucracy is "embedded" in the surrounding "social structure," that is, incorporating the preferences of businesses. A critical difference is that the business under the state autonomy framework presented in this study is subservient to the authority and subvention of the state; it is not independent. The relationship between the state and business is built on the preeminence of a political rather than an economic goal; the relationship guarantees the continued dominance of the center in the first place, while other objectives such as economic development are only incidental.

The cleavage between the center and the periphery is translated onto the political sphere as well. Secular and mostly leftist political parties claim to be representatives of the center, benefiting greatly from the existing political-economic system in place. Such parties as the Republican People's Party in Turkey and Istiqlal Party in Morocco identified with the independence movements, in a certain way, have been an effective mechanism for the center to shape the political arena in their respective societies. The periphery, depending on the political context, shied away from supporting parties of the center; oftentimes, Islamist parties proved to be the most serious alternative to the pro–status quo stance of the center parties. Antisystemic discourse of Islamist parties placed them clearly within the political, social, and economic alley of the peripheral groups. Politically, Islam features prominently in the discourse of Islamist parties; the lofty goal of Islamization of the state and society, albeit to differing levels, elevates these parties to positions such that they claim to speak on behalf of Islam.

The uncompromising stance of Islamist parties leads, rightly, to wide-ranging perceptions that far-reaching changes will take place once Islamists take power. Also, the perception that Islamists endorse democracy only with respect to its instrumental value in reaching to the envisioned Islamic system gained much currency among seculars more recently. Economically, redistribution of resources and emphasis on SMEs, seen as empowering the periphery and countering the dominance of big business, feature prominently in Islamist discourse. In line with the nationalist and protectionist economic discourse, Islamist parties do not have a preference for a liberal market economy; in contrast, states' active role in the economy with protective and subsidizing measures are viewed as critical to the interests of peripheral business groups. The Islamist political platform, when seen from this perspective, reflects the preferences of an excluded and marginalized periphery. Aydogan and Slapin (2013) find that "religious-secular divide" best illustrates the conventional left-right political divide. Along these lines, note that recent survey-based research corroborates the idea that Islamist parties draw their electoral support from a distinct social demographic, lending crucial support to the discussion above (Garcia-Rivero and Kotzé 2007; Gidengil and Karakoc 2014).

The center-periphery framework as a model of social cleavages in the Middle East maps the secularism-religion and socioeconomic cleavages succinctly. Building on the center-periphery framework, I now turn to a thorough discussion of a model of economic liberalization to conceptualize the contemporary political-economic conflict in the Middle East as it pertains to the moderation of political Islam.

Economic Liberalization

Economic liberalization, defined as the minimization of government involvement in the economy in favor of greater private enterprise through privatization and free movement of capital and goods across borders, intimately relates to social cleavages as it carries with itself the potential to bring the long-standing policies of state intervention that favored big businesses to an end. By extension, the way in which a country liberalizes its economy shapes the form of social cleavages that materialize, and the social foundations of Islamist politics. Hence modeling the relationship between economic liberalization and social cleavages becomes essential for teasing out its impact on Islamist politics.

The scholarly literature on economic liberalization offers limited help in modeling the effects of liberalization on social cleavages. The overwhelming majority of this literature focuses on liberalization's impact on distinct sectors and industries. Concomitantly, the emphasis is on the attainment of strictly economic interests as it pertains to individual industries and sectors without examining the wider implications for social cleavages and politics in general (Katzenstein 1985; Hiscox 2002; Mares 2005). A related problem surfaces in the form of the regional focus of such studies. Studies on the effects of liberalization engage either in global cross-national analyses (Adsera and Boix 2002; Milner and Kubota 2005; Reuveny and Li 2003) or on a subset of developing countries with levels of economic development and social structures considerably different from what we observe in the Middle East (Kaufman and Segura-Ubiergo 2001; Baker 2003; Brooks 2004).

A similar trend in the literature on economic liberalization is the focus on levels of liberalization and its impact on various dependent variables such as democratization, government spending, partisan politics, and social policies.[6] Here, the level of economic liberalization is usually operationalized as the ratio of imports and exports to GDP. Such analyses, by focusing on "how much" a country liberalizes, fail to integrate specific circumstances of different countries, and critically, they ignore the question of "how" a country liberalizes. Economic liberalization, rather than being a uniform process exposing sheltered domestic economic structures and agents to common market-based constraints and changes, in fact demonstrates great variance across countries in respect to its application and effects. In other words, not all liberalization is the same (Chaudhry 1994; Heydemann 2004; Adly 2009). In general, the state's potential to shape allocative decisions may tilt the balance in favor of one particular economic group as opposed to others (Bates 1981); the process of economic liberalization is no exception. When the state utilizes its potential to shape allocative decisions, it undercuts the impact of economic liberalization on domestic competition. The "how" question, in this regard, carries major implications for conceptualizing the impact of liberalization on Islamist politics.[7] Whether economic liberalization perpetuates preliberalization state-business relations or engenders competition on a broader scale is a crucial indicator of the "how" question. In particular, it lays bare a new economic cleavage arising between traditional beneficiaries of state protection and new economic actors able to compete in liberal market contexts.

The partial reform equilibrium model, originally formulated by Joel Hellman to account for the stalled-liberalization efforts in postcommunist countries, highlights differences in the pace of economic reforms (Hellman 1998). Although helpful in outlining the role of "winners" in the liberalization process and how they are able to prevent any and all unwanted reform initiatives, the partial reform equilibrium model fails to incorporate other actors and political considerations into the framework, stretching beyond purely economic concerns. The "winners" are capable of singularly imposing their preferences on others; hence the model reduces preexisting cleavages to nonfactors.

In a critical analysis, Kiren Aziz Chaudhry addresses the "how" question in her study of Saudi and Iraqi economic liberalization reforms in the 1980s. In contrast to Hellman's partial reform model highlighting the role of "winners" in liberalization, Chaudhry argues that distinct paths of reform pursued by Iraq and Saudi Arabia highlight the significance of "historical contingencies in determining social responses to economic liberalization" (Chaudhry 1994). Diverse patterns of business-state relations in these two countries and the extent of state involvement in the economy determine the future course of liberalization. Lengthy periods of *étatisme* in the region underscore the need for incorporating the "historically constituted institutional, political, and economic relationships" into the analysis in order to model liberalization and its societal impact. In criticizing purely economic perspectives in favor of a politicized approach to liberalization, Chaudhry states: "[The assumptions embraced] kept them from appreciating the interest political and economic elites may have in forestalling the creation of functioning national markets. Creating markets is politically dangerous. Functioning markets provide opportunities for mobility that undercut lineage and traditional rights of privilege, thus threatening the status quo. Markets create inequalities in wealth that may not match existing patterns of income distribution, status, power, and entitlements; they dislocate groups in both the political and economic realms" (Chaudhry 1994, 4). The dirigisme prevalent in the Middle East brings the validity of economic perspectives in conceptualizing the liberalization process into question. The role of the political elite in economic liberalization necessitates an alternative approach. Specifically, I emphasize the political aspect of economic liberalization to demonstrate how the center-periphery cleavage interacts with the liberalization process to create a cross-class coalition in support of MDPs in some countries, but not others. To this end, I distinguish between two types of economic liberalization: competitive liberalization and crony liberalization. I focus on two distinct aspects of an economic liberalization process in order to determine the type of liberalization in a specific case: (1) integration into the global economy, that is, level of effective protection, and (2) level of domestic competition and business concentration. I will discuss both in greater detail in chapter 2.

Competitive Liberalization

Competition characterizes this form of liberalization. Such economic competition benefits SMEs, which had previously been marginalized. The more that barriers to market participation are minimized, the more peripheral groups can participate in the liberalized economy and the more they can potentially benefit. The new shape of the economy thus will be more inclusionary and broad based in terms of participation. Competitive liberalization also entails a major redistribution of economic power from formerly protected and large businesses to SMEs. This is partly because liberalization permits the emergence or greater participation by peripheral economic actors, that is, SME owners, in the economy. Such peripheral business groups are able to compete in the global economy as the reforms remove the political and economic barriers to entry that were reminiscent of the closed economy.[8] The preliberalization socioeconomic status quo undergoes significant changes as a result of the rise of SMEs. For example, the level of competition in most industries increases considerably with liberalization, and level of monopolization decreases economy-wide. Once constrained either by law or by prohibitive costs associated with limited credit and market access, peripheral economic groups are able to more actively participate in the economy and challenge the dominance of traditional big business. Hence monopolization decreases over time to allow greater market access for peripheral groups. Decrease in monopolization may follow privatization of state economic enterprises and the death of state monopolies.

Crony Liberalization

Crony liberalization refers to a situation in which the economic elite that is traditionally well connected to the political elite in a closed economy maintains its privileged access to the decision-making mechanisms in the postliberalization period. The close relationship with the political elite ensures that big businesses continue benefiting disproportionately from economic resources and opportunities in the postliberalization period.[9] The Latin American experience with "embedded neoliberalism," in this regard, is an analogous process to crony liberalization, though with fundamental differences. The two are most comparable in the way the big businesses retain their regressive privileges in the postliberalization period.[10]

Crony liberalization differs from competitive liberalization in two important ways. First, the range of beneficiaries under crony liberalization remains vastly more limited than under competitive liberalization. Political considerations, that is, perpetuation of the privileged relationship between ruling and business elites, supersede economic considerations. An essential element of an open economy is the existence of competition in the economy (Roe 1999; Devarajan and Rodrik 1989; Pant and Pattanayak 2005; Stiglitz 1998). By maintaining the traditional state-business relationship structure, however, competition is effectively minimized under crony liberalization. Instead, monopolies define the structure of the economy, either in the form of protection for national industries or by allowing privatized state companies to dominate a given industry. Second, this particular type of economic liberalization fails to create a support base distinct from big business. The perception that a small group of cronies benefits from it dominates the public conception. Crucially, perception of this imbalance is particularly acute among members of peripheral groups. Crony liberalization differs from corruption. The goal with crony liberalization is not to attain petty favors and benefits; instead, it is a systematic way of tilting the socioeconomic balance to favor a certain group of the political and economic elite to the detriment of the population at large.

Two conflicting goals set the stage for the introduction of crony liberalization. Policy makers, facing low levels of economic growth, want to spur economic activity by encouraging integration to the global economy and by luring foreign investment. At the same time, the ruling elite want to maintain the mutually beneficial relationship for both politicians and crony business owners (Enderwick 2005). As Tarik Yousef argues, maintenance of control over economic and political power defines the ultimate goal: "Many governments of the Middle East had only been reluctant reformers to begin with, and when confronted by political opposition, they adopted policies that weakened the link between economic restructuring and political reform" (Yousef 2004, 111). Wary of the political implications of economic liberalization, many governments opted for a gradual pace and strict control over the liberalization reforms.

Crony liberalization limits competition in an economy by disproportionately favoring the traditional big business elite. Among the tools utilized to this end are politically manipulated privatization of state economic enterprises, protection of selected, big business–dominated industries, and favoritism in handing out government contracts. Peripheral businesses under crony liberalization largely remain underdeveloped, limited in size, and critical of the liberalization process. In contrast, competitive liberalization levels the playing field for SMEs and big business to compete, and redefines the preferences of the actors. The level of competition thus is the most critical outcome of the nature of liberalization shaping the postliberalization-era society and politics. This leveling of the playing field results in the emergence of interests vested in the continuance of openness in politics and economy, where the interest in the former rises due to its potential to contribute to the continuation of the latter by way of increasing rule of law, transparency, and secure property rights.

As a point of clarification, I do not theorize about the causes of distinct forms of economic liberalization, that is, competitive versus crony. I treat economic liberalization as an exogenous factor and focus on its impact over Islamist moderation and empowerment. Although I survey the specific circumstances that pave the way for the implementation of economic liberalization policies in closed regimes such as Egypt, Morocco, and Turkey in the following chapters, we can make the following broad observations. Economic opening decisions tend to follow economic hard times, prompting leaders to take action. When faced with acute economic conditions that demand immediate action, such as a balance of payments crisis, decision makers tend to have a smaller set of policy options to choose from; crisis conditions prompt policy makers to undertake more comprehensive liberalization reforms, removing most constraints in front of liberalization. In the absence of such crisis conditions, gradual reform programs better serve to ensure a particular form of postliberalization political-economic structure that is commensurate with the preferences of decision makers and their supporters. Hence, in general, the political elite's ability to cherry-pick reforms best suited to its interests negatively correlates with the severity of the economic conditions it faces. Finally, competitive and crony liberalizations represent ideal types; most cases will fall somewhere in between the two ideal states.

Theory

Prior to liberalization reforms, Islamist parties are the main representatives of peripheral Islamic groups in politics. MDPs' emergence is conditional on the initiation of liberalization reforms. In this context, the question is, how do different types of economic liberalization relate to Islamist parties? The distinction I draw between center and periphery in the previous section becomes critical because it allows me to model the way distinct social groups are affected by distinct paths of economic liberalization. In what follows, I offer a model to explain the emergence and strengthening of MDPs. Briefly stated, MDPs with a distinct political platform can emerge and challenge the dominance of Islamist parties as a result of changes in the social structure. Competitive economic liberalization facilitates the integration of peripheral groups to the global economy, which in turn leads to the transformation of their political preferences. MDPs, in this context, reflect the change in the preferences of the periphery with which Islamist parties now have incompatible platforms. Crony liberalization, however, perpetuates archaic forms of state-business relationship reinforcing preliberalization social structure, leaving peripheral groups marginalized; hence we do not observe a significant change in the political preferences of the periphery. Islamist parties under these circumstances continue addressing the preferences of peripheral groups. MDPs, even if they emerge, face considerable obstacles in establishing themselves as a strong competitor for power. The model I propose deals with the distribution of socioeconomic power in Muslim-majority societies and its reflection on the political space.

Competitive Liberalization and the Transformation of the Periphery

If peripheral groups, that is, SMEs and masses, indeed benefit from competitive economic liberalization, then the question becomes, how are the periphery's political preferences are affected by the new economic conditions? For peripheral business owners, it is possible to identify three principal policy areas where we should see a preference change: the economy, democracy, and the role of Islam.

The economy constitutes the most important element of SME owners' set of preferences. The disruption of economic openness would hurt their economic activities, both domestically and internationally. Thanks to access to global markets and the greater availability of domestic markets, SME owners do prosper, in terms of both number and size. Hence continuation of economic openness becomes a principal policy preference for SMEs. At the same time, their very existence as political and economic actors depends on this new liberal policy equilibrium. If the illiberal economic system makes a comeback, SME owners' property as well as their political and economic influence might face a major challenge by the traditional political and economic elite. Essentially, peripheral businesses develop a vested interest in the new, liberal economic order.

As part of a growing business class, liberalization means more than economic openness for peripheral businesses. Theoretically, it is the risk associated with a nontransparent regime that should lead peripheral businesses to support more democratic forms of governance. This is because peripheral businesses perceive democracy in this peculiar political and economic context as furthering their material interests by ensuring the rule of law, fair business opportunities, and secure property rights. The argument here is not that only democratic political systems can foster rule of law and secure property rights. Such an argument is not only empirically unfounded but also beside the point. There are circumstances under which nondemocratic regimes can be associated with rule of law and secure property rights; countries like Singapore or the United Arab Emirates (UAE) rank high in indices of rule of law and secure property rights.[11] The evolution of political preferences as far as SME owners are concerned is driven by socioeconomic changes where the legal infrastructure remains the same. Accordingly, SMEs should develop a strong preference for democracy. Commitment to an open political and economic regime draws from the risk of loss that peripheral business owners confront in an illiberal order. The greater the risk they face, the greater their inclination to avoid radical political discourse, and to support instead more moderate and transparent political platforms. In other words, the distinctive support for a democratic regime on the part of peripheral businesses should not stem from a newly evolved understanding of the inherent value of democracy as a political regime but instead should arise strictly from economic self-interest. To use Eva Bellin's terms, peripheral groups choose to become "contingent democrats."[12] Commitment to the liberal economy thus engenders an interest in transparency and political stability in the form of a democratic preference.[13] Similarly, peripheral business owners' interest in political—and economic—stability leads them to change their preference on the role of Islam. Islam featured prominently in their political agenda prior to economic liberalization with a holistic approach to the economy, politics, and society, eyeing a comprehensive transformation of the state and society. The unambiguous implication of this is that any such change is likely to bring polarization, instability, and uncertainty. Hence peripheral business owners prefer a nonpoliticized role for Islam, an emphasis on Islamic values but not a wholesale transformation of the state and society.

If SMEs do, in fact, benefit from such competitive liberalization and experience a transformation in their political preferences, what would be the mechanism peripheral SMEs utilize to voice their new policy preferences and make them known in the political arena? Ideally, formation of a business association would be the best means to organize and promote their common goals (Olson 1971). Otherwise, they would run the risk of remaining isolated and ineffective actors in the political and economic arena. Organizing around a business association offers key benefits.[14] A formal business association might help the members of this bourgeoning socioeconomic group to form distinct policy positions to make recommendations to policy makers. This is a nontrivial advantage for SME owners in promoting their policy preferences especially when the benchmark comparison is no organization. Also, collective action in such large proportions conveys a strong message to policy makers about the size and strength of the group. This perception of a powerful business association might enable SMEs to establish themselves as pivotal actors in politics and challenge others.

Peripheral masses may also benefit from liberalization. On the one hand, the economy-wide rise in prosperity affords the masses a chance to enjoy increased income. The growth of SMEs affords the peripheral masses to find greater employment opportunities in labor-intensive sectors of the economy. On the other hand, workers also face new risks associated with loss of income or employment as a result of increased insecurity in a free market economy. Hence political parties that offer a policy platform based on social programs and redistribution along with economic liberalization will be appealing.

Crony Liberalization and the "Same Old, Same Old" Periphery

Prior to economic liberalization, big business dominates the economic arena by its sheer size and historically "good" relationship with the ruling elite (Waterbury 1993). Statist economic policies pursued for decades in the Middle East not only reinforce the mutually beneficial relationship between the state and big business but also ensure the survival of the big business as its chief client. Crony liberalization limits competition in a nominally open economy by disproportionately favoring the traditional big business. The chances of a major transformation in the interests and preferences of relevant actors seem fairly low in light of low levels of economic competition, which is the major dynamic behind socioeconomic change. Under crony liberalization, big business continues to enjoy privileges in terms of credit allocation, market access, and contract awards, which largely leaves the preliberalization socioeconomic power structure intact (Waterbury 1993, 218–19). Maintaining the dynamics of the statist status quo ante thus is critical to the continued benefit of big business in this relationship. Under crony liberalization, SMEs largely remain underdeveloped, limited in size, and critical of the liberalization process, as it benefits only a certain group of individuals, who are politically well connected. Under these circumstances, SME owners' interests (along with the dissatisfaction of peripheral masses) lie in a sweeping transformation of the political and economic structure toward a more favorable socioeconomic distribution as envisioned by Islamist political parties, largely due to their effective exclusion from the political and economic system. Economically, peripheral groups remain aloof from liberalization. A liberal economy, which in this unique context refers to a crony model of liberalization, proves detrimental to the interests of peripheral groups. Politically, an Islamist system emphasizing redistribution, equality, and dominance of an Islamic identity appears to be the appropriate redress of the periphery's political and economic marginalization.

A key question at this point is the following: why do SME owners' economic and political preferences not remain the same under both types of liberalization? I answer this question with two interrelated points. First, the implicit assumption that the preferences of certain social groups or individuals should remain unchanged when societal conditions that give rise to them in the first place change ignores a fundamental attribute of human behavior, which is that humans respond to incentives. Unless the group in question is behaving on purely ideological grounds, this is an untenable assumption to make; we do not have this kind of evidence to suggest that SMEs do, indeed, behave on purely ideological grounds. What we do know about SME owners, just like any other political actor, is that their interest is focused on maximizing their benefits and remains relatively unchanged in a cross-national context. When specific conditions in the society change, such as a transition from a closed economy to an open one, or a change in how government support might affect economic outcomes, they do respond to such changes in the incentive structure.

Second, and more specifically, the crucial distinction between political Islam and social Islam rests on the latent capacity to polarize and destabilize the current political-economic system. Because of its antisystem character, political Islam does carry this potential. Social Islam, by contrast, does not pose a fundamental challenge to the existing system, and its ultimate goal differs from that of political Islam, which is to reach an amorphous ideal of an Islamic state. In this regard, SME owners simply pursue their interests, and the preference change reflects this.

Political Implications

Politically, parties in any modern political system should reflect the preferences and interests of the constituency they aspire to represent (Schmitter 1992; Strom 1990). Islamic parties are no exception to this general conceptualization; hence I expect Islamist parties and MDPs to respond to their perceived constituency's political preferences. The evolution of an Islamist platform toward a moderate Muslim democratic discourse depends largely on the periphery's response to the form that economic liberalization has taken throughout the 1970s and 1980s. In this regard, an analysis of the winners and losers of the liberalization process is instrumental to understanding the relative success of MDPs and Islamist parties.

Under a competitive model of liberalization, political Islam as a broad political discourse no longer serves the interests of peripheral groups. Political Islam, by being a reactionary response to the marginalization of peripheral groups, envisions far-reaching restructuring of the political and economic system that aims to secure the integration of the periphery to the center. In this regard, when peripheral groups lack the means and resources to overcome their exclusion from the system despite the fact that they would like to, an Islamist platform fits squarely with the preferences of peripheral groups before liberalization sets in. When, however, competitive liberalization enables peripheral businesses to benefit from the new system as winners, the antisystemic discourse of Islamist parties, which imagines sweeping changes in the state and society, would likely threaten both political and economic stability.[15] Stability is a central pillar of conducting business for business owners, especially so if these business owners are integrated to the global economy through liberalization. Hence the more moderate discourse of an MDP emphasizing Islamic values, liberal economy, and democracy meets the political preferences of peripheral businesses. Combined with its Islamic undertone and social policy focus, MDPs' endorsement of liberal economy thus speaks to the potential losers, that is, peripheral masses, as well. Accordingly, competitive liberalization processes create a new cross-class coalition of peripheral groups to whom the MDPs' moderate platform of social policy, Islamic values, democracy, and economic liberalization will appeal. Islamist parties' relatively radical platform, by contrast, is inconsistent with the new political preferences of peripheral groups in a competitive environment. MDPs' rise against the backdrop of political Islam is a clear indication to this effect.

Under crony liberalization, Islamist parties thrive to a greater extent than they do under competitively liberal economies. Persistence of archaic state-business relations and continued marginalization of peripheral groups justify the nonmoderate political preferences of the periphery. Crony liberalization distorts competition by severely limiting the potential winners from liberalization. Unless fair competition, as a key element of liberalization, accrues, it is hard to imagine how liberalization in this peculiar formation might lead to moderation at any point. Moderation essentially owes its existence to the leveling of socioeconomic competition. As long as severe inequalities in opportunities for competition persist, moderation is unlikely to follow. Continuation of preliberalization state–big business economic relationships leaves the periphery's preferences on politics and the economy intact. SMEs and other peripheral groups are effectively denied benefits from liberalization, while the domestic market is parceled among cronies by creating monopolies. Islamist parties have strong reservations against liberalization, particularly to current implementation. A closed or an open economy following the crony model does not differ by much, as the outcomes are awfully similar. Hence crony liberalization leaves Islamist parties' nationalistic and redistributive platform intact and fits well with the preferences of peripheral groups. Politically, reactionary discourse with a strong Islamist undertone continues to pervade the Islamist platform. Socially, the Islamist platform is conservative and envisions the Islamization of the state and society, which eventually would ensure equitable and fair distribution of resources as well as "proper" social order.

Distinct from its impact on peripheral businesses, crony liberalization also shapes the preferences of the peripheral masses. In this model, the political elite depends on the big business to reap the benefits of the new "liberal" economy. Yet the overall economic policy undermines the peripheral masses' perception of the liberalization. First, economic growth rests on the performance of the big business. If the big businesses perform well, their performance will have spin-off effects on the rest of the population. A larger economy translates into higher income and increased job opportunities for the population at large. Unless the economy grows exponentially, however, the masses will not experience a significant improvement in their well-being, particularly in view of high population growth rates. The case of many Arab countries is a good example. Second, the literature particularly emphasizes the increased purchasing power as the key cause of popular support for trade liberalization (Baker 2003; Milner and Kubota 2005). For example, Milner and Kubota state that trade openness "results in a gain in income for, and a reduction in the prices of imported goods bought by, those well endowed with the relatively abundant factor—that is, labor—in these economies" (Milner and Kubota 2005, 116). Additionally, export-oriented strategy is a key element of liberalization among developing countries. Exports ensure a steady source of income for imports, if not more. Hence in a liberalized developing economy, export promotion is likely to minimize current account imbalances. Yet crony liberalization, from this perspective, leads to depressed consumer demand, sharpening the negative attitude of peripheral masses against liberalization. If economic liberalization does not improve the lot of the masses and moreover is viewed as beneficial for only a select few, public opinion will overwhelmingly be against economic liberalization. Overall, Islamist parties with their platforms provide the perfect fit for the political preferences and demands of the peripheral groups under crony liberalization. The periphery's interest in a substantial change in economic policies for more redistribution finds resonance in the sharp and intransigent discourse of Islamist parties. Complementing the economic position of Islamist parties is the political understanding of Islam.

Conclusion

Table 1.1 summarizes the positions of Islamist and Muslim democratic parties on the two social cleavages in the Middle East, that is, the secular-Islamic and socioeconomic dimensions, before and after economic liberalization. In a closed

Table 1.1 Party Positions on Issues

A. Pre-liberalization				B. Post-liberalization		
Redistribution				**Statism**		
Secular		Islamist Parties	Islamic	Secular		Islamist Parties	Islamic
	Secular Parties				Secular Parties	MDPs	
Market Allocation				**Liberalism**		

economy, Islamist parties position themselves to reflect the policies preferred by the peripheral groups. On the one hand, they have an Islamist discourse on the secular-Islamic dimension, whereas on the other hand they opt for redistribution in a closed economy dominated by big business. After economic liberalization, MDPS position themselves closer to the Islamic dimension, albeit with a distinct role for Islam in their platforms in the secular-Islamic dimension. The socioeconomic dimension, however, proves to be the critical dimension. In the liberalized economy, the socioeconomic dimension is represented by a choice along the statism-liberalism continuum. Islamist parties envisage an extensive role for the state in the economy as it was prior to liberalization, while MDPs prefer a liberal economy. Critically, the postliberalization positions remain the same under both crony and competitive liberalizations for MDPs and Islamist parties. This is the very reason why MDPs prosper in certain contexts but not others. Under crony liberalization, MDPs fail to make an impact because their position on the socioeconomic dimension does not reflect the realities of the periphery. In cases where competitive liberalization reigns, MDPs speak directly to their constituencies' interests.

The premise of this argument is that Islamic political parties in Muslim-majority countries, as in any other modern political system, should reflect the preferences and interests of the constituency they aspire to represent (Schmitter 1992; Strom 1990). Briefly stated, I argue that MDPs are able to emerge and challenge the dominance of Islamist parties because of changes in the socioeconomic structure. Competitive economic liberalization facilitates the integration of peripheral groups into the global economy, which in turn leads to the transformation of their political and economic interests. MDPs, in this context, benefit from the change in the political interests of the periphery where Islamist parties' platforms become incompatible with the changing economic and social structure. By contrast, the process of crony liberalization perpetuates the more archaic forms of state-business relations that reinforced the preliberalization social structure, leaving the peripheral groups at the margins of political and eco-

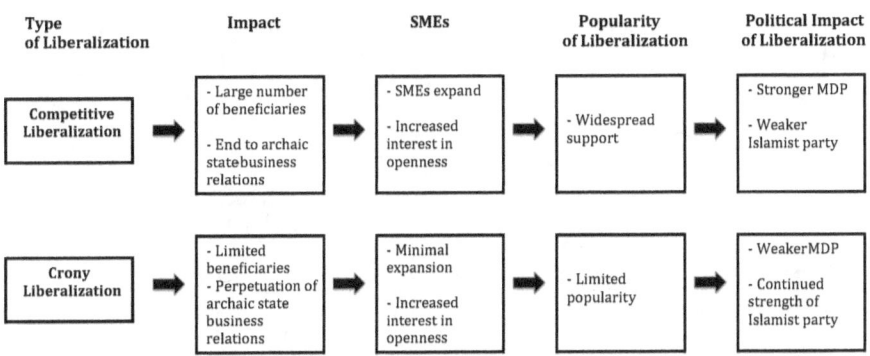

Figure 1.1 Causal Mechanisms.

nomic power. Hence we do not observe changes in the interests of the periphery in the crony liberalization context that would facilitate the rise of MDPs. Islamist parties under these circumstances are better able to address the political interests of peripheral groups, and thus remain strong. Even if MDPs emerge in crony liberalization contexts, they face considerable obstacles to establishing themselves as a strong competitor vis-à-vis Islamist parties. The model I propose to explain this dynamic thus places its central focus on the distribution of socioeconomic power in Muslim-majority societies and its reflection in the political space.

Specifically, then, I advance two sets of hypotheses. First, if there is competitive liberalization, then I expect to observe changes in the electoral support of SMEs for a more democratic political system, a liberal economy, and a social role for Islam instead of a political one. In this context MDPs are more likely to rise and prosper electorally. Alternatively, if there is crony liberalization, I expect to see Islamist parties remaining the major political representative of the peripheral groups with their emphasis on nationalist and protectionist economic policies and political Islamic discourse vis-à-vis MDPs. Figure 1.1 presents the causal mechanism succinctly.

With this analysis, my goal is not to compare mere levels of electoral support of Islamist and Muslim democratic parties. This would not only depend on core constituencies of such parties but also on contextual factors that directly influence electoral outcomes. Rather, the goal is to gauge relative societal support for MDPs and Islamist parties among the peripheral groups and to evaluate the extent of the social change as a result of liberalization. Accordingly, I bring evidence to test my theory by examining the relative electoral support for Islamist parties and MDPs. Because both types of parties speak to the same social groups, their relative strength should inform us of how the social base reacts to the distinct platforms of the two parties. To this end, I will compare electoral support of Islamist and Muslim democratic parties in recent legislative elections.

2 Modeling Economic Liberalization in a Comparative Perspective

IN ORDER TO make sense of highly politicized liberalization reforms and their impact on political and social processes in the context of a developing country, modeling economic liberalization is imperative. Building on the typology created in chapter 1, that is, competitive and crony liberalizations, I analyze the economic liberalization processes of each of the three cases (Egypt, Morocco, and Turkey) since the 1980s in order to classify them accordingly. In so doing, I first analyze the level of competition in each economy. The analysis will be instrumental in determining the economy-wide implications of peripheral businesses' size and power, which constitutes the backbone of my theory explaining the rise and success of Muslim democratic parties (MDPs), and the political implications of such economic change. Specifically, I focus on two concepts: (1) integration into the global economy, that is, level of effective protection, and (2) level of domestic competition and business concentration. Secondly, I present a thorough discussion of economic liberalization processes in Turkey, Egypt, and Morocco, respectively. In these brief case studies, I discuss the state's role in the economy, trade liberalization, financial liberalization, and privatization. The discussion reinforces the conclusions drawn in the first part of the chapter. Turkish economic liberalization (a case of competitive liberalization) offered greater opportunities for small and medium enterprises (SMEs) to integrate to the global economy, whereas the Egyptian economic liberalization (crony liberalization) prevented potential participation of SMEs in the liberalizing economy. The Moroccan case (semicompetitive liberalization) falls between those of Turkey and Egypt; some aspects of the economy are competitive and open to the global economy, while in other sectors of the economy, competition is still fairly restricted.

Evaluating Economic Liberalizations

In this first part of this chapter, I rely on the following two concepts to measure crony versus competitive liberalization in each country: (1) integration into the global economy, that is, level of effective protection, and (2) level of domestic competition and business concentration. A crucial observable implication of the

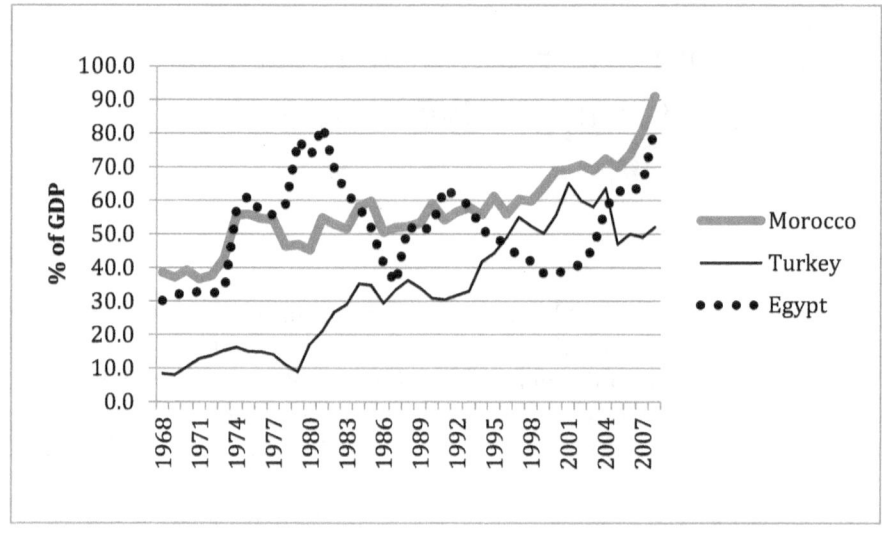

Figure 2.1 Trade as Percent of GDP. *Source:* World Development Indicators.

difference between crony and competitive liberalizations is the level of SME growth in a country. If SMEs are indeed empowered by the process of economic liberalization, collectively they should be able to control a larger share of the domestic market as compared with their role in the preliberalization period. By contrast, where the structure of the economy is dominated by big businesses and marked by lower levels of competition, resembling that of the preliberalization era, SMEs should play a smaller role in domestic activity. Collectively, these two indicators help determine which type of economic liberalization fits each case.

Comprehensive indicators of liberalization suggest that in the last three decades, the three countries have similar levels of openness, albeit with periodic ups and downs. For example, trade as a percentage of GDP shows that Turkey appears to be the least liberal among the three, with trade comprising less than 50 percent of the GDP despite increased trade levels in the last decade or so (Figure 2.1), while Morocco has consistently exceeded the 50 percent benchmark. Although Egypt exhibits the highest level of volatility, it fares closer to Morocco, with trade exposure above 50 percent of the GDP a majority of the time. Exports of goods and services detail a similar trend for all three countries, ranging between 15 percent and 30 percent of the GDP (Figure 2.2). The more qualitative indicators of openness, such as that of the Heritage Foundation, point to a similar picture, namely, that all three countries have comparable levels of openness (Figure 2.3). Yet, it is not the level of openness, but rather the quality of openness that matters for MDP development and success. In other words, it is the changes in the

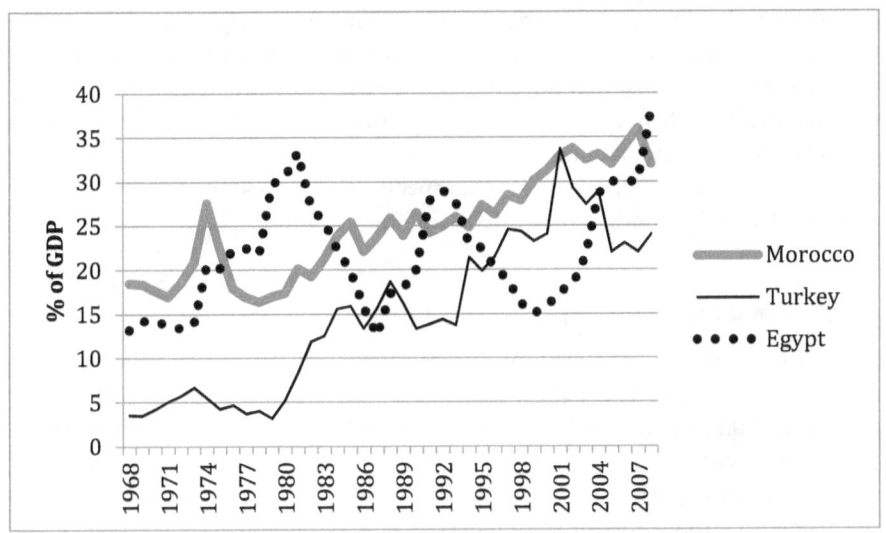

Figure 2.2 Goods and Services Exports (Current US$). *Source:* World Development Indicators.

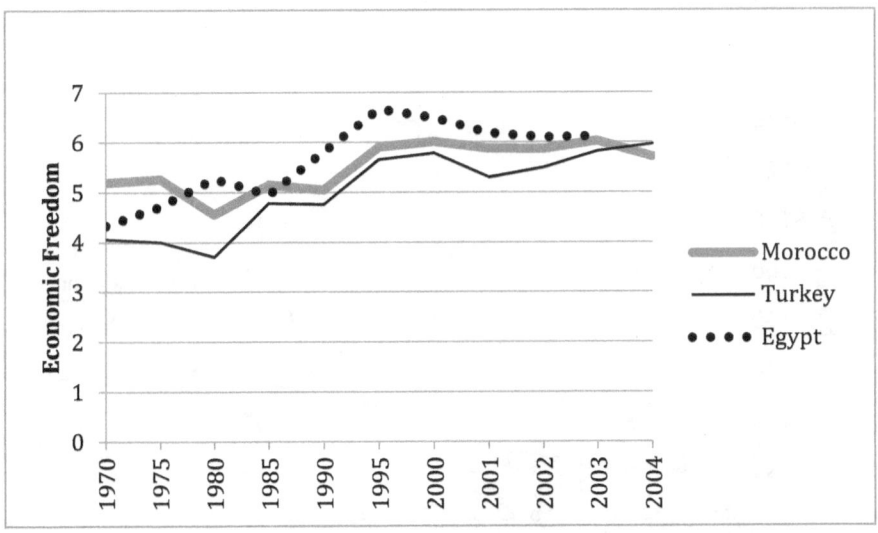

Figure 2.3 Economic Freedom of the World Index. *Source:* Heritage Foundation annual reports.

structure of the economy that affect the fundamental distribution of benefits in the economy. Who benefits from the new economy and in which ways? Provided that economic liberalization does not change the economic structure in such a way that the list of beneficiaries is altered, economic liberalization neither affects Islamist politics fundamentally nor enables MDPs to be electorally successful. Hence I will focus on three additional aspects of economic liberalization to obtain a better understanding of the depth of liberalization.

Integration and Protection

Indeed, the more specific components of openness, such as merchandise and manufacturing exports, convey a different message. Because they directly affect the integration of domestic businesses into global markets through production, these two measures are highly significant. Manufacturing and merchandise components of exports, unlike the overall measure of exports or trade, point to the productive and competitive elements of an economy. Despite its smaller GDP size, Morocco exports more merchandise than Egypt (around $10 billion for most of the 1990s), and Turkey, for the same period, has higher figures than both Egypt and Morocco (Figure 2.4). Additionally, Egyptian merchandise exports include a substantial amount of fuel exports, decreasing its net merchandise exports further still (Figure 2.5).[1] More specifically, manufacturing figures show

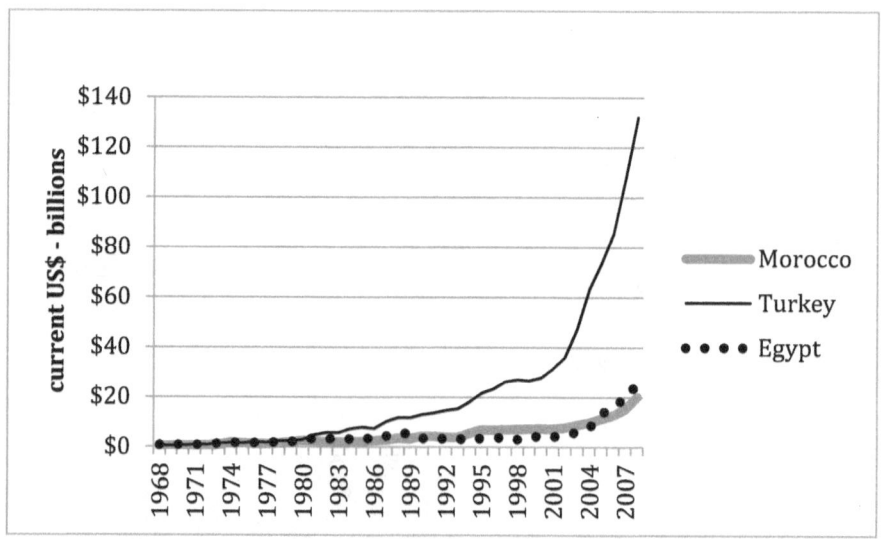

Figure 2.4 Merchandise Exports (Current US$). *Source:* World Development Indicators.

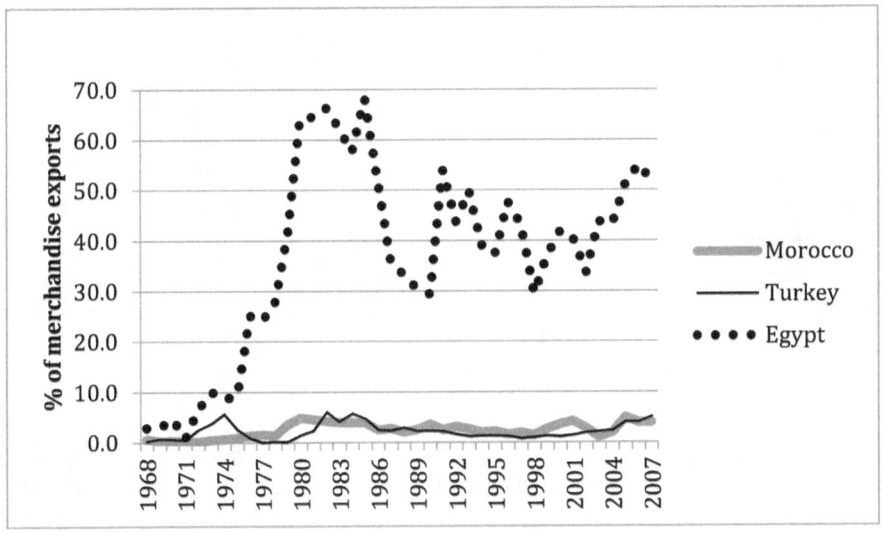

Figure 2.5 Fuel Exports as Percent of Merchandise Exports. *Source:* World Development Indicators.

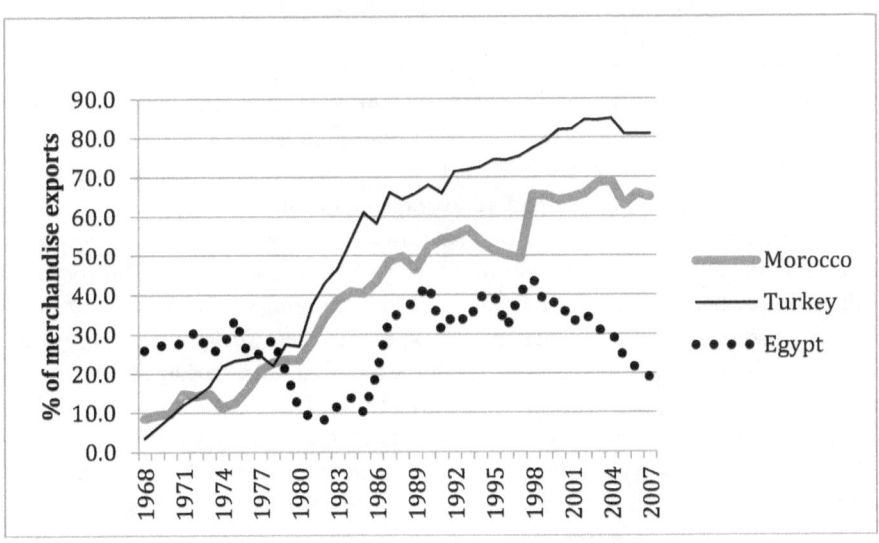

Figure 2.6 Manufactured Exports as Percent of Merchandise Exports. *Source:* World Development Indicators.

Table 2.1 Competition Indicators

	Egypt	Morocco	Turkey
Competition (overall)	4.08	4.28	4.55
Intensity of local competition	4.57	4.61	5.31
Extent of market dominance	3.41	3.88	4.04
Effectiveness of antimonopoly policy	3.31	4.24	4.34
Prevalence of trade barriers	3.87	4.17	4.91
Ease of access to loans	3.08	3.35	3.26
Trade-weighted tariff rate	21.83	12.70	4.00

Source: World Economic Forum (2008).

that only 30 percent of Egyptian merchandise exports are manufacture exports, whereas the same figure for Turkey and Morocco stands at around 70 percent and 50 percent, respectively (Figure 2.6). Considering the sizes of Turkey's and Morocco's economies, the relatively poor performance of Egypt becomes clearer, since the Egyptian economy was more than double the size of the Moroccan economy for most of the period since 1980. Nevertheless, the figures for manufacturing exports are heavily tilted in favor of Morocco. Empirical evidence on firm sizes, to be discussed next, will help to evaluate the significance of peripheral businesses in the two types of liberalization contexts.

Tariff rates, as a measure of effective protection, point in the same direction (Table 2.1). Average tariff rates tend to underestimate the level of actual protection in an economy; hence they may be deceiving. A country might have an overwhelming majority of its imports in high-tariff goods, while the remaining import categories have lower tariff rates without high levels of trade in these sectors. To avoid this problem, trade-weighted tariff levels may be utilized.[2] According to weighted tariffs, Egypt had an average tariff rate of 21.8 percent in 2008. The same rate for Morocco is 12.7 percent and for Turkey is 4.0 percent. The tariff rates indicate a higher level of competition in Turkey than in either Morocco or Egypt simply because domestic firms need to be as competitive as international manufacturers or, as a consequence, will experience being driven out of the market. Part of the explanation for this lies in the fact that both Turkey and Morocco are associated with the European Union in a form of economic integration. Turkey has had a customs union with the European Union since 1995, and since 2010, Morocco has been party to a free trade agreement with the European Union. This association allowed them to decrease their tariffs substantially. Because Egypt does not have such an agreement with an important trade partner of its own at this time, its global integration is greatly limited relative to that in the other cases.

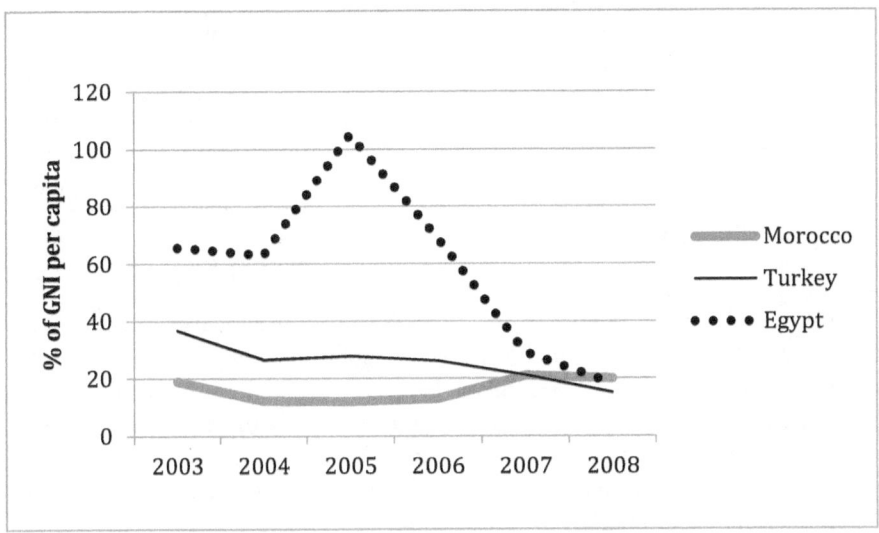

Figure 2.7 Cost of Business Start-Up Procedures (Percent of GNI per capita). *Source:* World Development Indicators.

On a similar note, the cost of starting a business as a percentage of GNI (Gross National Income) per capita puts Egyptian entrepreneurs at a disadvantage as compared with Turkey and Morocco and thus is an important indicator for small business ventures (Figure 2.7). The implication is that Egypt demonstrates a higher level of effective protection for domestic businesses, suggesting less efficiency vis-à-vis international firms, as Egyptian businesses can rely on state protection. These statistics show that the three cases differ in the extent of effective openness, a fundamental gauge of the competitiveness of liberalization and the domestic economy. Egypt, with higher protection and narrower integration into the global economy, provides an environment that is advantageous for traditional big businesses and hostile to the growth of new and smaller businesses, resembling crony liberalization. In contrast, Morocco and Turkey fall much closer to the competitive liberalization model, with a more hospitable economic milieu for the growth of SMEs in a competitive market.

Concentration and Competition

Firms' size distribution in the economy is a critical indicator of the level of concentration in an economy. A higher share for bigger firms in an economy implies a more concentrated market structure that is unfavorable to smaller and newer companies for two reasons. First, the cost of business would be disproportionately

Table 2.2 Egypt—Firms' Size Distribution in Manufacturing (%)

Years	<10	10–	25–	50–	100–	500–	Total
1980s	0.4	59.4	16.8	8.4	10.0	5.0	100.0
1990–1994	1.4	51.2	12.4	9.5	16.3	9.2	100.0
1995–2000	0.4	65.4	13.3	7.2	9.3	4.3	100.0

Source: Abdellatif and Ghoneim (2008).

high for smaller firms because the more established and bigger firms have access to an overwhelming share of the market, enabling the bigger firms to utilize economies of scale against potential challengers. Second, in a concentrated market, bigger companies are also more likely to possess a disproportionate influence in decision-making mechanisms, minimizing the economic and political power of their competitors. Additionally, higher concentration in a liberalizing economy implies the absence of competition.

The figures on the manufacturing sector over time and across cases are presented below. In Egypt, big businesses make up a disproportionate share of the economy (Table 2.2). Specifically, the dominance of companies with more than 500 employees is striking, with the share of companies in this range varying between 4.3 percent and 9.2 percent across different sectors of the economy. From the 1980s until 2000, the dominance of big firms over SMEs shows no sign of decrease, although there has been some variation. Egypt also stands in sharp contrast to international averages. Statistics indicate that SMEs generally constitute 95 percent of the firms in the OECD countries (OECD Observer 2000).

Morocco, on the other hand, displays a more favorable picture for SMEs. Big businesses' share among all firms varies between 1.2 percent and 1.9 percent throughout the 1990s and into the early 2000s (Table 2.3). In addition, the share of small-sized firms is markedly high. Finally, the data on Turkish firms lump all firms with more than 250 employees together; hence the case of Turkey is qualitatively different from the other two cases. Nonetheless, it does not invalidate the conclusions I draw (Table 2.4). The data suggest that on average, fewer than 2 percent of Turkish firms have fifty employees or more. From 1992 until 2000 the percentage improved slightly in favor of big firms, but the change is negligible. The share of firms with 250 employees or more stands at a mere 0.4 percent. In all three cases, the statistics on the distribution of firm sizes have a clear implication. Turkish SMEs claim a larger share of the economic production as compared with their Egyptian and Moroccan counterparts. Morocco, with a slightly higher percentage of big companies, also offers an SME-friendly economic environment, whereas in Egypt, big businesses unequivocally dominate the economy. Although the differences between cases seem to be negligible, the effect on the size

Table 2.3 Morocco—Firms' Size Distribution in Manufacturing (%)

Years	<10	11–	51–	101–	201–	500–	Total
1990	30.7	42.9	12.3	7.6	5.0	1.5	100.0
1991	31.1	42.5	12.1	7.7	5.2	1.4	100.0
1992	30.5	42.5	11.9	8.2	5.4	1.4	100.0
1993	28.3	44.5	12.3	8.0	5.3	1.5	100.0
1996	33.2	39.9	11.6	8.4	5.7	1.2	100.0
1997	34.2	39.8	10.7	8.0	5.8	1.5	100.0
1998	25.6	38.9	10.5	7.7	5.8	1.6	100.0
1999	36.0	38.7	10.6	7.5	5.4	1.9	100.0
2000	38.0	37.8	9.9	7.3	5.2	1.8	100.0
2001	37.4	39.0	9.7	7.0	5.2	1.8	100.0

Source: Annuaire Statistique du Maroc, various years.

Table 2.4 Turkey—Firms' Size Distribution in Manufacturing (%)

Years	<10	10–50	50–250	250–	Total
1992	94.3	4.0	1.2	0.4	100.0
2001	94.6	3.5	1.5	0.4	100.0
2003	94.1	3.5	2.0	0.5	100.0
2004	94.1	3.6	1.8	0.4	100.0

Source: Turkish Statistical Institute.

of production is much higher because of the major difference in company sizes and the potential to utilize economies of scale.

Data on competition levels present a similar trend. The World Economic Forum (WEF) identifies several indicators to assess the level of competition in an economy, such as the intensity of local competition, extent of market dominance, effectiveness of antimonopoly policy, and ease of access to loans (Table 2.1).[3] According to the WEF's qualitative evaluation of economies worldwide, the Egyptian economy is identified with less competition and prevalence of market dominance by larger firms, while Turkey fares better in terms of the pervasiveness of competition. Morocco lies somewhere in the middle but is closer to Turkey on this spectrum of competition.

With respect to the level of overall competition in the economy, Turkey is about a half point above Egypt and a quarter point above Morocco. Regarding other indicators of competition such as intensity of local competition, market dominance, and antimonopoly policy, Turkey's performance is markedly higher than that of Egypt up to a whole point. The Moroccan economy wavers between that of Turkey and Egypt on different indicators. On one such indicator, intensity of local competition, Morocco's score is almost identical to Egypt's, although on market dominance and antimonopoly policy, Morocco is placed much closer to Turkey. Hence overall the Turkish economy seems to be the most competitive among the three, followed by Morocco's middling competitiveness, and the uncompetitive economy of Egypt.

Crony versus Competitive Liberalization

The empirical evidence thus far suggests that each country's form of economic liberalization is qualitatively distinct. Based on the preceding discussion, I categorize each country on both components of economic liberalization in Table 2.5.

With features such as lower levels of competition, dominance of big firms in the economy, high levels of effective protection, and weak integration to the global economy, the Egyptian economy more closely resembles crony liberalization than it does competitive liberalization. The most recent example of crony relationships in Egypt is the privatization of public enterprises to investors on loans provided by state banks and the continuation of "protective policies," which effectively maintain the monopolistic industry structure. Among such privatizations are al-Nasr Boilers, al-Ahram Beverages, Asyut Cement, and the Egyptian Pepsi Cola Company (Farah 2009, 81). Turkey stands at the other end of the economic liberalization spectrum with opposite characteristics. SMEs have become the engine of the economy both in production and in employment in Turkey since the liberalization process began. Protection for domestic firms has been low since the beginning of liberalization, and economic integration with the European Union has only reinforced this trend. Similarly, manufacturing exports

Table 2.5 Classification of Economic Liberalizations

	Egypt	Morocco	Turkey
Integration & Protection			
Manufactures exports	low	high	high
Tariff rates	high	medium	low
Domestic Competition			
Concentration	high	medium	low
Competition	low	medium	high
Overall Categorization	Crony Liberalization	Semicompetitive Liberalization	Competitive Liberalization

and competition are significantly higher compared with other cases, placing the Turkish case closer to the competitive liberalization archetype. Morocco also performs better than Egypt in most indicators of economic competitiveness, with its liberalization taking a broader form with higher levels of competition and manufacturing exports and with a larger role for SMEs in the economy. Yet Morocco does not conform to either of the ideal types. Its performance is below that of Turkey on most indicators, while still standing closer to Turkey and competitive liberalization than to Egypt and crony liberalization. Hence I categorize Morocco as a case of semicompetitive liberalization.

Economic Liberalizations

Turkey

The Turkish economy, since the establishment of the republican regime in 1923, had been a statist one until the initiation of the economic liberalization process in 1980. The early period (1923–1950s) was marked by the overwhelming dominance of the state as an economic actor throughout the economy. Whatever existed of the private sector during this period was subservient to the demands of the state. However, in the late 1950s, the emphasis on economic policy was transformed into one of creating a large, local entrepreneurial class that would, in principle, be able to compete in the global market, but only after successfully completing the infant industry stage, a policy more concisely known, throughout the developing world, as Import Substitution Industrialization (ISI). The new policy of creating an indigenous business class proved at first to be on target, especially when growth rates soared and state protection helped the newly emerging industrial sector that focused solely on the domestic market as part of the ISI policy. However, in the medium to long term, the policy's problems became increasingly visible (Richards and Waterbury 1996, 25).

Self-sufficiency is a key goal in the initial stages of an ISI policy. Imports should, in principle, be substituted for domestic production, thereby lowering the payment made for imports. Building on the development of domestic industries, these domestic businesses were expected to start exporting in the long term. In Turkey, as in many other developing countries, the ISI policy did not work as expected. Specifically, three structural problems brewed throughout the 1970s: (1) failure to develop intermediate and capital goods industries, (2) the need for the importation of the technological foundation to develop industries beyond basic consumer goods production, and (3) the extraordinarily high levels of profits and protection enjoyed by the new industrial bourgeoisie (Pamuk 1981, 28–29).

As Turkey approached the late 1970s, a foreign exchange emergency surfaced as the result of an ISI economy that exported little and imported much. The income from exports was not sufficient to pay for imports, especially after an increase in oil prices (Pamuk 1981, 30). Domestically, the large industrial bourgeoisie enjoyed a favorable captive market, leading this economic group to be resistant to change for a long period of time. After 1980, the imbalance created by structural deficiencies in the ISI policy became the main determinant of change in Turkish economic policy, since it led to a balance of payments crisis.

The Turkish experience with economic liberalization was abrupt, beginning with dual crises at the end of the 1970s. This did not allow for much of an adaptation period on the part of business owners. Politically, unstable coalition governments and increased violence between rightist and leftist groups since the mid-1970s brought political chaos. Economically, the balance of payments crisis left the economic system untenable, and the end of the ISI era severely constrained options available to decision makers in addressing the economic problems. Therefore, radical reforms were undertaken in order to stabilize the economy. January 24, 1980, marked the official beginning of the economic liberalization era in Turkey. The Turkish government, headed by Suleyman Demirel, introduced a stabilization program under the auspices of the International Monetary Fund (IMF), alongside a wide array of economic policies devised to liberalize the economy. Turgut Özal was charged as overseer of the implementation of this program. Nonetheless, the political will behind such a radical reform initiative was lacking, with the military emerging as a critical actor. In the face of increased political and economic instability, the military took over the government on September 12, 1980, with a coup, which proved to be an important milestone in entrenching the drastic economic reform package initiated months earlier. The military was convinced, due in large part to the leading role of the future prime minister Turgut Özal in implementing the liberalization reforms, that economic reform was necessary and that a disciplined following of the program was in the best interests of the country.

When Turkey resorted to international borrowing to alleviate the current account deficit, such borrowing did not come without unambiguous conditions. In particular, the IMF loans came with a specific prescription regarding which policies the Turkish government would pursue to sustain the economy on fragile grounds. Simultaneously, a structural adjustment program was put in place to transform the Turkish economy from an ISI economy to an open and export-oriented economy in cooperation with the World Bank. In their entirety, these programs are called the Stabilization and Structural Adjustment Program (Senses 1991). In essence, the measures demanded by the IMF and the World Bank would lead to deep economic liberalization. In the long run, the aim was the integration of the Turkish economy into the global economy through free trade and free capital movement. In Waterbury's terms, the new focus of economic policy was to create an "export-led" economy (Waterbury 1992). Hence the beginning of Turkey's experience with liberalization was also the end of the ISI economy.[4]

In less than a decade, drastic reforms in the trade and financial sectors were undertaken. The reforms fall into four broad categories: (1) liberalization of domestic pricing mechanisms; (2) trade liberalization, that is, governmental support for exports and gradual reduction of quantitative import restrictions and tariffs; (3) financial liberalization, that is, free movement of capital and liberalization of bank time deposit interest rates; and (4) floating exchange rates (Cecen, Dogruel, and Dogruel 1994, 45; Togan 1996; Taşkin and Yeldan 1996; Snowden 1996; Bugra 2002). Such a fundamental shift in the Turkish economy toward a more open economy was late, however, mainly because the bourgeoisie that emerged and thrived under ISI policies was opposed to such reorientation, even though outward reorientation had benefits that were very obvious to the state. Turgut Özal, prime minister and leading figure in the economy after the 1980 coup, overcame domestic resistance by recourse to international constraints, in a process similar to what Putnam calls "two-level games" (Putnam 1988). A diehard proponent of the liberal market economy and a former World Bank economist, Özal utilized international pressure from the IMF and the World Bank to proceed with economic reforms and overcome domestic resistance from the bourgeoisie, yet these economic reforms had an unintended outcome. SME owners, or "the owners of regionally located smaller enterprises," made the best of this liberalization period, as Bugra duly notes (2002, 119), with SMEs growing dramatically during the 1980s and the 1990s.

SME owners successfully utilized the opportunities that the now-liberal economy afforded them (TR-1-B, interview). In their utilization, they were also aided by another aspect of the new trade policy, support given to the exporting sectors.[5] These sectors also included some larger companies, but mostly, it was smaller firms that had an advantage in flexible production and subcontracting. The exporters in the initial stages of the liberalization process were supported by export subsidies, tax breaks, and devaluation of currency (Bugra 2002, 119). In addition, the tariff rates were gradually cut in an effort to increase competitiveness of domestic firms with the rationale that domestic firms would be forced to keep up with foreign firms as they faced increasing international competition. The average tariff rate for manufactured goods was 11 percent, while manufactured consumer goods had a 17 percent tariff during the first decade of liberalization (Richards and Waterbury 1996, 245). Export figures show a corresponding increase (Figure 2.3).

The change that economic liberalization introduced became clear-cut in three statistics, pointing out the "challenge" that the peripheral economic actors posed vis-à-vis traditional big business's dominance. First, businesses with more than 500 employees dominated the value added in production prior to and immediately after liberalization. Yet over the course of the 1980s and the 1990s, they progressively lost their dominance. In 1985, their share in value added was 66.1 percent; in 1993, 58.5 percent; in 2001, 56.9 percent; and in 2004, 49 percent. Second, the highest increase in energy consumption was recorded in different parts of Anatolia, such as in Ankara, Kayseri, Gaziantep, and Sivas, rather than in Istanbul. The increase was particularly sharp for the period between 2002 and 2006. Finally, the biggest jump in bank credits is, again, recorded in different parts of Anatolia, such as southeastern and eastern Turkey, for the same period.[6] Collectively, these statistics imply an important shift in the dynamics of the Turkish economy: a shift in the centrality of economic production from Istanbul-based big business to the politically and geographically peripheral parts of Turkey. It was a change in the economic center of gravity that foreshadowed a political shift with the later rise of the Muslim periphery in politics.

Financial liberalization was the last element of liberalization to be entrenched in the Turkish economy. After what some called the first phase of liberalization between 1980 and 1989, the Özal government undertook a series of reforms to complete the financial liberalization phase (Yeldan, Metin-Ozcan, and Voyvoda 2000).[7] In August of 1989, Decree 32 ensured the liberalization of foreign exchange, and by April of 1990, Turkey informed the IMF of the full convertibility of the Turkish lira (Altinkemer and Ekinci 1992). This financial liberalization meant that businesses engaging in international trade would have fewer complications and problems.

Politically, the extent of the reforms was untenable in the face of their potential social costs. Surely, traditional big businesses of the ISI period stood to lose from liberalization. Nonetheless, governmental policies and the peculiar circumstances in Turkey at the time ensured minimal resistance to the reforms. The military coup in 1980, indeed, proved to be extremely functional for the center-right Özal government in this period, since the military was convinced of the necessity of the reforms. Generals also held that various interest groups and leftists were the ones responsible for the political chaos and subsequent violence that occurred throughout the 1970s. Trade unions and business associations suitably footed the bill (of blame for instabilities in this period) thanks to the heavy-handed measures taken by the military early on. Since the late 1970s, the major setback for the masses was the decreasing real income due to a consistently high inflation rate in the 60 to 70 percent range. Unsurprisingly, nominal incomes could not keep up with the increase in consumer prices. Throughout the 1980s, the Özal government tried to cushion the negative effects of liberalization reforms through high public spending in order to make sure it maintained the masses' support (Richards and Waterbury 1996, 247). The masses also benefited from cheaper consumer goods. This sector of the society, comprising the bulk of losers in this period, offered Özal its support by successive electoral vic-

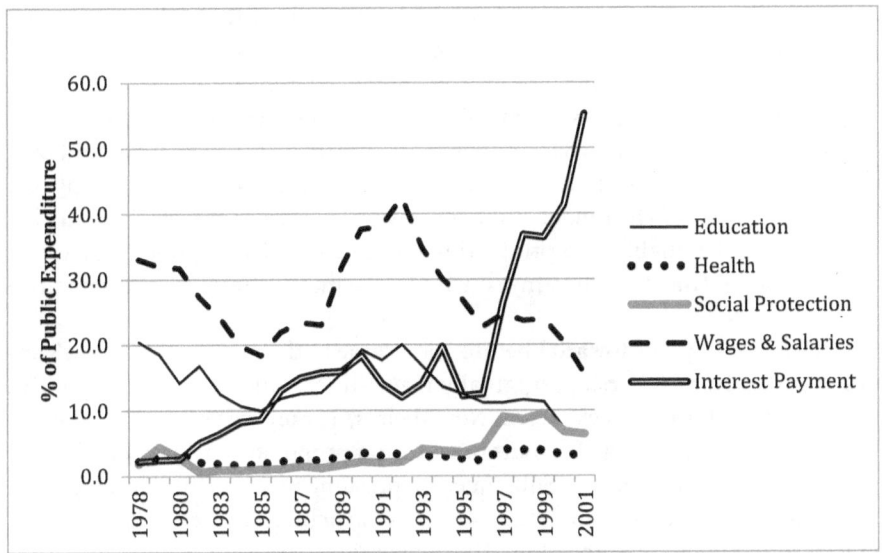

Figure 2.8 Public Spending by Category in Turkey. *Source:* International Monetary Fund, *Government Finance Statistics Yearbook*, various years. Data for 1982 are missing.

tories in 1983 and 1987 following the return to civilian rule in 1983 (Waterbury 1992).

Figure 2.8 shows itemized government spending. Through the first years of liberalization reforms, spending on wages and education declined, while health and social protection expenditures remained constant at their already low levels. However, beginning in the second half of the 1980s, spending on wages, education, and health care increased significantly despite the fact that the government was under an increasing debt and interest burden. In addition, governments between 1980 and 2000 utilized, to support the losers, an extrabudgetary account (Waterbury 1992). That was the equivalent of approximately 15 percent of total public spending throughout the 1980s and averaged at least 5 percent of public spending throughout the 1990s.[8]

As for big business, the military reaffirmed its conviction that political activism of civil society organizations was fundamentally destabilizing, a lesson learned prior to the 1980 coup. Hence civil society was severely limited to nonpolitical activism in large part due to the newly drafted constitution of 1982. The Turkish Industrialists and Businessmen's Association (TUSIAD), an exclusive business association established in 1971 representing big business owners, was one of the main targets of the depoliticization efforts of the military; the military was, indeed, successful in this endeavor. It was not until the early 1990s, when the military was largely out of power, that TUSIAD increased its political activism once again. By that time, however, economic liberalization was entrenched, leaving little room for opposing liberalization reforms. Economically, high inflation rates throughout the 1980s and the 1990s minimized the efficiency and productivity requirements of an open economy, helping big businesses adapt to a liberal economic environment. Ever-increasing consumer prices ensured that regardless of the quality and production cost of a good, such goods would in a short period of time be a firm investment in the market because of competitive prices.

A further impetus toward liberalization came in the mid-1990s. Turkey's application for EU membership, originally made in 1987, did not find the positive response from Europe as expected. Nonetheless, Turkey was offered an alternative mode of cooperation. The European Union proposed "customs union" as a step toward full membership. Subsequently, presumably when Turkey adapted to the European Union's underlying economic structure, Turkey would be embraced with full EU membership. The center-right coalition headed by Tansu Çiller accepted the offer and signed a customs union with the European Union in 1995, effective as of 1996, thus eliminating all duties and tariffs between the two parties. The sectors that were to be most affected by this union were industrial and processed agricultural goods.[9] The union exposed the Turkish economy, a developing economy with quite limited hi-tech export items, to one of the most developed regional markets on a global scale. According to trade data between Turkey and the European Union, over time, the Turkish economy has shown significant adaptability to EU standards in manufacturing and was not at all overwhelmed by a disproportionate flow of European goods into its market (Figure 2.9). Overall, Turkish liberalization is characterized by increased competition and new opportunities for SMEs while simultaneously the government has been able minimize opposition to liberalization by compensating for the losses of those social groups and sectors most hurt by liberalization.

Egypt

The Egyptian experience with economic liberalization is a completely different story compared with the Turkish and Moroccan cases, with substantially different implications for the fate of eventual Islamist moderation and the rise of MDPs. Liberalization, or the *infitah* (open door) policy, began with President Anwar Sadat's October Paper. Two decades under Gamal Abdel-Nasser's Arab socialism and the conflict with Israel left the Egyptian economy exhausted and with limited prospects for economic development. Particularly, by the time Nasser's Arab socialism was deemed obsolete (in the late 1960s and early 1970s), the economy

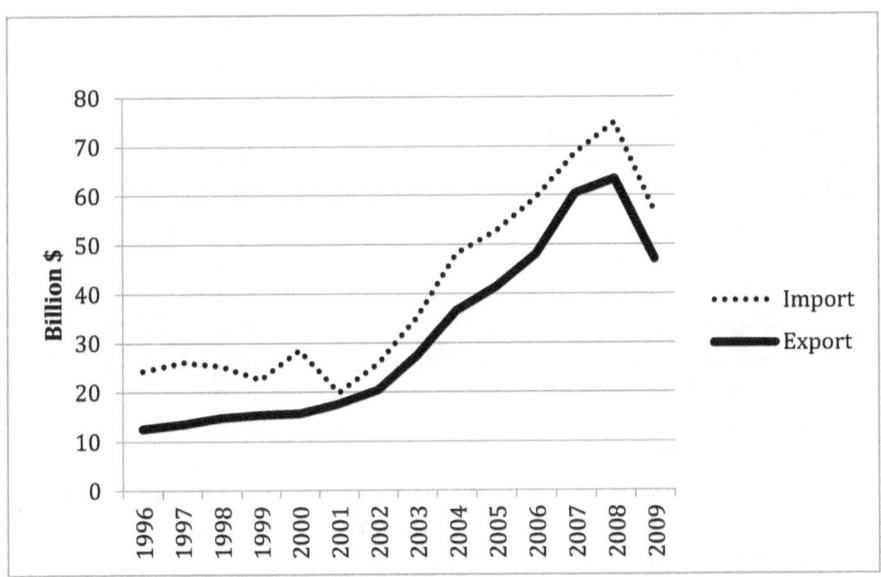

Figure 2.9 Trade between Turkey and the European Union. *Source:* Turkiye Istatistik Kurumu (Turkish Statistical Institute).

was devoid of private enterprise of any significant size. To eliminate potential challenge to his power, Nasser took away, by way of nationalization and land redistribution, the sources of power of the private sector and landed elite. The extent of state presence in the economy was such that by the late 1960s, the public sector constituted about 90 percent of nonagricultural production (Henry and Springborg 2001). Hence when the first liberalization reforms were undertaken in the early 1970s, one of the goals was to create a private business elite (Dillman 2001; Henry and Springborg 2001), similar to the classes of national bourgeoisie in other countries in the region, which would later replace the bureaucratic elite in Egypt (Farah 2009).

Even though Nasser himself initiated small-scale reforms toward a market economy, it was not until 1973 that a concerted effort to that effect emerged.[10] The goal of the October Paper was to attract foreign investment, including that of other Arab nations, and to promote domestic private investment (Alissa 2007, 3; Moustafa 2007). Accompanying the October Paper a year later was Law 43, which reduced the scope of qualifying conditions as a private business and also relaxed labor regulations to that end.[11] Simultaneously, the new constitution that was enacted and approved in 1971 guaranteed secure private property rights to erase the legacy of Nasser's Arab socialism (Rivlin 1985, 48).

During this first wave of liberalization, major exemptions and incentives were granted, mostly to foreign companies. Sadat had hoped to increase the share of the private sector to up to 30 percent of the economy. At first, the open door policy seemed to have a positive impact; in the next decade, the economy grew at substantially higher rates than it had in previous years. Yet most of the growth was due to various rents the state obtained in the form of increased oil prices and sales, remittances, and foreign aid rather than from real domestic production (Farah 2009). In terms of foreign investment, transnational companies had a sizeable presence in Egypt with investments of around $8 billion by 1995 (Ateş 2005). Nonetheless, the liberalization reforms did not deliver the anticipated outcome; the investment mostly came in real estate and luxury goods rather than in industries that would help increase domestic production, job creation, and integration into the global economy. Some even characterized certain ventures under *infitah* policy as leading to the "rape of Egypt" because such businesses were after quick and high profits at any cost (John Waterbury quoted in Farah 2009, 39). By 1991, the share of public enterprises in the economy was almost 65 percent (Anderson and Martinez 1998).

Hosni Mubarak, the recently ousted president of Egypt (1981–2011), undertook two other liberalization moves, first in the early 1990s as a response to increasing foreign debt and then in 2004 to improve the foreign investment environment. During the early 1990s, Mubarak's goal was to increase the role of the private sector in Egypt and increase competition by further opening the economy to foreign companies (Alissa 2007, 4). In 1991, the Egyptian government initiated the Economic Reform and Structural Adjustment Program (ERSAP) as a result of negotiations with the IMF and the World Bank. The program's immediate goals were to improve the balance of payments and reduce foreign debt to more acceptable levels, while the longer-term goals were the privatization of state companies and to instill a more liberal economy focused on attracting private investment. Financially, the program was deemed successful as foreign debt was substantially decreased, budget deficit was lowered to 1 to 2 percent of the GDP, and the current account turned to surplus in two years (Rivlin 2001, 106–108).

The program laid down a strict line of austerity measures including reduction in public spending, freeze on wages, and decrease in subsidies. While such austerity measures are typically known to affect lower classes the most, the timing of the program in Egypt could not have been better suited in order to minimize the negative effects on the masses. Egypt, under Mubarak's leadership, spearheaded Arab support for the Coalition Forces in 1991 when Saddam Hussein invaded Kuwait, and Egyptian military and political support was critical to the coalition. As a result, the West and the Arab world repaid Egyptian support in fighting Saddam Hussein with generous compensation. A substantial amount of Egyptian foreign debt was written off between 1991 and 1993, solving the most

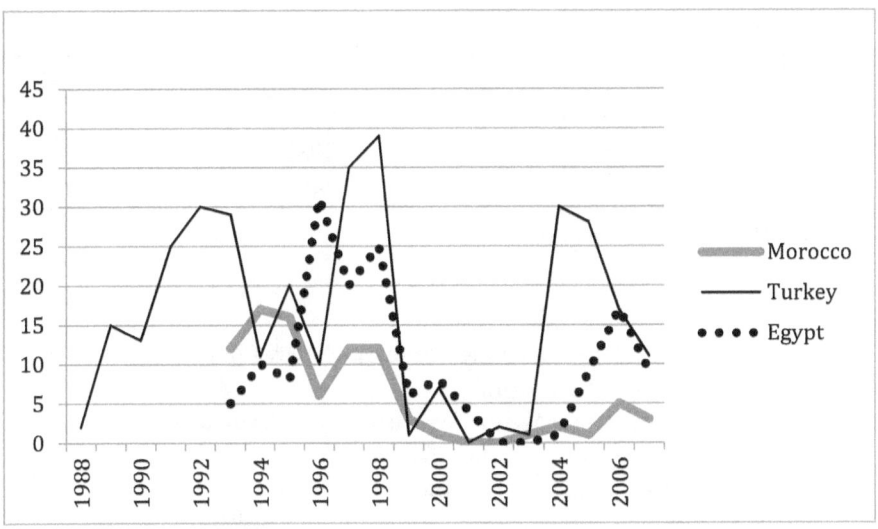

Figure 2.10 Number of Privatization Transactions. *Source:* World Bank Privatization Dataset.

immediate problem of the Egyptian economy at the time: "Twenty-five billion dollars of sugar coating had made the bitter pill of stabilization very much easier to swallow" (Henry and Springborg 2001, 140). The Egyptian debt was to both the United States and the wealthy Arab countries in the Gulf. Still, the austerity program had dismal effects on the society at large while maintaining crucial elements of an illiberal economic regime. Major problems that became evident regarding the liberalization reforms were limited transparency of privatizations, the distorted nature of credit access, noncompetitive market practices, and public procurement (Adly 2009). With respect to privatization, in the aftermath of Law 203 in 1991, which required the privatization of 314 public companies (16 percent of the total figure for state-owned enterprises [SOEs]), only about ninety companies were privatized by 1998 (Figure 2.10) (Kienle 2001). Moreover, the funds from privatization were not used to support the private sector in minimizing the state's economic role. Instead, the funds were either reinvested in state enterprises or funneled into public banks in order to provide credit to some well-connected business elite. As a result, the amount of privatization until 2007 was less than $15 billion despite the fact that Egypt was one of the most statist economies in the region with the largest population. Morocco, with less than half of Egypt's population, was able to privatize at a figure close to Egypt's (Table 2.6). In the words of Dillman, Egyptian privatization "could be seen as a

Table 2.6 Amount of Privatization (Million $)

	Egypt	Morocco	Turkey
1988–1999	$4,172.62	$3,099.13	$4,897.73
2000–2007	$10,631.86	$7,920.38	$27,792.42
TOTAL	$14,804.48	$11,019.51	$32,690.15

Source: World Bank Privatization Dataset.

self-interested state strategy, involving not so much deregulation as reregulation of the public sector" (Dillman 2001).

Similarly, credit access was severely distorted to favor a small number of well-connected business owners rather than a wider group of businesses and individuals. Credits from public banks, which overall held more than two-thirds of banking assets in Egypt, were extended either on the basis of political connections or to favored businesses without sufficient collateral. For example, Adly's analysis on loan concentrations yielded that until 2000, almost one-half of all credit extended to the private sector was received by only 343 clients; moreover, the top eight debtors received 6 percent of all credit equaling 12.4 billion LE (Adly 2009, 11). Irrespective of the motivations of political decision makers on why they chose to reregulate privatized public enterprises or why they chose to allocate credit on political bases, the poor privatization performance and preferential credit mechanisms reinforce the idea that Egyptian liberalization was not competitive, leaving narrow scope for the growth of SMEs.[12]

Since 2004, the emphasis has been on the privatization of SOEs and the creation of a favorable business environment in order to attract foreign investment. Successive technocratic cabinets formed under Prime Minister Ahmed Nazif undertook reforms to ensure a business-friendly environment, local and foreign alike (Rivlin 2009). The first wave of privatization was largely deemed a failure, and the second wave of privatization did not fare particularly well, either, for a number of reasons. First, the number of state companies that were privatized remained quite limited even though the value of the privatized companies surpassed the value of all privatization until 2004 (Figure 2.10). Second, although many state companies were privatized, most either did not enjoy full private control or were subject to renationalization after a while. When privatized companies' shares lost their value in the stock market, the government authorized buying the shares back with public funding (Henry and Springborg 2001, 141). The zigzags of the Egyptian state with respect to privatization seem to arise from two contrasting political concerns. On the one hand, international pressure constrains the options of the government as to what can be done with the public

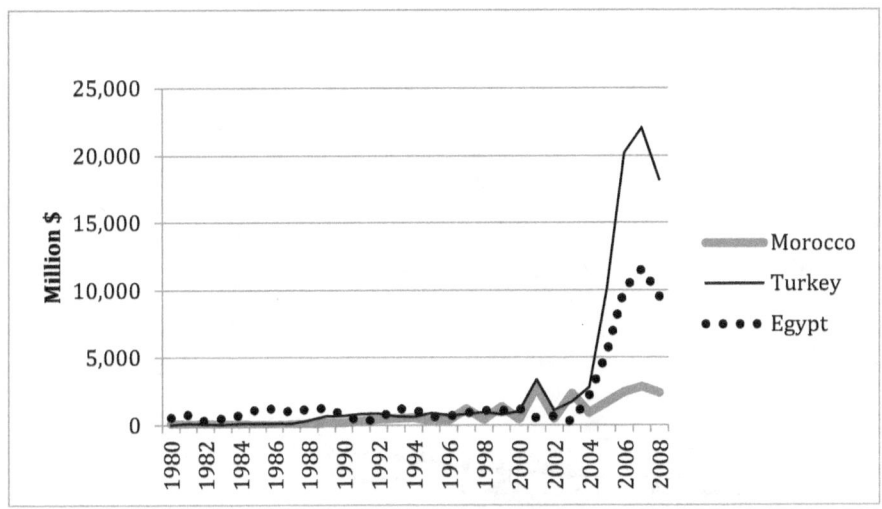

Figure 2.11 FDI Inflow. *Source:* United Nations Conference on Trade and Development (UNCTAD).

sector. International pressure is too important to dismiss outright, especially in terms of its potential implications for foreign investment in Egypt—an important source of investment to boost the economy. On the other hand, the state wants to maintain some form of control over public companies even in a phase of privatization, including distinct mechanisms such as partial privatization, renationalization, or allowing politically connected businessmen to buy the companies.

With respect to attracting foreign investment, the Egyptian government was relatively successful. The foreign direct investment (FDI) inflow and stock figures show that the Egyptian economy attracted substantial FDI, particularly in the post-2004 period (Figures 2.11 and 2.12). In 2006, Egypt surpassed the $10 billion benchmark with respect to FDI inflows, and the FDI stock was in excess of $38 billion the same year. These figures are significant in that as a percentage of Egyptian GDP they make up a substantial portion of the economy.

An interesting aspect of the new period of liberalization is that the Egyptian business elite found numerous influential positions within the cabinet, such as the appointment of Rashid Mohamed Rashid as the minister of foreign trade and industry in the first Nazif government, and the six appointments from the business world in the second Nazif cabinet.[13] Regarding the extent of business involvement in Egyptian government, Farah observes, "It seems that the state is not embedded in social networks, as Evans claims, but that business leaders are

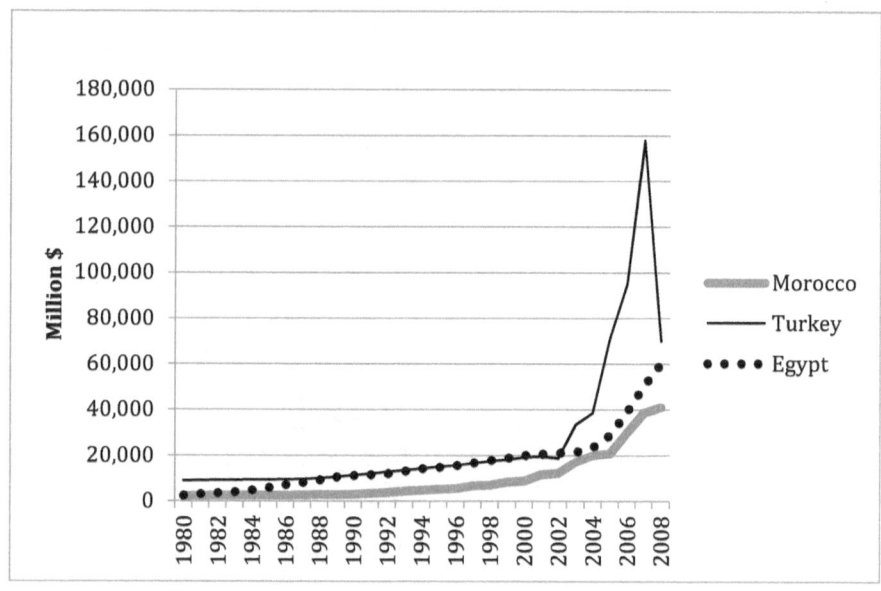

Figure 2.12 FDI Stock. *Source:* United Nations Conference on Trade and Development (UNCTAD).

now in charge of policy making under the rule of Egypt's neoliberals" (Farah 2009). Although this assertion is an overstatement of the influence of the business elite, it nonetheless points to their significant role. Among the reforms undertaken in this period was the reduction of corporate taxes along with personal income taxes to 20 percent (making it a regressive tax system), the creation of a new ministry in charge of investments, and fast-tracking privatization of SOEs with limited publicization of the sales. Such nontransparent schemes employed in privatization were deemed as "subsidizing the private sector at the expense of the nation as a whole" (Farah 2009, 50). Examples of nontransparent privatizations include the Qalyub Spinning Factory and the Alexandria Tire Company. These irregularities in the liberalization process reinforce the perception that economic liberalization in Egypt has been "piecemeal, corrupt, and highly contested" (Dillman 2001).

A related outcome of such nontransparent practices in liberalization reforms was the creation of monopolies and quasi-monopolies aimed at protecting the market shares of politically connected big business owners such as Osman Ahmed Osman, Ahmed Eizz in the steel industry, and Mohamed Nosseir in telecommunications and beverages (Adly 2009, 12–13; Henry and Springborg 2001). After a thorough statistical analysis, Abdellatif and Ghoneim conclude that these sectors are among the least competitive and are concentrated in the Egyptian economy (Abdellatif and Ghoneim 2008). Overall, the combined outcome of the privatization policy was the creation of private monopolies instead of state monopolies. This was essentially due to the protected nature of the Egyptian economy; the liberalization reforms since the 1970s failed to create a foundation for a competitive economy. In the absence of a liberal economy, privatizations resulted in "a series of privately owned monopolies which need to be neither responsive, low-cost nor dynamic" (Stevens 1993, 123–24).

As far as the masses are considered, the employment and income effects of liberalization were largely unfavorable. In a rapidly growing population, new job creation was quite limited. Egypt has the largest population of the entire region. According to estimates, the annual addition to the labor market is projected to be as high as 900,000. Throughout the period between 1980 and 2005, the working-age population increased by more than 80 percent and the labor force more than doubled, causing the demand for new jobs to be at record levels (Rivlin 2009, 96). In contrast, however, the growth in total employment (public and private) remained around 90 perent throughout the same period, according to official figures, failing to meet even the current demand.[14] Similarly significant is the fact that the contribution of the private sector to new job creation was limited. The Egyptian state contributed most to the growth of employment during this period with more than one-third of new jobs being created in the public sector (Henry and Springborg 2001; Rivlin 2009).

The feeble contribution of the private sector came about due to a number of reasons. On the one hand, the volume of new investment was quite limited in this period. Indeed, the comparison between pre- and post-ERSAP (1991) makes it clear that the investment numbers decreased by 60 percent throughout the period (Figure 2.13). The decrease was particularly substantial in public investments affecting employment in a country where the legacy of Arab socialism was still strongly felt.

On the other hand, the investment in the private sector came either in the form of the privatization of SOEs or in unproductive sectors that did not require high employment such as real estate and untradeable sectors (Rivlin 2009). In privatized public companies, the employees were oftentimes persuaded to leave their jobs through various tactics in order to maintain a sustainable labor force, making the job of new owners easier.[15] In terms of the low private investment figures, this problem emerged because of the specific nature of the trade regime following the liberalization reforms. Before 2000, the average effective rate of tariff was above 30 percent yet widely varying in different sectors. The outcome of such variation was twofold. First, investment shifted away from productive and labor-intensive sectors simply because the risks were higher in these unprotected sectors. Investors chose sectors such as furniture production and real

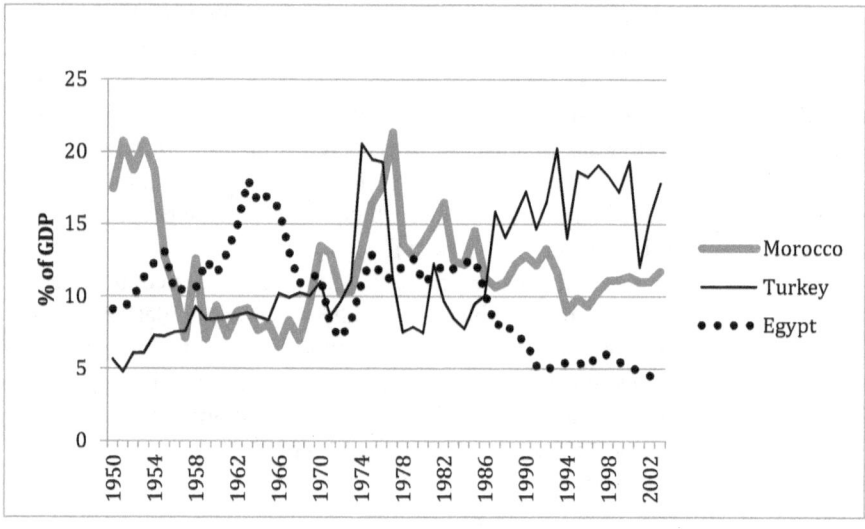

Figure 2.13 Investment Share in GDP. *Source:* World Development Indicators.

estate, where the protection was high and risks were commensurately low. Second, the sectors with lower protection also suffered from higher input prices. The higher tariff rates, along with nontariff barriers, raised overall costs of the exporters in their inputs, thereby further decreasing their international competitiveness. In the words of Paul Rivlin, these exporting sectors were being "taxed out of existence" (Rivlin 2009, 113). The effects of these economic reforms were most significantly felt by the masses in the form of income decrease. According to the Egyptian Household Survey (1999–2000), the percentage of Egyptians living under $2 a day is a staggering 52.7 percent of the total population (Farah 2009). The data on total government consumption also support the idea that the state failed to compensate the losers properly as the government's share in the economy declined significantly in the period since 1970 (Figure 2.14). This decline, moreover, was not picked up by the private sector either, as the investment figures indicate (Figure 2.13).

By restructuring government spending between its different components, that is, from interest payments to social protection, the government can diminish the impact of liberalization on potential losers in an alternative way. Total public spending by the Egyptian government from the 1970s until the early 2000s showed only minimal improvement, mostly in the last couple of years of this period. Public spending on wages, social protection, and health remained stable until the early 1990s, when the Egyptian economy was undergoing a major debt

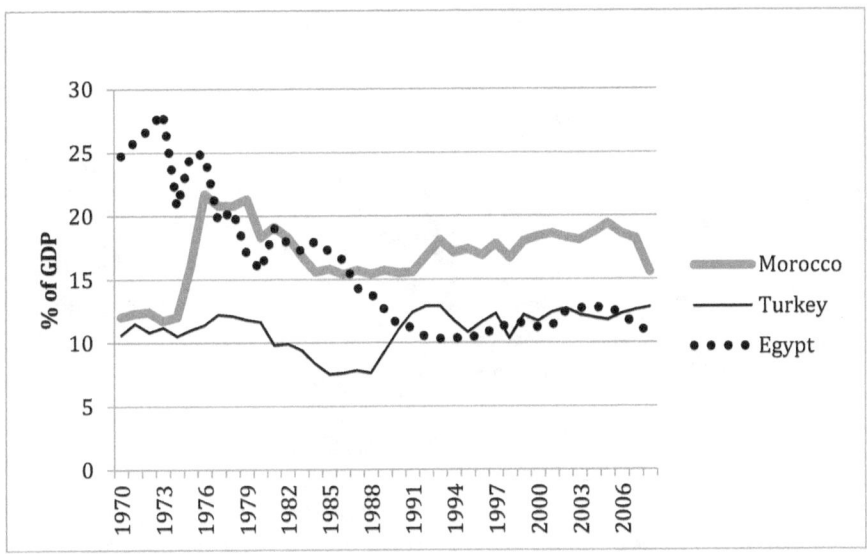

Figure 2.14 Government Consumption. *Source:* World Bank, World Development Indicators.

crisis and stabilized only after an IMF-brokered stabilization program. Although wages and health spending, along with the spending on education, recovered and surpassed their levels prior to the crisis in 1991, social protection spending dropped to less than 1 percent of the total public spending. The increasing interest payments incurred by the Egyptian government also exacerbated the decrease in various items on public spending (Figure 2.15). As a result, public spending on wages did not drop significantly in times of heavy foreign debt—as in the early 1990s—as Saeid Mahdavi's cross-national analysis finds for a set of developing countries; yet, social protection funds were cut substantially, aggravating the negative impact of liberalization on the losers, that is, the masses (Mahdavi 2004).

Overall, the liberalization process took more than three decades in Egypt and is still underway with extensive state presence in the economy and widespread protection for big business. In the words of Farah, extensive state presence in a liberalizing economy translated into "a conduit for widespread corruption, which penetrated all levels of the state" (Farah 2009, 52). Small and medium businesses were not able to find opportunities to integrate to the global economy, unlike in the case of Turkey. At the same time, the state failed to compensate the masses. The masses were among the most significant losers of this process in terms of both real income (decreased subsidies and wages) and employment.

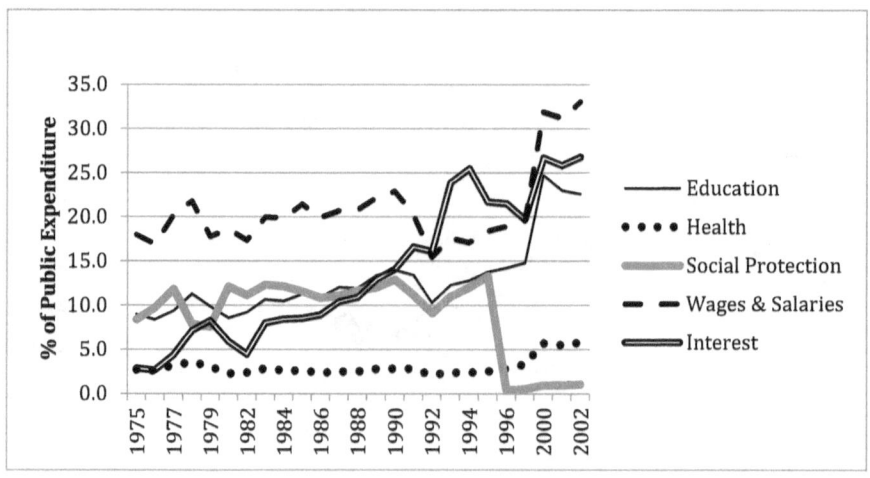

Figure 2.15 Public Spending by Category in Egypt. *Source:* International Monetary Fund, *Government Finance Statistics Yearbook*, various years. Data for 1980, 1998, and 1999 are missing.

Instead, liberalization policies were crafted to ensure that politically connected big businesses would be the winners.

Morocco

In contrast to the liberalization process in Egypt, Morocco's march toward a liberal economy is marked by an effort to integrate as wide a portion of the Moroccan society as possible. In that, the case of Morocco is similar to the case of Turkey. Prior to the liberalization reforms in the early 1980s, Morocco represented a typical state capitalist economy in the region. In a way, it was close to what Atul Kohli calls "state-directed development" in the developing world.[16] Although Morocco never adopted an Arab socialist economic paradigm, the state nevertheless dominated the economy, while private enterprise held a limited role. As in other parts of the Middle East, the private sector was not independent of the political tutelage of the state at any moment. Import Substitution Industrialization (ISI) became the dominant paradigm in the application of economic policies in the 1970s. The legacy of the ISI period was, as in the case of Turkey, the key catalyst in bringing about change in Morocco's economic orientation.

Even though some steps toward economic reforms were taken from 1977 onward due to the increasing ratio of debt to GDP, stabilization reforms did not find a welcoming audience in the society at that point. In particular, the decrease in government subsidies for basic food items was met with resistance in the Moroccan society. Following the second oil shock in 1979, matters were not any better for Morocco. By 1983, current account deficits became unsustainable at almost 13 percent of the GDP, and foreign currency reserves were depleted (Richards and Waterbury 1996, 237). Once again, the severity and urgency of the economic problems forced King Hassan II to heed the advice offered by international actors, that is, the IMF and the World Bank, in order to stabilize the economy and improve the balance of payments.

Morocco underwent a series of structural adjustment programs between 1983 and 1992 during which some elements of competitive economic liberalization were instilled fairly successfully. Indeed, the experience of Morocco led some to call Morocco the "textbook case" of successful economic reforms (Maghraoui 2002, 26; Richards and Waterbury 1996). Reflecting on the success of the Moroccan case, a World Bank official expressed, "Morocco is perhaps the only country in the world which has, at the same time, created a realistic hope for a durable solution to its foreign debt problem, put in place a basic program of structural adjustment, re-established a sound balance of payments situation, instituted monetary stability and stifled inflation while carrying through economic growth at about 4% a year" (quoted in Richards and Waterbury 1996, 237).

At first, high budget deficits and high foreign debt led the government to undertake austerity measures and eliminate price controls partially (Denoeux and Maghraoui 1998). As in any standard application of a structural adjustment program, the program laid out the end of ISI policy in Morocco, and instead tried to implement a new economic structure that focused on two basic goals. On the one hand, by privatizing state economic enterprises, removing state subsidies and price distortions, and floating currency, the state's economic role would be minimized (Pfeifer 1996; White 2001). On the other hand, the Moroccan economy would be integrated into the global economy by removing barriers to trade, encouraging an export-oriented strategy, and inducing private investment, especially foreign investment.

With respect to trade liberalization, most quantitative restrictions on imports were abolished by the early 1990s. In 1992, a mere 8 percent of imports were subject to import licenses, and maximum duties on imports were reduced to below 35 percent by 1993. Morocco also joined the General Agreement on Tariffs and Trade (GATT) in 1987 (Denoeux and Maghraoui 1998, 59). On the exports side, all restrictions on exports (i.e., export duties and licenses) were removed in 1984. As in Turkey, exporters were provided with subsidies and incentives. Additionally, the government established an agency called the Moroccan Export Promotion Center (CMPE) with the explicit goal of offering logistical support to exporters.

During this period, the Moroccan government also sought to attract foreign investment in order to create new job opportunities. To this end, in 1989, the government repealed the 1973 Morocconization Law, which stipulated that foreign investment was required to have Moroccan partners in order to have any investment in Morocco at all. In the same year, a new ministry, the Ministry of Foreign Trade, Foreign Investments, and Tourism, was established, both to address problems of foreign investors and to facilitate other bureaucratic hurdles (Denoeux and Maghraoui 1998).

Privatization in the Moroccan public sector came in the later stages of the economic restructuring—only after the late 1980s. The sluggish start of privatization was due in part to the limited role of the state in the economy when compared with other countries in the Middle East and North Africa. In the mid-1980s, state enterprises in Morocco made up only 17 percent of the GDP, no more than a small fraction of the Egyptian public sector (Denoeux and Maghraoui 1998, 60). In 1989, the Moroccan parliament passed Law 39-89, laying out the privatization of more than two-thirds of the state enterprises with the exception of sectors deemed "strategic" by the government such as electricity, telecommunications, railroads, and water. It was not until after the First Gulf War, however, that privatization actually began. In 1994, the "strategic" sectors were also included in the "accelerated privatization program" (Pfeifer 1996, 42; Rivlin 2001, 117; Denoeux and Maghraoui 1998, 61). Until 1998, privatization enabled the government to raise $1.9 billion, making Morocco one of the most successful privatizers in North Africa (Table 2.6) (Dillman 2001, 208).

During the 1990s, in the second phase of economic liberalization, a period that Melani Cammett refers to as deepened liberalization, the goal was to foster private investment so that it would make up more than 60 percent of the total industrial investment (Pfeifer 1996). Although the liberalization process entailed several problems including the absence of consistent coordination among different branches of the economic administration, it is deemed particularly successful at increasing the international competitiveness of Moroccan firms by enabling them to reach higher export levels. Cammett, in her study of Moroccan economic liberalization, points out the success of apparel exporters as a result of export promotion policies, an integral element of liberalization (Cammett 2007). The swift and comprehensive nature of liberalization reforms has been overwhelmingly attributed to this success in export promotion (Maghraoui 2002) as well as to King Hassan II's leadership role throughout the reform process. More specifically, Hassan II's perseverance in implementing the reform program was critical to the Moroccan success in liberalization.

The success of the "new men" (Richards and Waterbury, 1996), a new class of business owners relying on international trade, was emblematic of the success of liberalization reforms in creating business interests independent of the state. These business owners owned, largely, small and medium businesses, and contributed greatly to the relative success of the Moroccan economy (Denoeux and

Maghraoui 1998, 64). Trade liberalization helped small and medium-sized Moroccan firms to increase their productivity and compete with foreign firms (Haddad 1993). As for the big business owners, they were reliable supporters of the Royal Palace, *makhzen*, throughout the closed economy era. Economic liberalization did little to change this. For example, it is noteworthy that the chief representative of big business prior to liberalization, Confédération Générale des Entreprises Du Maroc (CGEM), largely maintained its support for the reforms, although at times it did not hesitate to voice concerns on various issues.[17] Morocco's dire and urgent economic state meant big business had only two options: support the liberalization reforms or face bankruptcy of the Moroccan economy. Not unexpectedly, they chose the former (Denoeux and Maghraoui 1998, 65).

King Hassan II's personal involvement in urging liberalization was critical in an authoritarian political setting. In contrast to what is observed in other economic reform efforts, the palace minimized the measures that could threaten the effectiveness of the liberalization reforms: "King Hassan took advantage of his triple role of broker, supreme leader, and businessman to push not only economic transition in general, but also the marginalization of political figures and business leaders reluctant to follow along" (Cohen 2004, 77–78). Being a business owner himself and thus interested in economic openness, the king found greater motivation to take a leading role in the liberalization period. *Makhzen* has been an influential actor in the economy by virtue of being one of the major business owners nationwide. For example, Omnium Nord Africain (ONA) is the largest holding company in Morocco, and the king is the largest shareholder, with about 15 percent of the shares of the holding (Rivlin 2009, 189). During the late 1980s and the early 1990s, ONA was the third-largest private enterprise in Africa (Dillman 2001, 209). By being the most significant businessman in the country, the king was still able to maintain a certain level of "patronage" in the postliberalization economy (Richards and Waterbury 1996, 239).

The masses were largely supportive of the economic reforms for two main reasons. First, the standard of living for most of the labor force did not decrease throughout this period. In rural areas, the agricultural sector actually experienced an increase in income due to the elimination of price controls and expansion of markets (Morrison 1991). In the same vein, the minimum wage started to increase in the late 1990s, especially in the manufacturing sector. According to a study by the Moroccan government, the number of people living below poverty level decreased by 41 percent between 1985 and 1991.[18] Second, public spending throughout the 1990s did increase, suggesting increased benefits for the masses. More importantly, the components of public spending that matter most for the masses do not show regressive trends, implying the lack of deterioration of the masses' well-being. For example, between 1978 and 1998, the share of wages, social protection, and education in public spending increased despite the fact that

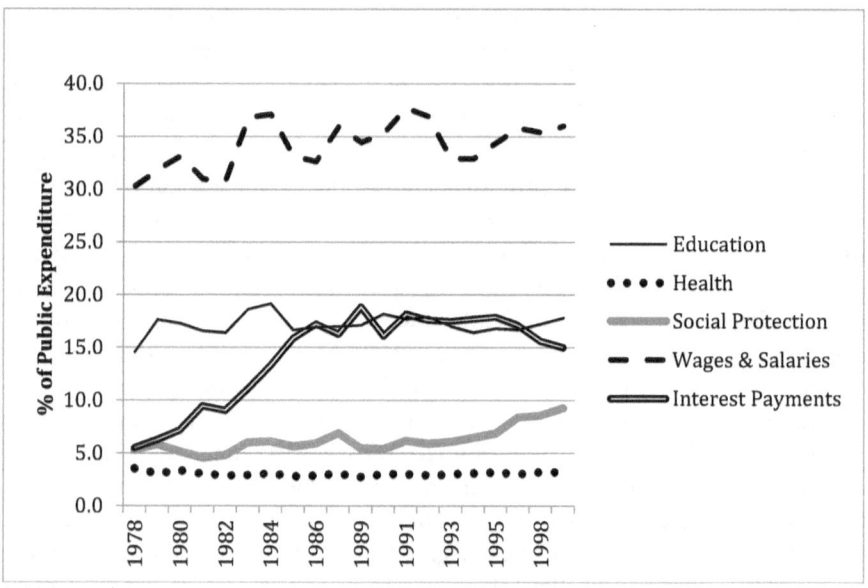

Figure 2.16 Public Spending by Category in Morocco. *Source:* International Monetary Fund, *Government Finance Statistics Yearbook*, various years. Data for 1988 and 1996 are missing.

Morocco was under a significant debt burden (Figure 2.16). Finally, the growth in new job creation was moderately beneficial in minimizing the number of losers in the entire reform process. Between 1989 and 2003, total employment increased by around 50 percent in urban areas, whereas the growth in the labor force was 40 percent, and the growth in total population was only 25 percent.[19]

Another dimension of the Moroccan economy's liberalization concerns the country's relationship with the European Union. An economic cooperation agreement with the European Union has been in the Moroccan agenda for an extended period of time. The year 1987 marks the origins of official Moroccan interest in a closer trade relationship in some fashion with the European Community (EC). King Hassan II applied for full membership in 1987. Although the application was quickly rejected, Morocco continued seeking some form of cooperation. Formal negotiations did not start until 1992, but in 1995, an agreement was reached to liberalize trade between the European Union and Morocco, and for this to be fully implemented in 2010,[20] eventually increasing the level of liberalization and competition in the economy.[21] According to Rutherford and colleagues, Morocco's interest in increasing the scope of its already-existing trade agreement with the European Community may be puzzling for some because

Morocco at the time already had "free access" to the EC market in industrial production without any obligation for reciprocity. What Morocco hoped to gain by increasing the level of access, however, was the inclusion of agricultural products in this free trade. European protectionism in agriculture was a major issue due to the weight of agriculture in the Moroccan economy (Rutherford, Rutstrom, and Tarr 1993). A similar free trade agreement was reached between Morocco and the United States (Rivlin 2009). Even so, foreign investment in the Moroccan economy currently is by and large very limited and increased only slightly in the post-2000 period. The only major exception is the telecommunications sector, where the bulk of investment came via privatization (Rivlin 2009).

Conclusion

In this chapter, I offered a typology of economic liberalization by focusing on two aspects of liberalization: integration into the global economy and level of domestic competition. The three cases (Egypt, Morocco, and Turkey) demonstrate great variance in the path that liberalization pursued, which ultimately has transcending effects over the future of Islamist party politics. Turkey, as the most successful case of liberalization, both integrated into the global market and achieved a high level of domestic competition, making it an example of competitive liberalization. As a result, small and medium business owners found an economic environment that was largely supportive of smaller businesses with various opportunities. Masses also benefited from increased income over time. Egypt, conversely, failed to foster a competitive economy and thus only selectively integrated to the global economy. As a result, smaller businesses—a key constituency of Islamist parties—found an adverse economic atmosphere with limited opportunities for growth. The crony liberalization of Egypt did not produce favorable economic conditions for the peripheral masses, either. Morocco lies between Turkey and Egypt as a case of a semicompetitive economy. Although the Moroccan state made great strides toward liberalizing the economy, the extent of liberalization fell short of creating a fully liberal economy. The semicompetitive economy provided some opportunities for smaller businesses to thrive, yet the masses found themselves experiencing little improvement in their standards of living. This discrepancy between the two key constituencies of Islamic parties in Morocco yielded a diverse set of political preferences for the Islamic constituency, which I explain in greater detail in chapter 5.

The economic analysis in this chapter serves a vital purpose. The theoretical foundation of the argument developed in chapter 1 rests on a thorough understanding of the dynamics of economic liberalization policies and the outcomes they produce. Who benefits from certain liberalization and in which ways deeply impact how the Islamic peripheral groups and, by extension, Islamist parties consider and realign their political preferences. Building on the analyses of economic liberalization in the three countries, I now turn to the politics of the moderation of Islamist parties.

3 From the Periphery to the Center
Competitive Liberalization in Turkey

THE TURKISH JUSTICE and Development Party (AKP) continues to occupy public opinion discussions in Turkey and beyond with its successive electoral success in 2002, 2007, and 2011. The general tendency is to attribute ever-growing electoral success of the party to its policies, which certainly play a key role in the outcome, but the origins of social support for the AKP are more complex than they may appear on the surface. The deep-rooted social transformation in the Turkish periphery as a result of the economic liberalization policies in the post-1980 period form the underpinnings of the AKP's shift from an Islamist stance toward a more moderate and democratic platform in the post-2000 era. In this chapter, I analyze the relationship between the transformation of the Islamic periphery and the rise of the AKP as a Muslim democratic party (MDP), and bring empirical evidence to support the relationship between the two. The Turkish case shows the correlation between transformation of peripheral political preferences and its impact on Islamist political discourse distinctly among the three cases to be analyzed in this book (Turkey, Egypt, and Morocco) due to the depth of economic liberalization in Turkey.

I first introduce the preliberalization socioeconomic and political context in the aftermath of the Ottoman Empire (1920s–70s) to illustrate the social cleavages that exist between a politically and economically powerful secular center and a marginalized Islamic periphery. This cleavage structure is critical to understanding how economic liberalization affects each socioeconomic group in the post-1980 period and the attitudes of Islamists concerning economic liberalization. Then I analyze the Islamist National Outlook Movement (NOM) and parties it has associated with since its inception in the late 1960s. In this, I focus on the social base of the group and its stance on various social and political issues opposing the domination of the center. The second part of the chapter pertains to the Muslim democratic AKP. Here, I provide an account of the original establishment of the party and then discuss various elements of its political discourse involving topics such as Islam, democracy, the economy, and social policy. Through this, I show that the AKP's political platform is qualitatively different from an Islamist discourse and that it directly speaks to the transformation that took place in its perceived core constituency (i.e., peripheral business owners and the peripheral masses). The final part of the chapter conveys evidence for the argument that the AKP owes its electoral success to capturing the changing political preferences of its core constituency—peripheral business owners (SMEs) and the masses. Field interviews with owners of small and medium businesses (SMEs) show that SME owners prefer political and economic stability, rule of law, and low uncertainty—what business owners generally prefer. These political preferences, in turn, are shaped by their material interest in continued prosperity. Such preferences indicate that peripheral business owners were able to undertake various business opportunities in the liberal economy—unlike in the preliberalization period. This observation allows me to draw the conclusion that economic liberalization in Turkey did indeed transform the Islamic periphery. The peripheral masses have also turned to the AKP due to the extensive social safety net offered by the AKP, as shown in the last part of the chapter. Empirically, I rely on primary sources and the interviews I conducted with AKP politicians and SME owners.

Early Republican Period (1923–1950)

Turkey represents the most vivid case of state-society relations with an Ottoman legacy. By extension, it also illustrates how the two-dimensional social conflict between the secular center and the Islamic periphery plays out as detailed in the theoretical framework of chapter 1. The War of Independence (1919–22) and its immediate aftermath institutionalized the conflict between these two broad social groups.[1] On the one hand, Ataturk and the Kemalist center's grip over the official means of politics and the economy became the defining feature of Turkish politics for the following decades. The credibility and reputation Ataturk and his friends earned in the War of Independence certainly reinforced the center's strong standing. On the other hand, those who were left out of the political calculation constituted the second group. Part of this second group was formed by the estranged prominent figures of the empire; the rest were the amorphous groups with Islamic sensitivities. To illustrate the ideological position of this second group, Şerif Mardin lists some of the group's policy initiatives as follows: emphasis on religious education, prohibition of alcohol consumption, and control of the military. Although such policies did not imply much in the way of the "cohesiveness" of the group, "the cluster" served as a "rallying point" against Ataturk and his followers (Mardin 1973, 181). The division between the two groups found its most concrete representation when a number of "new" parties were established to contest Ataturk's Cumhuriyet Halk Partisi, the Republican People's Party (CHP). Yet their experience in Turkish politics was short-lived, attributable to the threat felt by the Kemalist center. The Serbest Cumhuriyet Firkasi (the Free Republic Party) and the Terakkiperver Cumhuriyet Firkasi (the Progressive Republic Party) were shut down shortly after their foundation; their great potential in becoming the rallying center for the opposition was the primary reason for this. It was not until the late 1940s that the periphery was represented in the electoral platform.

The economic policies pursued in the 1930s and the 1940s complement the political and identity-based dimension of the center-periphery divide, that is, secular versus Islamic. Overall, economic policies of the period were largely representative of the statist ideology first introduced in 1931 at the Third Grand Convention of the CHP as part of the Six Arrows guiding Ataturk's reform efforts in the new republic (Tekeli and Ilkin 1982). The economic policy consisted of two pillars. First, the state would invest in industries where the private enterprise failed to invest, which in actuality consisted of an overwhelming majority of the economy. The creation and pervasiveness of state-owned enterprises (SOEs) was also facilitated by the fact that the world economy was experiencing the Great Depression, and the predominant economic rationale at the time favored protection over openness. The state was also present in the economy in a ubiquitous fashion, making the organization of economic relations feasible. The most critical political outcome of the state's far-reaching economic presence was that the state created its own support base by the very fact that such policies served the interests of a small group over the rest of the population. The patron-client relationship between the state and society finds great resonance in Turkish politics leading to the well-known aphorism *devlet baba*, that is, "father state" (Özbudun 1996; J. White 2003, 104). A statement by Ismet Inonu, who served as prime minister and president, is illustrative of the predominance of the statist economic mentality during this period: "Nonetheless, according to my opinion, for a business to belong to people [private enterprise] or to the state cannot be determined by the means required for that business. That it [the business] pertains to the whole society or to particular private interests will be the foundation to build the decision upon" (Tekeli and Ilkin 1982, 105). The first five-year economic plan (1933) Turkey devised is another indicator of the extent of state involvement in the economy. The state would, in accordance with the plan, establish factories to promote industrial production in areas such as textiles, mining, and chemical industries. However, the plan did not formulate any goals for the private sector, interestingly enough.[2]

Under the second pillar of economic policy, private businesses, deemed to be conducive to economic development, were to be created and promoted by state policies. Private business, in this regard, functioned under complete tutelage of the state.[3] A fitting example of this policy is the Promotion of Industry Law of 1927. The private sector actively tried to attract favorable state policies in attempts to survive in the nascent Turkish economy. The burgeoning private sector enjoyed protection against both foreign and domestic competition as part of state policy to grow a domestic private business sector over time.[4] Limits on domestic competition, however, clearly point to a dual structure in terms of the private sector. Not only did a group of relatively large private businesses exist, there were also smaller and less influential private business actors vying to compete for the economic dominance of the former group.

There were two ways the former group dealt with the latter. First, dominant producers in each sector developed structures to minimize competition. Of this, Tekeli and Ilkin note, "It was observed that whenever competition was being sensed in subsectors of the industry, they [dominant producers] had a tendency to form price unions or cartels" (Tekeli and Ilkin 1982, 220). Second, dominant private business groups actively lobbied government officials to limit production by smaller businesses. The key concept employed by the bigger domestic businesses was "surproduction"—implying overproduction for the domestic economy, which would eventually lead to decreased profitability rates. Most importantly, such businesses did not want to lose the rents they enjoyed in the form of protectionist policies, principally hoping to limit domestic competition (Tekeli and llkin 1982, 219). In brief, the statist policy, understood as consisting of both state-owned enterprises (SOEs) and heavy state assistance to the private sector, facilitated the growth of a big private business sector by decreasing both the cost and the risk that it assumed in the economy. *Étatisme*, over time, became the paramount export item of the new Turkish Republic.[5] In the 1940s and the 1950s, newly independent Middle Eastern countries followed suit in implementing the Turkish model of *étatisme*.

Social policies in this period paralleled the economic policies. The early republican period saw the systematic downplaying of social classes by the state. Instead, populism was the order of the day, one of Ataturk's Six Arrows, "guiding" the course of the new Turkish Republic. By virtue of the idea of populism, an entire nation was mobilized (Berkes 1964, 462–63.). Clearly, such a policy served to reinforce the existing cleavages along the center-periphery division by fortifying and sustaining the periphery's dim view of the center's economic and social domination. Concurrently, populism also ascertained the smooth operation of the Kemalist modernization project. Elimination of potential sources of conflict was viewed as imperative in internalizing the goal of modernization and minimizing opposition to modernization reforms. As other sources of social divisions, ethnic and religious identities were also suppressed along with socioeconomic conflict.[6] Mardin quotes the CHP on this very point as follows: "Do not go into the provincial towns or villages to gather support: our national unity will be undermined" (Mardin 1973, 182). The significance of this statement is due in part to its timing. It came immediately after the transition to a multiparty system in Turkey with the creation of the Democrat Party (DP) and was directly aimed at DP politicians. This warning by the CHP served to underscore the dominant perspective of the center over the rest of Turkish society. The policies of the early republican period led Anatolian provinces to become "centers of 'reaction'" against the political and economic elite's domination (Mardin 2006, 308). One AKP deputy called those marginalized to the periphery "children of Anatolia" (Mustafa Ozbayrak interview, 2008), whereas another AKP official argued that the periphery was the downtrodden population of Turkey (Reha Denemeç interview, 2008). An ironic testament to this cleavage between the secular elite and the periphery came in the form of news reporting in a 1940s Turkish paper that declared, "'It got hot and the people rushed to the beaches,' it read, adding that 'the citizens could not bathe.' Translation: Ordinary Turks [the people] crowded the privileged elite [the citizens] out of swimming areas."[7] This brief anecdote conveys the idea that despite the populist discourse of the Kemalist regime, the socioeconomic cleavage between a privileged class and a marginalized periphery of the lower classes was well entrenched.

Summarizing early social cleavages between the Islamic periphery and the secular center in Turkey, an AKP politician states:

> When the [political] system was established in 1923, which was already in practice prior to that, the Turks did not have accumulated capital at hand. In order to solve the infrastructure problem [for economic development], the idea of creating a class of wealthy [businessmen] prevailed. At that very point, a "capitalist development program" was put into practice with the hand of the state, as a result of which a group of people who made up the backbone of TUSIAD [Turkish Industrialists and Businessmen's Association] were made rich. This happened in Turkey by way of transfers of capital, ensuring protected domestic markets without quality control, high tariff walls, provision of incentives, tax breaks, grants, and cheap credit. (Ozbayrak interview, 2008)

While this observation outlines key elements of early Turkish history correctly, what is more striking is that it epitomizes the periphery's perception of the relationship between the state and big business. Benefits lavished on a few privileged big businesses and a relatively small group of urban elites incurred costs to the rest of society and the economy; in other words, the costs were socialized by way of taxes or higher consumer prices. In this regard, the development of TUSIAD— the business association representing the economic elite of Turkey—is emblematic of the center-periphery cleavage.

The Emergence of Political Islam

New political currents, political Islam included, emerged in the aftermath of the early republican period to politically represent the interests of peripheral groups. This came at a time when social cleavage between the center and the periphery was already entrenched. In Turkey, the origins of political Islam date back to the 1960s with the National Outlook Movement (NOM) of Necmettin Erbakan.[8]

Erbakan's leadership and the emergence of successive NOM parties are starkly contrasted with past experiences involving the relationship between Islam and politics. Until the late 1960s, center-right parties represented peripheral groups, not a distinct Islamist political formation. However, Erbakan's personal background and exclusive emphasis on peripheral groups transformed the shape of Turkish politics for decades to come. Prior to the 1960s, center-right parties of the period, such as the DP and the Justice Party, were able to incorporate the Islamic constituency within a broader coalition of oppositional groups against the CHP. Therefore, a political party that built exclusively on the Islamic and peripheral constituency did not materialize until the late 1960s (Sarıbay 1985, 91). Importantly, the leadership of the center-right coalition was not from a peripheral background.[9] It came instead from the heart of the bureaucratic elite and did not have a unique platform for the peripheral groups. Nevertheless, the fact that the center-right coalition offered an alternative to the CHP was sufficient to garner peripheral support.

The discourse and policy practices of the center-right coalitions entailed, however, key conflicts with the socioeconomic interests of peripheral groups. The rapid growth of private enterprise with the support of the center-right parties from its embryonic state to its growing into big business was a clear indication of this. Undoubtedly, the peripheral economic groups, that is, small and medium enterprises (SMEs), were not the chief beneficiaries of the economic policies of center-right coalitions throughout the 1950s and the 1960s. The fashionable Import Substitution Industrialization (ISI) policies of the period were also important; ISI policies were influential in nurturing a big domestic private business group, as was the dominant statist economic mentality. In brief, in the post-1950 democratic period, the periphery was incorporated into a broad center-right coalition that supported the ISI policies, yet the discord between its economic platform and the economic interests of the periphery reveals the effective failure of representation for peripheral groups in the party system. Consequently, Turkey was ripe for the emergence of political Islam.

The prevailing international context was another factor contributing to the rise of political Islam not only in Turkey but also in other countries in the region. The early 1970s saw the resurrection of political Islam as an attractive alternative to secular ideologies and parties in countries such as Egypt and Morocco (Ayoob 2008; Feldman 2008; Roy 1994). Region-wide failure of secular ideologies and programs enabled the Islamist groups to benefit from the opening in the political sphere.

The NOM addressed two distinct groups in society with an Islamist platform. First, lower socioeconomic groups constituted a significant chunk of its support base, particularly new migrants to urban areas. Indeed, throughout the 1970s and the 1980s, cities with populations over 100,000 saw vast numbers of migrants from smaller towns and rural areas with significant economic grievances (Danielson and Keles 1985). The second group at the core of the NOM constituency were owners of SMEs. These businesses faced effective discrimination in state economic policies. Erbakan's extensive expertise on the disadvantages of SMEs gave him a political advantage. He worked for the Union of Chambers and Commodity Exchanges of Turkey (TOBB) in the late 1960s, and at one point he was elected the president of TOBB with the support of SMEs. However, he was prevented from taking office due to opposition from the government and big business (Sarıbay 1985, 98).[10] Essentially, Erbakan built his political discourse on the marginalization of peripheral groups. Various studies shed light on geographic distribution and individual traits of the support base for the NOM. For example, in the 1973 general elections, the National Salvation Party (MSP) received its highest support in the least developed provinces with 15.4 percent of the votes cast, whereas its support reached 13.7 percent in provinces where the level of economic development was at a medium level, and support in the most developed provinces was at a low of 8.4 percent (Şen 2004, 45). Another study shows that the MSP's support within urban areas also showed variance based on the level of economic development. In Ankara, Turkey's capital, the highest support for the party came from new migrants to the city: "The MSP received below average support in upper and middle income districts along with old neighborhoods in Ankara. However, in new shantytown districts, which constitute the outskirts of the city, the party received an above average level of support. These findings are in line with the MSP program.... While the MSP could not find support in the older low-income neighborhoods of the central business districts, it found support in the new shantytowns" (Tekeli and Gokceli 1977, 67). NOM parties also emphasized Islam as a major motivation behind several policy initiatives. For Erbakan, "morals and spirituality" were key ingredients to success in other policy areas. The emphasis on morals and spirituality was also couched in terms of the "Communist threat" and a "materialist mentality" (Erbakan 1975). Although the extent of envisioned Islamization was more moderate as compared with Islamist parties in the rest of the Middle East, in the staunchly secular Turkish political system, the NOM's calls for morality and spirituality sufficed to produce the perception of impending Islamization and a radical Islamist platform. Other proposals of Islamization included "moral development" and "moral order" for the youth, strong support for opening religious schools, that is, Imam-Hatip schools, and nonconformist views of interest-based financial systems.[11] The MSP program laid out "national morals and virtue" as a main principle for forming governments (MSP program, article 9). Along the same lines, the NOM stated, "Our party will take every measure to ensure that moral order prevails in society, and justice and stability are reached without impeding economic progress" (MNP program, article 50). Thus, Islamist parties of the NOM sought to establish a greater emphasis on moral issues that were of concern to peripheral groups (and others who had been largely overlooked by the secular regime).

As for the economy, the NOM founded its policy on two pillars. First, the NOM was an ardent defender of a nationalist economic policy (Şen, 2004). Projects to the effect of a national drive for heavy industrialization were Erbakan's trademark, reflecting his developmentalist and interventionist approach to the economy since the beginnings of the NOM. An anti-Western undertone can also be found in the economic discourse of the NOM, including the EEC (European Economic Community) membership application. Throughout this period, the EEC was perceived as part of a neocolonial effort on the part of the West, adapted to contemporary conditions (Sarıbay 1985, 127). Hence the NOM staunchly opposed Westernization and greater integration with the West.

The second pillar of the NOM's economic policy was its emphasis on SMEs, which extended to a dislike of and an aversion to traditional big businesses. Erbakan couched his focus on SMEs as his approach toward addressing underdevelopment. SMEs were largely ignored and disadvantaged, and this created a problem throughout Anatolia—that is, beyond Istanbul—and it was a key cause of underdevelopment. He argued that the economic policies he offered would result in the "development of Anatolia" (Erbakan 1975).[12] Problems of SMEs, such as credit allocation and market access, occupied the top of the NOM's economic agenda. A distinct way the NOM promoted SMEs was the expansion of the ownership structure in large companies through a program called the "Widespread Private Sector." According to this initiative, established companies would have at least 100 shareholders, with no single shareholder holding more than 5 percent of the shares. The money raised through these companies would support interest-free credit programs to encourage investment in industries promoted by the state (Sarıbay 1985, 125; Erbakan 1975). Such a platform emphasizing a wide-ownership structure instead of productivity and efficiency was essentially an effort to increase the party's support base among small businesses in the face of the close relationship between big business and the state. The party's focus on the prevalent socioeconomic conflict in Turkey was evident in the party program, which highlighted the underlying socioeconomic conflict in Turkey by stating, "Instead of the presently applied limited-class private entrepreneurship, the state should undertake a widespread private sector policy to extend development nationwide and to mobilize unused forces that can assist in economic development" (MNP program, article 51). Additionally, the party program reflected Erbakan's trademark motto, "*Adil duzen*," or "Just order." It also addressed economic inequality between members of the center (i.e., big business) and the periphery (i.e., SMEs) (Erbakan 1975, 1991; Şen 1995). By calling for an end to all privileges and favors extended to the members of the select few, Erbakan successfully capitalized on the economic grievances of the peripheral groups between the 1960s and the

1990s via his populist discourse.[13] A closer look at the relationship between the state and big business hints at the reasons for Erbakan's focus on SMEs and the periphery in his political discourse.

From the early republican period until the early 1980s, big business in Turkey engaged in minimum risk ventures such as trade and construction instead of industrial production. It was not until the 1960s that a genuine local industrialist class emerged (Sarıbay 1985). Strikingly, this was also the period when center-right parties were almost "hijacked" by big business. Until the early 1980s, there were three critical ways that traditional big business benefited from its relations with the state in addition to the standard set of protective measures, including high tariff walls, cheap credit, and cheap currency. First, the state subsidized big businesses by selling inputs to these companies below market levels under a program called the Provision of Cheap Inputs Policy (Sonmez 1988, 119). The difference between the market price and the sale price was eventually subsidized by the state. Second, private companies enjoyed the partnership of state-owned enterprises (SOEs). If the partnership was on equal footing, it could have been justified in economic terms. However, private companies often would reap the benefits and profit of the partnership while SOEs carried the costs. Additionally, access to state credit and other incentives proved to be relatively hassle free for such private businesses because they were "trustworthy" companies due to their partnership with the state (Sonmez 1988, 121). This was effectively a self-fulfilling prophecy because the initial decision for partnership with such private businesses rested on political considerations. Finally, the state was also the major consumer of manufactured goods, in the form of either infrastructure projects or other government bids. Products from big firms found an easy market in the government. Not surprisingly, SMEs lacked such advantages in their business ventures (Bugra 2002).

Indeed, one businessman notes, "[Prior to 1980,] Turkey was being governed by state favoritism and a statist policy. The quotas [for import and export] were allocated based on the proximity of firms to particular political parties and bureaucrats. Such quotas were a form of privilege. These privileges enabled such firms to grow unfairly" (TR-15-B interview, 2008). Export and import limitations (TR-10-B interview, 2008), credit limitations (TR-8-B interview, 2008), and a dearth of foreign exchange (TR-7-B interview, 2008) resulted in a lack of genuine industrial development due to business owners' inability to import machinery and equipment for production, undertake new investments, and find customers. This period, in general, is identified by the common phrase "the period when Turkey was desperate for 70 cents" (TR-14-B interview, 2008).

The foundation of TUSIAD is helpful in understanding big business's relationship to the state. Until the early 1970s, big business in Turkey was part of a quasi-governmental and corporatist structure under TOBB.[14] TOBB was quite instrumental for big business because of the monopoly of these chambers in preferential policies such as foreign currency and credit allocation decisions. In a certain way, these chambers functioned as de facto patronage networks (Bugra 1994, 250; TR-11-B interview, 2008). Once these chambers and big businesses lost their privilege in foreign exchange and credit allocation, big businesses saw no further reason to stay on with the chambers. Instead, big businesses established their own business association, TUSIAD, in 1971 (Arat 1991, 136–37). The goal of TUSIAD was to limit membership to select business owners in order to maintain homogeneity of interest among members and increase the association's effectiveness in policy-related issues. By 1985, of the top 100 industrial businesses in the country, 80 percent were members of the association across various industries (Arat 1991, 140). From the 1970s until the 1990s, TUSIAD was regarded as "the biggest and most powerful business organization and pressure group" in Turkey and "the club of the rich" (Özbudun and Keyman 2002).

Overall, the republican period until the 1980s is marked with the overlap of the two dimensions of social conflict between the secular center and the Islamic periphery. Secularism versus Islam and socioeconomic dimensions were not crosscutting, so the opposition from both dimensions reinforced each other, particularly in the unique platform of political Islam. This lengthy introduction to cleavages and social conflict in Turkey provides a necessary foundation for understanding the structure of Turkey's political system and how external factors play their part. Having expounded on the origins of social cleavages in Turkey, I now move on to discuss the economic liberalization process and its transformative effect on the Islamic periphery.

Economic Liberalization and the Independent Industrialists and Businessmen's Association

Turkish economic liberalization, as discussed in chapter 2, is identified by its competitive character and the opportunities that the peripheral businesses were able to find in the postliberalization period. In this process, peripheral groups have been the main beneficiaries. Also, more generally, Turkey's economic growth in recent years is attributed to the dynamism of small businesses.[15] In 1991, vertical expansion of this burgeoning business class materialized with the establishment of a nationwide business association promoting their interests, the Independent Industrialists and Businessmen's Association (MUSIAD). The emergence of MUSIAD is emblematic of the rising economic power and interests of SMEs. With several thousand members nationwide, the organization has a much wider societal base than TUSIAD.[16] As a result of converging interests, SMEs organized around a nongovernmental civil society organization to ensure that their preferences and interests would be heard in policy formation. Of this, Özbudun and

Keyman state, "Since its inception, it [MUSIAD] has played a crucial role in linking business organizations with the rise of Islam; supporting, promoting, and protecting their economic interests; and developing a societal vision on the basis of Islamic principles. By creating a 'powerful network based upon trust relations' among Islamic economic actors, MUSIAD has become as significant and powerful as TUSIAD, even challenging the latter's dominance in Turkish economic life" (Özbudun and Keyman 2002, 307). Confirming this observation, a MUSIAD member expresses, "In addition to the business associations we are required to be a member of [per state regulations], there are also business associations that are voluntary, established by those individuals who share the same ideals, same views, and same feelings; based on that, we are members of MUSIAD. There, we have good connections and dialogue with our friends with whom we share values and to whom we offer support in commercial life" (TR-1-B interview, 2008). MUSIAD focuses on the problems facing SMEs throughout the Turkish economy. Among the problems MUSIAD highlights in different platforms are tax reductions, bureaucratic procedures, facilitation of credit, vocational training, and social security costs.[17]

Who are these business owners and what are their preferences? In terms of economic policy, SME owners support a liberal economy; after all, most SME owners owe their existence and/or subsequent growth to economic liberalization reforms in the post-1980 period. MUSIAD's approach to globalization is instructive in this regard. Özbudun and Keyman note, "For its [MUSIAD's] members, globalization creates interconnectedness among societies, economies, and cultures, and it sets 'the rule of the game,' which requires rational thinking, long-term strategies, and organizational capacities. In this sense, globalization becomes the new historical context for economic development. MUSIAD also attributes a positive quality to globalization because it is as a result of the globalization of market relations that a suitable ground was created for the rise and the success of economic Islam" (Özbudun and Keyman 2002, 307). Essentially, SME owners gained a new understanding of the potential benefits of new rules of the "game"; this stands in stark contrast to the preliberalization rules of the game when SME owners were largely sidelined.

With respect to democracy, MUSIAD has developed its position over time, approaching a liberal understanding of democracy since its foundation in 1990. MUSIAD views democracy as a guarantee of "good governance" and assurance of civil rights and liberties with particular emphasis on religious rights and liberties (Öniş and Turem 2001).[18] Finally, on a related note, Islam has been an important element of MUSIAD to the extent that at times, the MUSIAD acronym is jokingly referred to as the Muslim Industrialists and Businessmen's Association. However, the emphasis has never been on the application of an Islamic legal code or the Islamization of state institutions. Instead, MUSIAD calls for a strict following of Muslim values and ethics in conducting business, including business owners' approach to dealing with wages, labor rights, working conditions, and production standards.[19] The association fuses business interests, that is, liberal economy and democracy, with the identity of its peripheral membership, that is, emphasis on Islamic and conservative values.

MUSIAD's platform is built on two fundamental beliefs. The first one is the promotion of Muslim values and business ethics. Member businesses are asked to follow a certain code of ethics along the lines of socially responsible business morals. The second one is that MUSIAD underscores fairness and justice in terms of state incentives, subsidy programs, and economic policy-making, which has collectively defined the association since the early 1990s: "Compared to TUSIAD, however, MUSIAD appeared to place more emphasis on the issue of 'social rights' drawing attention to the importance of fair business-labor relations as well as the more equitable distribution of public resources among large and small businessmen" (Öniş and Turem 2001, 11). Over time, MUSIAD increased its public stature by policy recommendations and statements of policy positions on behalf of SMEs nationwide. In this regard, MUSIAD emerged as a direct challenger to TUSIAD. While the former represents the newly burgeoning peripheral SMEs, the latter voices the concerns and demands of traditional big business with its exclusive membership structure. As such, MUSIAD is a testament to the strength and significance of SMEs as a politically relevant group.

The socioeconomic conflict between the center as represented by TUSIAD and the periphery as represented by MUSIAD became most obvious around the February 28 "postmodern coup" in Turkey. February 28, 1997 marks the beginning of the period when secularist groups engaged in a public campaign against the Islamist Welfare Party (WP) and its supporters. The process was initiated by the military's demand for a list of reforms to be completed by the WP-led government in a National Security Council meeting. The "green capital," as the peripheral SMEs were called (due to their association with peripheral Islamic groups), faced a ruthless "witch hunt" (Öniş 2001; Özel 2003). The military, as the defender of the "secular" regime, even published a list of companies that it considered Islamist and encouraged discrimination against these businesses both legally and publicly. TUSIAD allied with the bureaucratic and military elite during this period and openly supported the removal of the Islamist WP from power. A strong stance against the "green capital," or SMEs, quickly followed. MUSIAD, as a result, received its fair share of discrimination from this highly publicized campaign.

A recent statement by a major business owner, Abdulkadir Konukoglu, attests to the rising prominence of peripheral businesses. Konukoglu recalls that in the late 1990s, he applied for membership in TUSIAD: "They [TUSIAD] did not accept us. They did not accept any businessmen from Anatolia. Right now, TUSIAD consistently says 'come and be a member.' We don't go. We don't need TUSIAD."[20] Konukoglu is a notable figure because he is a businessman from Gaziantep, and his experience is emblematic of many business owners from peripheral Turkey. In other words, Konukoglu is a representative of those peripheral business owners who rose to prominence in the last two decades or so following liberalization reforms in the economy. Currently, he is the CEO of the Sanko Holding with an annual turnover of over $2 billion and exports in excess of $200 million.

Along the same lines, TUSIAD president Umit Boyner, acknowledging the rising significance of smaller businesses, suggests, "Capital did not change hands. It spread throughout Turkey. This has been an important process for democratization of the country."[21] Sweden's former ambassador to Turkey (2001–5), Ann Dismorr, sheds light on the conflict between TUSIAD and the periphery by pointing out the level of distaste against the AKP within TUSIAD. She declares, "Many TUSIAD members support the banning of the AKP in their unofficial meetings. I cannot comprehend this because the recent surge of foreign direct investment into Turkey occurred due to political stability. From a Western European perspective, this is difficult to digest."[22] Despite the fact that the members of the secular center benefit greatly from the policies of the AKP, the depth of the social conflict between the two prevents the former from supporting the latter. Similarly, an AKP official reflected similar views about TUSIAD's predilection against the AKP. According to Yasar Yakis, TUSIAD members have expressed their interest in an AKP victory in the 2007 parliamentary elections, yet they personally did not intend to vote for the party, suggesting a fundamental conflict of interest and identity (Yasar Yakis interview, 2008).

In summary, MUSIAD became a more prominent actor as peripheral businesses' economic power rose in Turkish economy. In the post-1990 period, MUSIAD offers an important platform for voicing the concerns and demands of a large group of business owners. MUSIAD's emergence as a distinct business association focused solely on SME membership is a strong indicator of the rising significance of peripheral businesses, that is, SMEs, in the post-1980 period. It must also be noted that MUSIAD is not the only business association to cater to SMEs, nor do all small firm owners seek membership in business associations (Ozcan and Turunc 2011; Bugra and Savaskan 2012).

From Political Islam to Muslim Democracy

The creation of the Justice and Development Party (AKP) and its immediate domination of the Turkish political scene in 2002 represented the culmination of the brewing transformation of the periphery in Turkey. The AKP was founded in 2001 following severe disagreements with the more conservative-minded members of the Virtue Party over method and policy choice (Yakis 2002; Dagi 2005; Atacan

2006). The Virtue Party was the immediate successor to the recently banned WP, the longtime official representative of the Islamist discourse in Turkey. Difference of opinion about the Virtue Party's direction was an issue even before formal separation. The party congress in May 2000 was, in a way, the formal announcement of this rift between the reformists (*yenilikciler*) and the traditionalists (*gelenekciler*). The election for party leadership saw a real challenge from within for the first time in the history of the Islamist movement in Turkey. The reformist group, with Abdullah Gul (the former president) and Bulent Arinc (the former speaker of the parliament) leading the charge, contested the designated leadership of Recai Kutan in the party.[23] Erdogan, who is the current leader of the AKP, was also a member of the reformist group in 2000, yet was banned from politics at the time. The reformist movement united behind Gul's candidacy to take over the party leadership. Despite facing stiff opposition from Erbakan and the traditionalist wing to the extent of excommunication from the party, the reformist movement remained intact and challenged the incumbent party leader Kutan's nomination. The reformists lost by a small margin.[24] The close call in the elections and the positive response the reformist movement received from society gave the group the necessary momentum to break away from the Islamist movement. In the meantime, the Constitutional Court banned the Virtue Party shortly after the party congress in 2001 on the grounds that the party had been the locus of antisecularist activities, allowing the reformist movement a window of opportunity for official partition from the Islamist NOM.

The new party platform was a society-based one. Following a lengthy period of public opinion surveys and preparation, the new party was formed in 2001. In the establishment of the AKP, interviews with party officials revealed that the contours of the party policies were marked by the preferences of the society at large—specifically, SME owners and the lower classes. Peripheral businesses were effective in the process by the presence of many MUSIAD members within the AKP (TR-3-B interview, 2008). At the same time, the party also actively sought out specific policy preferences of SME owners by attending MUSIAD events. For example, one businessman attributed the success of the AKP economic policies to responsiveness to the demands of business owners (TR-15-B interview, 2008). Another businessman, along the same lines, recalled his interaction with AKP officials as follows: "At an *iftar* (fast-breaking) dinner last night, we had representatives of various public offices. During our conversation, we voiced some of the problems we encountered; they responded by saying that new regulations were underway.... On another occasion, we met with the Minister of Industry and chatted for a while. We realized that they are working hard, struggling [to address problems], interested [in the issues we are concerned about], and within the life [aware of the issues we face]" (TR-6-B interview, 2008). The AKP was informed of the concerns of peripheral businesses through MUSIAD reports and bulletins

(TR-1-B, TR-3-B, TR-15-B interviews, 2008). As for the lower classes, prospective AKP leaders conducted surveys among a large sample of the population. Among the issues highlighted in these surveys were democracy, employment, the economy, civil liberties, and EU membership (Yakis interview, 2008).

After its foundation, the AKP won three successive parliamentary elections in 2002, 2007, and 2011, as well as local elections in 2004 and 2009. The margins of victory in all three cases were particularly high by Turkish standards, and they included both structural elements and conjunctural factors. On the one hand, many voters cast their votes for the AKP in reaction to other parties and political actors. This was particularly evident in the 2002 and 2007 elections (Özel 2003, Öniş 2006a). Following the economic crisis in 2001 and the failure of successive coalition governments in recent years involving massive corruption and the rising distrust of established political actors, the voters were keen on choosing new faces. A great proportion of AKP supporters did not necessarily cast their votes for the AKP, but rather they tried to avoid others in the election, leading to a landslide victory for the AKP with 34 percent of the votes and almost two-thirds of the parliamentary seats thanks to the 10 percent national threshold for parties to receive any seats in the parliament (Özel 2003). The picture was fairly similar in 2007. The 2007 legislative elections were conducted under the shadow of extrademocratic interventions by the military and other secular elite actors including the judiciary and the CHP. The outcome was the unprecedented increase in the AKP's vote share to 47 percent, albeit with a decrease in seat share. An indirect measure of the AKP's success is the level of success of the Felicity Party (FP), the successor of the Virtue Party (VP). The FP under Kutan's leadership garnered 2 to 3 percent of votes in 2002, 2007, and 2011.

On the other hand, the results strongly indicate an overlap between the AKP's new discourse and the preferences of peripheral groups, both the lower classes and SMEs. It is not difficult to see the shift in the peripheral constituency's electoral support from the NOM to the AKP. In this regard, the AKP's existence is a direct response to the increasingly visible and changing demands and policy preferences of SMEs and other peripheral groups. Interviews with founding members of the party indicate that the AKP emerged to fill a void in the political space. The NOM's ideological persistence on several policy areas was far from reflecting the true demands of the electorate (Yakis 2002; Denemeç, Memecan, Ozbayrak, Yakis interviews, 2008).

One might ask at this point the following question: why do we observe a gap between the initiation of the economic liberalization process in 1980 and the emergence of an MDP in the early 2000s? The timing of the rise of the AKP rests on two distinct factors. On one hand, the rise of SMEs as the critical constituency to push for a transformation of the Islamist political discourse in the country did not thrive until the mid-1990s, both quantitatively and qualitatively. The societal push was not there to begin with. On the other hand, when the societal push was there after the mid-1990s, the party did not immediately respond to such demands. It was not until it became evident that the political obstinacy of the Islamist WP was threatening the economic interests of its constituency, first in the government in 1996–97 and later with its parliamentary opposition, that change materialized at the party level.

A brief aside must be made regarding the AKP's party identity. The AKP does not adopt the categorical title of an MDP. Some party officials argue that such a classification is based on religion and exclusive of non-Muslims or nonbelievers, from whom the party enjoys significant support (Denemeç, Ozbayrak, and Yakis interviews, 2008). Others, however, argue that the contextual elements of Turkish politics prevent the party from using this specific title; instead, the party adopts conservative democracy, a political stance marked by its commitment to both values of the society and democracy. Reha Denemeç, vice chairman of the AKP, likened the party's political stance to progressive conservatism essentially with the same commitments (Denemeç interview, 2008). In 2005, the AKP also became an observing member of the European People's Party (EPP), a conservative umbrella party across Europe having its roots in Christian Democracy.[25] The periphery and its political representative, the AKP, since its establishment challenged the "White Turks"—the secular urban upper class who "wielded the political and economic power in the country"—in their own game: democracy, a free market, secularism.[26] If that is the case, what are the distinctly new policy positions of the AKP?

Role of Islam

In the staunchly secular political context of Turkey, even a slight reference to Islam and religion is felt to threaten the secular indoctrination of many decades. The constant reference point is fear of Turkey becoming "another Iran." Hence historically the NOM's references to Islam and its Islamist agenda are largely diluted compared with those of other Islamist groups worldwide. In its new platform, the AKP repeatedly rejected any ties to political Islam as an ideology; similarly, the party explicitly states that it broke off with the tradition of political Islam, which refers to the idea that Islam serves as an instrument to accomplish political goals that envision the Islamization of the state and society. According to this view, even a slight reference to Islam could potentially trigger a turn toward theocracy like that of Saudi Arabia or Iran, a fear that has been a source of distress for some groups in Turkey. Nursuna Memecan, a member of the Turkish parliament from the AKP, had a personal experience to this end. She recounts,

> Recently, I visited my aunt whom I had not seen for a long time. She had her daughter there as well. My relationship with them has been a bit sour lately

just as it is with half of my family because I joined the AKP. Anyway, we chatted about nonpolitical issues for some time, and my aunt, who is very old, all of a sudden broke her reservations and said "So, you've become a deputy." I said, yes. My cousin, building on her mother's question, said, "There is a mayor from the AKP where I live; I am quite happy with his services, but I cannot sleep comfortably at nights. I fear that I will wake up one day, and it will be as if Iran is all around us." (Memecan interview, 2008)

The AKP downplays any reference to Islam in its discourse, although this could lead to the perception that the party engages in "creeping Islamization." For example, thoroughly rejecting claims that the AKP is after Islamization and sharia by emphasizing social preference, one AKP deputy maintains, "Regardless of how much you want to establish sharia, what the people want matters the most. Therefore, the situation in Turkey is not suitable to introduce any such system, and I do not believe there is a chance that it will ever be. I don't even think it will be suitable fifty years from today. Turkey is well on its course" (Ozbayrak interview, 2008). So instead, the party highlights conservative and Muslim values prevalent in Turkish society. According to Reha Denemeç, a "conservative" party identity refers to the advocation of conservative moral and family values in Turkish society (Denemeç interview, 2008). AKP deputy Ozbayrak argues that the AKP platform conceptualizes religion as part of individual liberties and as the main component of society's moral and ethical makeup, asserting, "We [the party] respect all the fundamental values in the make-up of this country and share them. What are these values? First, it is religion [Islam], then language, flag, national anthem, and primary principles emanating from our culture such as helping one another—loving and helping your neighbor in good and bad days" (Ozbayrak interview, 2008). In a similar way, a former AKP member, Yalcin Akdoğan, writes that conservative values include "tradition, family, and the protection of gains coming from history" (Akdoğan 2004). This shift from representing Islam to representing conservative and Muslim values of the society found resonance in the electorate and could reinforce the "social and economic networks" of Islam (Dagi 2006).

Emphasis on Muslim values (rather than on Islam) helps the AKP in two significant ways. First, the party is able to mobilize its core constituency around an identity. Muslim values speak to the peripheral groups' sensitivity on one of the two social cleavages, that is, religion versus secularism. Second, by focusing on social and moral values of society emanating from Islam, the AKP minimizes the polarizing and destabilizing impact of its identity discourse. Political Islam, by its very nature, is after a comprehensive transformation of the state and society toward an Islamist ideal. By extension, political Islam is a reaction against established secular order. Thus, an Islamist discourse is an open invitation to political polarization.

As is the case with other parties, the role that Islam holds in the context of the AKP is not straightforward, nor are the secularists' fears of it: "Its [the AKP's] politics have so far been respectful of secular freedom in most cases. But there are harder-line members who would like to see a more religious society, and secular Turks fear that highly personal questions like their children's education and rights for unmarried women could be threatened. In the country as a whole, religious Turks have felt like second-class citizens for generations, due in part to a legacy of Ataturk's radical, secular revolution in the early 20th century."[27] Despite varying shades of conservatism within the party, the AKP has been successful in maintaining the original party discourse on the role of Islam.

In 2007, the chief prosecutor engaged in a highly publicized campaign to ban the governing AKP on the grounds that the party had been the locus of antisecularist activities and that it was seeking to undermine the secular state. In this regard, the indictment prepared by the chief prosecutor Yalcinkaya is a good measure to assess the AKP's Islamic discourse and its stance on secularism. Since the prosecutor carefully documented all activities of the party pertaining to Islam and secularism, the indictment is a reliable document with respect to an analysis of the AKP's Islamic discourse. In this regard, the credibility of the document is assured.

The main thrust of the campaign was one piece of legislation passed by the AKP with the support of the Nationalist Action Party (MHP) emphasizing the "equality" of all citizens in receiving public services, including higher education. This legislation was part of an effort to allow veiled women to go to college—by making a constitutional amendment in the face of a long-standing ban. The Constitutional Court annulled the legislation immediately after its passage in the parliament, albeit with a decision beyond the court's constitutional jurisdiction. The indictment enables me to make two important observations regarding the AKP's Islamic discourse between 2001 and 2007. First, nothing in the indictment lends support to the argument that the AKP, in fact, promotes an Islamic agenda. The essence of the charges against the AKP was focused on the headscarf legislation and how it was viewed as a constitutional violation of the principle of secularism.[28] Moreover, the AKP emphasized the headscarf issue not as a religious problem but rather as part of individual freedoms (both religious and educational). Erdogan, in defense of the "headscarf legislation," insisted, "It should be known that we are not working for anything else other than to stop the unjust treatment against our girls at university entrances."[29] Other officials from the AKP echoed similar views (Denemeç, Ozbayrak, Memecan, Yakis interviews, 2008). Liberal seculars such as Ergun Özbudun, a constitutional scholar, concur with the AKP's take on the headscarf issue: "It's an issue of human rights, not secularism. . . . In the U.S., I had Jewish students wearing yarmulkes and nobody cared."[30] The editor of a social democrat daily, *Radikal*, also viewed this as an issue of liberties and criticized the staunch seculars for their illiberalism.[31] Emre Akoz went further and argued that several actions of the main opposition and staunchly secular CHP would certainly make the party favorites for a banning case if it were not for the nonstandard application of the laws by the secular judiciary. Among instances where the CHP utilized religion in politics (and hence violated the principle of secularism according to official Turkish interpretation) were the use of a veiled woman's picture on a campaign bus, the ceremonial honoring of a veiled woman with a party badge for membership, and use of Qur'anic verses and sayings of the prophet in party leader's speeches.[32]

The second point is in regard to the idea of secularism. The AKP, indeed, criticized the concept of secularism.[33] However, it should be noted that the party's critique was directed not at secularism as an abstract notion but rather to the specific interpretation of it in Turkey. Although Turkish success in secularism is emphasized in the West as a model for other Muslim-majority countries, the Turkish model has yet to find a welcome reception in the Muslim world, which can be attributed to the unique application of secularism in the Turkish context. Officials from the AKP branded Turkish secularism variously as militant secularism (Yakis interview, 2008) and Stalinist secularism (Ozbayrak interview, 2008); others dubbed it colonial secularism,[34] but Ahmet Kuru's recent analysis offers a more concise conceptual framework. Kuru argues that Turkish "assertive" secularism, usually dubbed as *laiklik* after the French model of *laïcité*, implies that "the state favors a secular worldview in the public sphere and aims to confine religion to the private sphere." The Anglo-American application of secularism, which Kuru calls "passive secularism," adopts "state neutrality toward various religions and allows the public visibility of religion" (Kuru 2006, 2009). The AKP's focus is on curbing the assertiveness of secularism and presenting an alternative that is more accommodative of religious practice of Muslims in the country. The nature of Turkish secularism hence is perceived to be restrictive of liberties and increasingly as a liability (US Department of State Religious Freedom Report 2010).

The case also had reverberations in Europe. The *Economist* harshly criticized the case for a lack of verifiable, objective evidence to make the case that the party had actually undermined secularism, reporting, "The Turkish prosecutor [Chief Prosecutor Yalcinkaya] insists that the European court will not take this view in the case of the AKP. Yet his charge sheet is long on assertions and short on hard facts. He cites newspaper articles and interviews to justify an otherwise unsubstantiated claim that the party is employing 'dissimulation' to bring in sharia law. That is not good enough."[35]

Despite the party's avoidance of Islamist language and Islamization, issues that are Islamic in nature such as the headscarf and Imam-Hatip schools have been regulars on the AKP agenda, but for what reason? Religion has largely been considered an integral part of individual liberties, yet at the same time, Islam is regarded as a personal matter, and Muslim values were critical to the traditional moral composition of the society. Reform efforts regarding the headscarf issue and Imam-Hatip schools, for example, are perceived as part of an initiative to ensure individual and religious liberties to those who have been effectively discriminated against throughout most of the republican period. The AKP's socially conservative but nonconfrontational stance on issues with an "Islamic" quality ensures the support of its core constituency. In brief, the AKP approaches various policy issues in a much less ideologically oriented way than does the Islamist tradition in Turkey. In this regard, it is possible to view the constitutional banning case against the AKP as an act of the "bureaucratic elite"[36] against the periphery's increasing dominance.

Periphery and Islam

If the AKP avoids Islamist discourse, it should be because of the preferences of the periphery, specifically that of SME owners. Indeed, we observe a great deal of overlap between the AKP's position on the role of Islam and what the peripheral business owners expect the role of Islam to be. Islam, for most peripheral business owners, is part of an individual's personal life, and not a matter of forcing others to observe similar religious practice, as we would expect in a theocratic system. In order to demonstrate this, I focus on two major issues. First, public discussions revolve mainly around secularism and the role that Islam plays in public life, most concretely illustrated by the debates on the headscarf. Second, I analyze recent political instabilities in Turkey that largely emanate from public discussions involving the AKP's Islamic identity and secularism. This is particularly important because it allows for the demonstration of how SME owners justify their political preferences regarding the public role of Islam.

Secularism and Religious Issues

Secularism has historically been one of the thorniest issues of political and social life in Turkey. With modernization and westernization as the primary goal, Ataturk took a strong stance against institutional religion, viewing organized religion as a major obstacle to achieving Turkish modernity. Specifically, it stood in the way of consolidation of Ataturk's power, which was a key issue in the aftermath of the Independence War. The Caliphate and Sufi orders, for example, were dealt with in this spirit, and a state institution was established to control religion (Diyanet Isleri Baskanligi). At times, individual religious practice was also violated by the state in the name of secularism. As discussed before, the Turkish version of secularism was notorious for its staunch character. Hence secularism as such has been a contentious issue in political life. Conservatives are generally deemed to be opposed to secularism because of marginalization of religion. Conversely, seculars have been the standard bearers of secularism. In this regard, SME owners' views are an important marker of the change in the Islamic peripheral constituency.

Overall, the SME owners interviewed for this research showed unequivocal support for secularism as a principle in government. However, this does not necessarily imply they approve of its current application and interpretation in Turkey. Two points stand out in particular. First, secularism is quite vague and not well defined. In this light, one businessman demands the "demarcation of the limits of secularism" (TR-3-B interview, 2008). Fuzziness about secularism is concerning because of the potential for it to lead to an abusive use of the concept, especially in political discourse. Targeting seculars' interpretation of the concept, one SME owner noted, "People do interpret secularism arbitrarily. For some, it means unveiling; for others, it means not praying. Yet for me—I am a devout believer—secularism means being able to perform daily prayers in business life, in civic life, and in social life without mixing those up. Secularism should not impede observing one's faith, yet in Turkey secularism is portrayed as being against religious practice" (TR-6-B interview, 2008). Clearly, for this business owner, the arbitrary and restrictive use of the concept constitutes the source of the problem. Reinforcing the same idea, one business owner referred to the case of the AKP to make his point, conveying, "Without a grain of hard evidence, people are able to constantly charge a party such as the AKP with antisecularism, [a party] that has taken this country the longest distance towards EU membership, that has registered significant liberalization reforms on civil rights and liberties for individuals and civil society organizations, and that has passed EU compliance laws" (TR-1-B interview, 2008).

Second, the application of secularism is viewed as too restrictive of individual religious liberties. For many SME owners, the principle of secularism prevents individuals from practicing their faith in their private lives. Hence a businessman defined the ideal scenario in which secularism does not pose a problem by expressing, "Secularism is a system where people's religious lives are not interfered with, and state affairs are distinct from religious affairs. In this system, individuals and institutions are required to respect each other" (TR-7-B interview, 2008). On a more personal level, another business owner revealed his disappointment over negative attitudes toward observant Muslims in the public sphere by stating, "Secularism in Turkey is widely manipulated. For example, secularism means that I should be able to pray in this very office; that is freedom of worship. Yet, in many institutions throughout Turkey, freedom of worship does not exist. People are being labeled in the name of secularism on whether they pray or fast" (TR-6-B interview, 2008). For many among SME owners, serious constraints on individuals' freedom of religion persist due to an "outdated" application of secularism.

Such sentiments regarding secularism resonate with the AKP's understanding of secularism as it is applied in Turkey.[37]

The controversy surrounding the headscarf relates intimately to the conception of secularism and the way religion is politicized. As such, it offers insights into the Islamic periphery's preferences on the public role of Islam. The headscarf has been banned in colleges and many other public offices for more than a decade on the grounds that it is a political symbol and is seen as politicization of religion and therefore violates the principle of secularism understood as the strict separation of religion and state. Many contested the grounds for the ban, claiming that distinction between different kinds of veiling styles was arbitrary and irrelevant. Hence in a country where more than half of the women wear a headscarf of some sort, the issue greatly vexed conservatives. For example, one business owner challenged the claim that the headscarf is a political symbol,[38] arguing that what matters is the essence (i.e., the fact that the head is covered) rather than the form of veiling (i.e., how it is covered) (TR-3-B interview, 2008). Another business owner derided the banning of the headscarf by placing it in a global perspective, suggesting, "Some people view secularism as restriction of religious practice. The issue is that if you are veiled, you cannot go to college. Why? It is because it is against secularism. In which part of the world is there such a perception?" (TR-6-B interview, 2008). The conventional restrictive view of secularism and religion by the secular elite dominated the public discourse for decades in Turkey, and the challenge from the Islamic periphery was significant. It is indicative of the gradual delegitimization of the secular modernization frame of mind reminiscent of the secularization thesis (Lerner 1958; Berger 1967; Inkeles and Smith 1976).

Along the same lines, one of the biggest business owners in Turkey, who built his business in the post-1980 liberalization period, raised a sharp criticism against the secularist perspective of a traditional elite business owner in the country by pointing out the discrimination in employment against women with headscarves. He says, "Many institutions and businesses do not employ women with headscarves. For example, most recently a leading businessman in Turkey [Rahmi Koc] came out and said, 'No one with a beard or a mustache can work in my company,' and we do not approve of this" (TR-6-B interview, 2008).[39] Just as the headscarf is viewed as politicization of religion, facial hair (i.e., a full beard or a mustache reminiscent of Islamic facial hair) is perceived as the men's version of Islamic observance. Hence this particular attitude reflects the secular center's view on religion and secularism.

Recent Political Instabilities

While the preferences of SME owners are important as they relate to religion's public role, their justification of such preferences and the rationale behind it is no less important. How do the preferences of peripheral business owners serve their interests? The interviews with peripheral business owners elucidate one key reason why they prefer a nonpolitical role for Islam: political stability. Overall, the perception is that if Islam is politicized and becomes a means of Islamization, then it directly affects the political and economic atmosphere of the country via heated public debates on the very fundamentals of the Turkish state. The risk is that a threat to Turkey's secular fundamentals is likely to draw the ire of the military and other secularist hardliners; in that case, uncertainty and instability would dominate the political and economic landscape. For SME owners, political and economic stability carries implications for their core material interest, that is, their business and property. The AKP's tenure in the Turkish government encompasses instances where the role of religion in political life became a crisis. Among these crises were the presidential elections of 2007, the headscarf legislation of 2008, and the AKP banning case in the Constitutional Court in 2008. These instances are valuable because they provide an opportunity to glean insights into the preferences of small business owners.

SME owners overwhelmingly took a critical stance in the face of these crises. They not only opposed a politicized use of religion and Islamization, they also disapproved of excessive concern with Islamization and threats to secularism in Turkey. Business owners justified their concerns with the crises in a number of ways. Largely, business owners have negative attitudes toward political instability because of the uncertainty associated with it and because it hampers business opportunities. Of this, one business owner proclaims, "The [AKP] banning case inevitably affected the economy. People do not like uncertainty. If you don't know the exchange rate tomorrow, can you exchange your foreign currency, or shop at all? In order to feel more secure, you save your savings. If you feel secure about your tomorrow, then you do not push your needs back; instead, you address those needs quickly" (TR-8-B interview, 2008). Another businessman echoed these sentiments, saying, "We became insecure [after the banning case]. Stability is the most important asset for businessmen like us. If there is stability, we can look ahead and plan accordingly. This would be reflected in the economy [positively]" (TR-9-B interview, 2008). Uncertainty also leads to lower levels of investment: "Currently, excessive insecurity pervades—buy no more than you need to, sell no more than you need to" (TR-11-B interview, 2008). Hence caution prevails among business owners under conditions of uncertainty that accompanied political instability following the cases of the AKP banning case and the headscarf legislation.

Uncertainty was also harmful to SME owners' interests because it negatively affected demand, preventing consumers from spending. Reflecting on how instability undermined his business, a business owner in the textile industry explained, "The people—businessmen and consumers alike—are affected. They might buy their bare necessities, but anything beyond that they might defer indefinitely. Small businesses, for example, do not purchase goods because of uncertainty; then, the other one does not produce and does not employ. Even a speculative statement can affect people, let alone facts. . . . Simply a negative outlook on the economy has the potential to undo favorable winds in the markets" (TR-16-B interview, 2008). The issue is further complicated at the macro level. The risk premium associated with political instability implies higher costs: "If costs are increasing, Turkey is viewed as a high-risk country. In that case, our credit costs are increasing" (TR-8-B interview, 2008). Indeed, Ayse Botan Berker, the office chief in Turkey for Fitch, a credit rating agency, makes it abundantly clear that the recent political instabilities in Turkey did indeed affect Turkey's investment rating. According to Berker, at a time when Turkey expected its rating to increase, Fitch decided to cancel the increase due to the rampant military coup rumors, alluding to the fact that political instability and threats to democratic governance harm the economic environment.[40] Exchange rates were also significantly affected by political instability. Consumption, especially in the domestic market, was negatively influenced by the sharp increase in exchange rates during the week when the indictment against the AKP was filed in the Constitutional Court (TR-8-B interview, 2008; TR-10-B interview, 2008). The general secretary of a big business association of various ideological stripes blamed political instability, that is, presidential elections and party banning cases, for the slow economic growth (TR-7-B interview, 2008; TR-10-B interview, 2008), whereas another business owner likened the political instability of 2007 and 2008 to being on the verge of a "catastrophe" (TR-9-B interview, 2008). Such ideas were also echoed by MUSIAD (Bolat 2007). Overall, although peripheral business owners have an Islamic identity and want Islam to be represented in the political space in some form, that is, social Islam, they also want to make sure that Islam is not politicized.

Foreign investment and international trade were undoubtedly impacted by political instability. Increasing political tension and uncertainty deterred many international customers. As an example, a businessman mentioned during an interview that one of his American customers canceled an order due merely to the increased instability in Turkey (TR-14-B interview, 2008).[41] On a broader scale, another business owner complained about the absence of foreign investment in Turkey, lamenting, "In the period following the AKP banning case, not a dollar's worth of investment was made in Turkey, and not a dollar's worth of privatization was made" (TR-6-B interview, 2008). Instability is also likely to lead to questioning of the government's legitimacy. One businessman questioned whether a government could function effectively when its fundamental legitimacy is at stake (TR-3-B interview, 2008). Although the unease about foreign investment is somewhat overblown, the underlying economic rationale seems to

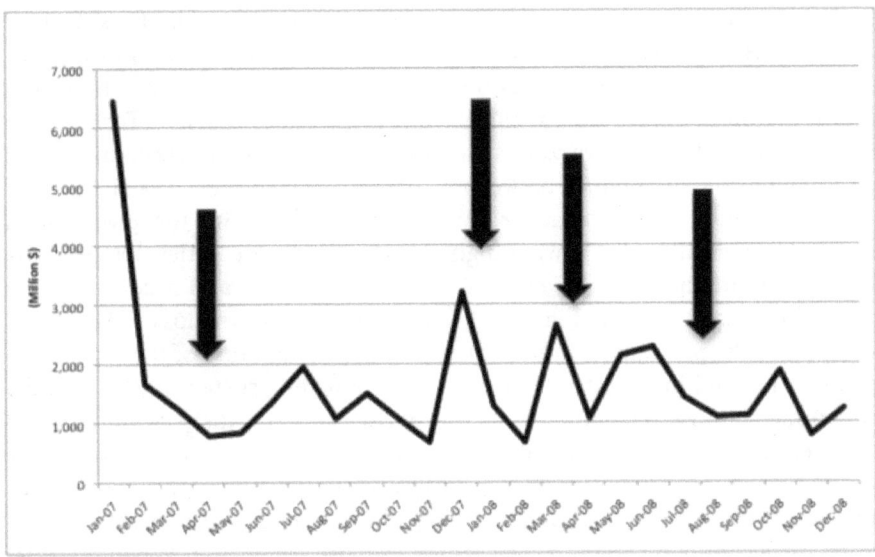

Figure 3.1 Foreign Direct Investment in Turkey in 2007 and 2008. *Sources:* Data from the Turkish Treasury. Presidential elections in April 2007; the Headscarf Legislation in January–February 2008; the Constitutional Banning Case against the AKP—Indictment in March 2008, Court Decision in July 2008.

reflect the course of events in Turkey at the time. During times of political crises, foreign direct investment (FDI) flow into Turkey declined significantly (Figure 3.1). In the period leading up to the presidential elections in April of 2007, foreign investment hit its lowest level in several months. Similarly, the headscarf legislation and the AKP banning case held a high correlation with lower investment figures.

From a different perspective, estimates regarding the economic impact of such political tension and instability are substantially high considering the size of the Turkish economy, which ultimately lends support to SME owners' concerns. The cost of the military's e-memorandum on the eve of the presidential elections[42] is estimated to be around $20 billion as a result of sharp fluctuations in the stock market. In the case of the banning case against the AKP, the bill is estimated at around $30 billion; the stock market, exchange rates, and foreign direct investment were projected to be most affected by this political instability.[43]

While the blame for the increased polarization and instability was equally divided between the AKP and the secularists, business owners also singled out the attitude of secular parties on Islam and secularism. They directed part of the blame for more than a year of instability in Turkey at the CHP—as the spokesperson of the secularist establishment—and other secularist institutions in Turkey. A small business owner's complaint is a case in point: "The CHP cannot stand the AKP and employs legal means [i.e., opposing AKP legislation]; as a result, the money and investment that was supposed to come to Turkey does not come. Military memorandums only worsen the situation." He continued by pointing out the dissonance between secularists' fear of social restriction and the reality under AKP governance: "When the AKP took over the government, was alcohol prohibited? Or were nightclubs closed down in the west [of Turkey]? No, quite the contrary; entertainment is increasing and becoming more liberal" (TR-10-B interview, 2008).[44] Others pointed out the loss of economic interests in the postliberalization era as the underlying cause of the increase in polarization and instability: "When the AKP gained its current position in the government, those benefiting from the statist and centralist system strongly opposed the slipping of political power from their hands because there is a resource[45] that some people [i.e., secularists] disproportionately exploit [since the foundation of the Republic].... They claim that they [the AKP] are Islamists; they cannot be liberals; they cannot espouse secularism. When the chief prosecutor filed the indictment, for a whole year they [the AKP] could not do anything" (TR-11-B interview, 2008). In other words, when secularists started losing their economic privileges, they resorted to foul play to prevent change. It is not only the peripheral business owners who complain about the polarizing attitude of the secularists, but also liberal and leftist business owners, according to the personal communication of a peripheral businessman (TR-1-B interview, 2008).

Democracy

In recent years, democracy has been a rallying cry for most Islamist parties; calls for democracy and public adherence to procedural democracy, that is, elections and multiple parties, are widely common. Hence a mere democratic discourse does not carry much weight as such unless we can qualify that with respect to human rights, minorities, and individual liberties. In this regard, a crucial distinction must be made between a majoritarian and community-based understanding of democracy on the one hand, and a more pluralist and liberties-oriented discourse on the other hand. Although elections are accepted in the former conceptualization in principle, the majority has the final say in all matters, regardless of its implications for the minority, and this could threaten minority rights.[46] In this scenario, individuals in society are largely viewed through their memberships in various religious groups rather than simply as individuals. In general, Islamist parties ascribe to this formulation of democracy rather than the one emphasizing rights and liberties at an individual level.

Democracy constitutes the main rallying point for the AKP as well. The party advocates a commitment to democracy both as a procedural system of governance and as a liberal value system. The AKP continues in the long-standing tradition of the NOM by ascribing to the procedural elements of democracy such as elections and a peaceful turnover of power. Despite some weak criticisms to the contrary, the AKP's credentials on formal democracy were never seriously questioned. Criticisms against the AKP's democratic credentials were usually fielded in the direction of its substantive subscription to democracy: is the AKP "sincerely" committed to democratic ideals? Hence the party's position on rights and liberties can provide a better idea as to what democracy means for the party as well as an opportunity to evaluate its "sincerity." Party discourse and policies pursued in the government thus far offer ample evidence to evaluate the AKP's stance on substantive elements of democracy (Yildirim 2013). Some of the issues that the AKP promotes as part of its democratic platform carry, in fact, Islamic undertones as discussed before, including the headscarf and Imam-Hatip schools. As sincere as the AKP may be in promoting these issues as part of its democratic and human rights discourse, such issues are not objective indicators of the party's emphasis on rights and liberties because they explicitly cater to the party's own constituency. Therefore, an analysis of other issues is imperative to assess the party position. Two issues stand out given the Turkish political context: long-standing human rights issues and EU membership.

Human Rights

Turkey does not have a good human rights record compared with that of most established democracies worldwide. Several issues are repeatedly reported in human rights reports such as the Kurdish issue, the status of ethnoreligious minorities including the Armenians and Orthodox Christians, and the Alevis—the Shia community in Turkey.[47] These issues are also important because they are among the most politicized issues regarding human rights and democracy within Turkey.

The Kurdish issue can be defined as the demand for greater cultural and ethnic rights for the Kurdish minority, and to a lesser extent the demand for greater regional political autonomy for the Kurdish-majority provinces in southeastern Turkey. Discussion of these issues was taboo in Turkish politics until less than a decade ago, when the AKP undertook important reforms that fundamentally changed the dynamics of the debate surrounding those issues. For the most part, the reforms are welcomed by Kurds and liberal seculars in Turkey, although significant criticisms are fielded regarding their noncomprehensive nature.

The AKP's Kurdish policy was to undertake revolutionary cultural reforms. Among the reforms were private and public broadcasting in Kurdish and education and publishing in Kurdish. The reforms do not amount to being "revolutionary" as such; yet, when the eight-decades-long suppression of Kurds as a distinct ethnic and cultural entity is put into perspective, the change in the statist and nationalist policy is striking. Until 2000, such reforms would be considered blasphemous against the sanctity of the Turkish republic. The emphasis on the cultural aspect of the issue enabled the AKP to couch the reforms as part of the democratization efforts called for by the European Union. This was particularly important to neutralize potential objections posed by the state bureaucracy.

More recently, the AKP announced the Kurdish Opening initiative, though it was renamed the Democratic Opening in order to alleviate the concerns of the bureaucracy and nationalists. According to the AKP, the initiative aims to solve long-standing democratization and human rights issues in Turkey, which the party claims are standing in the way of the progress in economic development and Turkey's active foreign policy.[48] Despite highly publicized discussions of the initiative, the exact contents and extent of it are far from being finalized. More importantly, the AKP government failed to follow through on the Kurdish Opening, which raised questions among liberals as to the party's commitment to the issue.

While the Kurdish issue became the focal point of discussions and media exposure, the challenges facing the Alevis seem to have taken a backseat in a predominantly Sunni country. In recent years, the AKP tried to engage more directly with the Alevi community regarding its demands. First, several prominent Alevis such as Reha Çamuroğlu, İbrahim Yiğit, and Hüseyin Tuğcu joined the ranks of the AKP. The explicit goal in this progressive union was to promote the party's Alevi initiative. Second, the party initiated a series of workshops designed to determine the demands of the Alevi community with the goal of incorporating them in future reform efforts. These workshops were conducted between June 2009 and January 2010 in seven sessions.[49] Even though some Alevi groups did not join the workshops for ideological reasons,[50] a significant majority took part in the series.[51]

The Alevi reforms thus far remain limited. One of the reforms deals with the official status of Alevi places of worship, or *cemevis*. Historically, *cemevis* received only semiofficial recognition, but full legal status would enable them to benefit from state funding in the same way as mosques. Currently, some local funding is diverted to support *cemevis* in an ad hoc manner.[52] Another outcome of the Alevi workshops was the change envisioned for religious education in schools. The proposed changes suggest either the canceling of these courses entirely or their transformation into comprehensive religious history courses. Either way, the Alevis would be relieved of the required Sunni indoctrination.[53] The most recent step taken to this end is the integration of the Alevi faith into religion courses beginning in the fourth grade.[54]

Historically, Armenians and the Greek Orthodox community enjoyed significant freedom as it pertained to their religious and cultural identities (Davison 1954; Inalcik 1991). However, with the onset of the Turkish republic in 1923, they have possessed few privileges beyond Turkish citizenship. Similar to the reforms regarding the Kurds and the Alevis, reform for the Armenian and Greek Orthodox communities has been protracted and limited. Reforms in this area are also couched largely within the framework of EU membership and democratization. Prime Minister Erdogan describes some of the reforms his government undertook as follows: "For instance we have made changes to the building codes so that they do not refer to 'mosques' but to 'places of religious worship.' We put government money into restoring the Armenian Church on Lake Van, and we have changed the law to help religious foundations [regain property confiscated by the state]."[55] The Law on Foundations was also a source of concern for non-Muslim minorities in Turkey particularly because it prevented such minorities from acquiring new property and reclaiming property seized by the state. The revisions to the law largely addressed problems in this regard.[56]

One of the thorniest issues concerning non-Muslim communities is the issue of religious schools. A dispute between the Turkish state and the Greek Orthodox Church in Istanbul over the Heybeliada Greek Orthodox Seminary became an international issue. Since 1971, the Greek Orthodox Church has demanded the reopening of the seminary because this reopening would be historically and culturally significant. At the same time, the Turkish government's condition on the patriarch's citizenship status puts the church in a bind: "The requirement that the Greek Orthodox Patriarch be a Turkish citizen is creating increasing problems for the Orthodox community given their rapidly dwindling numbers and their inability to train clergy in Turkey" (Jenkins 2004). In addition, the church also claims that the Greek Orthodox population in Turkey is limited in numbers, preventing the church from maintaining its very existence in terms of personnel. Nonetheless, as a state policy, the Turkish government has not recognized the ecumenical role of the church since the 1923 Lausanne Treaty, ultimately preventing a change in its policy thus far. As in the cases of the Kurdish and Alevi issues, the emphasis on the nation-state and its perception as a raison d'état prevents the Turkish government from taking more liberal steps toward the non-Muslim religious communities.

The AKP's largely accommodative approach to religious minorities drew the Armenian community closer to the party. According to a statement made by the church's Legal Commission member, Sebu Aslangil, prior to the 2007 parliamentary elections, there was a tendency to support the AKP within the Armenian community. The AKP's extensive efforts in passing the Foundations Law were instrumental in garnering this support, as it recognized the demands of the Armenian community.[57]

The AKP's human rights reforms include other areas of discourse and concern, including a willingness to address the constitution's infamous Article 301. Long renowned to be a means to keep those critical of "Turkishness" and the Turkish state in check, Article 301 limits freedom of expression, especially for intellectuals. The article requires prosecution of those who offend Turkishness and the Turkish state, an offense quite malleable and subjective in its formulation. Many likened the article to Damocles's sword hanging over Turkish democracy and freedom of expression. Among those prosecuted under Article 301 is Orhan Pamuk, the widely known novelist and the first Turkish Nobel laureate. The AKP government made changes to the article, particularly in its practical application, yet the change is far from fulfilling liberal standards. The change requires the president to authorize prosecution prior to any action by the judiciary; this was essentially a compromise solution to what was considered a political crime. Nonetheless, the change helped stop the "wanton application" of the law.[58] Also, the AKP passed legislation to eliminate the notorious State Security Courts and to reform the National Security Council, ensuring civilian majority in its first term in government. Both reforms were part of an effort to harmonize the Turkish judicial system with EU standards and to ensure the removal of remnants of military oversight over civilian rule. It is important to note that some contest the AKP's commitment to democratic ideas and argue that such reformist attitude on ethnic and religious minorities on the AKP's part does not necessarily reflect an ideological commitment; rather, contextual factors might explain the party's policy until recent times, argue Somer and Glupker-Kesebir: "Structural factors such as the reduction of the military tutelage and electoral strategies may better explain the AKP's Kurdish peace initiatives" (2015, 26).

EU Membership

The AKP's position on Turkish membership in the European Union is one of the clearest testaments to the democratic credentials of the party. The AKP unequivocally supports EU membership, thus stating in their most recent party program, "Turkey shall rapidly fulfill its promises in its relations with the European Union and the conditions, which the union demands of other candidate nations as well. Thus, it shall prevent the occupation of the agenda with artificial problems" (AKP Program 2007, section 6). The original party program marks a relationship between democracy and EU membership and states that democracy in Turkey should be made compatible with EU standards and that national legal reforms should be undertaken in order to comply with the Copenhagen Criteria (AKP Program 2001, section 2.5). Since the 1960s, EU membership represents one of the key ideals of Westernization for the Turkish Republic, in line with Ataturk's dictum that Turkey's goal is to "reach the level of contemporary civilizations." The

AKP's position on EU membership hence is not "sincere" for some because it represents a way out of the secular duress at the domestic level. Alternatively, one could argue that the main thrust behind the AKP's favorable position toward the European Union is the long-standing state policy on EU membership and the demands of the European Union to that end.

However, two factors indicate that the party's EU policy is, in fact, genuine. First, the party's position on the European Union, as it stands, is at odds with the old-fashioned Islamist opposition to the European Union as a "Christian Club" (Öniş 2006b; Gunes-Ayata 2003, 216). A leading Islamist intellectual, Abdurrahman Dilipak, once put the issue as follows:

> If Turkey enters the EU, then we should have to comply with European Parliament decisions. We should know that the parliamentarians from the first day will try to establish an Armenia and Pontus in the Eastern Black Sea and to reinstate the Byzantine Empire in Istanbul. If Turkey becomes a member, this will enable Israel to have a chance at membership, and then Turkey will be asked to merge with Israel. (Gunes-Ayata 2003, 216)

The Copenhagen Criteria demand pluralist democracy and individual liberties as one of the two criteria for EU membership, the second of which is a functioning market economy. Denemeç, referring to the Copenhagen Criteria, stated, "It is impossible for a country in the EU not to be a democracy" (Denemeç interview, 2008). The sharp contrast between the AKP's perspective on EU membership and that of the Islamist platform in Turkey leaves little room for doubt about the extent of the divergence. AKP officials argue that key rallying points in terms of the democratic credentials of the AKP are its EU membership efforts (Yakis interview, 2008) and intraparty democracy—the extent that democratic procedures are upheld within the party itself (Memecan interview, 2008).

Second, if the AKP was fundamentally opposed to the European Union and used the issue instrumentally, the expectation would be to see the party as "reluctant" reformers moving toward membership at best. Yet the AKP, especially in its first spell in government (2002–7), made EU membership a priority, obtaining candidacy status in December of 2004 as a result of extensive reforms designed to meet the EU criteria. Yasar Yakis, former chairman of the Turkish parliament's EU Integration Committee, noted that the popular demand for democracy is justification for the AKP's EU pursuit, declaring, "The response of survey respondents [conducted with 42,000 subjects in 2000] indicated that the people's priority was not Islam but rather democracy, employment, and the economy. . . . Until now, our efforts to complete EU reforms with commitment and steadfast resolution have been in order to establish democracy in Turkey on firm grounds"

(Yakis interview, 2008). This statement by Yakis confirms Kosebalaban's observation that the AKP views EU membership as an opportunity for increased democratization in Turkey (Kosebalaban 2005). Gunes-Ayata makes a similar case, saying, "There is no question about the sincerity of the AKP in this new endeavor. Integration with the EU is one of their major projects, through which they are hoping to change the structure of the state towards more pluralism, human rights, and fuller democracy" (Gunes-Ayata 2003, 217).

CRITICISMS

The AKP is not immune to criticisms; many have not been happy with the performance of the party in regard to democracy and human rights. First and foremost, the party is accused of being "democrat to itself" rather than being an advocate of democracy and human rights in Turkey. According to this critique, the AKP did not show the same level of democratic idealism when other parties faced similar ban cases as it did in 2007. The most illustrious case is that of the now-banned Kurdish Demokratik Toplum Partisi (DTP). Indeed, the AKP was much less vocal in its opposition to banning political parties as a principle when the issue was the DTP.[59]

Another criticism concerns the halfhearted manner in which human rights are advocated by the AKP. In particular, the party's determinism on issues related to its core constituency such as the headscarf and Imam-Hatip schools is contrasted with the way it handles other human rights issues. The criticism is that in the face of opposition to its reform proposals, the AKP backs down swiftly. A recent example was the series of public discussions surrounding a new constitution in 2007 and 2008. One of the key elements of the AKP's electoral manifesto in 2007 elections was the introduction of a new constitution. The current constitution drafted by the military government in 1982 is considered one of the main obstacles facing greater rights and liberties in Turkey. The military internalized the "lessons" of the chaotic period in the late 1970s and the individual was made subservient to the vague and malleable idea of "state interest" in the 1982 Constitution. The AKP, in an effort to initiate public discussions on the issue, publicized the first draft prepared by one of the most respected constitutional scholars of the country, Ergun Özbudun. Despite the fact that Özbudun is known as a secular and liberal intellectual, opposition mounted against the draft based on the idea that it was in violation of the long-upheld secularism principle. The soaring opposition to a new constitution from secularist actors such as the judiciary and the CHP proved sufficient for the AKP to backtrack. To the AKP's credit, this was a time of increasing pressure over the party, leading the party to pursue a cautious path. The proposal for a new constitution coincided with the Constitutional Court case to ban the party; hence to ensure survival, the party chose to shelve the draft indefinitely. The judiciary in Turkey is notorious for being statist, pro–status quo, and against the AKP on all grounds. Hence the party had little doubt that the barely avoided ban in 2008 would be a reality the next time. In 2011, the AKP made the drafting of a new constitution virtually the sole goal of the party, should they assume the government once again. Yet, at a time when new parliamentary elections are on the horizon, there is little that is accomplished in the way of a new constitution.

Although imperfect in application, the AKP has sound democratic credentials. The party's stance is neither revolutionary nor hostile with respect to democracy, yet it seems that the AKP engages in a cost-benefit analysis in terms of a democratic and reformist discourse vis-à-vis a nondemocratic discourse. Such a rational approach to democracy, concomitantly, does not require the individual members of the party to be more democratic than their counterparts in other parties, yet ensures democratic credentials of the AKP (Incekara interview, 2008). The following observation expresses this point concisely:

> The AKP is not a revolutionary, reformist, modernizing, aggressive party; if it was, we would have seen them change the political parties law and electoral laws, decrease the national threshold, end the dominance of party leaders, and demonstrate to us that they are different from others [parties] in their style [of politics]. No, they, just as others, wanted to rule with minimal loss of energy and to see what lies ahead when in power; that did not happen. Actual developments forced the AKP to adopt the role of a wrestler, that is, a victim-of-fate who must struggle with the status quo when the party was content with the role of a moderate reformer.[60]

PERIPHERY AND DEMOCRACY

Interviews with SME owners reveal that democracy is one of the most salient political preferences of such business owners in Turkey. In what follows, I first summarize the opinions and attitudes of peripheral business owners toward democracy and then explain the reasoning behind their preferences. For many business owners, democracy is a way to express individual opinions, especially as they pertain to politics, through the formal mechanism of elections. However, quite a few go beyond the minimalist or formal definition of democracy. Some support the idea that democracy is important for the whole society with emphasis on "respect for human rights" (TR-3-B interview, 2008). Citizen participation is the key to a democratic regime. Of this, one business owner expresses, "I see democracy more as participatory democracy. All segments of society should participate in governance, decisions, and efforts. It is not only voting in elections. It is more than that. This [participation] ensures that the society is more creative, open to innovations, and more competitive" (TR-15-B interview, 2008). Formal democracy, however, is deemed insufficient, as it might provide an avenue for the manipulation of the majority (i.e., the periphery) by the minority (i.e., the center) without real progress toward democratic ideals—similar to the apartheid regime in South Africa, as another explains, saying, "Democracy is conventionally defined as the rule of the people, but that is not the case in Turkey. The minority displays odd behavior in order to govern over the majority; this is not called democracy" (TR-6-B interview, 2008).[61] SME owners largely embrace the principles of democracy and support the AKP, but the reasons for this are the critical question. What does this democratic preference imply for the material interests of small business owners? And why is the AKP the party that they support as a means to achieve those ends?

An overwhelming majority of the business owners viewed democracy beneficial for their own businesses (95 percent). The justifications for democratic preference varied. Political stability is one of the oft-cited responses. Democracy is viewed as critical to continued stability in politics, which ultimately decreases the level of uncertainty in the system (TR-9-B, TR-11-B, TR-15-B interviews). One business owner with almost $200 million of annual turnover deemed democracy indispensable for economic stability, explaining the crucial role of economic stability as follows:

> For us, it [democracy] is essential for economic stability. Why? Because the investments we will make, our level of production, and others [business decisions] rest on this [economic stability]. When you make a sale, nobody pays right away; it [payment] is always in installments. When those payments are not made, if the country is economically or politically unstable, or if you cannot discern what will happen in the future, then those payments will be deferred indefinitely.... When payments are not made, everything in between production and sales will be held back... the customer is stuck, machinery is stuck, investment is stuck; what am I to do? I will be stuck as well. Therefore, stability is very important at the micro level. (TR-10-B interview, 2008)

Some went further and argued that political stability is a sine qua non of economic stability. One business owner asserts, "Political stability and economic stability are inseparable. For example, in the past 6–8 months, the cost of the [AKP] banning case was excessively high. We can't talk about the continuation of economic stability unless there is political stability. In other words, political stability means economic security.... It means the flow of economic investment to Turkey. The whole world can easily follow what happens. Hence, political stability and democracy are more important than economic stability, because they are preconditions of economic stability" (TR-1-B interview, 2008).

International trade constitutes another aspect of democratic preference. To explain how his decision was shaped by democratic governance, one businessman argued that wherever there is democracy, there is stability; hence his decision to trade with that country would certainly be "positively" affected by the presence of democracy (TR-9-B interview, 2008). Another businessman concurred and explained the positive effect of the legal guarantees associated with democracy, claiming,

In the last 3–4 years, the incoming foreign direct investment is around $28 billion. That means we were able to attract people here [Turkey] because of democracy. As you know, in Turkey there exist both arbitration courts and an opportunity to go to a foreign court in case of disagreements. Thus, this is also what we look for [when we invest]. No one wants to go and invest in a country where they cannot claim their rights. Democracy has such an advantage.... When we look at the figures for foreign direct investment into Russia, it is nil, even negative; those investments currently in Russia are also leaving. This is the benefit of democracy for businessmen. They prefer countries where people are trustworthy and free, where there is freedom of expression, and where legal defense rights are well established. (TR-6-B interview, 2008)

Along the same lines, bureaucratic red tape and its associated problems potentially affect business owners' decision making for doing business in a particular country (TR-1-B interview, 2008).

A second justification for a democratic preference is the expectation that democracy will ensure the rule of law (TR-15-B interview, 2008). In particular, when past experiences of the marginalization of small businesses are considered, the following statement becomes instructive: "Of course, democracy is important for me because of the rule of law and the systematized functioning of business. When you operate in an undemocratic environment, people's whims and spontaneous reflexes bind you. I don't have to be friendly with everyone; if the laws apply equally, I don't need to seek favoritism. I will have the opportunity to defend my rights without hesitation. In the past, it was not like this; the maturation of democracy is important in this regard" (TR-11-B interview, 2008). Another businessman had similar ideas about democracy and the rule of law, echoing, "Because democracy permeates all parts of our lives, we are able to conduct business and trade. Why? I sell goods to a person, but I know that if problems arise, I have the invoice in hand. I can go to court and collect my debt one way or another. This is due to democracy.... Democracy is an essential condition of the rule of law" (TR-10-B interview, 2008).

Just as the rule of law is vital to the health of a domestic business community, entrenchment of the rule of law is necessary in order to attract foreign investment (TR-15-B interview, 2008). For example, comparing Iran and Turkey in terms of the level of foreign investment, a businessman noted:

We research many countries for investment. This is our job as businessmen. We will go anywhere we see profit, and we will go anywhere we see opportunities for profit. In this sense, the first thing we look for is democracy. Everything else comes after that. We want to know that democracy reigns because if there is democracy, you can solve your problems easily. But if there is no democracy, investment in that country is not feasible. Why do people not go to Iran and invest there? It's because they don't believe there is democracy in Iran. Yet, the very same people come to Turkey for investment because there is democracy. (TR-6-B interview, 2008)

A closely related but distinct reason for support of democracy is the transparency that democracy is expected to court (TR-15-B interview, 2008). Specifically, local and central government budgets are a primary concern. Challenging the veil of mystery over Istanbul's municipal budget, a business owner observed, "Today, no one knows Istanbul's municipal budget, which is larger than [that of] many states around the world, nor can they determine the sources of revenue and how the money is spent. This is because there is no such announcement or statement. However, I think such statements should be made in the twenty-first century with its standard of transparency" (TR-6-B interview, 2008). Others, however, seemed more satisfied with the level of transparency, citing the cases of privatization and government bids broadcast on live TV. This is largely a result of the increased democratization in the country (TR-15-B interview, 2008).[62] In sum, businessmen's strong preference for democracy bodes well for the AKP's commitment to it, since the peripheral business sector forms an important part of its base. Potential benefits of democracy include rule of law, transparency, and political and economic stability, which in turn reinforce fairness and equality of opportunity in the economy for the peripheral groups.

Economic Policy

The transformation of the Turkish economy since the early 1980s has altered the views of former Islamists into that of a proliberalization stance. Comprehensive economic liberalization reforms precipitated wide-ranging social changes in the periphery, particularly among SMEs. Seeking to represent the periphery and address their preferences, a substantial difference emerged in the economic discourse of the AKP as compared with the Islamist economic discourse. The AKP has a strong preference for a market-oriented liberal economy. As the party program states, "Our party supports functioning of the market economy with all its institutions and rules" (AKP Program 2001, section 2). Well aware of the implications of a strong and liberal economy, the party program does not entail qualms about economic liberalization, which is typical of Islamist economic discourse. Serdar Şen, pointing out the distinctive economic perspectives of the AKP and the NOM, notes, "Instead of making statements indicating outright propaganda, a new holistic framework is drawn [in the AKP program] where goals are set forth, and the methods and tools to reach these goals are described" (Şen 2004, 73). In this regard, the AKP's economic policy can be analyzed by examining two broad issues: (1) the state's role in the economy and (2) integration into the global economy in trade, the financial sector, and foreign direct investment.

THE STATE'S ROLE IN THE ECONOMY

According to the AKP program, the state should only assume a minimal regulatory role in the economy: "[Our party] embraces the notion that the state, in principle, should be located outside of all kinds of economic activity. It defines the economic function of the state as regulatory and supervisory" (AKP Program 2001, article 3.1). Nonetheless, this renewed economic role of the state has implications for two groups in particular. On the one hand, the state will endeavor to remove or minimize barriers to liberalization and integration into the global economy by stripping itself of an active role in the economy. The regulation of economic activity to enable market forces to determine who benefits or loses is the most important responsibility of the state in this new period, according to the AKP. The private sector's role in the economy is reinforced by active restraint on the part of the state. The provision of incentives and subsidies to businesses when needed in global competition would be attuned to this. The party's increased support for SMEs in terms of exports and R&D funds in recent years can be viewed in this light (Yakis interview, 2008).[63] Considered from the perspective of a developing country, it is justified by the party to maintain its competitive edge in the global market. Moreover, the process is viewed as a gradual one; therefore, the state cannot remove itself from the economy instantaneously. The Turkish economy, like other economies in the region, has a strong tradition of statism, and so it is not unexpected that the state historically made its presence felt in every quarter of the economy.

State-owned enterprises (SOEs) are especially vital because privatization of SOEs conveys a strong message that the state is withdrawing from the economy. According to the AKP program, the party "views privatization as an important tool in the creation of a more rational economic infrastructure" (AKP Program 2007, section 3.1). Privatization in its entirety carries a number of implications. Private actors are gradually permeating the economy as the state gradually exits it. However, at the same time, the state is giving up a valuable tool of distribution and a patronage network. That is, SOEs conventionally provide employment beyond economically efficient levels for a significant portion of the population and provided inputs and consumer products at below market prices. As a result, protected businesses and the urban population benefited disproportionately from politically motivated decision-making mechanisms in SOEs. In addition, the state commits itself to addressing the demands of potential losers in liberalization and privatization reforms through an extensive social protection network. In other words, the state assumes a dual role. While trying to minimize its involvement to engage in full-scale liberalization, it recognizes the fact that there will be losers in this process, so it embraces these losses on the grounds that benefits of liberalization outweigh its costs.

By contrast, the Islamist WP assumed a critical economic stance throughout the 1990s; the party made a deliberate attempt at identifying big businesses and complaining about the way the economy was handled, albeit with no specific policy alternative. WP leader Erbakan stated, "We are not set against privatization or free enterprise. We are against copycat parties' current applications. [The party] is against the offering of state [resources] to certain individuals and entities. It will protect the rights of the state on every issue. The Welfare Party absolutely rejects the notion that the private sector consists of a number of monopolies, and that all the citizens drift into economic hardship. It advocates the Just Economic Order, which will enable all social classes to live humanely."[64] Here, we see a clear divergence between the Islamist discourse of the WP and the AKP's liberal economic discourse. While the WP criticizes privatization as a way of creating monopolies and underscores the need to distribute wealth, the AKP focuses on increasing the economic space available for the private sector, which in turn results in new opportunities for the party's own base, that is, SMEs.

The successor to the WP, the VP, portrays a more favorable view of economic policy-making with respect to liberalization and the role of the state. The VP program asserts, "When possible, it is necessary to exclude the state from commercial and industrial activities and have the private sector undertake such activities. The state will undertake security, justice, education, health care, and infrastructure as part of its essential functions; it [the state] will provide, as the overseer and guide, all the conditions of a free market economy in order for the private sector to develop" (VP Program 1999, 15). In addition, on privatization the VP stated, "Privatization will be emphasized to create an economy where market forces dominate, monopolies and oligopolies are broken, capital is distributed to the lower classes, competition is established in a productive economic structure through the use of new technologies, and finally the market economy functions within its rules, providing the state with the revenue to finance new state infrastructure" (VP Program 1999, 17–18). The VP's economic stance is significantly liberal compared with its predecessor the WP. The more liberal discourse of the VP can be explained by the influence of a large number of reformist members within the party who would later constitute the core of the AKP. However, the nationalist and protectionist turn in the economic discourse of the current Islamist Felicity Party (FP) is striking. The FP, in a period of full-scale liberalization, acts on the assumptions of the 1970s, saving certain sectors for the state, declaring in its party program, "The state will take the necessary measures to prevent cartelization, monopolization, black market activities, and unfair competition, and to remove those obstacles making production more difficult.... State investments will be limited to those areas where the private sector does not show much interest such as infrastructure, health, and education, and the areas deemed too sensitive to leave in the hands of the private sector such as some defense industry investments" (FP Program 2001, article 4.4). The regression of the FP from the fairly liberal economic stance of the VP to a more protectionist and nationalist position is indicative of the separation between the AKP and the FP in terms of their overall discourse.

Overall, the AKP views the state's role as limited to the creation of the optimal environment for a dynamic private sector, a significant portion of which consists of SMEs. Any active role for the state is perceived as a violation of the state's regulatory mantle. Indeed, such conceptualization fits well with a competitive economic liberalization model where the state offers opportunities to economic actors rather than the benefits themselves.

ECONOMIC LIBERALIZATION

The AKP's position on economic liberalization is unequivocally clear. The AKP espouses comprehensive economic liberalization with specific policy proposals regarding how to deepen Turkey's integration into the global economy, which is in sharp contrast to Islamist parties. Integration to the global economy always met skeptical eyes among Islamists because they were convinced that Turkey would be subjugated to dominant (non-Muslim) market forces, a reflection of both the nationalist economic conception of Islamists and the cynicism toward trade with non-Muslim countries, Western countries in particular. The nationalist discourse of Islamist parties is a legacy of the closed economy and a response to the exclusion of the peripheral groups from the economy. It carried well into the postliberalization period for the Islamists, however. In particular, under Erbakan's leadership, the NOM fielded strong reservations against the customs union with the European Union throughout the mid-1990s. The NOM highlighted economic redistribution rather than economic liberalization: "Our party accepts it as a fundamental principle to take up measures in order to redistribute welfare justly to the lower classes, and to overcome inequalities across regions and classes" (WP Program 1983, article 8).

Today, reservations against a liberal economy continue with the FP; instead, emphasis is on national and protectionist policies. For example, Numan Kurtulmuş, the outgoing FP leader, recently emphasized their espousal of "national solutions" and opposition to all solutions that do not place Turkey at the center.[65] The FP views the economy as more of an extension of rentierism. According to the FP program, the reason for the creation of a rentier economy in Turkey is "the ability of a small rentier group to shape decision-making mechanisms by bringing its active cadres to positions of power via its capital and media power" (Şen 2004, 76).

As part of its economic platform, the AKP highlights two specific components of economic liberalization: trade and the financial sector. Several members of the AKP mentioned the economic liberalization of the early 1980s as one of the turning points in Turkish history. Turgut Özal, the man behind the liberalization reforms and the former prime minister and president, was fondly remembered by AKP members with whom I conducted interviews (Denemeç, Ozbayrak, Tekin interviews, 2008). More specifically on trade, the AKP recognizes some difficulties and problems associated with the liberalization process. Yet instead of lambasting liberalization for the problems commonly associated with it, or even reversing liberalization, the AKP announced its commitment to liberalization in the first place, and then laid out a policy framework to address such issues within the confines of an open economy. Specifically, the AKP pursued a two-pronged policy to this end. On one hand, the government, under the direction of the party, encouraged the growth of exports as a way to secure Turkey's share in the global marketplace. A customs union with the European Union and other trade agreements are viewed as an opportunity rather than a threat (Ozbayrak interview, 2008). On the other hand, the AKP government expanded the scope of liberalization via a policy of bilateral trade agreements in the developing world, including in its immediate neighborhood. Of this, the AKP government program proclaims, "The structure and content of [governmental] action plans will rest on the idea that Turkey shall be the supermarket of the region and sustain it."[66] In this regard, the AKP's emphasis on international trade is a strong indicator of its liberal economic conception.

Indeed, in the six years from 2002 until 2008, Turkey's exports have quadrupled from $30 billion to more than $120 billion.[67] In particular, regional diversification of Turkey's international trade over time is striking (Table 3.1). This was largely due to the success of the "Anatolian Tigers," as AKP officials phrased it, referring to the non-Istanbul-based SMEs throughout Turkey (Denemeç and Ozbayrak interviews, 2008). The peripheral businesses have been one of the winning groups as a result of liberal economic policies.

By contrast, the Islamist FP is more critical of the increasing prosperity of the conservative and peripheral constituency in Turkey. For instance, the former FP leader Numan Kurtulmus argues that the public sector is viewed by some as a mechanism to enrich a group of people rather than the whole country: "This was the same during the previous government, and now it is no different. The only difference is that now it is the bearded and veiled people who ride SUVs as compared to others before."[68] The FP's Istanbul mayoral candidate in the 2009 local elections echoed Kurtulmus's views on the issue when he said, "SUVs and the headscarf cannot go together."[69]

Financial liberalization constitutes another element of the party's economic policy. Recognizing the importance of the financial sector, the party program avows, "The financial services sector plays an important role in the system of economic structure and in the network of relations, due to the strong forward

Table 3.1 Turkish Exports by Region (Billion $)

	EU	Middle East	Africa
2009	47.01	19.19	10.18
2008	63.40	25.43	9.06
2007	60.40	15.08	5.97
2006	47.93	11.31	4.56
2005	41.36	10.18	3.63
2004	36.58	7.92	2.96
2003	27.39	5.46	2.13
2002	20.41	3.44	1.69
2001	17.55	3.26	1.52
2000	15.66	2.57	1.37
1999	15.42	2.56	1.65
1998	14.81	2.68	1.82
1997	13.43	2.82	1.23
1996	12.56	2.59	1.16

Source: Turkish Statistical Institute.

and backward connections it possesses. Having an important role in the supply of money and purchasing power and its transfer into the economy, it is essential that financial institutions should operate efficiently and productively" (AKP Program, 2007, section 3.7). Building on this recognition, the AKP pursues a two-pronged approach to financial liberalization. First and foremost, the party wants to ensure that the fundamentals of the economy are sound and that political stability reigns in Turkey. According to the party, the absence of political stability prevents progress in this sector: "In the last two decades, Turkey has taken important steps in trade and capital movement towards integrating into the international system. The integration in trade has positively affected welfare. However, the integration in capital flows causes significant problems because of the absence of economic and financial stability" (AKP Electoral Manifesto, 2002). This observation builds on the financial and economic crisis Turkey experienced in 2001. Second, the AKP envisions Turkey becoming a major point of attraction in the region: "Our government's vision on the financial sector centers on the goal of strengthening the environment that will increase the preferability of Turkey as a regional financial hub" (AKP 59th Government Program, 2003). The investment figures below show a clear trend in attracting regional capital, to the credit of the AKP (Table 3.2). The overall FDI investment increased substantially throughout the 2000s, in particular since 2006.

Table 3.2 International Direct Investment Inflow by Region (Billion $)

	2002	2003	2004	2005	2006	2007	2008	2009
EU	455	555	1,027	5,006	14,489	12,600	11,103	4,604
Europe—Non-EU	64	70	6	1,646	85	373	290	295
Africa	0	0	—	3	21	5	82	0
US	2	52	36	88	848	4,212	859	236
Canada	7	6	61	26	121	11	24	52
Central-South America	0	0	—	8	33	494	60	16
Middle East	0	1	54	1,678	1,910	608	2,130	262
Other Asian Countries	65	59	6	78	17	797	160	298
Other Countries	24	2	—	2	115	36	1	12
Total	622	745	1,190	8,535	17,639	19,136	14,709	5,775

Source: Turkish Treasury.

PERIPHERY AND ECONOMY

During the interviews, peripheral business owners demonstrated that they clearly prefer a liberal economy, particularly in comparison to the preliberalization Turkish economy. The preliberalization economy is a source of bad memories for many business owners of the postliberalization era. Some lamented the official state favoritism of "big businesses" in the provision of subsidies and incentives, ultimately leading to monopolization in the economy (TR-3-B interview, 2008). Others attribute the absence of economic development and industrialization to the constraints on international trade and financing. Furthermore, others recall "special permit" requirements for imports of machinery, exports, foreign currency, or international credit, all of which were ultimately determined by political connections rather than economic needs (TR-10-B, TR-16-B, TR-7-B interviews). The encompassing nature of economic liberalization as initiated by Özal contrasts sharply with the pre-1980 picture, especially in the context of Anatolian cities as opposed to the home of the "big capital," Istanbul (TR-11-B interview, 2008).

SME owners' economic preferences centered around two major themes: (1) the state's economic role, and (2) the deepening of economic liberalization. Both are consistent with the AKP platform. The predominant view is that the state should limit itself to economic regulation, for a better business climate, and to a number of sectors where it can provide services for the public good rather than engage in "commerce": "The state must relinquish its stakes in the economy. In the contemporary world we live in, the state should collect taxes, be fair to everyone, provide fair competition conditions for everyone, provide health care, establish the rule of law, ensure security. . . . In this regard, the state [in Turkey] is evolving towards this ideal" (TR-11-B interview, 2008; TR-6-B interview, 2008).

The more pressing question is, however, why these business owners prefer a liberal economy. A major businessman in the furniture sector drew attention to the investment effect of the state's new regulatory role, stating, "As a businessman, I only expect regulation and supervision from the state. Of course, we do understand that when the Turkish Republic was established, the state had to undertake all kinds of commercial and industrial activities due to the absence of private capital. Yet, it's been years since even the Communist Bloc completed its privatization. . . . The state should regulate the investment climate. If you have not established the infrastructure yet, you will not be able to attract people and have them invest here" (TR-6-B interview, 2008). Another business owner conveyed the same message, albeit with slightly different wording: "I expect the state to remove the obstacles in front of Turkish industrialists. As an industrialist, I think we can run as we are expected to do so long as the [economic] terrain is cleared of rocks and mines, so to speak" (TR-7-B interview, 2008). State intervention in the economy is perceived to have damaging effects as illustrated by the rampant favoritism that existed prior to economic liberalization. Rather than being directly involved with the economy, the state should reduce the "labor and electricity costs" (TR-8-B interview, 2008), reduce interest rates (TR-15-B interview, 2008), and depreciate the currency (TR-11-B interview, 2008) in order to stimulate investment, according to SME owners.

Along the same lines, the absence of the state from the economy implies a competitive economic environment, which seems to be supported by almost all peripheral business owners because it emphasizes the equality of opportunity in the economy (TR-11-B interview, 2008). From a broader perspective, liberalization helps to improve the investment environment in the country. As articulated by one such business owner, "When we are not limited to the banks in Turkey, and can search for credit in banks abroad, we can make new investments in Turkey. Hence the simplification and liberalization of all such procedures and the decreasing number of bureaucratic procedures contributes to the development of Turkish industry" (TR-10-B interview, 2008).

As for the deepening of liberalization, the second economic preference, it is particularly revealing in exposing SME owners' interest in openness. Even though the period between 1980 and the early 2000s is viewed as an important phase of Turkish economic development and SME growth, some business owners explicitly referred to a qualitative distinction between the pre-2002 and post-2002 periods. Some even referred to the post-2002 period as the "second liberalization." The main difference between the two periods is the inflation rate:

> During that period [pre-2002], the inflation rate was quite high and companies were working inefficiently, but thanks to the high rate of inflation they were able to sell their products. The goods they produced would experience a price increase within a year at the 50 to 60 percent inflation rates. Thus, due to such price increases, companies would profit from whatever they sold; yet they were not efficient. In other words, a realistic production-cost analysis was not being conducted in order to reduce production costs. The state was a part of this cycle with the regular devaluations it offered to the business sector in order to keep exports at a certain level. In the post-2000 period, the economy reached its true indicators [dynamics]. Following the economic crisis in 2001, a second liberalization, that is, a real liberalization, enabled a cost analysis to be made [without having to rely on perpetual currency devaluations]. Efficient companies survived. In other words, the companies with higher productivity, a willingness to put forth much effort and a general positive capability did well. The economy got rid of such diseases [e.g., inflation and currency devaluations] for the most part. (TR-15-B interview, 2008)

In the same fashion, another businessman in the textile sector, speaking of his own experience with the second wave of "liberalization" explained, "The last five to seven years have been an adaptation period. We shifted to being a low-inflation economy from being a high-inflation economy. In the long term, this is a beneficial process, yet in the short term, the adaptation was difficult, including for my own firm. However, we have adjusted by this time. We reorganized the structure of our company accordingly" (TR-10-B interview, 2008).

Other business owners perceived the next step in deepening liberalization to be a systematic attempt to engage with other countries via free trade agreements and similar structures:

> The priority should be to liberalize the Turkish economy, not in terms of its domestic market, but by integrating with the global economic system; the domestic market is not important anymore. Recently, in the economic daily, *Dunya*, I've seen that the CEO of a construction firm made a statement that they were not interested in foreign business below $100 million. This is excellent; their benchmark for doing business is almost $300 to $400 million. This is a good indicator that demonstrates how far the country has come. When this is the case, the state cannot simply go ahead and ask them to limit themselves to the domestic market; that would be going against the current. (TR-1-B interview, 2008)

Even so, many problems remain in the way of greater economic integration and trade, including political or bureaucratic difficulties. Hence business owners call for greater political activism on the part of the state to eliminate noneconomic obstacles such as visa requirements (TR-1-B interview, 2008).

Social Spending

In this last section, I discuss a different aspect of the AKP's party platform: social policy. The justification for this shift rests on the fact that the electoral coalition that supports the party is made up of two groups: (1) SME owners as discussed in the previous sections of this chapter, and (2) the peripheral masses, to be discussed next. Social spending is a way to compensate the demands and losses of the lower and middle classes in a liberalizing economy. Although Islamic parties conventionally have been pro-social spending, the AKP's distinct approach to social policy sets it apart from this conventional position. Historically, the NOM viewed the issue of social policy as one of mutual aid per its Islamist discourse (Şen 2004, 291). In doing so, a traditional conceptualization of individuals' social responsibility is highlighted. Though an institutional structure to that end is supported, the state is, by and large, viewed as failing to systematically provide social protection. In order to fix this state failure, the MNP—the first political party of NOM—offered the development of "socialized mutual aid institutions" as a solution. This loose network was projected to offer help to a wide array of social groups such as those affected by natural disasters, those who cannot work, those who are unemployed, poor students, children in need of protection, senior citizens, widows, and orphans (MNP Program 1970, article 17).

The more contemporary parties of the NOM follow along the same line by emphasizing values and culture as a justification for their pro-social policy positions. The VP drew attention to the waning tradition of social help and offered state intervention as a way to address this problem: "As in every society in the world, the idea of social mutual aid and solidarity weakens day by day. The number of handicapped and hungry people increases constantly. Although the idea of protection and watching after the poor and handicapped people is widely accepted thanks to our nation's faith, it is evident that continuing such efforts at an individual level is difficult under current circumstances" (VP Program 1999, 8). For the latest representative of the NOM, the FP, the crux of the issue rests on the combination of the faith-culture edifice in society and a state social security institution: "We believe that the aforementioned faith and culture structure of our [society] is the insurance of the social security that we aspire to establish. We need to protect this structure of ours and do our best to improve it. The established systems may face a crisis at any moment and collapse. Even those countries with strong economies face difficulties in sustaining their social security systems" (FP Program 2001, article 3.12).

The AKP, on the other hand, views social policy in a significantly different light. First and foremost, social protection is viewed as a right on the part of the citizens, and thus the state has a responsibility to provide such services. According to the AKP program, "Our party understands social security as a constitutional right and accepts it as the responsibility of the state to ensure that every citizen benefits from this right" (AKP Program 2007, article 5.5). The underlying rationale in the provision of social protection differs from the more traditional view of the NOM. The basic thrust behind increased state responsibility in providing social protection is industrialization and increased urbanization (AKP Program 2007, article 5.5). Essentially, socioeconomic transformation lies at the origin of the problem for the AKP. The dislocations associated with a new socioeconomic structure systematically leave certain groups disadvantaged, so the goal is to address such dislocations endured by the "less fortunate" groups that make up the base of the AKP (Yakis interview, 2008). Such dislocations may arise from privatization of SOEs, restructuring of firms to adapt to a liberal economy, or the end of distributive policies of the statist era. On social policies, the AKP clearly has a vision to address a structural problem in a legalistic framework, whereas the NOM adheres to a more ad hoc framework based on culture and faith, that is, Islam. This focus on social spending increased the AKP's credibility as a social-democrat party in European eyes, according to AKP deputy Yakis (Yakis interview, 2008). Hence those who may suffer economic dislocation in a liberalizing economy belong largely to the core constituency of the AKP, the peripheral masses. Consequently, the AKP has a good reason to be fully supportive of an extensive social safety net.

The data on unemployment benefits during the AKP government since 2002 support the party's discourse on social spending. The number of people benefiting from unemployment insurance since 2002 shows a marked increase over time (Figure 3.2). Although the spike in 2008 is largely due to the recent economic crisis, the trend until that time is a clear indication of the AKP's policy of compensating losers in the new liberal economy. The actual amount of payment in this period closely follows the number of beneficiaries for unemployment insurance (Figure 3.3). These data explain the peripheral masses' support for the AKP.

In this chapter, I have shown that the deep-rooted economic liberalization process in Turkey in the aftermath of 1980, in the form of competitive liberalization, substantially shaped the future course of Islamist politics. The extensive economic liberalization reforms undertaken by Turgut Özal uncovered many opportunities for peripheral SMEs in the Turkish economy and beyond. Such new economic opportunities enabled peripheral business owners to operate under conditions close to a liberal market economy. Politically, for peripheral businessmen this meant that their political and economic preferences would undergo a major change to reflect their new material interests. Under political and economic conditions where political obstacles to doing business are limited and where business success largely rests on economic conditions rather than on political favoritism or intervention, peripheral businessmen support democracy, a

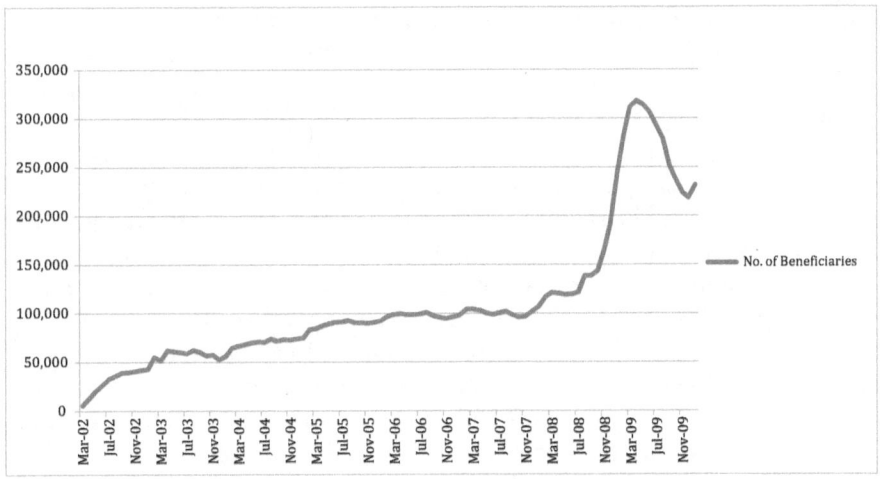

Figure 3.2 Unemployment Insurance Payments, Number of Beneficiaries. *Source:* Data compiled from Turkey Employment Agency's *Unemployment Insurance Bulletin* archives, various issues. The bulletins are available at http://www.iskur.gov.tr/LoadExternalPage.aspx?uicode=statikbultenindex.

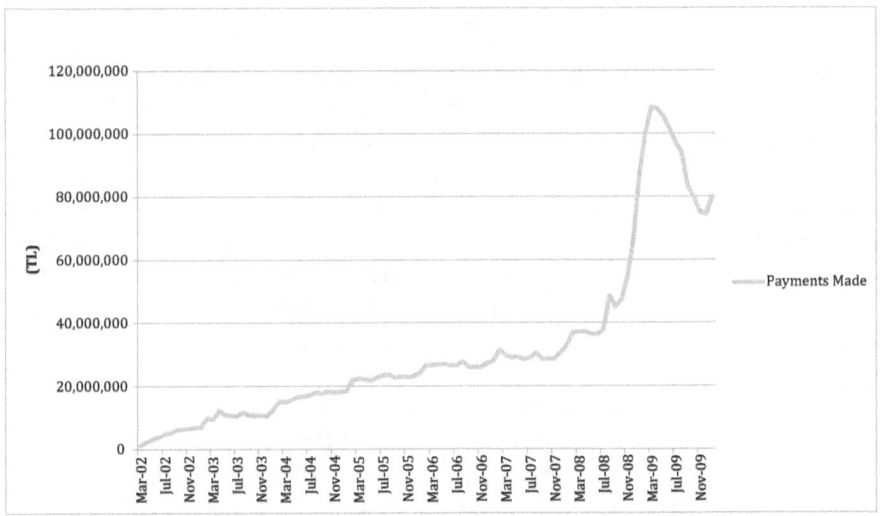

Figure 3.3 Unemployment Insurance Payments, Actual Payments Made. *Source:* Data compiled from the Turkey Employment Agency's *Unemployment Insurance Bulletin* archives, various issues. The bulletins are available at http://www.iskur.gov.tr/LoadExternalPage.aspx?uicode=statikbultenindex.

liberal economy, and a nonpoliticized emphasis on Islamic values. The expectation is that such political preferences will ensure political and economic stability, rule of law, and low uncertainty—issues of highest concern to peripheral business owners.

Concomitantly, the critical change in the Turkish Islamist movement in the late 1990s and the early 2000s (in the form of the AKP) was a direct response to these changes taking place in the Islamic periphery. The AKP, emerging with a Muslim democratic platform, duly emphasized Islamic values and social Islam rather than political Islam, democratic principles and individual liberties rather than procedural democracy, and a liberal economy rather than the nationalist and protectionist economic discourse of Islamists. In addition, the AKP underscored the compensation of the losers in the liberalization process, that is, the peripheral masses, in an effort to bring the rest of the periphery on board. Thus far, the AKP's new platform seems to have captured the periphery's changing political preferences, managing to keep the Islamist FP on the edges of Turkey's political space in the aftermath of their emergence. Along those same lines and perhaps more importantly, the AKP won successive elections in 2002, 2007, and 2011, while the FP received no more than a meager couple of percentage points in parliamentary elections.

Aftermath of 2011: An Islamist Reversion or the AKP's Impending Postmortem?

The analysis thus far depicts a greatly favorable picture of how economic openness paves the way for moderation, democratization, and greater political openness. Yet we observe a jarring turnaround in the way things have been unfolding in Turkey since 2011, which brings to mind, expectedly, the following question: Does the authoritarian turn in the AKP government since the 2011 parliamentary elections represent an Islamist reversion in the AKP's ideology? Alternatively, we can ask, do the post-2011 developments undermine the socioeconomic theory of Islamist moderation and democratization I offer in this book? I will first briefly overview the recent developments in Turkey since 2011 and then answer these questions.

For a long time, Turkey was the poster child for secular and Muslim democracy and was upheld as a model for the rest of the Muslim world (Altunisik 2005).[70] The fact that an Islamic party (i.e., the AKP) led the way in the most recent democratization drive only buttressed this perception. Turkey obtained official candidate status to the European Union, and accession talks were underway. As part of this process, many reforms aimed at establishing a pluralist, rights-oriented democratic system were undertaken. Ethnic and religious minorities were regaining their rights, having been heavily suppressed under the strict nationalist regime for decades. Military tutelage over the civilian, democratic process was greatly curtailed. All indicators were pointing in the direction of maturation of Turkish democracy after a long, hard-fought process. And all of this was happening, ironically, under the leadership of an Islamic party; it is ironic because historically, Kemalist leaders bragged about secular modernization and Westernization and how Islam was a thing of the past.

This was, of course, until the 2011 electoral victory of the AKP, the party's third straight win. The AKP campaigned on a platform marked by a new constitution that would usher in a new era in Turkish history, one in which pluralist democracy and individual rights and liberties would be firmly institutionalized. In other words, there was to be no return from democracy. This was in line with the AKP's political discourse in the decade leading up to the elections. The AKP won 50 percent of the votes, a large proportion in any parliamentary system. Despite its significant parliamentary power, popular demand for it, and no major opposition to it, the party never demonstrated serious ownership of the drafting of the new constitution, and some halfhearted efforts in parliamentary committees made sure that the idea was stillborn.[71]

Paradoxically, the post-2011 period also marks the beginning of the authoritarian trend in AKP governance. No major source of opposition to the AKP remained—the military was out of the picture; the parliamentary opposition was lacking and had been hopeless for a long time; it was only the society itself that could feasibly mount any oppositional challenge to Erdogan's rule. In the summer of 2013, a spontaneous, societal opposition came into existence around a relatively minor environmental issue, the protection of Gezi Park in the heart of Istanbul. Thanks to then–prime minister Erdogan's characteristically uncompromising stance and suppression of demonstrations, Gezi Park demonstrations turned into a societal outlet of opposition to the AKP's increasingly authoritarian and undemocratic governance (Arat 2013; Gurcan and Peker 2014). The tension came to a head at the end of 2013 (December 17) when multiple graft allegations and investigations surfaced. These allegations first concerned four ministers in Erdogan's cabinet, after which it became evident that Erdogan himself and his family were fully involved in an extensive corruption scheme, stretching several years prior (Bilgin 2014).[72]

More importantly, how did the AKP and Erdogan react to the allegations? Erdogan and the AKP responded to the accusations in three distinct ways. First, an Islamic movement (the Gulen Movement) was accused of establishing a "parallel" state within the bureaucracy, thereby organizing a conspiracy to overthrow the AKP government. Second, the AKP government reassigned hundreds of prosecutors and thousands of police officers and chiefs to different and peripheral locations within the country. Most critically, those prosecutors and police chiefs involved with investigating the corruption scandal were immediately reassigned to different positions and later investigated. Finally, several bills were passed in the parliament that undermine the separation of powers between the executive and judicial branches and violate basic freedoms such as access to the internet and freedom of speech (Yildirim 2015a).[73] These efforts clearly served to divert attention from the main issue, which was the widespread and endemic problem of corruption, and to prevent the progress of investigations.

The AKP and Erdogan were able to win three more elections following the graft scandal: local elections in March 2014, the presidential election in August 2014, and parliamentary elections in June 2015. In all three elections, observers noted how irregularities that favored the governing party were pervasive throughout both the campaign periods and during the actual elections (Rethink Institute 2015). For example, with the March 30, 2014, local elections, Turkey witnessed a rare case of widespread and systematic electoral fraud since 1950, undermining arguably its best democratic quality—free and fair elections.

Thousands of documented complaints about electoral fraud have been filed.[74] Such complaints include stuffing ballot boxes with prestamped ballots and voting by unregistered voters and noncitizen aliens. Many official ballot box reports entail lower counts for major opposition candidates. The districts with an anticipated pro-AKP outcome were reported first, while those districts hosting the greatest challenge to AKP candidates were reported last; this was aimed at tearing down the strength and morale of the opposition supporters. Once the vote count began, about forty or so major cities experienced extended power outages.[75] These outages are unusual (despite a statement by an AKP minister, attributing them ironically to poor weather conditions and cats),[76] as most of these cities did not have similar outages in the recent past. Erik Meyersson documents "a peculiar relationship" between higher vote share for the ruling AKP and the proportion of invalid ballots based on election data.[77]

Of note, the government tried to block news agencies from instantly accessing the election results as they were reported, subjugating everyone to the reporting of the state news agency (Anadolu Ajansi). Although in most cases such efforts yielded no results, the website of the premier reporter of election results, the Cihan News Agency, was curiously blocked with a systematic cyber-attack.[78] Similarly, the major Turkish daily *Zaman*, its English counterpart *Today's Zaman*, and the liberal *Taraf* newspaper had their websites under attack for most of the election day. These measures aimed to limit reporting by major opposition news resources.

Most concerning about these elections is their aftermath. In his victory speech, Erdogan declared that the opposition and enemies would "pay for this,"[79] referring to their opposition campaign in the face of corruption charges. Erdogan also suggested, "We will enter their lair," and charged the opposition with threatening the national security of Turkey. In a confrontational and arrogant fashion, as is typical of him, Erdogan utilized a rhetoric that was centered around vengeance and retribution. There is a great concern that such vengeful policies in this new era of Turkish politics would make even Joe McCarthy jealous with its witch hunt, undermining Erdogan's democratic credibility that had been built up in the last decade. It appears that Erdogan took the 45 percent AKP received in the polls as an acquittal of the corruption charges against him and as a mandate to engage in this personal vendetta against opponents.

AKP's electoral success post-2013 remains surprising. What explains the continued success of AKP at the polls despite widespread corruption allegations and a failing economy? As a party bent on winning the elections and showing its strength, the AKP used its administrative, political, and financial power to shape the election outcomes in critical contests. Three distinct factors explain the continued success of the party: media control, weakness of the opposition, and the haunting memories of the pre-AKP era. I will discuss each in turn.

When the corruption scandal first broke out in Turkey in late 2013, Twitter instantly became the primary outlet of opposition to Prime Minister Erdogan and the AKP.[80] Twitter was about dissemination of ideas, organization, and exposing the corruption and lawless rule of Prime Minister Erdogan and those around him. The results of the March 30 elections were instructive, however. Twitter was effective in terms of organizing the opposition and informing them about the extent and lavishness of the corruption the AKP was marred in. Yet this dedicated opposition was educated, young, urban, and relatively small in number; what appeared on Twitter (and other social media outlets) had limited impact on the rest of the society, which was large in number, less educated, older, and more suburban and rural than urban. The rest of society relied more heavily on traditional mass media, including television and print. In other words, the opposition created a world of its own on Twitter, essentially singing to the choir, unable to reach out to those outside the Twitter world. Thus the most effective arguments and evidence against AKP corruption did not get out to a large population in Turkey.

Arguably the most notorious aspect of democracy is the general public's openness to manipulation.[81] Erdogan is a savvy politician and exploits this potential weakness of democracy fully. His increasingly personalistic and authoritarian rule rests not on brawl but rather on media control, which is typical of the "velvet rule" of new dictators.[82] Erdogan's direct control of and influence over newspapers affect around 40 percent of all newspaper sales, including major, and seemingly mainstream, Turkish dailies like *Sabah*, *Milliyet*, and *Haberturk*.[83] Likewise, major TV channels like ATV, Star TV, Show TV, NTV, and the state television network TRT are all either directly controlled by Erdogan or influenced by his great sway on editorial control over the network's broadcast. Such expansive media control allows the AKP to shape the minds of many Turks who lack interest in various social media outlets and what they have to offer in terms of new information. The opposition rarely finds its way into these newspapers and television channels; instead, it remains home to implicit or explicit government propaganda. Hence while the AKP's dismissal of the corruption claims wins the hearts of the population at large, the opposition cannot make its case.

The latest episode in Turkish politics is instructive on the role of the opposition in democratic forms of governance. Opposition features as one of the most potent institutional guarantees of a democratic regime (Stepan 1990); it helps to ensure accountability by providing the threat of losing office (Manin, Przeworski, and Stokes 1999, 48). In systems where the opposition is no more than window dressing, the governing party remains largely unaccountable. Take away the real possibility of alternation of power, and all that is left is an effective one-party rule. The existence of a viable opposition breathes life into a democracy; the lack of a viable opposition leaves the majority rule (or at times even plurality rule) as the only yardstick of "popular will," impairing the most fundamental value of a democratic regime: accountability. The governing party knows that it can get away with virtually anything; hence it becomes more daring and acts with fewer reservations in terms of pursuing personal and ideological ends. The Turkish experience since 2011 epitomizes such a source of instability in budding democracies.

The main opposition party, CHP, suffers from its Kemalist legacy and fails to convince the electorate of its lack of hostility toward religion; the nationalist MHP appears content with having parliamentary representation, has little interest in taking part in the government, and does not question its leadership for its oxymoronic state; the pro-Kurdish HDP (Peoples' Democratic Party) is unable to shed its ethnic association in the eyes of the electorate and become a mass party. Additionally, the 10 percent electoral threshold keeps many smaller parties outside of the parliament, forcing the potential supporters of such parties to cast their votes strategically. Likewise, the opposition outside of the parliament is virtually nonexistent. The military no longer plays an important political role thanks to the Ergenekon process—a series of court cases that aimed to cripple a secularist secretive network that was accused of plotting against the government (Unver 2009). The media is largely controlled by the government, and societal opposition is crippled by the heavy-handed suppression of the police as demonstrated by Gezi protests. Under such circumstances, the AKP can use its legislative and executive powers unchecked and influence the judicial branch as well, effectively suspending the core of democratic governance: accountability (Taş 2015).

Finally, those who continue supporting the AKP are reminded by the consternations of the pre-2002 era. Unstable coalition governments and poor economic performance reigned throughout the decade preceding the AKP's rise to government. Moreover, pervasive corruption characterized politicians and government officials of the period. Haunted by the unpleasant imagery of politicians who fail in their principal duty of serving the people and who excel in corruption, many AKP supporters settle for the suboptimal outcome of politicians who serve but also engage in corruption.[84] With the recent economic downturn, the AKP is bound to lose more ground.

This latest episode offers a unique opportunity to evaluate the merit of the argument developed in this book in regard to the moderation of Islamist parties. There are two competing explanations. On one hand, one could argue that what we have been observing since 2002 is simply a façade as far as the AKP's Islamist moderation is concerned. An "Islamist turn" is a common suggestion.[85] This line of reasoning suggests that the AKP's "Islamist" character is finally catching up to it; the party reverted to its origins and dismantled its moderate cover. On the other hand, one could argue that the AKP has, indeed, moved past Islamist discourse and adopted a moderate platform such as a Muslim democratic one, yet the developments in the post-2011 period owe their existence to other factors, ones that primarily deal with the long-standing institutional weaknesses of Turkish democracy. I prefer the latter explanation and will explain why below.

The post-2011 AKP features a deep fusion of clientelism and authoritarianism that revolves around Erdogan's persona (Lancaster 2014; Özbudun 2014; Taş 2015). While it is accurate that the AKP exploited some religiously oriented issues such as the lifting of the headscarf ban and overtures to some Islamist groups across the region, the AKP's post-2011 policies have minimal resemblance to an ideologically oriented Islamist political agenda. As far as actual government policies are concerned, little in the way of an Islamist agenda has actually been discussed or implemented; many of the bills introduced by the AKP government facilitate the conditions for tighter state control over society. Most issues that we might be tempted to call Islamist are, in fact, simply symbolic yearnings for an Ottoman-era political order such as the janissary salutation corps at the new presidential palace[86] and AKP candidates donning Ottoman-style apparel in their campaigns.[87]

What we observe, rather, is political maneuvering to gain votes and solidify the support base of the party during electoral periods.[88] Erdogan controls the media and can manipulate public opinion with his sway over the media. Such religious or conservative rhetoric allows the party to appeal to the conservative vote in Turkey. Foreign policy is one exception to the AKP's policies in general. In foreign policy, recent AKP governments did steer in a direction that resembles Islamist solidarity of sorts with regional actors such as the Muslim Brotherhood in Egypt, Hamas in Gaza, Islamists in Libya, and lastly ISIS in Syria. Two points stand out. First, despite a series of overtures to Islamist groups and governments in the region recently, there has not been a fundamental break from the West; the United States still constitutes Turkey's major ally in the region, the EU membership process is officially still ongoing (despite lack of progress), and Turkey reestablished ties with Israel. Second, foreign policy falls outside the scope of the definition of Islamist moderation and moderateness that I employ in this study. Although foreign policy is an important issue area, it has little bearing on achieving the ultimate Islamist goal, that is, the establishment of an "Islamic state."

Moreover, I would suggest that the new emerging political system has few ideological underpinnings to it; instead, it is a truly personalistic authoritarian leadership with no clear ideological orientation. The AKP can be deemed Islamist not in the policies it promotes but in the way it conceives state-society relationships, the way it sacralizes state power and state control. The AKP's political platform remained largely intact. If recent developments belie an "Islamist turn," what accounts for this sharp change in the AKP?

The AKP's authoritarian turn since the 2011 elections has more to do with the poor institutional foundation of Turkish democracy and the lack of a viable opposition party or bloc in the parliament (which itself is an outcome of the weak institutional foundation of Turkish democracy) than AKP's ideological origins. In other words, whether the AKP endorses an Islamist, Muslim democratic, social democratic, or communist ideology is irrelevant. The unscrupulously corrupt and undemocratic actions and policies of some AKP members and the authoritarian direction of the party in recent times emanates from its conviction that no accountability exists in sight and no imminent danger of losing elections lies ahead. As Lord Acton once said, "Power tends to corrupt, and absolute power corrupts absolutely." Successive electoral victories and the lack of a viable oppositional challenge led the party to believe in its invincibility and unaccountability. Two examples will demonstrate this point.

The new presidential palace in Ankara was opened to service in the fall of 2014, yet the palace became the focal point of much debate in the public opinion. According to multiple court orders, the construction of the palace is illegal on protected land. Erdogan, nonetheless, was defiant in the face of legal challenge to the continued construction at the site. On one such occasion, Erdogan challenged opposition, saying, "If you have the power and courage, then come and demolish the building."[89] Clearly unfazed by the remote possibility of judicial or bureaucratic response, Erdogan ensured completion and later opening of the palace. In a similar way, prior to the June 2015 parliamentary elections, Erdogan (despite his constitutional mandate to remain politically neutral) encouraged voters to cast their votes for the AKP and added, "Give us 400 seats, let us solve this peacefully" in reference to a constitutional change to transform the regime from a parliamentary system into a presidential one as well as the resolution of the

Kurdish issue.⁹⁰ What is remarkable about this statement is the implicit threat to achieve his goals in a nonpeaceful way. As it turns out, the current phase of violence Turkey is plunging into since the June 2015 elections appears to confirm Erdogan's prophecy.

4 Stuck in the Periphery
Crony Liberalization in Egypt

THIS CHAPTER INTRODUCES a case of crony liberalization, Egypt, and examines its impact on the moderation of political Islam and the level of its success in its manifestation as the Egyptian Muslim democratic Wasat Party (WP). By discussing the Egyptian case of crony liberalization, I demonstrate that the economic liberalization policies pursued by successive Egyptian governments—in their entirety and as individual policies such as trade liberalization and privatization—have shaped the course of Islamist politics in Egypt. Egyptian economic reforms, initially framed as *infitah* (open door) and later as structural adjustment programs, served to create a local class of big business owners with interests directly tied to their connections with and relationship to the political elite. The distorted nature of economic liberalization, which in chapter 2 I called crony liberalization, enabled this group of crony business owners to maintain its privileged access to state resources, cheap credit, and the domestic market. This outcome was largely due to the selective nature of liberalization policies implemented in Egypt. These distorted economic policies also had some political ramifications. The socioeconomic structure created in the postindependence period, which pits the secular elite against the Islamic periphery in a political and socioeconomic conflict, remained intact, avoiding potentially destabilizing socioeconomic effects of economic liberalization, as in the case of Turkey. The peripheral businesses, that is, small and medium enterprises (SMEs), were largely among the losers of this process of liberalization, along with the masses, leading to an overwhelming dissatisfaction with liberalization. Consequently, even though a small group (the WP, Hizb ul-Wasat) hailed from the Islamist Muslim Brotherhood (MB) and adopted a moderate Muslim democratic political platform, it largely failed in representing the Islamic periphery. Instead, the MB continued its domination of the Islamic periphery via its Islamist discourse. In fact, the nexus of Islamic politics shifted to the right thanks to the rise of the Salafist Nour Party.

This chapter is divided into three sections. In the first section, I discuss the origins of the socioeconomic cleavages between the secular center and the Islamic periphery in Egypt. In particular, the events surrounding the independence of Egypt in 1952 will be discussed to underscore the division between the center and the periphery. I analyze the early phase of transition to a market economy and liberalization during Anwar Sadat's presidency. During this period, the big businesses, which were completely eliminated by Nasser in the 1950s and the 1960s, found a chance to reemerge. In the second section, I discuss the origins of political Islam in Egypt. Political Islam, particularly the MB, rose to prominence once again as a result of Sadat's lenient policy toward Islamist groups. The second phase of economic liberalization throughout the Hosni Mubarak presidency gave rise to dire consequences, which I discuss in detail to contextualize the rise of political Islam. In so doing, I highlight the MB's position on liberalization. In the third and final section, I discuss the origins of the WP and its moderate political platform with a focus on the role of Islam, democracy, economy, and social policy. The latter part of the third section presents evidence regarding the preferences and interests of Egyptian peripheral and big businesses, and compares them with the WP's platform to explain why the party failed to establish itself as a viable representative of the peripheral groups.

The Road to Independence and Thereafter: 1952–1970

Until 1952, the Egyptian state and economy were dominated only by a collection of small interest groups. Closely aligned with the interests of the British since the colonization of Egypt in 1882, this group consisted of state bureaucracy including the palace, the landed elite, and industrialists. Throughout most of this period between the 1880s and the 1950s, the agricultural export policy of the British forces reinforced the status quo by first supporting the agricultural production by the landed elite and then enabling the growth of a local industry mostly focused on the production of consumer goods based on food and textiles (Farah 2009, 29). A good indicator of the extent of the overlap of the interests of this early form of the center was the establishment of the first Egyptian bank, Banque Misr, in 1920 in order to foster industrialization. The founders of the bank were eight of the big Egyptian landed elite. In a few years, the bank helped in the establishment of an industrial business association, advancing Egyptian industries: the Federation of Egyptian Industries. In turn, the state provided funds to Banque Misr to lend to burgeoning Egyptian industries (Farah 2009, 29). Over time, the interests of the landed elite and the private business sector became increasingly intertwined. By the time Nasser took power in Egypt in the early 1950s, the landed elite, who held about 50 percent of cultivable land, were also the major shareholders of about 40 percent of joint-stock companies (Ibrahim 1994).

Egypt achieved complete independence in 1952. Although nominal independence from British colonialism was granted in 1921, severe restrictions were placed on King Farouk and the Wafd Party–led parliament as to what the Egyptian government could pursue in terms of foreign and domestic policy. A group of junior military officers in the Egyptian army led by Gamal Abdel-Nasser and commonly known as the Free Officers brought Egypt to complete independence in 1952 when they deposed King Farouk along with any remaining British influence in the country. The Free Officers materialized after the 1948 War with Israel with the goal of removing the king and British influence from Egypt. Nasser assumed complete control and the presidency in 1954. To consolidate power and to establish Arab socialism as the ideological framework organizing social and economic life, Nasser viewed it necessary to eliminate three principal sources of power in Egypt: private business, landed elite, and the MB.

As part of his policy to institute Arab socialism, Nasser undertook an extensive campaign of nationalization of the private sector and redistributed the cultivable land from the landed elite to farmers. On the one hand, by redistributing large plots of land belonging to the landed elite and introducing limits on how much land an individual or a family could hold, Nasser effectively eliminated the source of economic power of the landed elite. On the other hand, big business owners, many of whom were also closely associated with the landed elite, became increasingly uneasy and were hurt by Nasser's economic policies. Instead of utilizing incentives offered by Nasser to promote private investment, private businesses shied away from new investment. Deterred by prospective nationalization, they even retracted their current investment. Indeed, by the beginning of the 1960s, Nasser undertook an extensive policy of nationalization, expropriation, and "sequestration" in a preemptive move against any potential threat to his rule (Cooper 1982; Farah 2009, 35; EG-9-B interview, 2008). This move enabled Nasser to undercut the principal source of power in the hands of both private business, foreign and national alike, and the landed elite (Dessouki 1982).

Concurrently, Nasser eliminated another major political force in Egypt at the time, the MB. Even though the MB was supportive of the Free Officers and the revolution initially, the group increasingly turned critical of Nasser's secular aspirations and his failure to heed the MB's suggestions for a more Islamic regime (Osama Farid interview, 2008; Simms 2002, 572). Despite the fact that several high-ranking officers among the Free Officers were close to the MB, the Islamist group faced extensive persecution by the government; thousands of Brotherhood members were detained, and tens were executed. To echo Simms's Gramscian reading of the MB, the group offered a "counter-hegemonic ideology," challenging the very core of Nasser's regime:

> To the Brotherhood, Islam was the one true religion of God intended by Him to command authority over all human affairs for all people universally. This made it the indisputable centerpiece of their counter-ruling class ideology.... The Brethren went to the book of God and sought inspiration and guidance therefrom so that they knew for certain that Islam is this full, comprehensive meaning and that it must have supervision over all matters of life, that it gives its tone to all things, that all things must come under its rule, conform to its rules and teachings, and draw upon it. (Simms 2002, 573)

The model proposed by the MB fundamentally contradicted Nasser's vision for a secular and modern Egypt, much like the one Ataturk had in mind for Turkey.

Nasser's strategy also entailed populism; hence he was mindful of the peripheral masses and sought their support in his new Arab socialist regime. Nasser's land redistribution reform was accompanied by the promise that every college graduate would get a government job. The final element of Nasser's populism was the introduction of an extensive network of subsidies on basic foodstuff, energy, and health care, which Carrie Rosefsky Wickham calls the "Nasserist social contract" (Wickham 2002). Nasser himself summarized the goal of Arab socialist reforms in the following way: "I want a society in which class distinctions are dissolved through the equality of opportunities to all citizens. I want a society in which the free individual can determine his own position by himself, on the basis of his efficiency, capacity, and character" (Wickham 2002, 25). Indeed, some scholars characterized the Nasser era as having achieved a "high degree of income equality" as compared with other periods in Egyptian history (Abdel-Khalek and Tignor 1982). The parallel between what happened in Turkey until the early 1950s and in Egypt until 1970 is striking, despite the fact that such deemphasis on class conflict appears to go against the center-periphery division and minimize the power of the center. Class conflict was largely downplayed through an emphasis on populism and an extensive state role in the economy in postindependence Turkey. Unlike in Egypt, however, Ataturk engaged neither in nationalization of private businesses (as there was no private sector of any significant size) nor in land redistribution, because most of the land belonged to the state. Instead, the state distributed public land to increase agricultural production and reinforce its popular support.[1]

The 1970s were marked by the transition from an Arab socialist economy to a free market in Egypt—one of the most important legacies of Anwar Sadat's presidency. Although Nasser himself initiated some economic liberalization reforms in 1968 following the Six-Day War with Israel, these reforms did not bring the intended liberalization.[2] Sadat initiated the widely known *infitah* (open door) policy in 1971 in the wake of Nasser's death to reinstitute an economy that relied on the private sector for economic development. In order to attract foreign and Egyptian private capital for investment, Sadat introduced new laws and a new constitution.[3] An implicit goal of this new open door policy was to nurture an indigenous "capitalist elite" (Farah 2009, 24). This elite would lead the economy while simultaneously providing a strong base of support for the regime (Blaydes 2010, 34). Of note, of those who capitalized on the opportunities provided by the *infitah* policy, senior military officials were the major beneficiaries.[4]

The combination of open door policy and "windfall revenues" from oil enabled the government to expand its network of subsidies to peripheral masses, including increased state employment and expanded higher education (Farah 2009, 24; Wickham 2002, 37). Continued subsidies ensured the perception that the social contract established by Nasser was intact while simultaneously preventing a strong backlash from the masses against the open door policy, as was the case with the bread riots in 1977 (Soliman 2011, 39).[5] Remittances from workers abroad (mainly in the oil-rich Gulf countries) also relieved the Egyptian state with respect to social demand for services.

Overall, Sadat's *infitah* policy is deemed unsuccessful in terms of creating the range of economic activities that it originally promised (EG-8-B, EG-9-B, EG-12-B interviews, 2008). Most of the foreign and local private investment came in economic sectors, such as luxury construction and tourism, that had limited impact on economic development and industrialization. Economic growth during this period was largely based on increased consumption on the part of the government and the population (Cooper 1982, 106).

More importantly, however, the *infitah* policy had a sizeable effect on social classes. A formidable "socioeconomic-political coalition" was formed from distinct elements of the center. On the one hand, the remaining elements of the pre-Nasser landed elite and private business sector were able to utilize various incentives that the Sadat government offered to attract investment. Cognizant of what transpired in the 1950s and the 1960s, such capital holders invested in areas of the economy where risks were minimal and returns were comparatively higher. On the other hand, new groups such as former technocrats and managers of state economic enterprises emerged as influential actors in the Egyptian free market economy. Their expertise in the bureaucracy proved to be a great asset in their new economic ventures (Ibrahim 1994, 34). Collectively, these groups made up what Joel Beinin (2005) calls the "*infitah* class." By contrast, the peripheral masses were largely on the losing end of the open door policy. The masses failed to experience an improvement in income, unemployment progressively increased over time, and subsidies slowly withered away in the face of pressure from international financial institutions, but SME owners were also on the losing side, as they did not have many opportunities to take part in a liberalizing economy. In fact, relative to the big businesses in Egypt, SMEs remained as disadvantaged as ever during this time.[6]

The Rise of Political Islam and the Muslim Brotherhood

The humiliating defeat at the Six-Day War in 1967 and the inability of Nasser's Arab socialist regime to deliver on its "revolutionary promises" of economic development and international ascendancy led to the fallout between secular ideologies and the masses not only in Egypt but also in the rest of the Middle East, all throughout the 1970s (Wickham 2002, 35).[7] To make matters worse, the masses' disillusionment with Nasser's regime was juxtaposed with Sadat's favorable policy toward Islamic activism, one of tolerance and lenience, a policy aimed at erasing the bad memory of Nasser's heavy-handed approach toward Islamic groups. The policy also aspired to increase the regime's legitimacy, which was aided by the fact that Sadat enjoyed significant support from the right during his tenure in office (Blaydes 2010). Thus, starting in the mid- to late 1970s, political Islam emerged as the most important oppositional force in Egyptian politics yet again.

The MB has always been the "dominant" representative of Islamic activism in Egypt, although many other Islamic and Islamist groups have existed in Egypt since the early twentieth century (Wickham 2002). Established in 1928 by Hasan Al-Banna, the MB has focused on both political issues and *dawa* (Islamic missionary activity and religious education) as part of its mission.[8] Politically, the group focused on Palestinian independence and gaining complete independence from British influence in Egypt in its early history leading up to independence in 1952. The group owes its longevity and survival through phases of British and Nasserite suppression to its organizational skills and institutional structure between the 1940s and the 1970s.[9]

Although the MB became publicly active once again during Sadat's presidency in the 1970s, it did not pretend to be an important political actor during that period.[10] Throughout the 1970s Islamist activism increased its support base within the Egyptian society, with the college-educated young population constituting a significant part of this widened social base. In part, this expansion in Islamic activism was in reaction to the regime's inability to deliver services. For example, in the late 1970s, the waiting time for university graduates for appointment in a government job was three years. This waiting time had increased to almost ten years by the mid-1980s (Wickham 2002, 42). The expansion of the Islamic base was also due to economic alienation. The socioeconomic changes taking place at the time, as part of the economic opening, did not benefit a major segment of the Egyptian society. Islamic groups, particularly the MB, became the focal point of frustration with the government.

By the 1980s, the MB turned into a "quasi-party organization" functioning both as a political party and as an Islamic *dawa* organization aiming to increase the Egyptian population's Islamic education and awareness (Wickham 2002).[11] The MB, though technically illegal as an organization, participated in the 1984 and 1987 elections as a junior partner of the Wafd and Labor Parties. In both elections, the alliance, including the MB, received the highest vote share among the opposition parties.[12] The group's relative success in its first electoral experience in decades is largely attributed to two factors. One was that the MB was able to provide social services that the Egyptian state did not. Such services included health care clinics, schools, and charity assistance to those in need, as well as services that were more Islamic in nature such as financial assistance helping individuals perform Islamic pilgrimage (Wickham 2002, 99). The other was that the organizational superiority of the Brotherhood offered them an extensive grassroots presence. The MB was able to campaign on a unique platform declaring its panacea for Egypt's ill-run economy and society: "Islam is the solution [*al-Islam Huwa al-Hall*]." The MB saw itself as the unmistakable representative of religion, that is, Islam, in the political arena and encouraged the voters to cast their votes for Islam: "Give your vote to Allah, give it to the Muslim Brotherhood" (Wickham 2002, 92). Omar al-Tilmissani, a former general guide of the MB,[13] explained the goal in the group's political activism and run for parliamentary seats as follows: "We were completely serious when we joined in the elections. Our aim was to reach Parliament through a legal channel, the Wafd Party, because People's Assembly members enjoy parliamentary immunity. The brothers who will reach the Assembly will speak on behalf of the Brotherhood, will urge enforcement of the Islamic sharia laws, and will embarrass the government on this issue without fear of detention or torture. . . . Now some of them [Muslim Brothers] are People's Assembly members, watching the government and entitled to make it account for its actions" (quoted in Campagna 1996, 283).

As Wickham notes, the clear objective of the MB was to establish an Islamic state that would be "based on popular consent."[14] Nonetheless, the contours of such an Islamist program as advocated by the MB was not clearly explained, and this was the case for most other Islamist groups throughout the Muslim world until the 2000s.[15] Indeed, the MB's first draft party program was only disseminated in the summer of 2007 for public review. It was not until Mubarak was overthrown that the MB came up with a final political program.

The MB's oppositional discourse found resonance among various segments of the Egyptian society. Among the supporters of the MB were members of the middle class such as professionals and university graduates (Muhammad Habib interview, 2008). University students and graduates and professionals, as part of the middle class, were attracted to the ranks of the MB largely because of the "skilled and energetic" middle-generation leadership of the organization.[16] Among this middle-generation leadership of the MB, also called "Young Princes" of the MB, was the current WP leadership cadre (Stacher 2002). This middle-generation leadership included figures like Assam Sultan, Aboul Ela Mady, Abdul Moneim Aboul Fotouh, Issam al-Aryan, and Salah Abdal Karim. Janine Clark maintains that moderate Islamist movements, including those in Egypt, are movements of "the marginalized, educated middle class, not of the disenfranchised poor" (Clark 2004b). Asef Bayat, in agreement with Clark, states that "the backbone" of the MB originated from members of the middle class: "Political Islam in Egypt in this period [1980s and 1990s] reflected primarily the rebellion of the impoverished middle class who were frustrated by a feeling of moral outrage. Their high expectations, an outcome of their high education and thus social status, were dampened in the job market, which offered few prospects for economic success. A product of Nasser's welfare-state boom, this segment represented the losers of Sadat's infitah policy" (Bayat 1998, 157). This "lumpen intelligentsia" was a crucial component of the MB's social support (Wickham 2002).

The middle class was not the only socioeconomic group to offer its support to the MB; the lower classes also lent their support to the MB. Although Clark is certainly correct in pointing out the membership fee-based nature of some of the services provided by the Islamist groups catering to middle classes (in a way analogous to how social protection policies in the developing world cater to middle classes rather than to lower classes) (Rudra 2008), it only partially captures the dynamics of strategy of the MB. The support for the MB was pronounced in the "new urban quarters," as these areas were mostly inhabited by "the less well-off segments of society." The support of these lower classes, constituting part of the peripheral masses, was mostly due to the provision of social services and charity activities of Islamist groups like the MB. These services effectively turned such neighborhoods into "informal networks of mutual aid" (Ismail 2001). According to Osama Farid, a former MB member and an independent Islamist intellectual, the MB "has the sympathy of the people because they deliver. Islam is for delivering. What do you deliver for me? Medical care at a symbolic price, yes. When there is crisis, do you give me shelter? Yes" (Farid interview, 2008). For example, following the 1992 earthquake in Cairo and the floods in Upper Egypt in 1994, the MB was able to mobilize its resources, including professional associations, to offer help to those affected by the earthquake and flooding at a time when the government's help was limited at best. Another example illustrating the reach of the MB's efficiency in the provision of social services is the case of Gam'ia Shar'ia, an Egyptian charitable organization and part of the MB network. The association, according to Sarah Ben Nefissa, has 450 branches and 6,000 mosques. Moreover, according to the MB itself, one-fifth of all nongovernmental organizations in Egypt are controlled by the MB (Ben Nefissa quoted in Antar 2006). To summarize the lower classes' perception of the MB, "When the Muslim Brothers are asked, they open the drawer and they give you something. When you ask government officials, they open the drawer and they ask you to give something" (quoted in Walsh 2003, 34). Essentially, the MB was seen as "the only viable opposition to the status quo" by the lower classes (Bayat 1998). The lower classes are important for the MB because of its claim that it speaks on behalf of the marginalized and downtrodden Egyptians (Masoud 2014). The provision of such social services is an indication that the MB has the potential and the capacity to cater to the needs of the lower classes. Overall, the MB was able to "mobilize a wide variety of different segments of Egyptian society," as Ziad Munson argues. The strategies used by the MB—their unique organizational structure and discourse—ensured this outcome.[17]

During the first decade of Hosni Mubarak's presidency (1981–90), the MB was most politically successful in professional associations. Given the distorted nature of legislative elections throughout the 1980s and very low participation rates, professional association elections provided a genuine outlet for political competition in the country. Sami Zubaida observes that these professional associations were "the most advanced sectors of public life in Egypt, enjoying high status and speaking with an autonomous and respected voice" (Zubaida 1992). Among such professional associations, or syndicates, were the engineers', dentists', journalists', doctors', and pharmacists' associations.

The middle-generation leaders proved to be critical to the MB's success throughout the 1980s and the 1990s in professional associations. In this, the middle generation's transition from university life to professional life is recounted as a key factor (Wickham 2002; al-Awadi 2005; Brownlee 2002). Nabil Abd al-Fattah, a political analyst at the Al-Ahram Center for Political and Strategic Studies, draws attention to fundamental problems of the Egyptian economy to explain the MB's success in a bar association election in 1992:

> The syndicate [association] and its ruling council have not paid any attention to the problem of unemployment among young lawyers, or to matters such as modern legal training. The psychological state created by unemployment generates a flood of anger, and in the absence of any political role for the syndicate it finds no outlet or anything to channel it in a healthy direction. The young therefore turn to the most potent force in the community, the Islamist tendency, which largely embodies anger against the state and against the forces that made up the council of the bar association. The weakness of other political forces, the sterility of their arguments and their remoteness from the younger generation of lawyers have helped to create fertile ground for effective Islamist activity within the greatest bastion of liberal thought in Egypt. (Campagna 1996, 290)

Salah Abdal Karim, one of the middle-generation MB leaders, recalls his experience in professional associations, explaining their basis of popular support: "Even members who weren't necessarily sympathetic to the Islamic case supported us. We never identified ourselves as Muslim Brothers. We held all of our meetings in public in the syndicate headquarters, as opposed to the Muslim Brother veterans who were accustomed to conducting business underground" (Abdal Karim quoted in Stacher 2002).

This is a remarkable example in illustrating the severity of the socioeconomic problems Egypt faced at the time. Even the most liberal and secular sections of the society were drawn to the MB's sharp discourse criticizing the regime on issues such as the state of the economy. When the predominantly liberal and secular membership profile of professional associations is considered, the MB's success becomes clearer. In associations where the MB was in control, it utilized resources at the disposal of the associations in very effective ways, in order to provide services to the association membership. For example, in the Engineers' Association, the MB established "a private hospital, housing projects, a consumers' cooperative, a social welfare fund, group life insurance, and a social club for members," catering to the membership of the association (Beinin 2005, 127).

Nonetheless, within a short period of time in the mid-1990s, the Egyptian government brought most of the associations under its direct control to counter the increasing prominence of the Brotherhood as a political force, legally ensuring that management of professional associations was taken away from the MB (Brownlee 2002, 7).[18] Osama Farid concurred that the success of the MB in "delivering" services in professional associations led the government to take action against the MB in these associations, in a "very straightforward" manner (Farid interview, 2008).

The 1990s witnessed the MB's raising of its public stature, both in its discourse and in its support base, despite its outlawed but tolerated legal status. As a result of the problems in the economy and the perceived deterioration of the middle and lower classes' socioeconomic condition, the MB's political discourse became sharper in its critique of governmental policies, specifically highlighting the problems associated with liberalization and calling for an Islamic system. Bayat observes, "Islamism in Egypt represented an ideological package, which negated all the perceived causes of such a state of deprivation—economic dependency, cultural sell-out, and national humiliation (1967 defeat by the Israelis and then the Camp David Accords). In view of all the failed ideologies, chiefly Nasserite socialism and Sadat's capitalism, and of the conditions of western cultural, political, and economic onslaught, Islam was seen as the only indigenous doctrine that could bring about a genuine change" (Bayat 1998, 158).

Social costs of the slow-paced economic reforms became substantial concerns for the Egyptian government throughout the 1990s. The government lowered subsidies, and most salaries and wages remained stable or decreased; real wages, as a result, dropped for many throughout the country, ensuring further social unrest (Sullivan 1997, 69). Beinin notes that, indeed, many among industrial workers and public employees were the foremost protesters of the cuts in subsidies and declining real wages, which made them into the losers of the post-Nasser period (Beinin 2005, 131). This social unrest, in turn, haunted the National Democratic Party (NDP) and the Mubarak regime by spurring popular support for the major opposition force in Egypt, that is, political Islam and the MB (Blaydes 2010). Such renewed popular support for the MB added another layer of credibility to its unequivocal criticism of the liberalization process and the regime initiating this process.

The elections in 2000 confirmed the status of the MB as the strongest oppositional force in Egypt. After the 1995 parliamentary elections, opposition parties complained about the illegal tactics used by the Mubarak regime to ensure a favorable outcome: electoral fraud, harassment of voters, and use of force against opposition party members.[19] When Mubarak indicated that a nonpartisan body might monitor the upcoming elections of 1999, the Egyptian parliament, or the People's Assembly (Majlis Al-Sha'ab), passed legislation giving a supervisory role to the judiciary that would merely enable "committees of judges to float between polling stations." However, later in 2000, the Supreme Constitutional Court ruled that the judges "had to monitor every station as voting took place." Following the court's decision, the judges supervised the election in 2000: "Members of the judiciary . . . then supervised three rounds of elections and runoffs, from October 18 through November 24, across Egypt's 222 electoral districts (and 15,502 polling stations), providing unprecedented assurance that a vote cast would be a vote counted" (Brownlee 2002, 8).

The election outcome was highly encouraging for the MB as much as it was "embarrassing" and "disgracing" for the NDP and other opposition parties. Running its candidates as independents, the MB was able to win seventeen seats out of the sixty-three districts in which the group fielded candidates, whereas all other opposition parties won as many seats out of their 352 candidates, roughly corresponding to 3.5 percent of all parliamentary seats (Brownlee 2002, 9). Yet it is vital not to lose sight of the constant state manipulation of electoral outcomes in Egypt. Jillian Schwedler, rightly, highlights various techniques governments in the Arab world might employ to influence election results: constraints on voter and candidate eligibility, gerrymandering, electoral system choice, and other legal constraints on political parties (Schwedler 1998). Hence the election outcomes most likely do an injustice to the MB and other opposition parties in reflecting the level of their societal support. The case of Cihan Al-Halafawi in Alexandria is a good example of regime repression of the opposition. In the 2000 elections, Cihan Al-Halafawi represented the MB as an independent candidate in Alexandria. When she was about to win the election against the NDP candidate, a court suspended the elections. The legal battle continued until 2002, at which time a by-election was held in the district; yet the regime undertook various measures through which they secured a comfortable victory for the NDP candidate. Jason Brownlee reports, "Since Al-Halafawi and Ahmed's supporters were forcibly prevented from casting ballots, these legitimate victors were left with a few hundred votes compared to the three thousand they had garnered previously. Unbelievably, the NDP's candidates quintupled the number of votes they had taken in 2000" (Brownlee 2007, 148).

Although the MB faced intermittent crackdowns on its prominent members and leaders, for the most part, the early 2000s offered an auspicious environment for the group to expand its support base.[20] Income inequality worsened, and there was a growing perception that a group of big business owners coalescing around the dominating figure of Mubarak had greatly increased their prosperity; such perceptions only reinforced and justified the critical stance of the MB in regard to the whole economic liberalization ordeal. In the meantime, social service provision, which the lower and middle classes increasingly needed, accompanied the critical discourse of the MB. According to Mohammed El-Sayed Said, a political analyst at Al-Ahram Center, in 2000 "the group began lavishing money on charity and social projects during the month of Ramadan, a few weeks before voting commenced" (Said quoted in El Amrani 2005).

Prior to the Arab Spring revolution in early 2011, the parliamentary elections of 2005 were the greatest testament to the MB's success, and their overall picture even looked promising. For the first time since 1995, the group did not have even a single member in prison in the run up to the elections, according to Issam al-Aryan, former member of the Consultative Council and head of political bureau of the MB (Al-Aryan quoted in El Amrani 2005). Buoyed by their accomplishment in pressuring for judicial oversight in the 2000 elections, opposition parties, including the MB, were relatively more confident in securing a greater share of the seats in the parliament. Despite the fact that the regime engaged in various tactics to deter the opposition parties and their supporters, the 2005 elections were considered by far the fairest election in postindependence Egypt. In order to achieve its greatest electoral victory thus far, the MB put up a "vigorous fight." In reference to the MB general guide at the time, Mohammed Akef, El Amrani observes, "Although, as Akef pointed out, the Brotherhood competed in fewer than 170 constituencies, it put up a vigorous fight wherever it campaigned. It is a testament to the group's popularity and organizational skills that it managed to win 12 seats in the third round, despite the security forces' closure of polling stations and targeting of Brothers for arrest. By the end of the balloting, Akef claimed, at least 1,300 of the group's supporters had been detained" (El Amrani 2005).[21] Overall, the MB obtained eighty-eight seats (out of 444 seats) in the People's Assembly, the lower house of the Egyptian parliament. All the other opposition parties won a combined nine seats.[22] The MB's success was due to its unique platform, which combined strong social services provision with a critical stance against the government's economic policies.

Broadly, the success of the MB in the 2005 elections is attributed to a number of factors. Their provision of social services and effective grassroots organization top the list, although this is common among many Islamist groups throughout the Middle East, not something unique to the MB. For example, in preparing for the 2005 elections, the MB launched its electoral campaign much earlier in the year as compared with other parties, giving it a considerable advantage. As part of this strategy, the group also asked its members to register for early voting as well as encouraging those close to themselves to do the same (Antar 2006, 14). A more significant factor, however, is how well the MB's discourse resonated among its support base, a discourse that clearly emphasized the severity of the masses' losses resulting from the government's economic policies. In other words, the mere fact that the MB provides social services that the people desperately need underscores the regime's inability to undertake its basic functions.

Others point out ideological factors as the underlying causes of Islamists' prominence in the Middle East. For example, Fawaz Gerges notes that Islamist groups and parties aspire to present a completely different alternative to the dominant ideologies of the post–World War II era: "In this context of struggle between Islamist movements and established regimes, Islamism represents less a coherent ideology than a historic reaction to the inadequacies of market capitalism and Soviet communism, the doctrines that shaped the world in recent decades" (Gerges 1999). According to this logic, Islamists in Egypt view the government's socioeconomic policies, that is, economic liberalization, as fundamentally flawed. Similarly, Holger Albrecht and Eva Wegner point to the periodic nature of the Islamist upsurge. They argue that during periods of economic and social crises, Islamists tend to become "the major political challenge" for the secular Arab regimes, especially so since the Arab regimes are able to suppress other secular opposition groups with ease before they even turn strong (Albrecht and Wegner 2006).[23] This logic resonates closely with how contemporary Islamist thought reasoned on the role of Islam in the society and politics of the modern age. For example, Sayyid Qutb, one of the early theorists of the MB's ideology in the 1950s and the early 1960s, saw Islam and Islamic law as a viable system in the contemporary modern world (Qutb 2007). Andrew March, in his analysis of Sayyid Qutb's political theory, notes, "When we speak of modern Islamist movements and thinkers as belonging to modernity, this is most clearly discernible in their repackaging of Islamic law and ethics as an accessible and attractive 'system' ready to square off in battle as a fully formed, fully coherent alternative to Marxism, capitalism, and liberalism" (March 2010). The MB gained electoral success, building its legitimacy as an effective provider of social services and emphasizing its critical stance toward the regime (Al-Awadi 2005).

Despite the MB's soaring popularity, an internal division led to an eventual split in 1995. Some middle-generation leaders from the reformist wing took decisive action for a new platform and discourse in defiance of the MB leadership. Although the split of middle-generation leaders is projected as a case of organizational disobedience by the MB leadership, the discourse of the new party established by these dissidents was markedly different from that of the MB; the new party (the WP) outlined policies that did not, to a great measure, challenge the policies of the current regime. I now turn to the foundation process and policies of this new party.

The Wasat Party

The Egyptian Muslim democratic party (MDP), the WP, was founded in 1996 by some of the middle-generation leaders of the MB at the time, including Aboul Ela Mady, Salah Abdel Karim, and Issam Sultan. Since the early 1980s, the MB's participation in various political platforms and increasing success in the semi-liberal electoral platforms[24] created a desire to establish a legal political party that would represent the MB's ideological and political vision. This set off an intense internal discussion, out of which two major positions became discernible. The "old guard" of the MB wanted to abstain from forming an official and legal political party, largely because the founder of the MB, Hassan Al-Banna, held this belief (Moussalli 1993). Hence a move diametrically opposed to Al-Banna's principles would only undermine the group's legitimacy. Additionally, most of the old guard experienced the wrath of the secular Nasser regime throughout the 1950s and 1960s, having learned a lesson on how to survive and operate in a repressive regime. Moreover, legalization might have compromised the highly critical discourse of the MB. The old guard hence saw little use in defying the terms of an implicit coordination with the regime, that is, working as an illegal but tolerated group.

Conversely, the architects of the recent success of the MB called for a different direction, building on an increasingly pronounced Islamic activism in Egypt. Such activism began in universities in the 1970s and later spread to other sectors of the society. The middle-generation leaders of the MB, or the "young princes," included figures such as Issam Al-Aryan, Abdul Moneim Aboul Fotouh, Aboul Ela Mady, Salah Abdel Karim, and Issam Sultan. This group, also known as the reformist wing, recognized new opportunities for the MB, as the socioeconomic and political milieu the group now faced was significantly different from the one experienced by the old guard. Hence according to the reformists, strictly political tools gained currency, as opposed to the amalgam of religio-political activism of before. Of this crucial distinction, Mady explained, "Al-Banna's *dawa* [mission] is important because it developed Islamic movements in the first half of the twentieth century. But the problem is that Al-Banna's *dawa* did not develop after his death, especially in political issues. His *dawa* dealt with both religion and politics. It met the demands of his era. But, of course, the present situation in our society is different from that of Al-Banna's era. It is not suitable for us to directly apply Al-Banna's idea to our society, especially with regard to issues about Christians and political parties" (Mady quoted in Yokota 2007, 152). In particular, the "conflict in policy orientations" with respect to democracy, the role of Islam, and the economy was crucial in the configuration of the frontiers between the old guard and the middle generation (Yokota 2007, 151). This new party would be "part of, not an alternative to, the existing political system" in sharp contrast to the MB's conventional antisystem and critical approach to politics (Langohr 2001).

Despite the longtime resistance by the old guard, by late 1995, the reformist wing seemed to have won over the old guard in the discussion toward forming a political party, at which time the group provisionally and on an informal basis agreed to establish a political party as a distinct legal political entity. For Mady, who had been granted the leading role in this initiative, along with his fellow MB members, the timing was critical for forming the new party—the current political and socioeconomic environment was ripe for such an initiative. If time had been wasted, the opportunity might have escaped. At a different level, the internal conflict raised a significant concern: the old guard within the MB was strong enough to withdraw its support and prevent the establishment of the new party at any time (Mady interview, 2008). Rafik Habib, a former founding member of the WP and a Christian by faith, recounted Mady's reasoning during this period: "Aboul Ela [Mady] thought the older members of the Brotherhood were reluctant to allow a political party to be established, and his main concern was rooted in the notion that if they waited, the timing would not suitable. It would be too late and the chance to establish a party would pass" (Stacher 2002).

In 1996, seventy-four individuals applied for a license to form a new political party called Hizb ul-Wasat (the Center Party). Among these seventy-four individuals, an overwhelming majority—sixty-two individuals—were members of the MB. Following signals from the Political Parties Committee (PPC) that the Muslim Brothers would not obtain a license for a new party of their own, and the clear message from the MB deputy general guide Ma'moun Hudeibi to those associated with the WP to "withdraw" from the WP or "face expulsion," many MB members left the WP in a "wave of mass defection" (Stacher 2002; Wickham 2004). Nonetheless, Aboul Ela Mady and about fifteen other MB members persisted in their effort to found the new party, ignoring calls from the MB leadership. Later in 1996, Mady and several other members of the WP were jailed for five months, on what Beinin calls "fabricated charges that the Center Party [WP] was a front for the Muslim Brothers [MB]." In the same year, Mady and fifteen other members of the MB formally resigned from the MB (Beinin 2005, 126; Wickham 2004). By 1998 when the group reapplied for a license, the diversity among the founding members was striking: twenty-four former Brotherhood members, three Christians, and nineteen female members (Stacher 2002).[25] This renewed application and the composition of founding members were also indicative of the fundamental difference between the MB and the WP. The contrast was more than just about the tactics or being a part of the MB; it was about creating a political party distinct and independent from the MB. Nonetheless, Islamic discourse would still be a central element of the party. Hence even though there was a vague agreement between the old guard and the reformist wing in regard to establishing a party, each had its own fundamentally different ideas about what shape the party would assume.

In contrast to the WP's perception of the causes of the split, for the MB, their opposition to the WP was largely unrelated to policy issues. Most notably, the WP was viewed as an initiative that violated the institutionalized internal decision-making mechanisms of the Brotherhood. According to the former head of the group's political bureau, Issam Al-Aryan, the "impatience" on the part of the "dissenters" was the cause of the split: "The decision making process is institutionalized in the Brotherhood. It takes time to consult (*shura*) and some of our former colleagues were urged to bypass this process and take steps to form a party early" (Al-Aryan quoted in Stacher 2002). Others both within and outside the group pointed to the same cause—because the WP initiative violated the hierarchy within the MB, the split was beyond its control (Shadid 2001; Wickham 2004; Farid interview, 2008). For example, AbdelHamid Al-Ghazali, the former head of MB's political bureau, Consultative Council member, and advisor to the former general guide Muhammad Akef, speaking of the split, comments:

> The cause for this estrangement of the WP from the MB is that the leaders of the WP did not listen to the orders of the Guidance Council in order to withdraw the first application of this proposed party because we believe this party will never get the approval from this so-called PPC [Political Parties Committee]. In our movement, if you are a member by your free will, you should adhere to our principles. One of our principles is that if there is a discussion, which has been done by the Guidance Council of the movement, before reaching a decision, you could say whatever you like. But after reaching a decision that you should not make an application for a party, and you go against this, this means you do not want to be a member. (AbdelHamid Al-Ghazali interview, 2008)

Furthermore, the MB was exceedingly vigilant, concerned about not only what a move to disturb the status quo with the regime might imply but also what the extent of real change could be, both of which clearly indicate how weighty the old guard's opinions are in the group's philosophies. In particular, one of the leading figures of the MB, Ma'moun Hudeibi, questioned the futility of the WP initiative: "Are there really any parties in Egypt, religious or nonreligious? To have parties means to alternate power. Parties compete in elections—real elections; people vote for something, and they change something. Can that happen here?" (Hudeibi quoted in Shadid 2001, 258). Hence it appears that the old guard relinquished its support for a new party proposal because of their distrust of the political system. Al-Aryan reasons about the state response to the MB, suggesting, "If their [the WP's] step is some sort of harassment against the government, or if the government thinks that, it should take intense action against the Brotherhood if they want to try and make a party" (Stacher 2002).

Note, however, that the distinctive perceptions of the split between the MB and the WP have a unique implication. The vigilance on the part of the MB was to ensure that any prospective action must have little bearing on the group's political discourse and ideological standing because the MB feared it did not have control over the WP and that the government's response might cause a major change. In other words, it was because the MB perceived the WP as an initiative with a potential to cause a shift in the discourse and strategic goals of the movement, rather than a mere tactical change, that is, from running as independents to a legal political party. Yet for the leading figures within the WP, the establishment of the WP represented the ideals of the reformist wing within the MB, and of the Wasatiyya movement, in a broader conception.[26] But when the WP initiative came to a "closed road" at the end of 1995, some of the reformists under the leadership of Aboul Ela Mady decided to push forward regardless of the MB's support or authorization (Aboul Ela Mady interview, 2008). For the leadership of the WP, the split was indicative of the change in the strategic thinking about the end goal of a new political party. Hence the discourse of the new party had to be commensurate with the "present" situation of Egyptian society and reflect the "policy orientations" of the reformist wing. Therefore, this was more than a mere tactical change. It was a change in the basic discourse of the movement. Hence even though it might seem like a rather simple case of imprudent action on the part of WP leaders and an effort to achieve a fait accompli, for shrewd politicians such as Mady, Sultan, and Abdel Karim, the mechanics of the split were designed to ensure a successful split from the MB for a whole new party and platform. If that is the case, what constitutes the platform of the new WP? The four distinct components of the WP platform—the role of Islam, democracy, economy, and social policy—and its comparison to the MB's discourse are discussed in the next section.

Islam in the Party Platform

Islam, in WP discourse, plays a central role, yet it is fundamentally distinct from conventional Islamist formulations. The party identifies itself as a moderate and civil political party with an Islamic reference (Mady interview, 2008; WP Program, 2004), which is in sharp contrast to the MB's promotion of an Islamist discourse at the very center of its platform. In the words of its founder, Al-Banna, the MB advocates "the most powerful system—the Islamic ideology; and that [they] are offering to mankind the most just law—the Sacred Law of the Qur'an" (El-Ghazali 2001, 119–20). Along the same lines, the MB's former general guide Akef stated, "We believe that the establishment of Shar'a Allah is the most efficient way out of all internal and external problems, political, economical, social and cultural, and will happen through the formation of the Muslim individual, the Muslim family, the Muslim government."[27]

For the WP, Islam is a "civilizational" element in their party platform rather than simply a religion, In this original formulation, "Islamic civilization," as the founding identity element of the WP, refers to the idea that Egyptians of Muslim and Christian origins share in the same "cultural framework" offered by the Islamic civilization created throughout the centuries by both Muslims and Christians, "partners on the basis of citizenship, not religion" (Mady interview, 2008). Conceived in this way, the concept of Islamic civilization is more comprehensive and encompassing of "others" in a Muslim-majority society than the "Islam as a religion" framework (Takayuki 2007), a particularly important emphasis in Egyptian society because of its sizeable Coptic Christian minority.[28] One of the original founding Christian members of the WP, Rafiq Habib, concurs and states, "Christianity is a part of Islamic civilization as well as other elements. When we talk about Islamic civilization, it means we talk about the value system. This fundamental value system unifies Christians and Muslims because civilization is not a religious doctrine" (Habib quoted in Takayuki 2007, 153).

In the case of the MB, for example, one of the most debated articles of the 2007 draft party program stipulated that women and Copts were not qualified to run for the head of state position (*al-imamah al-kubra*) (MB Draft Party Program 2007). Critics, rightly, claimed that such a condition violated the concept of equality of all citizens, a principle that the MB purportedly accepts. That being said, the principal idea behind this clause was that since the end goal is to establish an "Islamic state," the head of the state should be Muslim and male, according to the justification offered by the MB (R. Habib interview, 2008). Some within the MB, such as Mahmoud Ezzat and Muhammed Habib, defended the clause by saying that the head of state represented the Islamic *ummah* (nation), and hence can be occupied only by a male Muslim (Abdel-Latif 2008, 9). Issam Al-Aryan maintained that the position is a symbol for a "Muslim state" and likened it to the position of the king of Britain (Al-Aryan interview, 2008). All other positions are open to women and Copts, according to these MB officials.[29] Others have justified the inclusion of the clause on the grounds that it was intended for the sake of transparency and "to be frank to everybody" (Al-Aryan and Al-Ghazali interviews, 2008). Others, such as Abdul Moneim Aboul Fotouh and Issam al-Aryan, however, disagreed with the explicit mentioning of such a clause and recognized its implications from a democratic and citizenship perspective (Fotouh interview, 2008; Al-Aryan interview, 2008), preferring silence on the issue since the dynamics of the Egyptian society will not allow for a woman or a Copt citizen to be elected to this position anytime soon. The interviews made it clear that a revision on this clause is almost certainly needed and that this issue regarding the presidency is seen as an "administrative problem" (M. Habib interview, 2008).

In contrast, by emphasizing Islamic civilization, the WP is able to avoid potential problems emanating from adherence to both Islam and a pluralist notion of democracy, avoiding religious conflict. According to the WP program, women and Christians are eligible for all public offices (WP Program 2004, 7). The WP's emphasis on Islamic civilization as a "cultural framework" is almost identical to the role of Islam in the Turkish Justice and Development Party (AKP), where Islam represents the set of common values and serves as cement for the society.

For the WP, the goal is not to represent and instill Islam in the politics and society as the MB ventures to do, but rather to promote Islamic values already prevalent in the society in a fashion akin to Christian democratic parties (Mady interview, 2008). To this end, Islam offers only "guiding principles." The WP's adherence to sharia as a general guiding principle is far from being a strict adherence to a religious doctrine, but rather a way to emphasize its adherence to an Islamic identity. To this effect, the party program states: "They [the WP] believe that the interpretations of sharia they offer, although illuminated by the general goals of sharia and its fundamental principles, are nonetheless human interpretations, and as such, may or may not be correct. Hence they are open to debate, criticism, and revision, and change depending on time and place" (WP Program 2004, 4). The MB, in sharp distinction to the WP, envisions a state "that combines both religion and state" (MB Electoral Program 2005, introduction). In brief, the WP's position on the role of Islam is more moderate, that is, less politicized and more focused on Islamic values, than that of the MB's Islamic discourse.

The WP separated religious *dawa* activities from political activities, a move similar to the one by the Party for Justice and Development in Morocco. The conjoint nature of the political and religious activities, as in the case of the MB, constitutes a principal source of concern about Islamist parties (R. Habib interview, 2008). When the MB makes a statement, for example, it is not clear who the audience is. Does the MB speak to its membership who already adheres to the group's principles as an Islamic movement, or is the audience the population at large, that is, the electorate, who do not necessarily subscribe to the MB's Islamist worldview and over whom the MB does not have an authority? For WP leader Mady, the fact that the party separated "the preaching job and political job, and specializes in the political job only" is a testament to the unpoliticized role of Islam within the party. It also sends a clear message as to who their audience is. This separation between preaching activities (*dawa*) and political activities also afforded the party versatility in its political stance, enabling the party to work with other parties without any preconditions and reservations on various issues, according to Mady (Mady interview, 2008). Emphasizing this "flexibility" of the party, WP founding member Eman Kandil underscores the absence of an "ideological orientation" from the party discourse (Kandil interview, 2008).[30]

One of the fundamental issues facing Islamist parties is their monopolistic claim about speaking on behalf of Islam. In other words, Islamist parties render themselves as the (official) representatives of the faith. For example, the former head of the political bureau in the MB, Abdel Hamid Al-Ghazali, notes that the "Islamic point of view and Muslim Brotherhood point of view... are identical," implying that views beyond that of the MB face condemnation simply because they are not MB views (Al-Ghazali interview, 2008). Indeed, several members of the WP criticized the MB due to its claim about speaking for Islam. WP official Kandil claims that the MB "consider themselves the only right way" on every issue, including Islam (Kandil interview, 2008). The WP official for the youth branch, Ahmed Hamid, explained that an important part of the discussions he engaged in with his father, who has been a member of the MB since the chaotic days of the 1950s and of the much-disputed militia force of the MB, al-Nizam al-Khas, centered on this issue: "I am a Muslim, but I cannot say that I am Islam. I cannot say that I am talking in the name of Islam. This is the difference between my father and me. My father used to say that 'Islam said that' while he meant that 'Ikhwan al-Muslimin said that.' So, I would get into debates with him oftentimes about why he said Islam when he meant Ikhwan al-Muslimin, and he used to say 'We [MB] are Islam.'... You can take thoughts, ideas, principles from religion, but you cannot say I am the religion" (Hamid interview, 2008). This core issue is addressed by the separation between the religious and political activities of MDPs, as in the case of the WP in Egypt. Mady, for example, claims, "Although we are confident that we have a distinct contribution to make, we do not believe we are always right or that we hold the monopoly over truth" (Mady 2008, 8). Leading figures within the MB, by contrast, explicitly state that "Islam is Muslim Brotherhood and Muslim Brotherhood is Islam," suggesting that the MB's views and Islamic perspective are identical.[31] Indeed, WP leader Mady criticizes the MB on its exclusive notion of Muslimness: "Membership in the Muslim Brotherhood is dependent on your religion—everyone should be Muslim, not only Muslim but a special kind of Muslim. Not all Muslims can be members of the Muslim Brotherhood" (Mady quoted in Stacher 2002).

The separation between religious and political activities is crucial from a democratic perspective as well. Religious organizations' main audience is their own membership, and they require conformity and strict following of the organization's principles. However, political parties deal with issues that concern a whole population rather than just their own constituency. Hence political parties are, in theory, more open to compromise and negotiation as compared with religious organizations because they do not deal with "absolutes." Amr Hamzawy, Marina Ottaway, and Nathan Brown underscore this democratic implication and draw an analogy to the European experience on the same issue: "It is not only important that the party and the broader organization have separate identities but also full (and not merely formal) autonomy. Returning to the earlier example, Christian Democratic parties became accepted as legitimate political players when it became clear the party leadership made its decisions on its own without accepting instructions from the Church" (Hamzawy, Ottaway, and Brown 2007). Hence the lack of separation between religious and political activities of the MB presents a formidable problem for the MB.

In the application of sharia, the MB largely rests on the conviction that Egyptians overwhelmingly favor the application of sharia. Hence when asked whether the MB will use coercion to ensure the observation of sharia, MB officials responded by pointing out the popular support for sharia in Egypt; popular decision will be determinative, and the people will be the ultimate referees (Al-Aryan and M. Habib interviews, 2008). Complementing the MB's position on the application of sharia is the grassroots approach to Islamization. For the MB, reform of the individual and societal acceptance of an Islamic system constitute the primary goal because only after that can an Islamic state be established. Muhammad Habib succinctly summarizes the group's position on this issue: "Islam has its specialty, it has economics, [it has an] economic system, it has political system, and it has [a] social system and so on. But we cannot enforce people to do this or that. The people or the nation must agree with the system [the sharia]. [If people do not agree with sharia], as they like, [there is] no enforcement" (M. Habib interview, 2008). Hence the group's long-term perspective on Islamization affords them their current position on the application of sharia, which appears to be compatible with procedural democracy.

Democracy and the Wasat Party

As in the case of other MDPs, the WP's adherence to a democratic discourse rests on both procedures and principles of democracy. The WP leader Mady unequivocally expresses the party's adherence to all democratic procedures such as elections and peaceful rotation of power. This emphasis on procedural elements of democracy, however, is not radically different from the MB's approach to democracy. What sets the WP's democratic position apart is the embrace of a pluralist and "inclusive" conception of democracy (Kandil interview, 2008). According to Joshua Stacher, the WP "argues in favor of democratic reforms, human rights, women's rights, and the inclusion of Christians in its party project" (Stacher 2002, 415). The emphasis on such notions is a clear indication of the party's pluralistic and liberties-oriented nature. Mady maintains that "most democratic principles are not against Islam.... Some very small issues are not acceptable, but the majority, as I said, is acceptable of the principles. But all the [democratic] process is acceptable." For Mady, only "excessive sexual freedom" seems to be at odds with their understanding of democracy, commensurate with the conservative values of the Egyptian society conceived more broadly (Mady interview, 2008).

The WP's emphasis on the idea of equal "citizenship," instead of playing up ethnic or religious identity, aims to demonstrate the internalization of democratic values and principles in the party (Mady, Kandil, and R. Habib interviews, 2008; WP Program 2004). The focus on citizenship helps the WP address two specific problems associated with Islamist parties in general, one being the status of non-Muslims in a polity where Islam constitutes the principal source of rights, as discussed previously. The other is the equality of men and women. By supporting full citizenship rights to women, including the much disputed exclusion clause of the MB on women's right to be become the president, along with non-Muslims, the WP illustrates another distinction between itself and an Islamist platform (WP Program 2004, 7). One of the female members of the WP, Eman Kandil, views the party's position on women as "exciting" and expressed it as a key factor in her decision to join in the ranks of the party (Kandil interview, 2008).

Another dimension of the WP's democratic discourse is the focus on "popular sovereignty" as the source of legitimate state power (Kandil interview, 2008).[32] The MB, historically, adhered to the notion that sovereignty belongs to God, which created a continuous source of tension with the group's statements on democracy. Cognizant of this problem, the WP reinforced its democratic credentials with the following statement: "The people are the source of all powers; legislative, executive, and judicial branches of government must be separate and independent from one another in a context of general balance. This includes the right of the people to legislate for themselves the laws which are to their interest" (WP Program 2004, 6). The acceptance of popular sovereignty as a principal guiding rule also sheds light on the relationship between democratic and Islamic principles. Although Islam figures prominently in the party's discourse, what people demand is what ultimately matters, and the legitimacy that a party and law can derive is primarily due to popular preference.[33]

At times, it appears that officials from the WP make a careful effort to address the issues pointed out as problematic in the MB's democratic discourse.[34] Others also underscored a tendency by the WP to distinguish itself from the MB, particularly to convince state security that its separation from the MB was genuine and not a Trojan horse to be used by the MB once the WP obtained legal party status. Fahmy Howeidy, a respected Islamist intellectual in Egypt, concurred by referencing his conversation with WP leader Mady on this issue (Fahmy Howeidy interview, 2008).

For decades, the MB has strongly favored democratic procedures, that is, separation of powers, peaceful transfer of power, and fair elections. Issam Al-Aryan, the former head of the political bureau of the MB, in regard to the group's position on democracy with reference to Islam, explains: "We believe that Islam is an overall solution for all problems, and in Islam we have some general rules and principles that are compatible with democratic principles. Islam respects multiplicity, respects choice of people, gives the right to people to decide which is better for them, respects the rotation of power, respects human rights, respects freedom, of course" (Al-Aryan interview, 2008). In a similar vein, former deputy general guide Muhammad Habib outlines the fundamentals of the democratic system envisioned by the MB: "We are hoping to settle a democratic regime, a real democratic regime based on multiple parties, peaceful change of power, and the nation as the source of power" (M. Habib interview, 2008). This understanding of democracy is in line with most Islamist thought throughout the Middle East and is partly due to the authoritarian regimes that the Brothers operate within. The disproportionate emphasis on "political" liberties instead of a comprehensive endorsement of individual rights and liberties stems from the belief that "the cornerstone for tackling our [Egypt's] basic problems in every aspect is through political reform. . . . The basic emphasis for any reform should start from political reform. Without political reform nothing can be done in any aspect of our society" (Al-Ghazali interview, 2008). Nevertheless, Hamzawy, Ottaway, and Brown make it clear that the endorsement of procedural elements of democracy might, indeed, be genuine: "The position of the Brotherhood on its respect for democratic legislative procedures is clear, and does not require, in our opinion, any further elucidation: Brotherhood members elected to parliament have proven over the years to be respectful of democratic procedures, often more so than the incumbent government" (Hamzawy, Ottaway, and Brown 2007).[35]

The thorny question is, however, on the relationship between sharia and democracy. The MB holds that sharia is perfectly compatible with democracy (Muslim Brotherhood Electoral Program 2005), yet the MB does not clarify concerns about the implementation of sharia and its compatibility with democracy at any length. Antar states, "Particularly, it does not provide concrete hints as to what the implementation of Islamic law means for the judicial, legislative, or economic system, or as to what the central body responsible for legislation would be" (Antar 2006, 19). The MB is aware of the ambiguities. Abdul Monem Aboul Fotouh, a former member of the Guidance Council of the movement, mentions that the movement needs a clear vision distinguishing between its missionary and political activities: "There is a debate within the movement about the possibility of transformation to a political party that carries out the movement's reform agenda. Another possibility is establishing a separate political party, with a clear delineation of responsibilities between party and movement. We differentiate clearly between political and religious activities, although repressive state practices have often led to conflation of the two, which would not happen in a free society" (Aboul Fotouh, n.d.).

Nonetheless, the MB further presented observers with doubts about its position on the relationship between sharia and democracy. The 2007 draft of the party program circulated by the MB includes a clause that establishes a legislative supervisory role for a council of ulama (Islamic scholars) (MB Draft Party Program 2007). Essentially, the role of such a council is to oversee whether the legislation passed in the parliament is compatible with Islamic law (sharia), a function similar to that of a Constitutional Court with the exception that it reviews the legislation only insofar as it relates to Islamic law. A similar body called the Guardian Council was, indeed, established in the Islamic Republic of Iran following the 1979 revolution. The MB, however, was quick to backtrack on its proposal, recognizing the criticisms and the potential implications for democracy. Such a body, essentially, contradicts the basic idea that the only legitimate authority with respect to legislation is the parliament. Issam Al-Aryan, the former head of MB's political bureau, explained the problem as follows: "It will be a contradiction between this [ulama council] and the parliament. Now, the parliament clearly in the [revised] draft is the only body which legislates the laws. And high court is the only body which reviews the laws; that is clear for us" (Al-Aryan interview, 2008). Despite Al-Aryan's statement, Muhammad Habib, the former second man in the MB, makes it clear that Islamic compatibility of legislation continues to be the guiding principle of the MB's take on the issue: "Any law, we take the tools of democracy, but any law coming from the parliament should be agreeable to the principles of sharia. We do not make *harams halal*, and *halals haram*.[36] This is the principal difference between us and the West's understanding of democracy. Every social, political, economic activity must agree with the principles of sharia" (M. Habib interview, 2008).

The MB also came under fire from seculars for its position on women, as it was not deemed to be up to par with a liberal understanding of democracy. For example, the MB's 2005 electoral program calls for women to "participate in the elections and to have membership in the legislative councils and the like, but within the limits that keep her honor and dignity," which resonates well with the idea that women should be "protected everywhere" (MB Electoral Program 2005, first section).[37] The problem from a liberal Western point of view is determining who the authority is in keeping women's "honor and dignity." Or, in a broader context, the MB guarantees "some rights" and "some liberties" so long as they are compatible with the principles of Islam (MB Electoral Program 2005, first section). The WP leader Mady, rightly, challenges the Brotherhood on its "deliberately ambiguous position" on the constitution and democracy (Mady interview, 2008). Ambiguities on many issues as discussed previously appear to harm rather than benefit the MB's democratic discourse.

In his introduction to a book on the MB's parliamentary performance, Akef makes it clear that democracy, as a procedure, serves a specific end. Unlike in the case of democratic procedures, the MB does not have a fundamental attachment to democratic principles and values. Akef writes: "The MB's aim in participating in the People's Assembly [Egyptian parliament] or other elected councils is to serve the establishment of the Islamic State from which the country and worshipers will benefit" (Akef quoted in Antar 2006). To put it differently, there is significant evidence in the words and actions of the MB that it will adhere to democratic procedures; the case of democratic principles, however, is far from clear. The MB still struggles to come to terms with democratic principles in view of the role of Islamic law and its compatibility with democracy. Hence hasty conclusions about the MB's "hypocritical" democratic stance may be premature. To quote Samer Shehata and Joshua Stacher on the MB's democratic credentials, "While a healthy dose of skepticism toward any political organization is prudent, commentary on the Brotherhood frequently leaps to unsubstantiated conclusions that paint the group as a monolith bent on oppression and rule by force in the future" (Shehata and Stacher 2006). After all, the MB is the group that was overthrown from government by a military coup.

Overall, the MB's stance on democracy focuses on procedural democracy with an emphasis on elections, peaceful turn of power, and majoritarian decision making while remaining silent on principal adherence to a pluralist and rights-based democratic conception. Therefore, the MB's position is in line with an Islamist ideology. The WP, however, goes to lengths to prove that its democratic credentials are solid, particularly in regard to individual liberties and minority rights.

Economic Policy

The WP's economic vision sketches out the blueprint for a liberal economy. The party endorses "open markets and free capital," where the role of the government is "to facilitate the growth of the private sector by removing unnecessary red tape and contradictory regulations." The state's role, in this context, refers to the regulation of the economy, which should in principle ensure the operation of a free private sector without "monopoly or exploitation" (WP Political Program 2004, 10–11). However, the economic crisis of 2008 certainly tilted the party's discourse toward greater state involvement in the economy (Mady interview, 2008). According to the WP political program in 2004, the party views an "appropriate legislative and regulatory environment" crucial for successful economic enterprise and a precondition for "a healthy investment environment" (WP Political Program 2004, 10). Contrasted with the economic discourse of the MB, the WP is certainly more accepting of a liberal economic system. While the MB offers an economic system "derived" from Islam, or based on a "market economy in Islamic perspective," and fundamentally opposed to the use of interest in the economy,[38] the WP does not have such a goal of fundamentally reorganizing the economy. The WP's position on the economy is most clearly demonstrated by the language the party uses to increase Egypt's integration to the global economy and the tools offered to that end. Broadly conceived, WP leadership views Egypt's economic system favorably: "We are not far away from the [economic] system in Egypt now with the exception of corruption" (Hamid interview, 2008).

LIBERAL ECONOMY

A critical component of the WP's economic discourse is geared toward the entrenchment of a truly liberal economy. Throughout the party program, the WP makes references to the need for a liberal economy and the ways to deal with obstacles in achieving this goal (WP Political Program 2004, 15). Inefficiencies, according to the party, are major factors preventing the establishment of a liberal trade regime, and customs procedures, perhaps, are the most problematic of these inefficiencies: "Developing and simplifying customs procedures and ensuring that procedures in the air and sea ports facilitate, rather than cause delays to the entry and exit of goods. A better estimate of customs tariffs is needed depending on the real price of the product" (17).

The Arab free trade agreement (FTA) has been a key element of the WP's economic discourse.[39] It is viewed favorably as a means of promoting a more liberal economy both in Egypt and in the Arab world more generally. However, actual steps taken toward an Arab FTA lags significantly behind the goodwill toward such a goal, claims the WP. The major problem is "the absence of political will" to create a competitive regional economic bloc. In order to reenact the stillborn Arab FTA, the WP envisions that the FTA should "include a gradual lifting of customs and similar internal fees and elimination of administrative, monetary and quota restrictions on the trade between the different countries" (WP Political Program 2004, 23). The core idea behind the party's take on the Arab FTA is greater integration to the world economy. Indeed, one of the issues the WP underscores with respect to liberalization in the Egyptian economy is Egypt's position in the "Global Competitiveness Report." The WP claims, correctly, that Egypt's ranking in the report prepared annually by the World Economic Forum has declined steadily since the mid-1990s (WP Political Program 2004, 15).

A related issue that the WP raises, as it relates to the state of the Egyptian economic liberalization, is the problems that the Egyptian private sector faces. One such problem is the high level of government debt. For the WP, government debt implies that "the government is crowding out the private sector in terms of domestic borrowing." In turn, the decreased amount of credit available for domestic borrowing negatively affects "the interest rate, job opportunities and income distribution" (WP Political Program 2004, 17). In the same vein, the party calls for ending the public financing of state economic institutions, which announce annual losses of LE5 (approximately $1 million), according to the party (WP Political Program 2004, 18).

Development of the Egyptian banking system is also viewed as a potential problem, preventing greater private investment. The Central Bank of Egypt assumes a key role, due especially to its autonomy, which will likely help it to maintain a lower interest rate, according to the WP, eventually "encourag[ing] investment and hence, development" (WP Political Program 2004, 16). Note, however, that the WP does not find that interest intrinsically creates problems with the economy, a stark contrast to Islamist discourse, which monolithically opposes interest.[40]

On privatization, the WP takes an aggressive stance, calling for privatization of most state economic enterprises. WP official Ahmed Hamid states, "We cannot talk about privatization in this case. Why do we have six million government employees? To control the country. So, we need to continue with privatization, we cannot continue paying this many people" (Hamid interview, 2008).

While the WP is quite specific in its economic observations and policy recommendations, the MB takes a more comprehensive approach and emphasizes the underlying socioeconomic divisions in the Egyptian society. For example, the MB states, "The failed economic policies are responsible for [severe socioeconomic divisions] because they did not take into consideration the poor, and basically cared only for the upper class, i.e., the businessmen and corrupt bureaucracy" (MB Electoral Program 2005, third section). In the same light, the former head of the MB's political bureau and a leading economic advisor to the group railed against the pervasive nature of monopolistic practice in Egypt: "As far as market economy is concerned, we are—by our Qur'anic verses—against any monopolistic practice. One of the basic weaknesses of our economy is that it is suffering from really excessive monopolistic practices by some leaders of the regime's party. For instance, iron and steel, which is monopolized by Ahmed Eizz who is the second man in the regime. We are against this; we are against corruption, which is in every economic activity of our society and very destructive" (Al-Ghazali interview, 2008). By discrediting the network of monopolistic corruption in the hands of the political and economic elite, the MB makes direct appeals to the periphery in Egypt.

Infitah policy also takes its fair share from the MB's critique of the Egyptian economy. Although in principle the MB is not against liberalization of the economy, it is unequivocally opposed to its current practice on the grounds that "power and wealth are married" in Egypt: "We are against *infitah* as it is practiced because it does not have a program, no clear-cut program; it is a chaotic *infitah*, and it is molded with corrupted people and corruption. We are not against *infitah* as such." Al-Ghazali continued to specify the mechanism that sustains such a "corrupt" system, underscoring the selective nature of the process:

Only a few select people are taking the ticket of being an NDP member. They are also taking the membership of the Majlis Al-Sha'ab [People's Assembly] only to benefit themselves. For example, Hani Surur, who is trading in contaminated blood baths, and he was under trial. There is Mamdouh Ismail of this boat that sank in the Red Sea, causing more than 1,000 casualties as if it was war. Nothing has been done. Hisham Talaat Mustafa, who without any responsibility spent millions for a playgirl and ended up by killing her. These are people who are not responsible, not really feeling the problem of the ordinary Egyptian. (Al-Ghazali interview, 2008)

These prominent Egyptian business owners have been the face and score sheet of the regime, for the MB.

As opposed to a liberal market economy, the MB calls for a market economy with extensively protectionist and nationalist policies reminiscent of the 1960s and 1970s, where the state assumes an "interventionist" role (Al-Ghazali interview, 2008). To this end, vaguely construed concepts such as "self-sufficiency, self-industry, [and] self-development" are employed in the MB's electoral program, where self-development is defined as a system "based on increasing the utilization of the local resources without using them up nor resorting to loans and external aids, [and it] is our way for achieving the comprehensive development" (MB Electoral Program 2005, second section).[41] The MB's overall economic policy is far from being thorough (Howeidy interview, 2008); instead, it highlights socioeconomic conflict in broad terms and calls for a grand reorganization of the economic system along Islamist criteria.

The MB's position on the current economic liberalization reforms such as privatization is highly critical of the government. Though the MB has historically favored a market economy with an Islamic twist, its criticism of the economic reforms—presumably toward a market economy but mostly reinforcing the current socioeconomic structure—is aimed at the perception that the MB is standing up for the interests of the marginalized and lower-income Egyptians. Hence at times, the tone of the MB's critiques went as far as praising "the gains of the socialist Nasser era" with an excessively nationalist rhetoric (Hamzawy, Ottaway, and Brown 2007).

Emphasis on SMEs

In view of the potential social base of the party, the WP also, in its program, places great emphasis on supporting SMEs. The WP views SMEs as the "backbone" of the Egyptian economy and maintains that this sector of the economy should become "the basis and stimulus for other production sectors" (WP Political Program 2004, 20). Specifically, SMEs should be supported to undertake specific functions for the party. For one, the government should put in place a strategy to support "export-oriented projects" by SMEs, targeting foreign markets. Secondly,

SMEs should be supported to offer viable "alternatives to imported goods." Eventually, SMEs of both kinds will help in "sustaining development and raising the standard of living." Nonetheless, the WP underscores several problems associated with how SMEs are currently handled in the Egyptian economy, including (1) scarcity of funds, (2) difficulties in marketing, (3) complicated bureaucratic procedures, and (4) lack of administrative and technical support (WP Political Program 2004, 22).

The MB is also critical of the current economic policy on SMEs and middle classes. The main problem for the MB, however, lies in with the regressive structure of the tax law. According to the MB's 2005 electoral program, "The new tax law needs another reform because it reduced the stock companies' taxes while it canceled the given exemption to the professionals such as the engineers, doctors, and accountants. All the previous factors lead to the absence of trust in the economic policies management and in those who are responsible for the economic policy due to the spread of corruption in all sectors" (MB Electoral Program 2005, third section).

To summarize its economic policy, the WP seems to have submitted itself to the global trend toward greater international economic integration and wants to ensure that Egypt is a part of this trend. A WP official made the following statement regarding the party's view on Egypt's contemporary economic trend: "After current worldwide globalization, we cannot discuss globalization; there is globalization. The money is transferred over the borders; the goods are transferred over the borders. I cannot say that I will not be in the globalization movement" (Hamid interview, 2008). The MB, however, takes a critical perspective on the current liberalization drive and does not view it favorably for the peripheral groups in Egypt who, for the MB, shoulder the burden of this process, as opposed to big businesses and other components of the secular and central coalition. Nonetheless, the MB is harshly criticized in various corners because "it does not provide any specific plans or financial policies to reach these goals" beyond a mere broad perspective on the economy (Antar 2006, 19).[42] With respect to the peripheral business owners in Egypt, distinct positions of the WP and the MB have unique implications. The WP's perceived overidentification with the exclusive and cronyistic economic policies of the regime undermines its favorable discourse on SMEs. The MB, in contrast, holds its unwavering position vis-à-vis the regime by its foundational criticism of economic policies, including liberalization. Hence peripheral business owners should in principle relate more closely to the Islamist discourse of the MB. Notwithstanding the thorough discussion of the economic discourse of MB above, it is important to note that relative lack of coherence and overall weakness of Islamist parties' conception of economic policy-making is one of their main weaknesses (Roy 1994). Indeed, the MB's poor economic performance in its brief stint in government between 2012 and 2013 is a testament to this weakness.

Social Policy

Egypt's relatively poor population certainly affects the social policy of political parties in the country. The WP's position on social policy is decidedly expansionist in orientation, especially when coupled with Islamic emphasis on social protection. According to the WP program, the party believes in the principle of social equality which "demands that basic necessities for all citizens must be fulfilled." The party calls for the expansion of the social safety net beyond those who contribute to the system, such as in the case of pensions. The main objective for the WP is to "care for" those with limited income (WP Political Program 2004, 31). To this end, the party offers several mechanisms. Among the solutions are (1) tax exemptions for low-income people, (2) taxation only on production, (3) participation of civil society in the social safety net, (4) management of *zakat* (almsgiving) and *sadaqat* (donation),[43] and (5) separation of the social welfare budget from the rest of the state budget. The last measure would, in particular, guarantee the safeguarding the interests of the poor through social protection. Charitable endowments (*waqf*) are also expected to partake in the provision of such services (WP Political Program 2004, 12).

Zakat and *sadaqat* also assume unique roles in the WP program, certainly uncharacteristic uses for these two forms of Islamic streams of revenue. Both items in the social safety net need to provide the economic fundamentals for greater SME investment and production. According to the party program, "the role of *zakat* could be extended to support and fund small and medium enterprises (SMEs) which would contribute to overcoming unemployment and poverty." Similarly, the program calls for "rationalizing and providing guidelines for the expenditure of *sadaqat* and *nudhour* to support SMEs and put the productive family scheme into practical implementation" (WP Political Program 2004, 12).

More recently, the WP framed its discourse around the idea of the Third Way, following Tony Blair's success in Britain (Mady and Hamid interviews, 2008). The problem for the WP is more intricate than simply adopting a discourse that merely combines basic elements of a free market economy with an extensive social safety net. The way economic liberalization is handled in Egypt clearly contradicts the interests of peripheral groups. As I have shown in chapter 2, neither peripheral masses nor peripheral businesses benefited from the liberalization process, yet the discourse of the WP largely fails to represent such disappointment. Instead of voicing strong criticism of the implementation of liberalization in Egypt and distancing itself from governmental economic policies, the party appears to be complicit in this exercise, by failing to stand against it. Unlike the AKP in Turkey, which was able to build on the success of the liberalization program and compensate for the dislocations by way of increased social spending and unemployment benefits, the WP has been unable to strike a balance between supporting a liberal economy and social protection, or a constituency to support its endorsement of the status quo. The outcome, as disheartening as it is, consists of minimal levels of support among the peripheral businesses and masses for the WP. Even though the party moved toward the left because of "the poor problem" (R. Habib interview, 2008), the economically liberal orientation overshadows the emphasis on social policies.

The MB's program on social policy is structured along the same lines, and it constitutes the other side of the MB's economic policy, as it is viewed the responsibility of the state to ensure social justice. The group's long-standing emphasis on social welfare and charity networks is a testament to the upholding of the social justice principle. The MB, like the WP, relies heavily on *zakat* and *sadaqat* to structure its social spending. According to the 2005 electoral program, the MB declares, "*Zakat* institutions should be in charge of distributing wealth and income within an integral Islamic system."[44] The MB views *zakat* and *sadaqat* as essential parts of its broader Islamic economic outlook: "Our [the MB's] economic program is based on the market economy in Islamic perspective, which means we believe in private ownership as long as it gives its obligations toward society paying *zakat*, paying other donations for the poor. This is what we call economic obligations" (Al-Ghazali interview, 2008).

Similar to the WP's proposition, the MB calls for an institutional body to oversee the distribution of *zakat* and utilize the funds for addressing other economic issues as well: "Establishing a civil institution in each governorate to collect and distribute the alms in order to guarantee a suitable standard of living for the poor. It is also possible to use this money to establish projects for reducing the rate of unemployment" (MB Electoral Program 2005, third section). Unlike the WP, however, the MB unequivocally opposes the implementation of economic liberalization in Egypt and distances itself from the regime's economic policies: "The Muslim Brotherhood watches the local and the international development, and sees that the absence of democracy, and the imposition of the emergency law since October 1981 up till now has led to the monopoly of wealth and power by a few persons; consequently, corruption has spread everywhere" (MB Electoral Program 2005, third section).

Business World and Political Preferences

This section offers interview data on Egyptian business owners' political preferences with respect to the four distinct elements of an MDP: Islam, democracy, the economy, and social policy. The interviews are conducted with both peripheral SME owners and big business owners. I offer evidence to demonstrate that the perception of the status quo with respect to socioeconomic classes continues for SME owners. As a result, their political preferences reflect their perceived marginalization in the political-economic system of Egypt, a reaction to the status quo vis-à-vis the center. In order to show the continuity of the preliberalization structure, I rely on interviews from both big business owners and peripheral business owners in Egypt. The interviews demonstrate that the perceived sense of economic exclusion and the "corrupt" nature of the relationship between the state and big businesses constitute the key policy area that the peripheral business owners view as essential for their interests. The interviews make it clear that favored policy preferences on Islam and democracy remain overwhelmingly subordinate to the economic preferences; without a resolution to the fundamental economic plight of the periphery, it appears, talk about other issues is devoid of any real substance. For the big businesses, economic interest seems to constitute the main nexus of their political preferences. The continuation of the economic status quo is imperative; their preferences on Islam, democracy, and social policy only seem to reinforce their economic interests vis-à-vis the rest of the Egyptian society.

Islam and Democracy

Democracy as a political preference featured low in the agenda of several business owners, big and peripheral alike. Theoretically, I would expect that business owners in Egypt, particularly peripheral business owners, should have a favorable view of democracy because in principle, it ensures a political system favorable to doing business.[45] Yet, unlike in Turkey or Morocco, Egyptian peripheral business owners shied away from establishing direct links between democracy and the role of Islam in politics on the one hand, and economic liberalization and their businesses on the other hand. This peculiarity indicates the complicated, intertwined nature of politics and the economy in Egypt. In a country such as Egypt, where the economy is characterized by intricate relationships between politics and business, crony relationships and corruption become the direct target of peripheral businesses. Democracy, as such, is insufficient to explain the problems of the Egyptian society and economy, according to one businessman (EG-2-B interview, 2008). If democracy is taken as a mechanism to hold elections and offer a peaceful turn of power, it might become a means to perpetuate the current political economic structure. Such conceptualization of democracy, as a result, does not offer much in the way of the rule of law or other principles that democracy would offer. Hence the peculiarity of the Egyptian peripheral business owners' views on democracy becomes more revealing in this vein.

The interviews with peripheral business owners did not reveal a clear-cut explanation as to why and how Islam in politics might affect their business in one way or another. Islam, clearly, was one of their main political preferences (EG-3-B, EG-5-B, EG-10-B interviews, 2008), yet instead of establishing discernible mechanisms on how Islam might help or undermine their businesses with a political role, they focused on the perceived corruption in the entire political system. Without a comprehensive solution "encompassing social, economic, and political issues," no single policy change is likely to bring about desired and equitable outcomes, one peripheral businessman argued (EG-2-B interview, 2008).[46]

As for the big business owners, their stance on Islam and democracy is, surprisingly, more straightforward. Compared with the peripheral business owners, big business owners' preferences on democracy are more pronounced, as they perceived it to be directly—and negatively—related to their own interests. In line with what many have suggested, democracy implies redistribution from the rich to the poor.[47] The fact that an overwhelming majority of the Egyptian population is poverty stricken reinforces the big business owners' perception that democracy is likely to harm their prosperity via extensive redistribution. Any change away from the status quo, unequivocally, implied harm to their interests. In principle, all business owners supported a democratic regime, but when asked about its implementation in the current Egyptian society, big business owners hesitated to display favorable views. One reason was the strong perceived association between democracy and political Islam, that is, Islamists winning democratic elections. Politicized Islam is perceived to be detrimental for their own businesses and for the Egyptian economy in general.

For example, a businessman who operates in various sectors of the economy with an annual turnover of more than $700 million praised democracy as a political system. Echoing modernization theory's rubric on the relationship between democracy and education, he highlighted potential implications of a democratic regime in a society where poverty and illiteracy reigned:

> The problem with democracy is that it is something nice, everybody likes it, but due to poverty and illiteracy, in democracy [people] will be in favor of not market policy, not market economy. On the contrary, they will prefer a socialist system. Of course, as a businessman, I don't like it so much to be honest with you. We are very unfortunate that the world has gone into this economic slump [the 2008 crisis], and especially these days because this will strengthen the other party's side [those who want democracy]. They will say, "See the capitalist system did not work anyway; the Mecca of capitalism has fallen down badly and even not knowing what to do." So, in Egypt democracy—full democracy—is not very healthy. (EG-4-B interview, 2008)

This businessman established an explicit link between a democratic regime and redistribution. Ironically, however, in his account, a democratic regime is viewed as incompatible with a capitalist market economy.

In a similar way, another big businessman and chairman of one of the major business groups in Egypt called for higher levels of education in order for people to be able to make "the choice" in a democratic regime: "To have true democracy, you have to have an educated population that is knowledgeable and able to make free choices. . . . I would definitely like to see a democratic regime in place coupled with a massive educational reform to allow for total eradication of illiteracy and the ability of every Egyptian to have the knowledge necessary to make the choice" (EG-11-B interview, 2008). The concern for this businessman is the potential that people might make incorrect choices, an attitude and a distrust emblematic of educated and secular elites when talking about the peripheral and largely Islamic population. The businessman did not elaborate on what "the choice" is, yet the rest of the interview was clear in pointing out that it was not the policies and platforms favored by lower classes and peripheral business owners, that is, political Islam and redistribution. He argued that "Islam should never be used as a political cover by people with political ambitions," a clear reference to the MB (EG-11-B interview, 2008). God and democracy, in this formulation, do not go together: "It is not democracy anymore because when there is God, there is no democracy" (EG-4-B interview, 2008).

Another big businessman, a leader of one of the major business associations in Egypt, was abundantly clear in detailing the potential future he was concerned about:

> As in any country, democracy is better for business; in [an] Islamic country, it is very difficult. You don't want to see a full democracy; then, you will find Islamic fundamentalists in power. I am sure there will be a big chaos for the coming ten, twenty, thirty years. . . . You can see it in Iran after the revolution. . . . In a country like Egypt, if you do not have a good program for foreign investment in the country, and encourage investors to come and work, they will not. So, if there are Islamists in this country, then there is no tourism, there is no alcohol, there are no cinemas. . . . Democracy is very good for business, but is it good for this country? No. (EG-8-B interview, 2008)

Drawing on the same analogy, a businessman challenged Islamists with respect to their economic policies: "They will start saying, 'We will form charity organizations' to touch the masses. But, at the end, what good will they do for the economy? I did not see Iran do something great for the economy" (EG-4-B interview, 2008). Another businessman echoed the perceived weakness of Islamist discourse on economic policy: "The people from the MB have criticized everything, but I have not seen anything from them, their economic agenda; what kind of real agenda do they have? It's only a hidden agenda" (EG-9-B interview, 2008).

To summarize, peripheral business owners certainly hold a favorable position on democracy and Islam, but these opinions do not necessarily expose clear mechanisms on how either one would improve their interests in isolation from other political and economic issues that they perceived more directly and more crucially linked to furthering their interests. A comprehensive discourse that aims to curtail the special relationship between big business and the state is imperative.

Economy

In contrast to their positions on democracy and the role of Islam in politics, the economy constitutes the main policy area where peripheral business owners revealed an unequivocal opposition to the current state of affairs and challenged big business owners' stances and actions in many ways. This not only implies that the cleavage between peripheral and big business owners is a comprehensive one encompassing the economy, politics, and society but also indicates economic conflict's primal role. Unless peripheral businesses are integrated into the system and offered economic opportunities to benefit from it, change, that is, moderation, in their political preferences seems a distant possibility. In light of the Turkish case, this concept becomes much clearer. The economic issues that were highlighted by the peripheral business owners centered on three issues: (1) problems associated with the overall process of economic liberalization, (2) privatization, and (3) the relationship between politics and the economy. I will address these issues as they relate to the Egyptian periphery's stance on each.

ECONOMIC LIBERALIZATION

Peripheral business owners, in principle, view economic liberalization as a process leading to the establishment and strengthening of a functioning market economy. A market economy, according to Islamic economic doctrine, is the ideal economic system. Nonetheless, for many, this process is perceived as being a long way from completion due to the starting point of the liberalization process. Unlike many other countries in the developing world, Egypt is in the process of making a transition from a centrally planned economy to a free market economy. Hence necessary precautions and preparations must be ensured along the road, although according to several peripheral businessmen, successive Egyptian governments have failed to do so (EG-1-B and EG-2-B interviews, 2008). A prominent businessman from the periphery with past ties to the Islamist movements like the MB observes, "We are coming from the very far left designed to be left; everything was centralized; you cannot take me all of a sudden to the other side, to the far right. It is very difficult; I am not prepared; the president, the government, the business people, the people—no one is ready for what you are doing. In the newspapers, there are so many people on strike, and [they] refuse and resign; they want to share in this process" (EG-3-B interview, 2008). One of the major concerns with the whole process of economic liberalization was the manner in which it was presented to the public as an "inevitable" process rather than as a choice made by the government. By presenting economic liberalization as "inevitable," the government aims to prevent substantive discussions on the necessity and benefits of liberalization and the method in which it is undertaken by the government, according to this businessman (EG-2-B interview, 2008).

More specifically, the two major problems associated with the liberalization process are its selective nature and the extensive role the state plays in the economy: "We already started down the path of economic liberalization for a long time now; however, Egyptian liberalization path is plagued by two issues. One, the economic liberalization that exists is not comprehensive; it is selective. Secondly, the hand of the state is quite strong in terms of what is liberalized and what is not. Therefore, it does, to a large extent, interfere in market forces." The problem for this businessman in the textile industry is not the process itself, but rather the inability of the government to give "hope" that it will reach the goal it set initially (EG-12-B interview, 2008).

Some business owners, in the same vein, pinpointed the "gradual" nature of liberalization as a political strategy to ensure certain outcomes (EG-7-B interview, 2008), whereas others have attributed the problems associated with economic liberalization to poor organization and planning rather than political calculation:

> It was just getting away from a socialist economy, central market to open market. It was a very slow process. It was unorganized and not well planned, which actually did not yield its results. Actually, on the contrary, it had some bad effects where you find some people making money out of nowhere. So, a lot of people got richer, and at the same time, it did not help the market. But it was a trial, and Anwar Sadat was really in a hurry to implement it and he wanted it for political reasons. He wanted to prove to the U.S. that we are on track and we are on your side after twenty years of socialism. (EG-10-B interview, 2008)

Nonetheless, both agreed on the observation that monopolization was rampant in the new and "liberal" Egyptian economy. The oft-cited examples of such monopolization were the cases of the cement[48] and iron and steel industries. Ahmed Eizz, needless to say, topped the list. Eizz is recognized as the "second man" in the Mubarak regime (Al-Ghazali interview, 2008). He was both a wealthy businessman and a politician close to no less than Hosni Mubarak himself. One businessman notes, "In the steel industry, we don't have enough [competition]; Ahmed Eizz is in control of the big part of the steel industry. It is because it is a very expensive industry to establish, but also Ahmed Eizz is an influential man; nobody wants to go out and compete against him" (EG-8-B interview,

2008). Indeed, this association with the Mubarak regime allowed Ahmed Eizz to become one of the primary symbols of resentment against the regime itself in the early phase of the Arab Spring demonstrations in the country in 2011.[49]

The poor state of the government policy on SMEs merely reinforced this perception of widespread monopolization. Several business owners claimed that until 2005, no specific policy targeted SME development and growth in Egypt, unlike in many other liberalizing economies in the developing world. One businessman in the medical industry, for example, cited the case of incentives offered to smaller businesses. In Egypt, the export incentives amounted to 8 percent of the exported goods, whereas in Turkey, tax breaks provided at least a 20 percent incentive, according to this businessman (EG-7-B interview, 2008). With the beginning of the Ahmed Nazif government in 2005, SMEs became one of the targets of the government, according to another businessman: "The light was shed on [SMEs] only two to three years ago, when people started taking them seriously. I think they [the government] are applying the Chinese model. . . . To our astonishment, everybody is saying it was very successful because there were no bad debts; bad debts for this kind of businesses are very small. I see now more institutions, banks going toward this model of businesses and lending, supporting" (EG-8-B interview, 2008). The banking crisis throughout the 1990s and the early 2000s also angered peripheral business owners. As discussed in chapter 2, during this period, banks extended loans to business owners on political and personal connections instead of borrower credibility. As a result, a substantial portion of loans during this period was not repaid, leading to increased public mistrust in the whole liberalization process (EG-10-B interview, 2008). Overall, the perception of the liberalization process has been a rather problematic one from the perspective of peripheral business owners. One noted, "I would argue that the Egyptian economy needs two things: a level playing field and more competition. There is no doubt that those two things are to the benefit of the economy and of the consumers" (EG-12-B interview, 2008). It goes without saying that competition certainly would benefit peripheral business owners.

Conversely, big business owners' attitudes toward economic liberalization were much different than those of peripheral business owners. Economic liberalization is largely viewed as a "necessity" that needs to be undertaken "for a whole rethink for the issue of economic growth and economic development in Egypt" (EG-11-B interview, 2008). Yet they, like the peripheral business owners, also complained about the implementation of economic liberalization in Egypt. However, their complaint was focused on the tardiness of the process rather than on the outcome and the immediate effects of liberalization. One of the businessmen likened the liberalization process in Egypt to a "roller-coaster" where periods of reversion would follow periods of liberalization, until 2005 or so (EG-9-B interview, 2008). The Atef Ebeid government is one such example: "From 2000 to

2005, when Dr. Atef Ebeid came to power, things were almost reversed.... It made a very bad impact on foreign investment, even on Egyptian investors. All the laws and regulations done in previous years were in one way or another either reversed or put into standstill" (EG-8-B interview, 2008). Similarly, others characterized the progress of liberalization as a "system of trial and error" where the Egyptian government made mistakes on a continual basis and then put in an effort to correct such mistakes. In one such example, a businessman recalled, "You can even hear today our minister of investment coming out and saying 'We made mistakes last May when we canceled some of the tax benefits of free zone operations'" (EG-11-B and EG-8-B interviews, 2008).

Lack of leadership in economic liberalization is also cited as a problem: "One step ahead, two steps back, staying many years waiting to change a law, and cowardice from people's reactions. So, they are not taking any bold economic steps. Had Sadat been living, people would have been very different, because Mubarak is a cautious man" (EG-4-B interview, 2008). The absence of an institutional mechanism and of stable leadership throughout the economic reform process are, time and again, pointed out as issues undermining the whole liberalization experience. The absence of leadership is also a feature of the Egyptian case, setting it apart from its Turkish and Moroccan counterparts. The leadership of Turgut Özal in Turkey and that of King Hassan II in Morocco proved to be staples of economic liberalization in both countries, as outlined in chapter 2. The lack of an institutionalized liberalization process is closely associated with the lack of leadership in Egypt: "The economic liberalization that is taking place [in Egypt] is a process that is assisted by certain personalities in government and in politics. It is still not an institutionalized process, which is necessary for the sustainability of any liberalization. It is personalized; so, if we have one good minister of economy, he can undertake the necessary steps for liberalization. If the new minister, for example, comes, he can change that. Until the system is institutionalized, then sustainability of such liberalization has lower impact" (EG-11-B interview, 2008). Overall, big business owners' reactions to the liberalization process differed fundamentally from those of peripheral business owners. While peripheral business owners view the whole process as fundamentally flawed and structured to benefit only a subset of Egyptians, big businesses field criticism to spur liberalization, ignoring its distributional implications and the losers of the policy. The fact that peripheral businesses oppose Egyptian liberalization whereas big businesses endorse it is a good indication as to who the beneficiaries and losers are in liberalization policy.

The interviews with business owners also reveal that the need for consistency in economic liberalization both over time and across sectors is equally important. One business owner noted, "To have the benefit of liberalization, it needs to be sustainable and it needs to be continuous; it cannot be a situation where you open the door and close the door. It needs to be a situation like the Czech Republic. You have to prepare all the necessary steps for liberalization and there are several steps. And then liberalize, and then rehabilitate, fix what you made wrong. But if you keep liberalizing over a period of twenty plus years, you lose the core of liberalization. It becomes a process; it does not become an end-objective" (EG-11-B interview, 2008). Such consistency would also assure that Egypt would be able to overcome the immediate problems and difficulties associated with liberalization just as "Turkey bit the bullet" in its own liberalization experience (EG-11-B interview, 2008). Critique of the exceptions granted to certain sectors in the liberalization process was common: "Still, some government members look at certain areas strategically, consider them untouchable. Certain industries, certain land property, certain activities are still looked upon as the domain of the government. So, you will see that in the area of, for example, privatizing of airports or building of airports, it is still a very selective process" (EG-8-B interview, 2008). A businessman who established his business in the *infitah* period and saw it grow substantially in the liberalizing Egyptian economy attributed the problems to the people rather than to the Egyptian government: "Government policies are not problematic; you cannot blame government for everything. The problem is to follow guidelines; the people go outside the guidelines. The government says we will offer vocational training; how many workers will show up? Ten percent? Twenty percent?" (EG-9-B interview, 2008).

Big business and peripheral business have diametrically opposed views on economic liberalization in Egypt. While big business perceives it to be a process of insufficient persistence and courage to complete the transition to a fully liberal economy, the peripheral businesses are highly critical of the effects of the liberalization reforms and of the widening gap between the two groups. In view of the WP's and the MB's take on economic liberalization, it seems clear that the WP's overidentification with the current liberalization regime in Egypt undermines the legitimacy of its claim to represent the Islamic constituency in Egypt. While peripheral businesses did not endorse the liberalization process in Egypt, the WP underscored its inevitability.

PRIVATIZATION

Privatization became the most politicized aspect of the liberalization process in Egypt. Peripheral groups and big businesses demonstrated fundamentally contrasting views on privatization. Peripheral businesses invariably opposed the practice of privatization in Egypt, claiming that the Egyptian economy and society were not mature enough for privatization yet. One businessman with ties to the MB asserted, "Why are we selling a factory? Because of bad management. Management is very cheap to buy. Why sell the factory, why sell the assets of my country? And privatization is not like what Thomas Friedman said, a golden jacket; or, the end of history, and I have to do it. No; who said so? Then, we start to nationalize companies again, it is wrong" (EG-2-B interview, 2008). Another businessman underscored the mismatch between the privatization program and the realities of the Egyptian society: "The government plan was probably not able to fit with the social, economic, political status of the country. And the private sector was not, again, ready for carrying such a big responsibility, and the plan does not exclude the major and important sectors. The government should postpone or delay, make them at the end of the road. And invest more" (EG-1-B interview, 2008).

As important as the opposition to the notion of privatization is, the implementation of the privatization program by successive Egyptian governments is plagued by a quagmire of mismanagement and corruption. One peripheral businessman complained about the lack of transparency in privatization:

> So, the environment was not designed properly to implement this privatization. Again, it was not transparent from day one. They did not inform the people what they are going to sell and why. And we know stories that some ministries, for example, want to put a specific company into the private sector. . . . Forget about monopoly and under-the-table stuff; they don't spend money on maintenance, and they make this company make losses, so the man who comes can buy the company that is worth 100 million [in Egyptian pounds, the equivalent of $20 million] for 20 million [in Egyptian Pounds, the equivalent of $4 million], to this extent. (EG-3-B interview, 2008)

In the same way, another challenged the poor management of the privatization process and below-the-market sale value of privatized companies:

> I am against the way people apply this privatization. This privatization program should bring to the country—this is what the government says—LE500 billion. Do you know how much it ended up actually? LE17 billion. People ask, "Where is the money?" [The money was lost to] corruption, bad management. There are some sectors that should be managed by the government. Here [in Egypt], you cannot live without the presence of the government [in the economy]. I cannot go for privatization. So, people are not against privatization here. But people think the way they apply it, and the timing, they are improper and incorrect. (EG-2-B interview, 2008)

On the whole, the periphery's sentiment is that the process was managed badly and that it did not benefit the society as a whole: "The people who are negotiating these contracts did not do the job well. There are a lot of conditions that could be eliminated or postponed, and you really make the benefit out of this agreement. I think, in Egypt, the experiment of privatization was not successful; people did not benefit out of it" (EG-3-B interview, 2008).

Like the small business owners, big business also complained about the privatization process, but for completely different reasons. For the most part, privatization is a highly endorsed idea among big business owners, and it is seen as an essential element of the liberalization of the Egyptian economy. In this regard, one businessman praised the former Egyptian government headed by Ahmed Nazif because of its emphasis on the privatization process: "And then, we found big relief in 2005 when Dr. Ahmed Nazif came to power. Of course, with the new team there with the businessmen and with Mr. Gamal Mubarak as an organizer for this team, we found huge steps towards privatization and free economy and open markets. We are still in this process. I cannot say that we have achieved all [of] what's needed. It's very difficult in a country like Egypt where bureaucracy is very much entrenched in its roots" (EG-8-B interview, 2008). This stance on privatization stands in sharp contrast to the peripheral business owners' take on the issue.

Another business owner who, in 2002, bought one of his companies through the privatization of a public company criticized the hesitancy on the part of the government: "I think it [privatization] is very important. Privatization was not a very popular exercise here in Egypt; people did not like it so much. In some cases it's been very successful; [in] some cases it failed. Egypt is now going back; now, they want to distribute the remaining [companies' shares] to all the population of Egypt" (EG-4-B interview, 2008). Looking at the big picture, another businessman called for swift action and planning to complete the privatization process with an analogy to the case of the Czech Republic:

> When I used to visit Czech Republic, they used to have a calendar, very clear, and they used to have a date whereby the ministry of privatization would be canceled. Because its role would end, and therefore the government would no longer own assets that interfere in the economic realm. And by doing that even when there is a crisis, the government no longer has assets that it is managing. But we have—as long as I can remember since 1991—been privatizing, so seventeen years privatizing. And, as we privatize we still create state-owned entities. A month ago, you could see the minister of investment announcing the creation of a LE300 million entity for investment in Upper Egypt. There is a contradiction, and this contradiction, sadly enough, causes distortions, and these distortions have effects in the economy as a whole such as the continuous subsidization process that we have. (EG-11-B interview, 2008)

Once again, peripheral business owners' unambiguous opposition to the idea of privatization and its implementation in Egypt contradicts the WP's support for the idea of privatization in principle. The interviews made it clear that neither peripheral businesses nor peripheral masses are perceived to be among the beneficiaries of liberalization in Egypt.

MARRIAGE OF BUSINESS AND POLITICS

The crux of discussions in Egyptian public opinion with regard to the liberalization of the economy is the "marriage" between business and politics. For the peripheral business owners, the fate of the Egyptian economy is left "in the hands of ten or fifteen businessmen," and the public at large is excluded from all discussions (EG-2-B interview, 2008). The extent of intimacy between business and politics is such that several members of the Egyptian business community also served members of the Egyptian cabinet at different times. The perception of this intimacy, however, varies vastly between peripheral business owners and big business owners. For example, one peripheral businessman highlighted the difficulty in differentiating between personal and public interests of those businessmen serving as ministers in the government: "It [economic liberalization] benefited a particular group of people. Unfortunately, in the third world countries, there are common factors concerning the money, the loans, the aids, and the chances for using authority to become rich in an illegal way. Remember, members of the parliament and the ministers of this government—they are all business people. How can we differentiate between their personal interests, their mega big companies and the country's benefits?" (EG-3-B interview, 2008). Indeed, the public perception of business owners and politicians suffered greatly, depending on the events at the time. For example, one businessman noted that in the heyday of corruption during the early 2000s in the Atef Ebeid government, "the businessmen were looked at as traitors, as enemies, as robbers" (EG-8-B interview, 2008).

One of the main criticisms fielded by the peripheral businesses was the lack of debate and engagement with the broader public. For example, one businessman pointed to the "lack of public debate" as the cause of policy shifts: "This, unfortunately, comes from lack of public debate, from lack of careful study before undertaking necessary steps and for a lack of conviction that you can engage with public opinion and find out how to take steps that you don't have to reverse one year later or six months later" (EG-11-B interview, 2008). Another peripheral business owner I interviewed called for greater participation in the economic liberalization process in light of the perceived failure of the reforms: "It is very important now to open the room for more people to share their [views on] economic reform and about what we really should do especially after what happened" (EG-3-B interview, 2008).

For the big businesses, however, the overlap between the political and business interests was, indeed, a positive development. The interviews I conducted revealed that it was not the potential problems arising in the form of public interest being overwhelmed by the private interests of the businessmen-cum-government officials that represented the business-politics relationship. It was rather the benefits and normalcy of such mutual influences that were underscored by the big business owners. Several business owners emphasized the fact that with the most recent cabinet under Ahmed Nazif (2004–11), the government is discernibly open to the demands and suggestions of the business world (EG-6-B interview, 2008). One businessman declared, "In the last couple of years, they [the government] reformed the tax laws, made land available for industry, industrial zones, [the] industry modernization program—they are giving support to all factories, supported the industry in the last five years, and offered training" (EG-4-B interview, 2008). Another businessman cautioned that the fast pace of the reforms, thanks to the "good relations" between the business world and policy makers, might lead to "political instability," which in turn would affect the progression of economic reforms (EG-9-B interview, 2008).

Others pointed out the fact that in every country, those business owners with substantial wealth are more likely to have more leverage and influence in politics; in this regard, what is happening in Egypt is no exception. Of this, one businessman stated, "Of course, in any government, there are businessmen using their influence with politicians or using their money to pose influence. It's everywhere, and Egypt is not an exception. Of course, there are a lot of businessmen and they got a lot of leverage, which people think they should not have gotten. But, I don't see it as something very odd" (EG-8-B interview, 2008). Another businessman remarked on big businesses' influence: "It's everywhere, not only in Egypt. You're more powerful, you're more influential. It's the law of the business. The bigger you are, the stronger you are" (EG-9-B interview, 2008). Nonetheless, for this businessman, a good relation with the political world is not a necessary condition for a successful business: "It is not as gloomy and as dark. I am working and I have nothing to do with the government. *Alhamdulillah* [thank God], I am expanding. Of course, in some cases, a close relationship with the government might mean favorable business" (EG-9-B interview, 2008).

Others defended the close relationship between the two on various grounds. For example, one businessman emphasized the private sector's role in economic reforms: "They're claiming that business and politics are married together and that the government works only for the private [business] people. . . . At the end of the day, it's the private sector that's pushing the government [for reforms], but nobody wants to recognize that, and there is not a strong lobby for the private sector to advocate that" (EG-4-B interview, 2008). Another complained about the "anti" sentiments brewing against business and business owners in Egypt and its potential implications for the future of market economy in Egypt (EG-8-B interview, 2008).

At the end of the day, the "marriage" between business and politics overshadows potentially all favorable views on a liberal market economy. The views of the WP and the MB could not be fundamentally more different in addressing the same social base. The WP views it as sufficient to put an exclusion clause on corruption and almost endorse the whole liberalization experience in Egypt, whereas the MB calls the regime on this "marriage" between business and politics, and demands a wholesale reorganization of the socioeconomic system to benefit a larger group of Egyptians (Al-Ghazali interview, 2008).

Social Policy

Business owners of all stripes recognize the problem of poverty and the need for subsidies for a significant portion of the Egyptian population. For the peripheral business owners, the mere fact that a substantial portion of the population is in constant need of subsidies is sufficient to curb the implementation of liberalization reforms (EG-1-B, EG-2-B, EG-3-B interviews, 2008). For the big business owners, however, despite the fact that poverty constitutes an important problem, it should not be allowed to prevent further liberalization in any significant way. One exposed the "dilemma" that the government faces, saying,

> The problem is not what to do. The problem is how to do it with the circumstances [of the country] being what [they are]. You cannot go and say we want to make such and such. You face a lot of troubles. You cannot go and say we're going to free the dollar. You'll find disasters, inflation, and the poor people will be affected. There are a lot of poor people; if you don't have these poor people, you would not have as many problems running the government. But the problem is that there are lots of things that tie their hands all the way. (EG-8-B interview, 2008)

It is the expectation on the part of the people that "the subsidies will exist forever," and that creates "distortion," having an immediate negative impact on the economy (EG-11-B interview, 2008). Hence some business owners think it is "too late" to cut subsidies now as opposed to having done it "ten to fifteen years ago" (EG-5-B interview, 2008).

The expectation among some business owners was that the population would start feeling the benefits of the liberalization process, alleviating some of the concerns along the way: "The problem is that when the economic liberalization process began, it did not trickle down to the population; still, not many people felt it yet. Unfortunately, now with what's happening in the world [the 2008 global crisis], we will go back this year [in terms of economic growth, and the] FDI [foreign direct investment] will be reduced substantially. So, to have this trickle-down effect, we must sustain high growth rates for five or six years; then you could feel it" (EG-4-B interview, 2008).

Another businessman went further and insisted on proceeding despite the potential suffering among the masses: "They [the government] know what [needs] to be done, but they're always facing the anger in the street and they don't have the free hand, as they should.... When they privatize the companies, for example, they always find criticism that 'they're selling the country,' and everybody attacks them that 'they're thieves and they're stealing and they're taking bribes under the table.' I am not telling you they don't—they might be—but everywhere there is a process you have to go through. I have to get rid of this big burden of [the] public sector" (EG-8-B interview, 2008).

Party Support Levels

To summarize, the WP's political platform does not have a significant resonance with that of the peripheral groups, masses, and SMEs. For the masses, the lack of emphasis on social provision fails to address the significant needs of the poor. Instead, the more substantial social provision of the MB has made that party more relevant to the needs of the peripheral masses. Importantly, peripheral business owners are not happy with the façade of economic liberalization, the causes of which are beyond a single policy area, be it democracy, Islam, or the economy. Also, unlike how the WP reduces all problems in the liberalization process to a simple case of "corruption," peripheral business owners view the problems of the liberalizing economy from a wider perspective. A comprehensive system of structural change is necessary for the peripheral business owners. As it stands, the WP's stance is more representative of the big businesses than it is of the periphery.

The MB, however, maintained and built on its sharp discourse against the regime. Specifically, the group was able to muster a broad coalition of social groups around its vague but accurate platform aimed at (1) the socioeconomic problems accumulated around the idea and practice of economic liberalization and (2) democratic problems. Unlike the complacency of the WP in trying to become a voice of democracy and moderate Islam, the MB tapped into the concerns of its perceived social base.

The evidence presented here on policy platforms of the WP and policy preferences of Egyptian business owners has a clear implication. Despite its moderate stance and extensive support for economic liberalization, the WP remains largely a marginal party in Egyptian politics. Some have called the party "elitist" and pointed to its "salon" character (Wickham 2004). The core supporters of the party gather around a nonprofit organization called Egypt for Culture and Dialogue (Misr lil-Thaqafa wal-Hiwar). By most accounts, the WP is a marginal party "without a mass base" (Wickham 2004, 223). Before the revolution in 2011, the party's support was estimated not to exceed a couple of percentage points at best (R. Habib, Howeidy, Hamid, Farid, and Al-Anani interviews, 2008). In the 2011–12 parliamentary elections, the WP received 3.7 percent of the votes and 2 percent of the seats. The fundamental reason for this electoral failure is the failure of the

WP to align itself with its target audience on the basis of the nature of economic liberalization that has taken place in Egypt, that is, crony liberalization. Although various liberalization reforms were largely implemented over the course of the last three decades in Egypt, they failed to create a strong support base for the WP; SMEs did not register much growth or expansion, and the population at large did not benefit from liberalization at all. Thus, the WP's conciliatory and affirmative position on liberalization and its nonconfrontational discourse do not speak to the peripheral groups, who instead choose to support the Islamist MB for its critical discourse on the economy and the state.

The MB remains the major "dynamic socio-political force" in Egypt after phases of repression and change (Stacher 2002). Others have called the group "the nation's only real political party" (Shehata and Stacher 2006). After the 2005 parliamentary elections, the MB held one-fifth of the seats in the Egyptian parliament, the People's Assembly, with eighty-eight deputies. This made it by far the largest opposition group in the parliament. While all other secular opposition parties in the parliament held about 10 percent of the seats in total, the National Democratic Party representing the Mubarak regime controlled the remaining 70 percent. At the 2011–12 elections, the MB's 37.5 percent vote share translated into 44.9 percent of the seats in the parliament, making it the plurality winner by almost twenty percentage points. It is important also to keep in mind that these figures from the first post-Mubarak elections should be regarded as tentative indicators and not absolute markers of societal popularity.

Post–Arab Spring Egypt

The Middle East, since late 2010, is going through one of the most tumultuous phases of its recent history. Revolutions, civil wars, and electoral fraud highlight the news from the region on a regular basis. Islamists are part of the discussion in virtually all cases. My natural inclination is to evaluate these developments through the theoretical lenses presented in this book. Hence I ask, does the rise of the MB to the power and its later removal suggest a direct refutation of social theory of Islamist moderation theory I introduce in this book? In what follows, I will address this question in light of post-2011 developments in Egypt.

As far as Islamists are concerned, the key question revolved around the impact of Islamists on the fate of the revolution. Two basic positions exist on this point: By pushing for a conservative or theocratic agenda, Islamism will lead to an "Islamic winter," or Islamism is "the first genuine expression of popular sovereignty" (Pecastaing 2012).

The MB's initial hesitancy to join the ranks of Tahrir protesters at the end of 2010 gave way to tacit approval for individual members to flock to the square as the protests continued (El Sherif 2011; Al-Awadi 2013). Later on, the MB offered its organizational prowess in the service of Tahrir demonstrators (Farag 2012). On February 11, 2011, the Supreme Council of the Armed Forces (SCAF) announced Mubarak's departure, suspended the constitution, and took over power in a transitional capacity (Brown 2013, 2). The military, for the most part, kept a low profile in the aftermath of the February 11 announcement until the 2013 coup. The military's early public quietism emanated from its ability to control, influence, and manipulate the government in the early postrevolutionary period and a desire to ensure that the military was not associated with the Mubarak regime. Ultimately, this would allow the military to appear more democratic and legitimate in the eyes of the protestors (Masoud 2011; Ashour 2012).

In this transitional period (early 2011), amendments in the political parties law paved the way for new political parties to form. Simultaneously, restrictions on "religious contention within the state" were also lifted (Brown 2012b, 535). Soon after, the MB established its own political party in April 2011: the Freedom and Justice Party. Early signs from the party and the MB itself indicated that the party was not planning on dominating other parties or on securing the presidency (Brown 2012b, 545), but rather on coordinating with them in order to ensure a positive effect in Egypt's political landscape. This was, in part, a reflection of the "pluralism" inherent in the revolution, of which the MB was merely one element (Masoud 2011). Yet the "electoral ambitions" definitively undermined the early statements by the group (Brown 2012b, 545).

The MB was divided on how to proceed in the aftermath of the revolution. The "reformists," or the youth, as it is sometimes referred to, within the MB preferred a greater level of cooperation with liberals and seculars to put pressure on the military to usher in democratic reforms while the conservative-dominated Guidance Bureau of the MB chose to align the group with the SCAF to gain tactical advantage in the upcoming elections (El Sherif 2011, 359). The reformists' search for a "secular common ground" with non-Islamists found no resonance among the conservatives (Farag 2012, 219).

Once again, one of the key manifestations of the lack of moderation for Islamist movements and parties was the unwillingness to separate the MB from the new Freedom and Justice Party (FJP). The old guard, or the conservatives, within the MB found ways to keep the party "on a very tight leash" and maintain organizational control over the FJP (Brown 2012b, 547). The self-perception that the MB is "greater than a party and less than a state" allows the organizational leadership to project the "totality" of Islam as the guiding principle for the party, thereby subduing the party to the wishes of the MB organization (El Sherif 2011, 360). In the words of Brown, "The movement's approach had always been to assert that all of these realms were within its purview, that none should be sacrificed for another, and that the various activities are complementary products of a single vision of a reformed individual, family, and society" (Brown 2012b, 545).

The timing of the first parliamentary elections helped well-organized groups, particularly the MB, to gain advantage over other revolutionary groups and dictate the terms of the constitution drafting process. SCAF's eight-point proposed constitutional amendment received 77 percent approval from Egyptians on March 19, 2011, paving the way for the parliamentary elections to be held early and for the new parliament to form a constitutional drafting body. Of note, the MB (along with other Islamists) successfully turned the referendum into "a matter of religion" by suggesting that "approving the amendments was virtuous and would please God, and anyone who rejected the amendments was evil." In the process, the MB also worked closely with Salafis and utilized mosques extensively.[50] The preservation of Article 2[51] in the amendments was a key motivator for many in the conservative fold (Farag 2012, 218). The fact that Islamists such as the MB could be better organized for early elections and might use this opportunity "to erect, if not a theocracy, then a deeply illiberal democracy" constitutes the primary concern underlying liberals' skepticism of the Brotherhood (Masoud 2011, 121).

In the months leading to the parliamentary elections of 2011–12, the MB markedly changed its stance on the revolutionary legacy by contesting a much larger number of seats than it had suggested early on. As a result, the secular members of the Democratic Alliance for Egypt (to which the MB belonged) left the alliance prior to elections.[52] The parliamentary elections of 2011–12 gave Islamists a major victory. The Democratic Alliance led by the FJP won 37.5 percent of the votes and 235 seats out of 498 elected deputies (47 percent); the FJP's own share was 213 seats (42 percent). The Islamist bloc led by the Salafist Al-Nour Party received 27.8 percent of the votes and 123 seats (24 percent). Collectively, MB- and Salafi-led blocs won more than 60 percent of the votes and 70 percent of the seats in the parliament, a major victory by all indicators. Particularly, the FJP's electoral success is partly attributable to the idea that the MB organization appeared as a "credible" party (Roy 2012).

Following the parliamentary elections, the Constitutional Court dissolved the parliament on June 14, 2012, on the grounds of bias in election laws in favor of party candidates as opposed to independents for the parliament to be reinstated by the president on July 8 (Al-Awadi 2013). In the midst of discussions on the role of the military in the impending Egyptian democracy,[53] Mohamed Morsi, one of the top leaders of the MB, assumed the presidency on June 30. Morsi came to power on the heels of the first democratic elections in Egypt in decades, following Mubarak's ouster. The MB's decision to field a candidate in the presidential election was also a surprise, coming in repudiation of earlier statements by the group against it (Al-Awadi 2013, 545). At the time, no one anticipated the series of decisive actions Morsi would take in the months following his inauguration. Arguably the most significant of Morsi's actions was the dismissal of Field Marshal

Tantawi, the defense minister, and Lieutenant General Sami Enan, chief of staff of the armed forces. This unprecedented move against the military by a civilian authority whose power rested solely on electoral support provoked conflicting reactions from different corners of the Egyptian society. Perhaps the most striking of these reactions came from the MB itself. In January 2013, a former top Brotherhood leader boasted, "It took you [Turks] twenty years to solve the problem of civil-military relations, but we did it in two years."[54] Later in the same year, the Egyptian military removed Morsi from power, forcing the MB to face one of the worst crackdowns on its organization since the 1950s. Additionally, Field Marshal Abdel Fattah al-Sisi took over the government, suspending the constitution, which had been drafted merely a year prior, and finally became the president in June 2014.

This brief but intense episode of Egyptian politics in those two years shattered any appearance of a genuine democratic transition. The initial euphoria surrounding the removal of Mubarak from power gave the impression that Egypt was headed toward a bright democratic future. Yet the structural problems of Egypt were largely bracketed. It was assumed that with Mubarak's departure most problems of Egypt would disappear, as if the whole political, economic, and military structure that enabled Mubarak to rule for such a long period of time was immaterial. As it turns out, the presumed rupture with the old regime and the military had never materialized.

Going back to the question posed at the beginning of this section, whether the MB experienced a change in its ideological platform, the MB's actions on three interrelated issue areas offer a good insight to whether the MB shows any sign of moderation and which factors underlie its ideological stance in the post-2010 period: competition with Salafis, the new constitution, and party policies.

Competition with Al-Nour

The notion that the MB's ideological stance not only deals with the religious sphere but extends to all areas of life determined the MB's dealings with other actors in the postrevolutionary period as well. Rather than choosing to deal with liberals and seculars on the principle of compromise, the MB, through its policies during this phase, helped move Islamist versus non-Islamist to the position of principal ideological conflict in Egypt. Despite little sympathy for Al-Nour, commitment to a conservative Islamist platform accounts for the MB's alignment with the Salafist Al-Nour Party on many issues and their competition for the conservative vote.

There are two dynamics at work here. On one hand, as Olivier Roy suggests, the Arab Spring veiled "large reservoirs of underlying conservatism" in the Arab world (Roy 2012, 9); this is most apparent in the Egyptian context. The MB understands well that to improve its popularity and win greater political influence inside and outside of the parliament, appealing to the conservative electorate is the key. The support base for all parties in the postrevolutionary era is "malleable and unpredictable," which contributes to the MB's urge to compete with the Salafis for the conservative vote, which is viewed as the safe bet (Lust, Soltan, and Wichmann 2012).

On the other hand, the democratic process comes with a straightforward implication. The MB will face stiff competition in its conservative Islamist ideology. The swift (and successful) entry of strictly literalist Islamist fundamentalist groups such as the Salafis into politics means that the MB can no longer "claim a monopoly over the expression of Islam in the political sphere" (Roy 2012, 6). Shadi Hamid offers a striking analogy: "They [the MB] have to compete with newly established Salafi parties that believe in a strict, literalist Islam, producing a 'Tea Party effect' where the center-right is dragged further rightward."[55]

Put differently, the fact that the MB is "politically pragmatic and fully capable of embracing the give and take of democratic life" (Norton 2012) or that the group increasingly embraced pragmatism and avoided "religious and dogmatic propaganda" (Al-Anani 2012; Hamid 2011) does not prevent the MB from reading the political landscape correctly. As Hamid puts it in reference to Islamist conservatism in society, "If the popular demand is there, someone will need to supply it."[56] Hence the competition with the Salafist Al-Nour Party aims to up the ante on conservatism, not moderate politics, despite the fact that the MB values pragmatism and the democratic process in the aftermath of Mubarak's removal from power affords the MB the greatest inclusion in the political system since Nasser's time.

For MB leaders, the suggestions in the immediate postrevolutionary period about "a natural Brotherhood-Salafi alliance" are baseless. Nathan Brown, in this regard, agrees with such statements and argues that "on a societal level, the Brotherhood and the Salafi movements regard each other as rivals rather than partners" (Brown 2012a, 9). The MB and Salafis are "fated to be rivals" over the same constituency (Roy 2012, 12). Indeed, the social dynamics at play are confirmed by the MB's and its members' search for support in the post-2013 coup period, when the MB organization came under increasing pressure by the Sisi regime (Tadros 2015).

The 2012 Constitution

The 2012 constitutional drafting process and the new constitution proved to be among the best indicators of the dynamics of the MB's ideological stance. On one hand, the process allowed the MB to incorporate its vague approach to sharia and how it might be incorporated into the legal framework. On the other hand, it showcases the MB's distinct relationship with the Salafis in Egypt. Forming a formidable Islamist bloc within the Constituent Assembly, the MB-Salafi group was able to ignore secular concerns voiced on many issues (Casper 2013).

Despite its many criticisms by secular liberals, the 2012 constitution falls short of being the "blueprint for theocracy or for renewed dictatorship," as Marc Lynch puts it (Lynch 2013, 4). The constitution certainly features an uptick in reference to religious emphasis, yet the vagueness that envelops the MB's approach to the religion-state relationship characterizes it. Seven out of 236 articles include "an explicit reference to religion; a mere three refer to Islam" (Albrecht 2013). Of those that mention Islam, Article 2 remains the same with the 1971 constitution ("Islam is the religion of the state and Arabic its official language. Principles of Islamic law [sharia] are the principal source of legislation").

Article 4 of the constitution stipulates that the state-supported Al-Azhar University in Cairo should function as a consultative authority: "Al-Azhar ulema are to be consulted in matters pertaining to Islamic law." Despite this boost in Al-Azhar's seeming authority, no specific mechanism for such consultation is laid out.

Article 219 of the constitution aims to clarify the language in Article 2 as to what constitutes "principles of Islamic Sharia." The article states, "The principles of Islamic Sharia include general evidence, foundational rules, rules of jurisprudence, and credible sources accepted in Sunni doctrines and by the larger community." Article 219 maintains the basic vagueness in approach to Islamic law. Although it does serve Salafi insistence on elaborating further what is meant by "principles" in Article 2, it brings in new questions and uncertainties. While further specification is welcomed by Salafis, others stipulated that Article 219 has "no actual effect"[57] because it was not clear who would decide on these sources, Al-Azhar or the Supreme Constitutional Court (a secular and liberal legal institution with no religious law background). Rachel Scott puts it thusly: "Calls for the enforcement of sharīʿa are often unclear about the kind of institutional structure that would regulate the interpretation of sharīʿa. Who would be responsible for the interpretation and application of sharīʿa in the context of the modern Egyptian nation state? Such questions relate to the issue of how the Muslim Brotherhood constructs and defends religious authority when they present their proposal of an Islamic state" (Scott 2012, 132). This uncertainty is also supported by the MB's ambiguous, or confusing, attitude toward sharia provisions: "Contrary to the mentioned assumptions, the Muslim Brotherhood tends toward preserving existing institutions. This includes retaining al-Azhar as the representative body of religious authority, at the same time as keeping the Supreme Constitutional Court as final interpreter of the sharīʿa provision of the Egyptian Constitution (in Article 2). On the other hand, there are also controversies within the Brotherhood about the role of the 'ulamāʾ of al-Azhar vis-à-vis the Supreme Constitutional Court, a question that also occupies the Azharites themselves" (Scott 2012, 131).

Overall, it would be fair to suggest that the 2012 constitution failed to provide "a common platform" to carry on with the ideals of the 2011 revolution (Pioppi 2013, 62). The MB's "go-it-alone" attitude, which undermines compromise and the creation of a shared framework for people of various ideological stripes, and the disproportionate influence Salafis wielded in the drafting body are the main reasons for this failure.

Muslim Brotherhood and Freedom and Justice Party Policies

The MB, and the FJP, emphasized "political reform, education and social services, and economic development" in their discourse during this episode (Brown 2012b, 547). The MB did not have an extensive opportunity to deal with actual policy issues during its brief stint in parliament and in the presidency, with the exception of very urgent issues that required immediate attention, usually economic in nature.[58] Overall, however, we can observe that Morsi's rule was marked by poor economic performance, exclusion, and alienation (Tadros 2015).[59] To be fair, Morsi also faced insurmountable pressure from the international community and domestically (i.e., from the military, the bureaucracy, and the courts), depriving him of an opportunity to address Egypt's economic problems in a timely fashion.[60]

In this period, we do not observe a significant change in the MB's stance on the economy from its former position. The MB's stance on the economy has remained consistent, although many of its statements are vague and lack specific solutions to Egypt's economic woes. The priority, again, is addressing the ailing Egyptian economy with private economic investment and foreign investment. Following the revolution, the Egyptian economy has been thrown into an economic chaos, with dwindling foreign currency reserves and increased interest rates of Egyptian bonds, making it difficult to borrow funds. A large budget deficit, rising unemployment, and quickly deteriorating infrastructure made things worse (Pioppi 2013). During the brief tenure of the MB in power, many were concerned that the MB is ill equipped to handle economic crisis.[61] Businesses that were interested in investing in Egypt were put off by the "crony capitalism" that ran rampant in former Egyptian regimes, hindering investments in the country.[62]

In general, the MB wants a democratic state based on sharia law. Sharia remained a pillar of the FJP's platform, with references to the *umma* (the Islamic community) and democracy (Al-Awadi 2013, 544). There exists, at the same time, significant differences within the organization on how sharia law should influence Egyptian law. The MB has only vaguely addressed how it intends sharia law to influence general Egyptian law, and this has not changed over time. The main justification for promoting sharia law deals with national identity and culture: "Islamic Sharia is the most important component of the Egyptian personality, and the most important determinant of the Egyptian identity, since it is for

Muslims the true faith and religion, and for non-Muslims it is culture and equal citizenship." Similarly, the MB justifies it on the grounds that it will promote a fairer and more equal society.[63]

Egypt's Coptic Christians were concerned in this period that they would be marginalized and dominated by the MB and sharia law, while Western nations were concerned that implementation of the sharia law will "derail" liberal democracy in Egypt. An important aspect of the MB's stance on sharia concerns the "spreading and deepening" of the understanding of sharia to guide Egyptians, which reflects MB officials' disinclination to impose religious law against their will.[64] This position is essentially a reflection of the MB's uncertainty and vagueness as far as the implementation of sharia is concerned, as discussed in greater detail earlier in this chapter for the pre-2011 period. This approach is also reflected on the constitutional drafting process in which the MB was content with not "entrenching more robust language on Islam" (Brown 2012a, 11) and leaving the "religious agenda" fuzzy (Brown 2012b, 547). Nonetheless, the Salafis' potent presence in the political scene after 2011 challenged the MB's more lenient stance on Islamization of the state and society. The MB's competition with the Salafis for the conservative electorate further complicates how the MB caters to the societal demand on religious conservatism, further pushing the MB to "reassert their own presence throughout Egyptian cities, towns, and villages and reclaim the religious constituency they regard as naturally theirs" (Brown 2012a, 16).

Briefly, the MB (former president Morsi in particular) failed in undertaking economic policies to offer a smooth transition period and address the "dire socioeconomic situation," maintained its commitment to a conservative Islamist outlook while avoiding an explicit religious agenda, and acted in an exclusive manner that resulted in "Brotherization" of the state and ever-greater polarization of the society, especially in regard to other opposition groups that took part in the revolution (Al-Awadi 2013; Pioppi 2013; Tadros 2015). Indeed, the MB's "run-alone attitude" and failure to reach out to other groups led an otherwise extremely fragmented and divided non-Islamist opposition into an alliance, the National Salvation Front, under Mohamed el-Baradei, Hamdeen Sabahi, and Amr Moussa's leadership (Pioppi 2013, 61).

The revolution and its aftermath provide us with an invaluable opportunity to see the inclusion-moderation argument in action. If the argument holds, we should have observed discernible moderation in the MB's program or policies because the legalization of the movement and its ability to compete legally as a political entity and to assume governmental roles indicate ultimate inclusion in the political system. Neither the MB's rise to power nor its fall, however, suggests any implication on the group's political moderation or democratization. As I demonstrate previously, the MB's ideological stance or its policies show no signs of moderation during this time frame. By contrast, the MB chose to compete in the conservative political domain and alienate other non-Islamist actors in the postrevolutionary period.

My social theory of Islamist moderation, by comparison, captures this dynamic well. The political developments since late 2010 left the economy intact but impaired; there is no discernible progress in socioeconomic inequality, especially one that would benefit the core Islamist support base. In other words, the underlying conservatism of the Islamic constituency remained unscathed (hence the competition with Salafis). The basic implication of this constancy is that the MB's conservative Islamist ideology is bound to remain largely unchanged unless there is a corresponding change in the fundamental economic structure. Even if the MB remained in power and the 2013 coup did not materialize, we would not have observed a significant moderation or democratization in the MB's ideology.

Most recently, we observe that the MB organization is gradually veering in a violent direction. The shift in the leadership of the organization from the old guard to the younger members, close alliances with various Salafi figures, and explicit calls for "retribution" on the Sisi regime are indicators of a metamorphosis in the movement toward demoderation, not seen since the organization dissociated itself from Sayyid Qutb's radical ideology (Brooke 2015; Brown and Dunne 2015; Fahmi 2015; Tadros 2015). What we might be observing currently is likely a categorically different "exclusion" than one to which the inclusion-moderation hypothesis would apply. The Sisi regime does not only exclude the MB from the political structure but puts on an effort to completely eradicate the Brotherhood organization from the Egyptian landscape. Whether Sisi might succeed in his venture remains to be seen, yet crucially the MB's slow descent into violence represents more of a destitute attempt at "retribution" to the violent suppression perpetrated by the regime leading to hundreds or even thousands of deaths and many more imprisonments and less a shift in the ideological disposition of the organization to incorporate fundamental reorientation of the goals of the group.

To reiterate, Islamist parties' popularity in the post-2011 period has less to do with the external institutional environment that implies inclusion in or exclusion from the political system in Egypt and more to do with the socioeconomic layout of the society. It is true that conservative Islamist parties did have an advantage as far as their lopsided electoral victory in the 2011–12 elections is concerned, yet their dominance of moderate parties such as the Muslim democratic WP is so great that better organization is an insufficient explanation.

Given the WP's current platform, the chance that the WP will rise electorally in the short term is quite unlikely. On the one hand, with respect to the peripheral businesses, that is, SMEs, positive change toward greater integration to the global economy or opportunities to that effect is virtually nonexistent. On the other hand, the absence of compensation for those dislocated by economic liberalization in the WP platform undercuts the credibility of its economic program and is one of the key reasons why the party was not able to muster support from the masses. The party seems to only reappropriate Islamic charity with respect to social policy. By contrast the MB and Salafis understand well where the societal preferences lie and compete against each other in garnering a greater share of this Islamic constituency with a conservative political discourse.

5 Pathways from the Periphery
Competitive Liberalization in Morocco

THE MOROCCAN MUSLIM democratic party (MDP), the Party for Justice and Development (PJD), has been partly successful in garnering the support of the Islamic periphery via the Islamist Al-Adl wal-Ihsan (AWI). This has been largely due to the state of Moroccan economic liberalization, which, unlike that of Turkey, is far from being a competitive model. Even so, with the wide array of opportunities offered to smaller businesses and new actors in the economy, it proves to be more competitive than the Egyptian economy. This semicompetitive character of the Moroccan economy provides a suitable opportunity to observe the losers and winners of the liberalization process among the peripheral groups and the distinct political preferences of these groups. In Turkey and Egypt, distinct elements of the periphery were unified in their loss or gain as a result of the liberalization process, but in Morocco, as a result of this clear separation between the losers and winners within the periphery, we are able to observe societal support for Islamist and Muslim democratic parties that is distinct, yet comparable in size. The losers in the periphery, mostly the masses, identify with the Islamist AWI, whereas the relative winners of the periphery, that is, peripheral businesses, side with the liberal discourse of the Muslim democratic PJD. The result is a divided peripheral constituency, which weakened the PJD's electoral strength.

The Moroccan case makes a valuable analytical contribution to the theory developed in this book. It is a critical test of an alternative hypothesis, namely, of the impact of democracy on the rise of MDPs. In terms of popular support for MDPs, the contrast between Turkey and Egypt is often attributed to the difference in degree of their democratic governance. However, the case of Morocco allows me to eliminate a state's level of democratic governance as an alternative explanation—Morocco and Egypt have similar levels of political liberalization but varying levels of support for MDPs.

The remainder of this chapter is divided into five sections, the first of which provides a history on the development of the center-periphery division in Morocco and briefly discusses the effect of economic liberalization. The second section introduces the evolution of political Islam in the country, specifically in reference to Al-Adl wal-Ihsan and the rise of the PJD. In the third section, the political discourse of both political groups is analyzed. The fourth section makes a connection between the parties and the peripheral businesses—expressly, the political preferences of these businesses. The final section brings evidence for the relative standing of each party in the Moroccan society and concludes.

Moroccan Independence

Morocco became independent in 1956, ending its status as a French colony and protectorate. Prior to independence, however, the basic structure of the socioeconomic and political system for the postindependence Morocco had been slowly entrenched. At the time of French colonialism, the royal family was the central authority in Morocco and symbolically represented the unity of the nation, yet local administrative authorities, established by France, had a stronger grip on power than the monarch. Particularly in the first half of the twentieth century, the sultans were highly discredited in the eyes of Moroccans due to their complicity in the face of foreign occupation (H. Munson 1993, 125). The status of the *makhzen* as the true center of power was only established in the struggle leading up to independence (Cammett 2007, 82).[1] Nationalist groups, at the forefront of the struggle for independence, increased their loyalty to the king over time as a genuine "symbol of the Moroccan nation" on the path to independence. Additionally, the triumphant return of Mohammed V from exile in 1955 was a particularly decisive moment (Shahin 1997, 34; H. Munson 1993, 125; Bendourou 1996).

As in the case of Egypt, the economic relationship between Morocco and France, and more broadly between Morocco and Europe, helped in the creation of a privileged class of merchant businessmen who were, for the most part, protégés of European consulates in Morocco. Among the privileges enjoyed by this merchant class were exemption from "Islamic market taxes" due to their extraterritorial status, elite educational opportunities for the families of these merchants, and agriculture and industry investment by the colonial administration (Cohen 2004, 38–41). Yet this favored status was not enjoyed exclusively by the merchant class; the rural elite also shared in this privileged access to resources during the colonial period because Morocco, with its agricultural economy, provided rich agricultural production resources for the French administration. Not surprisingly, the French returned the favor to these two classes by offering them greater privilege. The colonial experience in Morocco also helped in the emergence of a very small group of businessmen working in industry, although an overwhelming majority of industrial business activity during this period was directly controlled by the French colonial power.

Along with the merchant class, these business owners were called the "Fassi" entrepreneurs and families. In the earlier part of the twentieth century and following independence in 1956, these Fassi elite dominated the economic life in Morocco. Although these elite families were not necessarily from Fes (the former capital and the traditional center of power in Morocco), they had privileged access to political and economic power. As John Waterbury expresses, being Fassi is "a frame of mind" and depends on one's family and origins.[2] Alongside the convergence of the economic interests of this class of business owners, their sociocultural background and goals began to show coherence as well. In the words of Shana Cohen, "Social and cultural modernization, as well as the common goal of national independence, brought more coherence and structure to the elite as a social group. The older, prestigious families of Fes sent their children to the same elite French schools and used advantageous marriage alliances among themselves to promote political and business interests, setting up the kind of interlaced political and corporate networks that would govern independent Morocco" (Cohen 2004, 41). Eventually, Fassi elite would form the core of the Istiqlal Party (Tessler 1982, 39).

The homogeneity of economic and sociocultural interests eventually led this group of Fassi business owners to establish a common nationalist front in the struggle against French colonialism as the 1950s approached. The Fassi business owners' goal in their anticolonial struggle was twofold. As their principal concern, they wanted to achieve an independent Moroccan state—a desire shared with most other Moroccans. In a second and more self-interested way, however, they fought against "French capital and for control of domestic industry and commerce" (Cammett 2007, 85; Cohen 2004, 41). The increasing favoritism offered to French businesses during Morocco's time as a French protectorate helped the native elite unite against the French administration.

The aftermath of World War II brought a global wave of anticolonial movements, and the end of French colonialism in Morocco was no exception. The struggle for independence was a collaborative effort, involving several social segments of the Moroccan society, including Fassi elite business owners, the monarchy, and the Istiqlal Party.[3] The postcolonial structure was developed under the shadow of the influential actors of the independence struggle by utilizing the preexisting state apparatus and policies. Although the initial years of the independent Moroccan state were fraught with conflict between the Istiqlal Party, which favored a symbolic role for the king, and the monarchy, which was intent on eliminating any viable alternative to its power, Hassan II's reign (1961–99) effectively resolved the conflict between these two parties (Bendourou 1996, 109; Waterbury 1970, 268).

After independence, King Mohammed V ignored calls from opposition groups to transform the political system into a more pluralistic and modern polity, and instead consolidated his power, creating a constitutional monarchy. Patronage networks and clientelism became the cornerstones of the "new" system. Waterbury, in regard to those assuming power after independence, notes the following: "They have taken up the old defense of patrimony, not for their fathers but for their own account. Yet the result is the same. With a modern veneer they have adopted the tried and true techniques of building clientele groups and alliances with patronage, encouraging far-reaching systems of mutual obligation, and utilizing their power for defensive purposes" (Waterbury 1970, 110). Nonetheless, the *makhzen* allowed multiple parties to function in the political system, a move Cammett considers aimed to preclude the "rise of a single influential body that could capture mass allegiance" (Cammett 2007, 83).

Mohammed V, in an effort to undercut the power of the Istiqlal Party and the Fassi elite associated with it, diverted early investment funds to agricultural sectors and thus ensured the support of the rural elite. As a skilled politician, Hassan II (who rose to power in 1961, succeeding Mohammed V) continued the policy of Mohammed V and tried to court rural elite and the military to his rule. He did so in various ways such as through the allocation of former French properties and through his economic policies, that is, favorable tariffs and monopolies (Cohen 2004, 44). Hassan II also revived the waning religious legitimacy of the monarchy to secure his rule (Cohen 2004, 38; Shahin 1997, 31).[4] This was also a move to undercut the powers of potential sources of dissent, including the ulama (Islamic scholars) and Sufi orders. The borders of the center and the periphery of the new Moroccan political economic structure thus were demarcated in the early postindependence period. The king, as in many other countries throughout the Middle East, forced his dominance in the religious sphere by directly controlling the public display of Islam. The extent of this religious control is so vast that even Friday sermons are made in the name of the king (Burgat and Dowell 1997, 169).

Eventually, the new political economic structure proved to be quid pro quo for the leaders of the Moroccan independence; some Moroccans were more equal than others. After the early 1960s, the Fassi elite constituted what Cammett calls "the embryo of a cohesive indigenous industrial bourgeoisie" (Cohen 2004, 44). Through various means such as intermarriage, education, and commerce, the core of the postindependence center of political and economic power remained intact. To use Waterbury's term, the rise of a "state bourgeoisie" was assured (Waterbury 1991).

The special relationship between the political and nonagricultural economic elite was entrenched in two ways in the postcolonial period. First, members of Fassi families cultivated good relationships with the political elite, enabling the former to obtain "key positions in the administration, national banks, parastatal organizations, and producer organizations" (Cammett 2007, 85). Second, economic policies were crafted to "appease a small network of elites" (Cohen 2004, 43). While favorable economic policies were partly the undertaking of the political elite in an effort to cultivate a local business class to forge economic development and modernization in a newly independent Morocco, they were also greatly helped by the new Fassi members of the political elite. The extent of informal networks between the political and economic elite was such that the boundary between the two was only "theoretical" and blurry at best. Such "dense" networks led to favorable policies in many forms. Protective trade policies, government contracts, import licenses, and easier access to bank credit were virtually guaranteed for the Fassi elite (Cammett 2007, 86).

The weight of the royal family in the economy was sizeable and complementary to that of the Fassi elite. The king is the largest businessman in Morocco. For example, Omnium Nord Africain (ONA) is the largest holding company in Morocco, with more than 25,000 employees and activities ranging from banking to mining and tourism. The royal family is the largest shareholder of the company and thus is effectively in control of it. This economic weight of the king was also reinforced by the fact that Hassan II was a peer of the Fassi elite in terms of education, culture, and social relations (Waterbury 1970). Therefore, a small core of political and economic elite in postindependence Morocco tightly controlled economic power.

A local Moroccan industrial bourgeoisie slowly arose, beginning in the early 1960s. These industrial producers in sectors such as textiles, food, and construction served exclusively the domestic market. Investment in these sectors was also in line with an import substitution industrialization policy. "Built-in consumer demand" and "state incentives" were key elements of private investment in these sectors (Cammett 2007, 89). Compared with Egypt and Turkey, Moroccan industrialists were in an advantageous position in the postindependence period. Whereas in Egypt (in the post-1970s) and Turkey (until 1980) industrialists enjoyed a good relationship with the political elite and enjoyed their support, in Morocco, industrialists were able to cultivate the sociocultural ties they established in the pre- and postliberalization periods for exclusive and favorable policies. In addition, the Fassi elite "leveraged their importance in the nationalist movement to penetrate the state and influence economic policy" (Cammett 2007, 89).

Economic policy pursued by Morocco in the postindependence period is illustrative of the preferred status of the Fassi elite as part of the center. Beginning in the late 1950s, trade policy progressively changed to erect trade barriers in order to shelter local producers from international competition, and thus, by the end of the 1960s, trade protection was in full swing in Morocco. Similarly, other economic policies were developed with the intention of nurturing a native industrial business class. For example, a regressive tax system was adopted to facilitate transfer of wealth to the wealthy: "Tax collection acted as a simple change of rapport of forces at the interior of the old system: the traditional bourgeoisie assuming the advantage at the expense of the army, the city [business elite] at the expense of the rural areas [rural elite]" (Laroui quoted in Cohen 2004, 40). Policies such as "tax exemptions, incentives, and subsidies" accumulated to surpass public spending on social programs, and were devised to transfer public funds to a particular class of people, that is, the Fassi elite (Cammett 2007, 92). As a result, the exclusive interest of the Moroccan political elite in promoting the economic interests of the Fassi elite led to two problems not only unique to Morocco but also pervasive in the rest of the developing world: "Both equity and the trajectory of economic development suffered from the control of the commercial and landed elite, who were relatively uninterested in and unmotivated by the potential of significant industrialization" (Cohen 2004, 43).

Protective economic policy was entrenched in the early 1970s following a series of policies designed to promote the private sector. Among such policies were import duties, currency appreciation, and import licenses. Most importantly, however, the Moroccan government implemented a policy called "Moroccanization." The policy aimed to transfer majority ownership of foreign companies to Moroccans in order to enable a greater percentage of Moroccans to "share in" Morocco's wealth. In this, French companies were the primary target of the government, a legacy of the colonial past. According to various legal regulations undertaken in the early 1970s, Moroccan nationals were to hold at least 50 percent of "capital and managerial positions for any given commercial, financial, or industrial firm." Moreover, under this policy, Moroccans were the only individuals allowed to fill executive positions.[5]

The Moroccanization policy did not serve its intended goal of encouraging "middle-class" ownership. Instead, the existing socioeconomic cleavages were intensified; those who benefited most from this policy were already well off. Shana Cohen notes, "Although the middle class profited from this decade of phosphate boom and debt accumulation [the 1970s], Moroccanization itself reinforced the economic and political resources of the Moroccan bourgeoisie more than it promoted greater equity. High-level administrators and wealthy businessmen took advantage of international and domestic connections to secure access to capital and the sale of shares in the companies themselves" (Cohen 2004, 45). In effect, the process of Moroccanization led to the increased concentration of capital in the hands of "prominent families" who owned "a cluster of companies linked by financial and personal relations as well as their relationships to the same decision-making center" (Cammett 2007, 95). These "prominent families" lobbied the king and his advisors, successfully, for the inclusion of the private sector, when in the early phases of the Moroccanization policy, the potential beneficiaries were limited to only the public sector. Hence some in Morocco have called the policy "Lamranisation" and "Larakisation" after two such prominent families (Cammett 2007, 96).

In the meantime, two failed coup attempts in 1971 and 1972 by officers with "rural origins" alerted Hassan II to the need to secure his rule by way of repositioning himself vis-à-vis domestic actors. Hassan II responded to this threat by first strengthening his alliance with the urban Fassi elite, much to the dismay of the rural elite. Partly, the shift from a rural to an urban support base was due to land distribution. In the next few years after the coup attempts, the policy of land distribution gained momentum, weakening the rural elite. In one single year (1972), land distribution surpassed that of the previous sixteen years of the postindependence period, combined (Cammett 2007, 96). This shift proved to be the most notable indication thus far that the rural elite no longer enjoyed the advantageous position of the postindependence period in relation to the urban elite. The urban elite, as a result, reinforced its position as the most prominent domestic group. Second, Hassan countered the rural threat by "occupy[ing]" the army with the newly emerging issue of the Western Sahara (Cohen 2004, 66). Although it is not clear whether Hassan II honestly intended to tie the hands of the military with this issue or whether he was, in actuality, a believer in it, the fact of the matter remains the same: he clearly utilized the issue to his own advantage.

While developments in the economic realm were unfolding, sociocultural modernization and the creation of a national identity (as in Egypt and Turkey) were high on the agenda of the center of Moroccan society and politics, that is, the Fassi and political elite. Cohen notes, "Regardless of party affiliation and ideological stance, intellectuals and political leaders agreed that the objective of state intervention into education and employment was to establish a model of individual fulfillment. This model would bind together all those who followed it, encouraging the 'sameness' . . . that nationalist politicians and intellectuals regarded as critical to the popularization of the modern conception of citizenship" (Cohen 2004, 51). The Moroccan economic policy in the postindependence era involved heavy state intervention: political and economic power was controlled by a small but dominant group of political economic elite with close connections to the government.

The Origins of Economic Liberalization

The mid-1970s witnessed an expansion in public spending in Morocco; the phosphates industry accounted for most of the newly available budgetary funds. Following the sharp increase in the price of phosphates in the international markets, Hassan II increased the central government's budget accordingly for investments and public projects. However, when the price of phosphates returned to its previous level toward the end of the decade, it was evidence of the hard times to come (Denoeux and Maghraoui 1998, 56). By the end of the 1970s, the Moroccan government, under the pressure of the Western Sahara campaign and increasing domestic unrest, was still attempting to maintain the high levels of spending that the phosphates income afforded in the mid-1970s. As a result, the debt level increased substantially and the government "half-heartedly" implemented two short-term stabilization programs, in 1977 and 1980 (Cohen 2004, 65). At this time, the programs did not succeed for two main reasons, the first of which was the "lack of political will," which ensured that even the slightest societal resistance would hinder the complete application of the program. Additionally, the programs did not envision a fundamental change to the basic Import Substitution Industrialization–oriented structure of the economy; instead, demand management was the preferred method to deal with the crisis. Consequently, substantial decreases in government spending ensued as part of an economic restructuring program that begin in 1983 (Denoeux and Maghraoui 1998, 57).

By 1983, Morocco was effectively "bankrupt" (Denoeux and Maghraoui 1998, 57); hence this was, by all means, a critical and ideal time to restructure the economy. By then, Morocco's foreign exchange reserve was virtually depleted. At $11.8 billion, the foreign debt stood at 84 percent of the GDP and 300 percent of export earnings. Although Hassan II publicly endorsed and encouraged the implementation of the earlier stabilization programs in the late 1970s and the early 1980s, he was not able to succeed in securing such reform. The lack of enthusiasm on the part of the bureaucracy was characteristic of countries in a similar situation. Likewise in Turkey, for instance, the bureaucracy's lack of enthusiasm in the face of pressure for greater political and economic openness is regarded as an expression of the established interests' resistance to fundamental change. In Morocco, however, as the 1980s drew to a close, the king's persistence resulted in a change of attitude on the part of the bureaucracy, and other elements of the center, toward the recognition of the vital need for a restructuring of the economy.

In 1983, the Moroccan government adopted an "all-out liberalization drive," and this was to include every sector of the economy. At first, the reforms were recognized as ad hoc responses to the economic crisis that Morocco was experiencing, just as before: "It was not until 1988 that it became apparent that the reforms were guided by the embrace of a liberal economic agenda. . . . In his address to parliament in April 1988, the king presented the rationale behind Morocco's neo-liberal economic restructuring. That rationale was then quickly adopted by the state elite and used to justify subsequent policies" (Denoeux and Maghraoui 1998, 62). In the meantime, the ill-fated Moroccanization Law was also abrogated in 1989. In summary, the liberalization reforms that were undertaken by the government were to increase the level of competitiveness, efficiency, and export capacity of the Moroccan economy, and the private sector was to be an integral part of this economic transformation.

The Moroccan experience in economic liberalization is, by and large, regarded as a successful case, and this success can be attributed to several factors (Barkey 1995, 122). To begin with, the personal involvement of the king in the face of "a recalcitrant administration and political class" proved to be decisive (Denoeux and Maghraoui 1998, 62). Hassan II's persistence, coupled with the objective fact that Morocco was almost bankrupt, ensured that other actors would be on board during the reform process. The king's involvement was significant, for it minimized the Fassi elite's potential opposition to the end of a protectionist era. Similarly, societal dislocations were largely limited and hence did not create a strong and sustained popular opposition to liberalization reforms.[6] Finally, in contrast to several other countries in the Middle East, Morocco never implemented a fully socialist economic policy, which potentially facilitated its transition to a liberal economy (Barkey 1995, 122; Cohen 2004, 77).

For this study, the rise of a new and influential entrepreneurial class of SME owners is the most pertinent result of the economic liberalization reforms in Morocco. Largely by virtue of subcontracting relationships with European markets, this new class emerged in the immediate aftermath of the liberalization of the Moroccan trade regime in the early 1980s. As in Turkey, the export promotion strategy of the Moroccan government was certainly also a contributing factor in this development through the Export Code and the creation of the Moroccan Center for Export Promotion (CMPE). In this regard, Cammett's discussion of the textile sector, the sector that reaped the most benefits from trade liberalization, proves useful. Cammett finds that between 1983 and 1997, the number of apparel firms increased threefold from 264 to 738. The number of employees in the same sector increased more than seven times, from 16,397 to 116,923 (Cammett 2007, 97–98). While the figure on the number of firms clearly points to the greater involvement of non-Fassi peripheral business owners to the global economy, the figure for employees is an indication of the greater involvement of lower classes in a liberalizing economy by way of employment.

The new class of SME owners is much less dependent on the national market and state support than the Fassi elite, who were almost exclusively focused on the domestic market. Hence what happened in the global markets was more critical to the well-being of these new business owners. The perceived opportunities in the liberalizing Moroccan economy enabled them to take part in this new venture. Equally important, however, are the implications of this newfound opportunity over socioeconomic divisions. Although the preferences of SME owners will be discussed later in this chapter, it should suffice for the moment to say that a "level playing field" and "equality of opportunity" are the most oft-repeated demands of this new group of business owners—business owners who had formerly been disadvantaged by the exclusive structure of economic policies (Cohen 2004, 67). Indeed, the magazine *La Vie Economique* reports that this "new elite" was claiming "equality of opportunity" in the economy. Democracy is also quite fitting with the general outlook of this "new race" as it "demands a financial system which permits social mobility, in offering to savers different products and to entrepreneurs the financial resources responding to their needs" (*La Vie Economique* quoted in Cohen 2004, 67). Concomitantly, Moroccan SME owners resemble Turkish SME owners in terms of their modest origins, how they benefit from economic liberalization, and their political preferences.

In contrast to the Turkish case where MUSIAD became the institutional representative of SMEs, the Moroccan SME owners did not resort to a separate institutional body to voice their demands and concerns despite the fact that they had distinct interests and that these interests were not institutionally represented: "They [SME owners] do not appreciate the nepotism and obscure accounting of older Moroccan patrons, and certainly, they dislike the small circle of established businessmen, landowners, and intellectuals that govern political parties and exclude them from political power" (Cohen 2004, 68). Nevertheless, the Moroccan SMEs joined in the existing business associations and tried to open a new block within the organization to voice their concerns.

Political Islam in Morocco

Political Islam's ascent into the Moroccan political scenery occurred during the 1960s. Though far from being officially represented in the legal political space, as in many other countries throughout the Middle East at the time, Islamist groups made headway and slowly started building their societal support bases during this period. The rise of Islamist discourse was not divorced from the socioeconomic realities of the Moroccan society. Mark Tessler observes, "The religious revival is particularly pronounced among young urban men with some but not extensive modern education, and . . . their heightened religious consciousness derives in substantial measure from economic and political discontent. . . . And if their intensified interest in religion reflects a belief that modern and Western political formulae are inextricably linked to bourgeois privilege and exploitation of the masses in contemporary Morocco, then an Islamic revival clearly signified latent opposition to the present political system" (Tessler 1982, 60). Bourgat and Dowell agree with Tessler's observation and view "social demands" as the central line of Islamist discontentment with the regime in Morocco (Burgat and Dowell 1997, 142). Unlike in Egypt and Turkey, no single dominant Islamist group existed in Morocco, historically; instead, Islamic movements remained largely "fragmented" (Shahin 1997; Zeghal 2008). Despite efforts for unification at various times, distinct Islamist groups preferred to continue their mission on their own; hence competition has been more significant in Morocco (Hamzawy 2008).

The official title of the king as Amir al-Mu'minin (Commander of the Faithful) and its perceived control of the religious space in the country dominate the religious discourse in Morocco, which Clifford Geertz views as the "key institution in the Moroccan religious system" (Geertz 1968). Alaui kings have used religious legitimacy since their ascent to the peak of political power in Morocco three centuries ago. Their legitimacy is also underpinned by the fact that the royal family comes from the lineage of the Prophet. Even though the recourse to legitimacy has been constant to varying degrees throughout history, it has particularly been emphasized after Hassan II's rise to power and gained an institutional structure with state religious institutions serving to that end. Nonetheless, it is important to emphasize that Islam and Islamist groups in Morocco have had a notable and independent role aside from the king's monopolistic claim over the religious sphere.

From a comparative perspective, however, what happened in Morocco is not extraordinary. In Egypt, the secular political authority has tried to bring religion under its direct control since independence. In this regard, Al-Azhar University—traditionally, the bulwark of Sunni Islam worldwide—was put under state control; administration of the university is appointed by the state, and it is under the state's direct financial control. Similarly in Turkey, the secular regime established by Ataturk wasted no time bringing the official religious discourse under its direct authority. To this end, the caliphate was abolished in 1924 (a potential rallying point against the secular regime of Ataturk), and a new state institution was established instead, the Directorate of Religious Affairs (Diyanet Isleri Baskanligi). In all three countries, the official religious discourse failed to bring religious activism under complete control of the state. Socially strong Islamic movements, groups, and parties emerged to challenge the official discourse. As a result, the fusing of formal political and religious authority thus does not imply the effective centrality of both in the society.

Indeed, in Morocco the king's official religious discourse owes its existence in large measure to the king as a "strong man" and the government-controlled media's propaganda; hence there is no automatic and indispensable relationship between the official sanction over religion and the Moroccan people's perception of this official discourse.[7] Although the state strives to control the religious space and speak in the name of Islam, this effort largely does not resonate with the society. In the words of Bourgat and Dowell, "In spite of the specific character so often emphasized by the King in the 'religious field,' the Islamists appear undiminished as the most popular of its challengers" (Burgat and Dowell 1997, 181).

In what follows, I present a brief account of the trajectories of two contemporary dominant Moroccan Islamic groups: Al-Adl wal-Ihsan (Justice and Charity) and Harakat al-Tawhid wal-Islah (Movement of Unity and Reform). The PJD descends from the lineage of the latter group. The analysis in this section lays the foundation for a better understanding of each group's political discourse, which will be discussed in the following section.

Al-Adl wal-Ihsan

AWI, under the leadership of Sheikh Abdeslam Yassine, has been—for an extended period of time—both a major Islamist group and a major opposition group in Morocco. Even though most other political parties are formally part of the "opposition," what sets AWI apart from others is its direct opposition to the monarchy rather than the implicit or explicit recognition of it by all other parties. The origins of AWI date back to the early 1970s. At that time, Yassine was a member of a Sufi order called Qadiri Budshishi Tariqa (Zeghal 2008). Sufi orders oftentimes are not sympathetic toward political activism in Morocco or elsewhere. As one member of the order stated, "We do not have the pretension to change the world; all we want is to be left in peace to be able to educate and purify Moroccan society from within; we are against any political manipulation of religion; we are *turuqis* [brotherhood of followers], not Khomeinists" (quoted in Shahin 1997, 55). In the particular case of Budshishi zawiya, Yassine grew increasingly restless about the fact that the order did not stand up against the regime and "ask for justice" (H. Munson 1993, 163; Tlaidi interview, 2009) and as a result, eventually broke with the Sufi order in the early 1970s and set out a path for himself, enmeshing Islamist ideology with a Sufi background—a relatively unique configuration compared with other Islamist movements globally.[8] To this end, Yassine outlined his early political thought in his own books.[9]

The breaking point for Yassine and his embryonic movement was the "audacious" 1974 letter he penned to King Hassan II, titled *al-Islam aw al-Tufan* (Islam or the Deluge) (H. Munson 1993, 163; Willis 2004, 58). In his letter, Yassine advised Hassan II to be a just ruler and follow the examples set by virtuous leaders from Islamic history such as Omar bin Abdulaziz of the Umayyad Dynasty (ruled between 717 and 720).[10] King Hassan II, notorious for being heavy-handed against challenges to his rule and legitimacy, dismissed the letter at once and decided to take action against him. At first, Yassine was put in a mental hospital; later, he was put in jail and then on house arrest for the remainder of the period until Mohammed VI became the king in 1999 (Willis 2004, 58). Although the letter does not seem to show blatant opposition to the regime, Hassan II was likely offended by pervasive undertones that challenged his religious legitimacy. Yassine, essentially, accused Hassan II of using the religion to "camouflage" his "liberal" ideas (H. Munson 1993, 164). The movement's current spokesperson and the daughter of Abdeslam Yassine, Nadia Yassine, summarized her father's "symbolic action" as follows: "He [Yassine] thought that this [letter] is the end; he does that for God knowing that he is going to die right after it. They actually did not kill him, [which was unexpected] because the king was known for killing his opponents, systematically. Especially when the fight was about religious or spiritual legitimacy since he constructed all his power on this religious legitimacy. . . . It was a very dangerous discourse" (Yassine interview, 2009).[11]

Over the course of the next decade or so, Yassine tried to increase the popular base of his movement. In the late 1970s, he founded the organization called Usrat al-Jamaa. In the words of Nadia Yassine, it was just an "embryo" and an informal community. At this time, the community was formed around the movement's magazine *Majallat al-Jamaa* (Shahin 1997, 194). The legal formation of the association and the magazine appeared to contradict the conflict between the state and the movement, at least at first. Nadia Yassine accounts for this seeming contradiction by referencing Hassan II's political calculations: "You may wonder why the authorities allowed him [Yassine] to have a magazine right after he went out of a mental institution. In the meanwhile, there was the Iranian revolution. He [Hassan II] was very cunning, very politically cunning. So, he thought maybe it's better to know what is going on inside their minds, inside the minds of radicals [AWI], rather than have the surprise that the Shah had [in Iran]. So, he gave the permission for launching the magazine" (Yassine interview, 2009). In 1979, Yassine attempted to unify Islamic groups in Morocco, but he was unsuccessful. It was not until 1987 that his movement became a major political actor. The Moroccan government's increasing crackdown on the group seems to have worked to increase its publicity and popularity (Willis 2004, 58). In particular, when the government arrested the leadership of the movement during Majlis al-Irshad's meeting, the popularity of the group received a major boost (Tlaidi interview, 2009).[12] The year 1987 is also when the movement took the name Jamaat Al-Adl wal-Ihsan (Community of Justice and Charity) (Hamzawy 2008, 8). The regime and the movement, however, seem to be at odds on the legality of the group. The regime claims that the group is legally nonexistent because Moroccan authorities did not approve the association's paperwork. The group, in contrast, claims that according to the legal framework at the time of application, the association was legalized by the state when the authorities accepted its paperwork at the time of submission, which is supported with the receipt from the authorities. Nadia Yassine claims that it was only after the whole ordeal regarding AWI's official application that the state changed the regulations on associations, requiring a formal approval by the state following the submission of paperwork. Hence the regime's effort to apply the new law retroactively in the case of AWI is against fundamental legal logic, according to the movement (Yassine interview, 2009).[13]

A major development in the movement's historical timeline is the establishment of its "political circle," which some termed the "heart of the organization" (Cavatorta 2007). Even though Yassine's movement was political right from the beginning, the creation of a special body charged with political activities within the organization happened only in 1998. According to the officials in the movement, the rationale for the political circle is to present an alternative to the current system, a "backup plan": "The members who are involved in the circle are in charge of debating these issues, to propose alternatives, to create bridges with the civil society. Our basic theory is kind of radical, but the possible propositions are not radical. It is not possible to do anything with this system because it is locked" (Yassine interview, 2009).

When Mohammed VI was enthroned in 1999, succeeding his father, Hassan II, he ended the house arrest of Abdeslam Yassine—a move that was widely recognized as an effort to co-opt AWI. Against all odds, Yassine drafted another letter to the new king in 2001. This time, he explicitly called for Mohammed VI to return the wealth of his family to the poor of Morocco. Following the letter, the government intensified its stance against the movement to such an extent that it even disallowed the movement's annual youth summer camps. Despite state action against the AWI, the "open door" policy of the movement after 2002 drew a significant social base. This new policy essentially was a way to respond to the state's increasing containment of the organization, "a way to speak with people." It enabled the movement to receive thousands of people in members' houses and make documents and publications available for their review (Tlaidi interview, 2009), resulting in an expanded support base for AWI.

Despite its growing social base, AWI did not take part in Moroccan elections, in part due to its rejection of the monarchical regime, even though this could have opened the way to a possible governmental role. AWI demands that Islam have such a decisive role in society that the king's powers would, by all means, have to be revised in the event of an Islamic transformation. Hence this is a chief reason for their strong opposition to the regime as it currently exists. Essentially, AWI views the king's overtures to Islam with great suspicion. Nadia Yassine justifies their reservation to the system as follows: "We prefer to keep our strength; our strength is on the confidence of our people, their trust; we don't want to be puppets in the government. It is a big treason if we integrate when the system is locked in such a way" (Yassine interview, 2009). Participation in a regime characterized by the monarchy's tight grip on power thus would have constrained AWI's political scope for maneuver, and therefore it chose to remain outside of electoral politics in Morocco.

Along the same lines, AWI does not view the limited scope of reforms enacted by the king to be conducive to the model it sets forth, and therefore it does not formally participate in politics. Compromise in implementing the group's vision seems unacceptable to AWI, while it does not want to become complicit in a failed reform effort much like the Moroccan MDP, PJD: "If we do [participate], we will be like the PJD. PJD's members are very sincere, but when they enter the system, the little waves cannot stop the currents of the big river. They are obliged to play the game, and we don't want to play their [the regime's] game. We believe that the real opposition is to be out of the system. The little stack of dust that stops the machine. It is the only way to counteract. We are not actually doing it, but we are trying" (Yassine interview, 2009; Cavatorta 2007). Nonetheless, the group increased its political activism and involvement in Moroccan political life significantly. In recent years, AWI participated in demonstrations such as the ones in front of the Moroccan parliament and the mass rally in Casablanca in March of 2000 against the reforms of the family code (Willis 2004, 58).

In particular, AWI began publishing regular political reports on issues of interest such as health care, education, and the economy. The movement justifies its increased involvement and activism in politics in recent years as an effort to demonstrate that it is "ready" for power with alternative policies. Abdel Wahed Al-Mutawakkil, who heads the political circle of AWI, sees no inherent contradiction between the expression of political ideas and the lack of participation in the formal political space:

> To participate in the official institutions is one thing, and to be there, to work, to express your ideas, your views regarding many issues, is something different. So, we are present. All the people and all the observers know that Al-Adl wal-Ihsan [AWI] is there and many people think that if they are talking about real change in Morocco, they cannot do it without Al-Adl wal-Ihsan [AWI]. . . . We are working, we are trying to do our jobs, preparing ourselves, trying to enlarge our following. And, waiting for the opportunity when it is possible to really participate, and when our participation really has a meaning and impact. Not just to participate in some institutions that have no real power at all. (Al-Mutawakkil interview, 2009)

In essence, the principal reason for AWI's critical stance on the regime, that is, the monarchy, has not changed, despite its vocal role in national political discourse. Also, no real change is imminent in the movement's political discourse because the movement leadership firmly opposes any and all electoral participation as long as the monarchy controls power.

However, the increased vocal expression of views on the part of AWI seems to send a different signal to others in Morocco. Bilal Tlaidi, a member of the PJD's national congress, views the change as a strong indication that AWI is slowly shifting toward the PJD's position, that is, participation in the existing system:

> AWI recently started to talk about public policy; this is the first time that AWI talk[ed] about public policy. That means that they are focused on public policy. Earlier, they were saying that there is no difference between the regime and its policies; we don't need to criticize the policies of the regime because our problem is with the regime. Now, they criticize the policies; there is a change. They used to say, "When there is milk, you cannot separate the milk from the cow, because it's from the cow. If the milk is not good, that means the cow is not good." Also in 2009, they started to talk about the use of the language of "together," which means we cannot have the solution unless we cooperate with other parties and groups. (Tlaidi interview, 2009)[14]

The creation of the political circle in 1998 and the antisystem stance of the movement also make sense from an organizational and mobilizational perspective. Such a strong political stance "allowed Al Adl to differentiate itself from PJD, to recruit young members interested in standing up to the regime." The competition with the PJD is even more evident in AWI's mobilization drives after each election (Spiegel 2015, 9).

When we look at whether the movement has been successful in its political mobilization, it is fair to suggest that the group is an important political actor. As an example of the group's societal influence, Khalid Bekkaoui and Ricardo René Larémont cite the following rallies and how many people attended these events:

- February 1991: Tens of thousands of AWI members marched to protest the Gulf War in Rabat.
- December 1998: Approximately 100,000 protestors demonstrated against Anglo-American strikes against Iraq.
- Summer 1999: Tens of thousands of young members of AWI camped at beaches.
- September 2000: Approximately one million people participated in a rally led by AWI in support of Second Intifada.
- March 2000: Approximately one million people marched in defense of the Moroccan family. (Bekkaoui and Larémont 2011, 45–46).

Overall, AWI is formally banned yet tolerated by the monarchy, therein enabling the group to take part in social and political life, like the Muslim Brotherhood's (MB) murky status in Egypt before 2011. It is this social and religious activism that yields strong societal support for AWI, reinforcing its political discourse. Despite its strong criticism of the monarchy, AWI does not condone the use of violence; rather, the movement undertakes its political activism through "legalistic and pacifist action" (Amghar 2007). Because AWI attracts a large support base, regardless of the fact that it does not participate in electoral politics, the Moroccan MDP, the PJD, as a result, suffers from a lower support base, especially among the lower classes, as we will soon see.

The Movement for Unity and Reform and the Party for Justice and Development

Al-Shabiba Al-Islamiyya (the Islamic Youth Association), the predecessor of the Party for Justice and Development (PJD) and the movement associated with it, the Movement for Unity and Reform (MUR), was established in 1969 under the leadership of Abdel Karim Muti' and Ibrahim Kamal. Sayyid Qutb, the Egyptian MB's prominent and highly controversial leader in the 1950s and 1960s, greatly influenced Muti' early on, to such an extent that Muti' viewed Moroccan society in a state of *jahiliyya* (pre-Islamic ignorance), legitimizing the use of force to reach the goal of an Islamic state if necessary. Similarly, political participation was viewed as un-Islamic (Tlaidi interview, 2009; Shahin 1997, 182). In the aftermath of the assassination of a socialist daily's editor, Omar Benjelloun, several members of Al-Shabiba were implicated in the event, including Muti'.[15] The king took decisive action by banning the organization in the late 1970s and persecuting many members (Wegner and Pellicer 2009, 159).[16] Al-Shabiba's leader Abdel Karim Muti' left Morocco in 1975, but maintained its control over the group for several years to come (H. Munson 1993, 161).

Following the dissolution of the Islamic Youth Association, many in Al-Shabiba turned to a new and legal organization established in 1981 by the younger leaders of the group at the time such as Abdelilah Benkirane, Abdallah Baha, and Mohamed Yatim: Al-Jama'a Al-Islamiyya (the Islamic Group).[17] The formation of this new group entailed several revisions in the basic organizational structure, ideology, and practice. The most telling change was in the ideology, namely, the group's belief that although society had deviated from Islam in many ways, it was still Muslim, and thus not *jahili*. In this way, it is evident that this new group had broken away from Qutb's ideas and from its former leader Muti'. The group's new self-professed duty was "to contribute to the reform of the society and the state.... Its application of Islam is not complete. So, our duty is to push the decision makers to apply Islam step by step, not all at the same time" (Tlaidi interview, 2009). Eva Wegner and Miquel Pellicer note that Al-Jama'a's goals reverberated classical Islamist discourse: "According to a charter published in the late 1980s, the organization's goals were to renew the understanding of religion, to advocate the implementation of sharia law, to achieve a comprehensive cultural renaissance, to work on accomplishing the unity of Muslims, to confront ideologies and ideas which they believed were subversive to Islam, and to raise the educational and moral level of the Moroccan people" (Wegner and Pellicer 2009, 160).

The new organization's foundational principle complements the change in ideology. Unlike the discourse in the 1970s, Al-Jama'a officially recognized "the political and religious legitimacy of the monarchic regime" mindful of the recent history and its conflict with the regime (Wegner and Pellicer 2009, 160). The decision to remain within the legal framework of Moroccan politics is a natural extension of this shift in the group's foundational principle.

In another radical break with its past, Al-Jama'a deliberated on political participation in the current Moroccan political system. Although the notion of political participation was still viewed as un-Islamic (*haram*) by many members of the group, the leadership published a report called "The Paper of Political Participation." The report thoroughly explained the rationale behind political participation, which included the desire (1) to reach a wider population, (2) to break the "siege of secularists" who constantly pointed the legality issues of the group, and (3) to obtain parliamentary immunity for the group's leadership, which would ensure safety of *dawa* activities (Tlaidi interview, 2009).[18] It is clear that at this stage, the group is predominantly interested in safeguarding the religious mission (*dawa*) activities rather than achieving other political goals. Such a stance, ensuring their ability to spread *dawa*, fits squarely with an Islamist discourse.

The report also outlined potential strategies to realize this goal of political participation. Such strategies included establishment of a political party, alliance with an existing party, running as independents, and establishment of a pressure group. In the meantime, Al-Jama'a Al-Islamiyya changed its name to Harakat al-Islah wal-Tajdid al-Maghribiyya (the Movement for Reform and Renewal in Morocco) in a formal move to reassert its commitment to the rules of the political game in Morocco. This name change took place in 1992 (Shahin 1997, 191).

The Party for Justice and Development

The PJD followed a distinct route to its current platform as a moderate and Muslim democratic party compared with its counterparts in Egypt and Turkey. The PJD experimented in formal politics in different forms throughout the 1990s. The first initiative for a political party came about in 1992 when the group proposed the establishment of the National Renewal Party (Hizb Al-Tajdid Al-Watani). The government swiftly refused to grant license to the initiative (Mustapha El-Khalfi interview, 2009). Events unfolding in neighboring Algeria were one of the reasons for the refusal. The civil war that began in 1991 after the FIS's (Islamic Salvation Front) lead in the first round of parliamentary elections made the political situation untenable for Hassan II to allow an Islamist party at the time (Tlaidi interview, 2009).

Upon refusal by the government, the group sought an alternative mechanism for political participation without challenging the governmental decision on the issue. Instead of establishing a brand new party, the group resorted to joining an existing party's legal umbrella. After talks with parties such as the Istiqlal Party, the National Union of Popular Forces (Union Nationale des Forces Populaires, UNFP), and the Democratic Independence Party (Parti Démocratique et de l'Indépendance) failed, the Movement for Reform and Renewal concentrated its efforts to secure the cooperation of Abdelkarim Al-Khatib's moribund party, Mouvement Populaire Démocratique et Constitutionnel (Constitutional and Democratic Popular Movement, MPDC) (Desrues and Moyano 2001, 30; Tlaidi interview, 2009). Al-Khatib proposed three conditions for a potential merger between the two: the acceptance of the monarchy, denunciation of violence, and an Islamic identity. None of these constituted a problem for the movement, and it agreed to Al-Khatib's conditions. The merger would enable Al-Khatib's party to gain popularity once again and to revive its position in Moroccan politics, whereas the Movement for Reform and Renewal would have legal access to political participation (Hamzawy 2008, 8; Tlaidi interview, 2009). In 1996, the national congress of the MPDC convened following the agreement between the movement

(MUR) and the party (MPDC) to choose the new leadership cadre composed of both (El-Khalfi interview, 2009). In 1997, the MPDC participated in legislative elections, and won nine seats (Willis 2004, 55; Desrues and Moyano 2001, 30).[19]

The current form of the PJD was finalized in 1998 with a name change. Formerly a part of Al-Islah Wal-Tajdid (Movement for Reform and Renewal) and Mouvement Populaire Démocratique et Constitutionnel (Constitutional and Democratic Popular Movement), the new PJD made its political platform both substantively and substantially distinct from that of its predecessors. Islam became a "point of reference" for the party but not the central tenet of the party platform (El-Khalfi and Amara interviews, 2009). Emphasizing the pragmatism of the party, PJD parliamentarian and current minister of Industry, Trade, and New Technologies Abdelkader Amara maintains that the "idealist model" gave way to the current platform of the party in order to be able "to find solutions to the daily problems of citizens, especially in economy, social life, education, and health" (Amara interview, 2009). Another PJD official, Mustapha El-Khalfi, pointed out the "public policy framework" the party employed after 2002, underscoring the key role of the "functional separation between religious activities and political activities" (El-Khalfi interview, 2009).

While the movement's political opening unfolded, there were other developments on the *dawa* front. Throughout the first half of the 1990s, many Islamic groups across the country were having discussions on creating a union among themselves. The most tangible progress was achieved between two major groups in 1994: Harakat al-Islah wa al-Tajdid al-Maghribiyya (the Movement for Reform and Renewal in Morocco) and Rabitat al-Mustaqbal al-Islamiyya (the League of the Islamic Future). Although the discussions were proceeding positively toward a union, one issue remained contentious between the two sides. The league raised its concerns over the impending political merger between the Movement for Reform and the MPDC, arguing that the merger with MPDC would present them with a situation they had not negotiated in their unification discussions earlier. Against this, the Movement for Reform pressed its concern that it did not want to lose its unique opportunity for political participation when the circumstances were favorable. At the end of negotiations, with the exception of one group (al-Dawa of Fes), the league agreed to the union with the Movement for Reform and Renewal in 1996. The union led to a new name and the nation's largest Islamic movement at the time: Harakat al-Tawhid wal-Islah (Movement of Unity and Reform) (Tlaidi interview, 2009).

The PJD's platform evolved from political Islam toward a Muslim democratic platform in the post-1998 period. In 1998, the main discourse of the party was focused on issues related to Islamic identity and Islamization of the state and society, as we would expect from an Islamist discourse. Even though the separation of the political party from the main body of the Islamic movement was complete, functional boundaries between the two appeared to be less clearly demarcated. The 2002 and 2007 electoral programs were more successful in delineating the "public policy framework" that PJD officials underscored. The programs clearly demonstrate that "public affairs" and problems around corruption take precedence over issues of Islamic identity (*al-Huviyya al-Islamiyya*) (El-Khalfi and Tlaidi interviews, 2009).[20] Bilal Tlaidi, a member of the PJD's national council and a researcher on Islamic movements, sheds light on the party's internal discussions on this issue:

> [At an intraparty discussion in 2002,] they [party officials] evaluated the experience and they found that the PJD focused on Islamic identity, morals. The question arose "Are we an Islamic party, or a political party with an Islamic reference?" The PJD, in the final analysis, chose to be a political party with an Islamic reference. When you say an Islamic party, the issues of Islamic identity and morals should be the main priority for the party. When you say you are a political party with an Islamic reference that means the priority is public policy, but the solutions suggested by the PJD is based on Islamic values, not political Islam. (Tlaidi interview, 2009)

For party officials, the profound transformation of the party from its advocacy of political Islam to a party with an Islamic reference was reflective of changes taking place at the societal level. As former PJD leader Uthmani stated, "It is impossible for societal changes not to change parties" (Saad Eddin Uthmani interview, 2009). In essence, the change in the name of the party was more than a mere cosmetic change; rather, it was a fundamental reorientation. Others in the party confirmed, "In reality, what happened in 1998 was a change in the name of the party that reflects change in policy" (El-Khalfi interview, 2009). One of the female legislators from the PJD, Nezha El-Ouafi, underscored the changes taking place both in Morocco and the world, and the concomitant necessity for the party to transform itself in order to "keep up" with the changes in their own constituency (Nezha El-Ouafi interview, 2009). Major issues arising in Moroccan society included economic development, democracy, and social justice (Amara, El-Khalfi, and Uthmani interviews, 2009). Interviews with party officials make clear that the party put a careful effort in formulating the new platform, and the new party was the product of a serious effort to match the party program with people's preferences. In other words, it was the product of a shift from an "idealist" model to a "pragmatic" model (Amara interview, 2009). One PJD official noted, "As a political party we have to do our best in our programs to be close to the citizen and propose solutions to the daily problems. And we considered that it is a good jump from the view of Islamist movement to a political party" (Amara interview, 2009). Nonetheless, Islam continues to be one of the central tenets of the party, as it offers the identity and value base for the party: "And these two issues [justice and development] should be based on our Islamic authenticity. It [Islamic authenticity] is Islamic references, Islamic values, new interpretation of Islam that allow us to connect modernity with Islam" (El-Khalfi interview, 2009).[21]

The critical question is whether the new platform of the party, indeed, coincides with the preferences of the people. PJD officials claim it does. In particular, two critical groups constitute the target audience of the PJD. One group is the poor of Morocco, who are in need of "good governance to fight corruption and social justice," and the other group, the middle class, including SME owners, demands an "improved social and economic condition" in Morocco (Uthmani, El-Khalfi, Karbal interviews, 2009). Moreover, what brought these two distinct socioeconomic groups together was their shared identity and conservative values; the PJD's constituency thus included "the religious people in the society who are thinking that our party [the PJD] is not only a credible party, but a party that is defending Islamic values of the society" (El-Khalfi interview, 2009). The PJD, with its new platform, claims to have addressed major issues in Morocco while submitting itself to the values of the society. Very briefly, the new mantra of the party captures the sentiment of its own constituency while striving to be "a party of all Morocco": *Asalah, Adalah, Tanmiyah* (Authenticity/Origins, Justice, Development) (El-Khalfi interview, 2009).

An important aside must be made on the PJD's political participation, as it constitutes a critical distinction between the party and AWI. Although AWI criticizes the PJD for being part of the system with its political participation,[22] the PJD thus far has acted carefully to make a crucial distinction between two kinds of participation. For one, they are fully supportive of being part of the official opposition as a legal party and have competed in parliamentary and local elections since the mid-1990s. In addition, they repeatedly declined formal and informal invitations to be a part of Moroccan government at different times until very recently, recognizing an opportunity in the post–Arab Spring context. For example, in 1997 when Abderrahmane Al-Youssoufi invited MPDC (PJD's predecessor) to be part of the government led by Al-Youssoufi, the party turned down the invitation due to the uncertainty surrounding the true capacity of the new government "to change things." Instead, the party chose to be in the opposition while retaining a position of "critical support." Such a position would ensure that the party could "distance itself from possible failures and difficulties" of the new government (Willis 2004, 56). Similarly, following the 2002 general elections, the PJD decided to not participate in the government, as "the benefits of being the strongest opposition party outweighed any gains to be made by becoming part of a governing coalition" (Willis 2004, 73).[23] Had the PJD decided to take part in the government, it would have received six or seven ministerial posts in the cabinet (Wegner and Pellicer 2009, 165). To AWI's credit, however, the PJD emphasized the fact that its opposition was on specific policies and not "systematic" (Willis 2004, 73). Despite the party's refusal that it has been part of the system, in a circuitous way, it accepted the claim.

PJD Platform

Islam

The PJD's emphasis on Islam in its party discourse has decreased over time. The party programs from 1997 and 1998 put strong emphasis on "identity issues," envisioning a major role for Islam in political and social life, which ultimately made Islam the principal concern of the party. Hamzawy notes that between 1997 and 2002, PJD legislators brought up issues mostly related to Islam and Islamic identity such as "non-Islamic banking, alcohol consumption, Islamic education, immoral practices in the tourism industry, and reforming the cinema industry to ensure that it complied with Islamic teachings" (Hamzawy 2008, 12).

However, the 2002 electoral program downgraded identity issues in the platform and instead prioritized more socioeconomic and democratic problems in Morocco, according to El-Khalfi. Indeed, the policy agenda of the party prior to the 2002 elections reflects this change. Only one of the main policy issues is related to Islam, and the rest deal with the more immediate needs of the Moroccan society.[24] The transformation was complete with the 2007 platform, which was announced prior to the legislative elections that year. According to the program, Islam (*asalah*, "authenticity") as an element of the platform was discussed only after more pressing issues such as education, investment, and economic production. For El-Khalfi, the order of the issues as discussed in the electoral program was not a coincidence; it was a testament to the priorities of the party itself (El-Khalfi interview, 2009). Nonetheless, many seculars in Morocco continue to "think negatively of the PJD as a threat to their secular lifestyles," complained Driss Bouanou, the youth leader in the PJD (Bouanou interview, 2009). This skepticism underscores the depth of the divide between the secular center and the Islamic periphery. Even as the PJD downplayed the role of Islam in the party platform, secular Moroccans viewed the party with suspicion.

The PJD in Morocco defines itself as a political party with "Islamic reference" along the same lines as the Wasat Party (WP) in Egypt (Amara and El-Khalfi interviews, 2009). Officials in the party likened the concept of "Islamic reference" to a core system of values and ideas in forming the party platform; the policy positions devised within the party conform to the Islamic base of reference. One PJD official drew an analogy with other ideologies, stating, "It [Islamic reference] means that the reference is Islam as if you say, for example, for another party the base of reference is communism or socialism" (Amara interview, 2009).[25] Essentially, the party's emphasis on Islam as a point of reference amounts to being a guiding principle rather than a specific policy initiative. To this end, the party avoids using the term "sharia" in its discourse despite the fact that it conceives it more as a guiding principle than a set of specific laws (Uthmani and Bouanou interviews, 2009). Along the same lines, PJD official Mustapha El-Khalfi challenges those charging the PJD with a "narrow" focus on Islamic issues: "Islam is calling for social justice, economic development. So, indirectly by working on social justice, economic development, we are working to implement what Islam in principle is calling for. We think that as a party we are not a sectarian party, we are not a party for only religious people. We are a party for all citizens. And we defend the idea of citizenship" (El-Khalfi interview, 2009). Similar to how the AKP in Turkey defined the values it upholds as part of its conservative platform, the Moroccan PJD underscores issues such as the family, education, and societal values (El-Khalfi and Bouanou interviews, 2009) in addition to its the principal attachment to the "Islamic identity" of Moroccan society (PJD 2007 Electoral Program [Together to Build a Just Morocco]; Amghar 2007).

The formal separation between the PJD and its founding organization, the MUR, is an important indication of the PJD's credentials on their distinct Islamic discourse.[26] The MUR, in contrast to the PJD, strictly engages in *dawa* (roughly translated as Islamic missionary activity) and religious education activities devoid of political activism. The PJD, however, addresses a wider audience and engages in political activities only: "The movement will focus mainly on religious activities, education, culture, social welfare and so on. And the party will focus on the management of public affairs, political activities, and public policies. The relationship between the two takes the form of political partnership based on strategic cooperation but functional separation of each one" (El-Khalfi interview, 2009).

In a thorough analysis of the extent of separation of the movement and the political party, Wegner and Pellicer make important observations on this issue. Formally, membership in the movement was not a condition for membership in the party. Wegner and Pellicer show that in practice, the separation was genuine. In 2002, out of the 179 PJD candidates for a parliamentary seat, only fifty-six were MUR members (31 percent). Of those forty-two PJD officials who were elected to the parliament, there were twenty-two MUR members (52 percent). This figure stands in sharp contrast to the 1997 elections when all MPs were MUR members, save for one. Reinforcing the authenticity of the separation is the fact that currently, a lower percentage of intermediate-level and local-level officials in the party are members of the MUR (Wegner and Pellicer 2009, 159–61). Wegner and Pellicer also point to other issues that attest to the autonomy of the party from the movement, including financial independence, institutionalization of party structure, parallel structures, and "independent mobilization of resources."[27]

The implication of this "functional separation" is the absence of a monopolistic claim to speak on behalf of Islam in the political arena (Wegner and Pellicer 2009); or, in El-Khalfi's words, they are not presenting "the truth" (El-Khalfi interview, 2009). The separation enables the party to open up to others in the society and "learn" from them when necessary. This openness resulting from functional separation between the party and the movement sets it apart from Islamist groups' integrated approach to politics and religion such as the AWI. A PJD parliamentarian and currently the minister of Industry, Trade, and New Technologies, Amara, claimed that the AWI's current position—that "before starting to participate they have many conditions"—poses the biggest problem for their discourse and gives the impression that "they are the only actor having the truth" (Amara interview, 2009). The PJD's approach prevents "dividing the society" as the party abstains from employing polarizing discourse on the basis of Islam (El-Khalfi interview, 2009).

Willis, in observing the PJD's political priorities, also quotes the former PJD leader, saying, "Both [Uthmani and Benkirane] went on to stress, probably not disingenuously, that the party's real priorities lay with the issues of justice, corruption, and economic development rather than the veil or amputations, Othmani stating that: 'We have already said, and we repeat, to the Moroccan people: our party wants to prioritize the economic and social development of the country, not the *sharia*'" (Willis 2004, 66).

Islam constitutes the main reference for AWI, as is the case for the PJD. In building its political discourse and ideology, Islam has been the principal yardstick with which the movement (both Abdeslam Yassine himself and the political circle more currently) outlined its position on various issues ranging from democracy to the economy. The movement's head of the political circle, Al-Mutawakkil, states, "We are Muslims, and we live in a Muslim country, and we believe that we have many ideas and many principles if they are really applied, the situation of our country, of our people will be better" (Al-Mutawakkil interview, 2009).

A key difference between the Islamic discourse of the PJD and AWI concerns the issue of moral education. Much like the Egyptian MB and the NOM in Turkey, for AWI the moral education of individuals as Muslims takes precedence over any discussion of the application of Islamic law. For example, Nadia Yassine states, "Right now, Muslims are in dire need of much change. This is the actual work, work on the person—*dawa*. My father said many times that we have to change this Wahhabi attitude [of pointing]; we have to point to ourselves" (Yassine interview, 2009). To this end, the movement organizes spiritual retreats (*ribat*) where those who attend, members and nonmembers alike, engage in fasting, *zhikr* (remembrance of God), silence, and Sufi education. In contrast, the PJD has no such agenda. The main reason behind this difference is the separation of the religious and political activities of the movement between the PJD and the MUR.

On the issue of sharia, AWI's position shows a marked contrast with conventional Islamist discourse. The group is certainly committed to the principles of sharia, yet it makes a distinction between the principles of sharia and the specific laws of it. Nadia Yassine underscores the dynamic nature of sharia, and cautions against a static and "patriarchal" interpretation: "Last week, I saw some men and women being stoned; it's not my sharia. The sharia that we know, the Muslims know, and the people come to know is nothing but jurisprudence chosen by autocratical power, patriarchal reading of Islam, chosen by autocrats. 'Sharia' in Arabic means to dig a path, especially through water. The water is the symbol of *rahmat* [mercy], not of coercion, not to stone this one or that one. . . . I think that we need to rediscover the rights of Muslims and forget a little bit about their obligations" (Yassine interview, 2009). Al-Mutawakkil concurs with Nadia Yassine on sharia and emphasizes the necessity of having all the conditions in place prior to any application of a specific law. For example, when talking about theft and the punishment for it according to sharia, Al-Mutawakkil commented as follows:

> Before we talk about thieves, you have to give people enough to eat, to provide enough for them. . . . Once, Omer bin Khattab [the second caliph in Islamic history] did not apply this law because there was starvation and people did not have enough to eat. When in Morocco you have about 6 million people that live on $1 every day, can you talk about sharia in that situation? And 8 million people are threatened to fall into that category. In Islam, you don't apply a law blindly; if you want to apply a law, you have to take care that all the circumstances are there in order to apply the law, or it's going to be against Islam. (Al-Mutawakkil interview, 2009)

In brief, AWI favors sharia, but with important stipulations before any application of it can even be considered.

In summary, the PJD adheres to an Islamic identity in its political platform, as it constitutes the social fabric of Moroccan society, yet it does not view it as part of its agenda to increase the level of Islamic morality of the people. AWI, however, views it as important for the society to have an increased level of Islamic moral education.

Democracy

The Moroccan PJD resembles the Turkish and Egyptian MDPs in its commitment to a democratic regime with guarantees of individual liberties (PJD 2007 Electoral Program). PJD official Amara defines democracy from the party's perspective as follows: "Democracy for us [the PJD] means transparency; it means clean elections; it also means to respect human rights, to respect freedom of expression and so on" (Amara interview, 2009). Former party leader Uthmani emphasizes people's participation in "elections and decision-making mechanisms," with which Amara concurred (Uthmani and Amara interviews, 2009).

In this formulation of democracy, democratic principles and pluralism constitute key elements of the party discourse. For example, as a party, "we value both people's opinions and their individual rights and liberties," states Uthmani

(Uthmani interview, 2009). Likewise, Amara states, "To be sure, other rights such as freedom of expression and rights of minority should be taken in account" (Amara interview, 2009). Nezha El-Ouafi concurred with the emphasis on individual rights, and expressed full support (El-Ouafi interview, 2009). In the words of one PJD official, the PJD is a party that "believes in democracy like Christian democratic parties do" (El-Khalfi interview, 2009).[28] Nonetheless, El-Khalfi, clarifying the party's position on individual liberties, states, "We believe in individual liberties, but we are making a difference between the private sphere and the public sphere." The individual is completely free to act as he wishes in the private sphere; in the public sphere, however, other individuals' rights are also involved in determining the limits of individual freedom. The difference essentially applies only when individual actions impinge on others' rights (El-Khalfi interview, 2009).

A concrete example sheds light on the PJD's democratic stance. In 2004, during the family code (*Mudawana*) reform discussions, the PJD objected to the reform efforts on the grounds that they were against society's Islamic values (Willis 2004, 56). The perception among conservative Moroccans, including the PJD's base, was that the new bill would "strip the country of its Islamic identity and heritage," and that the "secularist and francophone elites" were supporting the bill. The PJD faced a socially conservative constituency and the need for reforming an outdated family code, leaving the party in a precarious situation. Although the movement that the PJD hailed from (MUR) was "strongly opposed" to the bill, the party barely opposed the proposed bill. In the National Council of the party, the vote on the issue was very close: eleven more votes to oppose the bill, out of 280 total votes (Wegner and Pellicer 2009, 165). The legislation was accepted in the parliament despite the PJD's objections. The party, however, accepted the reforms ex post facto on the grounds that it was the outcome of a democratic process.[29] This case is illustrative not because the PJD opposed a secular family code, but rather because the party demonstrated a "willingness to compromise when faced with political issues that might appear to conflict with its interpretation of Islamic values," a feature in contrast with AWI's insistence on the supremacy of Islamic nature of the code over the democratic deliberation process (Glennie and Mepham 2007).

Like the PJD, AWI endorses democratic procedures without hesitation. More importantly, this endorsement comes despite AWI's strong reservations against Western influence and dominance in Morocco and beyond: "Democracy is freedom of speech, freedom of assembly, possibility to organize free elections, possibility to elect your leaders, to elect your representatives. All of these mechanisms, I think, are very important, and we have no reservation regarding these. We think humanity has managed to find a way to deal with dictatorship, and that is very important to learn. Even if it [democracy] originates in the West, it is not something that belongs to the West. It belongs to the humanity, and everybody should be able to benefit" (Al-Mutawakkil interview, 2009). The political context that AWI operates within is certainly a critical factor in shaping the movement's preference on democracy, as with any other political party. Democracy is useful insofar as providing a mechanism for accountability in the system, which incidentally aims to curtail the extensive powers at the disposal of the regime formed around the persona of the king (Glennie and Mepham 2007).[30] Nonetheless, the current practice of procedural democracy in Morocco is hollow, and the elections are a "nonevent," as they function to buttress the current system (Willis 2004, 61).

When we turn to a more pluralistic notion of democracy, emphasizing democratic values and principles, the picture becomes murky for AWI. AWI's stance on democracy and individual liberties takes the form of a vaguely defined notion of Islamic democracy lacking clear-cut implications. AWI opposes the "taking" of values and principles from the West and "applying" them in the Moroccan context, specifically in reference to democracy. The culture and ideas in Morocco are different from those of the West, and hence require a different synthesis, according to the movement (Al-Mutawakkil interview, 2009). A distinct interpretation needs to be made with respect to the application of democracy in Morocco. As an example, Nadia Yassine underscores the spiritual legacy of Islam in order to create the new democratic understanding (Yassine interview, 2009). Although AWI respects individual choice and freedom, two issues complicate their conceptualization of a new democracy.[31] On the one hand, AWI emphasizes the religious and spiritual aspect of a new and Islamic democracy, but the contours of such a new model are not clearly laid out. Cognizant of the potential problems such an interpretation might pose, Yassine outright rejects analogies to the concept of *velayat-e faqih*[32] in postrevolutionary Iran as a mechanism to ensure the "Islamic" aspect of democracy. Yet she is not able to offer a concrete alternative to it as to how the spiritual and temporal authorities might have their own spheres (Yassine interview, 2009).

On the other hand, unable to develop a specific formula to address this quagmire, AWI appears to rely on the Islamic sensitivity of the people and their innate capacity to find a middle ground between Islam and democracy; this will occur mechanically, for AWI. In a way, an invisible (and unclear) hand of the Moroccan people will address the issue. For example, Al-Mutawakkil maintains, "There may be certain things that are not allowed from an Islamic point of view [in a democracy]. But, again, despite this, we believe that our people would make the right choice and would enact laws that are not against their own religion, that is, automatically. People are Muslims inside, they love Islam, and they are not after making laws against Islam. . . . You don't expect such a thing" (Al-Mutawakkil interview, 2009). On the same issue, Abdeslam Yassine also envisions a "democratic equilibrium" where the spiritual and temporal spheres do not violate each other's "turfs," where the exact mechanism is unsubstantiated (Yassine interview, 2009). The major problem here is not that AWI might, in an undemocratic fashion, undertake action against a majority decision that is perceived to be against Islamic values. AWI expressed its respect for the choice of the majority on different occasions, and its adherence to procedural elements of democracy provides ample evidence to that end. Rather, the problem stems from the fact that AWI puts its faith fully in the hands of the electorate to secure the envisioned Islamic nature of the regime rather than devising an institutional solution to this predicament. It is this uncertainty that puts seculars at unease, quite similar to the uncertainty emanating from the unclarified and unqualified discourses of the Egyptian MB on democracy and Islam.

In summary, the PJD adheres to a democratic political system both in terms of its procedural elements (i.e., elections, turn of power) and in its principles (i.e., individual liberties, pluralism, and protection of minority rights). AWI's democratic discourse, however, remains somewhat ambivalent due to its emphasis on Islamic spirituality and inability to clarify potential implications of such an emphasis for democratic principles.

Economy

The particular kind of liberalization undertaken in Morocco (semicompetitive liberalization) affected the economic discourses of the PJD and of its most significant rival, AWI. In view of peripheral winners (SMEs) and losers (peripheral masses) of the liberalization process, each party tailored its economic policy to its respective constituencies. The PJD adheres to a liberal economic discourse without reservations while simultaneously drawing attention to the problems associated with Morocco's integration to the global economy. Similar to the economic discourse of the WP in Egypt and the AKP in Turkey, the PJD recognizes the "reality" of greater economic globalization and Moroccan integration into global markets and underscores Morocco's "need" to be a part of this process (Amara and El-Ouafi interviews, 2009). One PJD official summarized the party's position on economic liberalization as follows: "Globalization, we [the PJD] think, is a phenomenon we cannot stop. What we shall do is to prepare our economy, our companies, and businessmen and face this globalization and to take part in this globalization. But we think, unfortunately, the government did not do anything special to take part in this globalization" (Amara interview, 2009). PJD legislator and current minister of Higher Education and Scientific Research Lahcen Daoudi explains the "need" for Moroccan economic liberalization in the following way: "In Morocco, economic opening is a necessity because we are a small state. It is not possible for us to develop with our domestic market only; we don't have oil, minerals, or gold" (Daoudi interview, 2009). Noureddine Karbal, also a member of the Moroccan parliament, states that as a party they are "believers in [economic] liberalization" (Karbal interview, 2009). Another PJD official went further and claimed that "everyone is benefiting from economic liberalization," and hence as a party, they are happy with liberalization as an economic policy (Bouanou interview, 2009).

More specifically in the Moroccan context, free trade agreements (FTAs) signed by Morocco in recent years have been a point of contention. Among the FTA partners of Morocco are the United States, the European Union, and Turkey. The PJD carved its position on these FTAs carefully, mindful of their socioeconomic implications for the country. For example, PJD official Amara criticized the government for its perceived failure to undertake necessary measures ensuring an optimal outcome for Morocco, instead of rejecting FTAs outright, which is what many Islamist parties choose to do: "As a political party, clearly, we [the PJD] are not against FTA, but to conclude and sign an FTA with the US, which is economically a big country, means that our state has to prepare for this agreement. That's what our government did not do. And if you see the results of the economic balance between the US and Morocco, you will find that for Morocco it is always negative; and also when you see this balance with Turkey, it is always negative" (Amara interview, 2009). Another PJD official underscored Moroccan SMEs' participation in the liberalization process: "We have a good relationship with them [SMEs] because as a party in our platform we called for that the country should have economic openness toward the West and Europe in a way that takes into account the interests of the small and medium businesses in the country. For example, having a free trade agreement with the US, having a free trade agreement with the EU, that will help this part of the Moroccan business. So we defend these ideas" (El-Khalfi interview, 2009).

The PJD formulated its economic discourse on the basis of a "public policy framework" oriented toward "tackling the priorities of the society." Such a framework enables the party to be cognizant of various aspects of the Moroccan society and economy in a time of increasing economic liberalization and to move beyond zero-sum views of economic opening, which is characteristic of Islamist discourse. In other words, the party adopts a liberal economic discourse wholeheartedly while pointing out the problems in the way Morocco is integrating to the global economy. To this end, the latest PJD electoral program (2007) spotlights issues such as investment and production before identity issues. As in the case of the WP in Egypt, the program made a reference to Morocco's placement in the global development index as well as highlighting specific development issues by relying on statistical data (PJD 2007 Electoral Program). El-Khalfi adds that the public policy framework of the party lays out detailed measures on the problems faced by the Moroccan economy: "Measures that tackle all levels related to how we are going to finance funds for these measures, what the implications of these measures on the legal and legislative framework are, who is going to be in charge of these measures, at the institutional level, at the legislative level, at the financial level, the interactions between all these institutions that could be related to specific measures" (El-Khalfi interview, 2009). Reinforcing the public policy framework adopted by the PJD is also attested by the actions of one PJD mayor. Much like the AKP in Turkey and the WP in Egypt, PJD officials are much less reprehensive of the use of interest in financial transactions. Upon criticisms that he used interest to finance certain development projects, even from within the MUR, the mayor responded as follows: "I don't even realize, for me that's fine, this is not really what we are concerned about.... Now, we realize that it is not enough to have principles to be able to set up a budget. The citizens judge you on the basis of your efficiency" (Wegner and Pellicer 2009, 167). Others in the party pointed out the fact that there were regular meetings with French trade chambers in Casablanca as evidence of the party's economically liberal stance (Karbal interview, 2009). Clearly, pragmatism prevails over ideology for the PJD in economic affairs (Amghar 2007, 2).

PJD officials did not hesitate to point out the government as the culprit in regard to economic problems: "Since the 1980s, in Morocco we started to talk about making the economy effective, productive by modernizing the law, the statute of companies, from family companies to modern companies, by giving more facilities and funds for companies, by education and formation, a lot of things that are well known. The problem is that the government did not prioritize this" (Amara interview, 2009). Outgoing PJD leader Uthmani, in the same spirit, pointed to three problems of the Moroccan economy preventing greater integration into the global economy: economic management, legal framework, and education (Uthmani interview, 2009). The party program also called for specific economic goals addressing issues such as GDP growth rate, public debt, and the government budget (PJD 2007 Electoral Program).

One key component of the PJD economic platform is the call for a solution to the economic problems of small and medium businesses. The chief reason for this call is the party's identification with SMEs and the perception that small and medium business owners in Morocco constitute an integral part of its social base. The trend of closer identification between the PJD and SMEs has been more pronounced since the mid-1990s, according to PJD officials (El-Khalfi and Amara interviews, 2009). The concentration of SMEs in urban areas partially accounts for the PJD's strength in urban areas, one party official claimed (El-Khalfi interview, 2009). The party's approach to the question of SMEs is two-pronged. SMEs should be supported, as they constitute the main element of Moroccan businesses; without a stronger SME base, the economy is likely to suffer. Secondly, the PJD maintains that SME participation in the liberal Moroccan economy would boost competitiveness of the Moroccan economy vis-à-vis competitors. Hence "positive discrimination" should be applied for SMEs, which would "allow them [SMEs] to enhance their competitiveness against big economies who use liberalization to enter to our [Moroccan] market" (El-Khalfi interview, 2009). Additionally, Amara stresses the need for greater SME involvement in the economy: "They [SMEs] shall be included in this development by giving them the possibility to participate in this [liberal] market . . . to facilitate [for them] to have money from banks . . . the transformation from family companies to new forms of companies" (Amara interview, 2009).

Unlike the PJD, AWI takes a highly critical stance on economic liberalization and on the overall economic policy. Its stance resembles very closely that of the MB in Egypt. Removal of corruption and a wholesale change of the system are the prerequisites of any discussion about potential benefits of a specific policy, according to the movement. In the face of the problems that Moroccans are facing, AWI maintains hope that problems can be addressed: "The problem is that we can overcome the present predicament but not with the present regime; we need change in order to overcome this imbroglio. We need a different system. You want to talk about development? People should endorse you. People are marginalized; they have lost all trust in political parties and political regime." The main motivation behind the demand for the "change" in the system is the persistent "problem of mismanagement" and that the political system is "corrupt to the core." As an example, Al-Mutawakkil cites the case of foreign aid to Morocco. He argues that because the government is corrupt and the foreign aid money goes to "the pockets of some people" instead of to the intended projects, foreign donors more recently choose to deal directly with civil society organizations rather than with the state (Al-Mutawakkil interview, 2009).

As for the process of economic liberalization in Morocco, the attitude of AWI is no less critical: "Neoliberalism is not Mother Teresa. It's made to benefit some groups of people; others are left out. It's the law of the jungle. In Morocco, it's the already rich ones [who are benefiting from it] who represent about 1 percent of the population. And the rest [are] starving. Liberalism is a good thing if there is equality. We are in the underdeveloped world, so we don't have much chance in this competition" (Yassine interview, 2009). Another official from AWI points to a small group of big business owners as the beneficiaries of this particular form of liberalization undertaken in Morocco: "There are twenty families or so. These are businessmen closely associated with the regime. Those people are close to the regime, and many of them have some functions within the regime. [Since the time of Hassan II,] you cannot make money or become rich unless you have the agreement of the regime. It is impossible. You have to deal with them in order to do your business. Otherwise, it is not possible for you to do anything. So, those people are the beneficiaries, but the rest are suffering" (Al-Mutawakkil interview, 2009).

The implication is that competition in the Moroccan economy is minimal, as "the businessmen are afraid" to compete with the monarchy, which is "everywhere" (Al-Mutawakkil interview, 2009).

Nadia Yassine thinks that the economy is a challenge beyond the national borders of Morocco; it is, in other words, international. The level of inequality is not sustainable, and no solution exists in the given parameters of the international economic system; hence it is not possible for Morocco to address the issue by itself. For Yassine, it is only "spirituality," that is, Islamic spirituality, that can help humanity to "change the reality" (Yassine interview, 2009). Overall, the economic outlook of Morocco is not bright, and economic liberalization did not deliver what many believed that it would deliver, according to AWI. This sharp and critical stance on the economy is in direct contrast to the PJD's position.

Social Policy

Both the PJD and AWI have favorable views on social spending and the protection of the less fortunate in society. Favorable opinions on social justice are attested by the mere fact that both parties have "justice" as part of their names. Their justification for the need for social policy differs, however. For the PJD, the issue of poverty is an outcome of economic modernization and integration into the global economy. It is considered as a necessary evil and needs to be addressed by the government. The social policy of the PJD calls for minimizing poverty and addressing the problem of unemployment, a principal source of poverty. As part of its social policy discourse, the PJD tackles universal health care coverage and a progressive tax system in its 2007 platform (PJD 2007 Electoral Program). Specifically, the party draws a connection between its popularity in the urban areas and its economic discourse: "Within urban areas we are the first party; we are weak in the rural areas. This reflects that the party is the product of the challenges, the contradiction between modernity and our identity, Islamic identity, identity of the country. And this reflects that the intellectual core that guides the movement has emerged in urban areas, within universities, schools, high schools, and they developed a discourse. That is in some way related to the needs and challenges of the urban people" (El-Khalfi interview, 2009). For AWI, however, poverty is rampant and the economic disparity between a small minority of business owners and a politically well-connected group, and the rest of the people are worsening each day: "When you look at social statistics, you will see that the situation of the Moroccan people is going back; it is deteriorating. If there are any benefits, only a small minority would benefit from those, but the crushing majority is really suffering" (Al-Mutawakkil interview, 2009). In order to support his case, Al-Mutawakkil referenced the deplorable living conditions of many Moroccan families, including family houses in alleys of one meter wide, two to three families living in one house with a single toilet, and hospitals of "poor quality" (Al-Mutawakkil interview, 2009).

AWI's social dimension (Al-Adl) also has an intricate relationship with its spiritual dimension (*al-Ihsan*). In the words of Abdeslam Yassine, "An angry stomach has no ears"; hence unless a certain level of "social equality" can be established, the ideological message of AWI is unlikely to find a welcoming audience: "We are not seeking paradise on earth, but a certain social equity. Only then we can transmit honorably this message [of Islam], and have it accepted by the people" (Yassine interview, 2009).

When the PJD and AWI's discourses on the economy and social policy are considered in tandem, each group's somewhat distinct societal base becomes more easily identifiable. Observers note that the PJD's support is largely middle class, urban, and SME owners, whereas AWI speaks to the poorer sections of the Moroccan society and commands a more "popular base" than the PJD does (Willis 2004, 71). This observation is also shared by Nadia Yassine of AWI: "They [the PJD] are very selective in choosing their members, and there are subjective and objective reasons. [The] subjective reason is that they choose to have a special kind of member; they prefer to have intellectual, middle-class membership—a certain profile, not like us. We have a wide variety of people. [The objective reason is that] the people do not appreciate the discourse of the PJD because they are not against the regime. They have started to lose their popularity because they are more and more in the system" (Yassine interview, 2009).

Emad Eldin Shahin, a scholar on Islamic movements in North Africa, concurs with Yassine and notes that the MUR and the PJD appeal more to intellectual and middle-class groups whereas AWI has a stronger base among the lower classes (Shahin 1997, 195).

SMEs and Political Preferences

Islam

The peripheral business owners interviewed for this study showed unequivocal support for Islam in Moroccan politics and favored a party emphasizing "Muslim values." Particularly striking was not that a majority of these business owners believe in the importance of Islam in politics but rather that their reasons for believing this were largely the same. Several business owners expressed that Islam has "good" values to offer and that Morocco could benefit from it (MA-14-B, MA-4-B, MA-7-B, MA-2-B interviews, 2009). One businessman working in the home textiles industry considers it essential for the continued Islamic character of Moroccan society; hence he stated quite simply, "Muslim values should be integrated into the state and government" (MA-9-B interview, 2009). Another businessman in the yarn industry approaches the question in a more self-interested manner and dismisses secularism (which is largely understood to be the French version of secularism, laïcité): "Personally, I am a Muslim, and I would like to give the same education I received to my kids in a Muslim environment. I am against laïcité" (MA-7-B interview, 2009).

To illustrate the exact way Islam should be involved in politics, one business owner, for example, notes that the utilization of "tolerant" Islam is certainly a "good" use of Islam, referencing the nonpoliticized use of Islam, just as we would expect from an MDP (MA-4-B interview, 2009). Another businessman, drawing an analogy with confessional parties of Europe, was quite explicit in the way in which he believed religion should be included in a democratic political system. He explains, "For example, in other countries, Christians may create a political party, and they are not using the name of the religion to force people. They are just taking principles [from Christianity,] and they are using it in a good way" (MA-3-B interview, 2009). Another business owner, working in the apparel sector and in subcontracting arrangements with European companies, concurs, suggesting that Islamic banks are comparatively better than those of Europe and that other rules in Islam could have a positive effect on society as well (MA-14-B interview, 2009).

Although it is possible to make an argument that the royal title of Amir al-Mu'minin (Commander of the Faithful) may be the primary reason for a favorable opinion on Islam in Morocco, not all businessmen actually "buy" the king's use of Islam in his political discourse. A business owner who started his own business after many years working for an international company in Morocco challenges the king's Islamic legitimacy: "The king is Amir al-Mu'minin. Maybe he is using it to show off or to be respected. It's another way to be respected. Army, money, companies, religion . . . that's another form of legitimization [for the king]" (MA-9-B interview, 2009). Reflecting a similar thought, another business owner argues that it should actually be the political parties who "defend" Islamic values and Islam; hence a specific party's position on Islam is not to be regarded as "extraordinary" (MA-6-B interview, 2009).

SME owners responded in an overwhelmingly positive way about the discourse and policies of the PJD. One businessman argues that he believes the party is venturing to reconcile Islamic values with a modernizing social and political context: "This party [PJD] is trying to bring some answers when they try to say, 'Islam is not in opposition to modernity, and we should integrate it'" (MA-8-B interview, 2009). A businessman who most likely identifies himself with AWI refers to an Islamic role in politics as a "need": "There are many associations that are trying to do the same [religion and politics]. This is a need. Whoever is practicing his religion has a need to say 'I am practicing my religion, but also I don't want to feel in opposition like in Europe [as a Muslim]. . . . I want to feel part of this.' They [the PJD] are going in the right direction" (MA-9-B interview, 2009).

The Turkish Justice and Development Party (AKP) was even mentioned when the PJD's economic discourse was discussed: "I think they [the PJD] have some very good things for us, both Moroccans and businesses. There are very good economic policies from this party. Uthmani [the former PJD leader] emphasized the economy and offered good ideas. . . . Like the AKP in Turkey, they've developed so many things in the economy."[33] This business owner continued to say that the PJD "listens" and is "flexible, adaptable, practical," and perhaps most importantly, that the party made the Moroccans feel that "we are on the same boat" (MA-13-B interview, 2009).

Overall, peripheral business owners demonstrate an overwhelming support for a political discourse encompassing Islamic values—the same type of political discourse that the PJD has already executed. Islamic values hence are preferred to political Islam, a more politicized and pronounced version of an Islamic discourse.

Democracy

Moroccan business owners expressed a great deal of support for a democratic regime as it pertains to their businesses, although the exact rationale for such support showed variance across the interviewed business owners. Their perceptions of the state of Moroccan democracy were also at odds. While one business owner declares "Democracy is good for business" (MA-7-B interview, 2009), another takes a broader perspective, emphasizing democratic progress over time: "Democracy always benefits people. We are very satisfied by our democracy right now; it is not like in the days after independence" (MA-2-B interview, 2009). Another businessman from Fes appears to find comfort in the relatively democratic standing of Morocco. He also believes that democracy can lead to political stability, which he considers to be the underlying cause of foreign investment in Morocco: "Democracy always brings benefits to the economy, to social life. . . . In a country without democracy, we cannot find political stability. Investors are always looking for stability, political stability, and democracy affords that. Morocco is a democratic country; it surely is not like a European country. But compared with Tunisia or Egypt, we are more democratic. That's why we attract more investment" (MA-5-B interview, 2009). Another business owner concurs with the political stability effect of democracy, and adds, "Stability helps business; it encourages investments" (MA-4-B interview, 2009).

In the same vein, a businessman from the Ain Sabaa neighborhood of Casablanca views democracy as an "essential" element of the economy. Nonetheless, unhappy with the level of democracy in the country, he claims that lack of democracy is a key source of mismanagement: "It [democracy] is essential in the economy. Democracy is good management, and we cannot do good business in bad management all around us. Administration, many enterprises of the state, the laws are not good; to be fair, not to give this money and this favor to someone... this is democracy. Democracy is good management for the state. We ask the companies to have good management; we also ask the state to have good management. Democracy is the guarantee of this good management" (MA-14-B interview, 2009).

One of the business owners I interviewed challenged the purely formal definition of democracy in Morocco, stating, "Democracy is multiple parties and parliament; does that mean we are a democratic country? No" (MA-9-B interview, 2009). He continued to emphasize the "rule of law" as the true essence of a democratic regime: "At the end, what does democracy mean? There is law, and everyone respects the law. Of course, there is the practice, people choose whom they want, et cetera, but the main issue is this: justice, laws, and everyone following the same laws" (MA-9-B interview, 2009). Along the same lines, the owner of a textile company in Fes claims that democracy's emphasis on the rule of law is likely to prevent "cheaters" in the business world: "The more democracy, the better. Democracy, first of all, helps stop the cheaters in business—rule of law" (MA-3-B interview, 2009). Education and freedom of expression were also among the issues mentioned by business owners, as they relate to the business world: "More democracy for me means an easier way to express my demands.... Democracy is also helping the level of the conscience of all people in my country and improving education and such. I need better education for my business" (MA-8-B interview, 2009).

The contribution of democracy to the growth of a middle class in Morocco was another issue alluded to by a business owner: "In the past years, we had the very rich people and the very poor people, no middle class. With democracy, we are noticing that we have this middle class growing and this is beneficial for the whole economy" (MA-3-B interview, 2009). Other business owners took a broader view of democracy and evaluated it from the country's overall perspective. For one businessman, democracy is the gateway to becoming a "modern" country, while at the same time, it guarantees "open markets" in Morocco. The "survival" of Morocco is dependent on democracy, according to this businessman (MA-6-B interview, 2009).

Economy

In competitive economies, SME owners should benefit from economic liberalization. Where cronyism persists, their growth is stymied, and so is the strength of this critical base for MDPS. Overall, given the extent and kind of economic liberalization, the expectation is to observe a group of SME owners who will largely be supportive of policies spurring liberalization and competition.

ECONOMIC LIBERALIZATION

Looking at the views of Moroccan SME owners on economic liberalization, it becomes clear that their perceptions varied in great measure in accordance with their businesses' orientation, that is, export oriented versus import competing. Whether they directly benefit from liberalization or are harmed by it is a reliable indicator of their stance on liberalization. A businessman in textiles who exports his entire production to various European countries expresses favorable views on liberalization, citing his own case: "Economic liberalization was very beneficial for all Moroccans. As I stated before, I started as a simple businessman and now have my own companies. For the Moroccan economy, textile is not the first industry [benefiting from liberalization]; we have tourism, agriculture, services as well" (MA-2-B interview, 2009). Others maintained that economic liberalization should be "defended" (MA-13-B interview, 2009), and that government should try to "take off barriers" to free trade, which will eventually lead to "less problems" in the economy (MA-14-B interview, 2009). The mere fact that Morocco is one of the few countries globally to have FTAs with both the United States and the European Union contributes to Morocco's developing economy, for a businessman (MA-1-B interview, 2009). Specifically, the new and liberal economic environment was deemed conducive to doing business. One business owner states, "The economic conditions are healthy; all the conditions [are favorable] to make your business" (MA-8-B interview, 2009), whereas another reinforced an earlier statement, saying, "Whenever you think there is an opportunity, you go for the opportunity," referring to the opportunities offered by the opening economy (MA-9-B interview, 2009).

An immediate impact of a liberalizing economy is the increased level of competition from both domestic and foreign companies. In this regard, several business owners underscored the increased level of domestic competition and their eventual dissatisfaction with it, as Moroccan industries are deemed "weak and fragile" (MA-4-B interview, 2009). One business owner in Casablanca attributes the increased domestic competition to the following condition: "Many people understood that there was an opportunity to invest and they started to do that, and also because there are no entry barriers. They could start with old machines; [new] investment was not important" (MA-7-B interview, 2009). The need for decreasing the costs of production was raised as a critical outcome of this increased competition in order to remain competitive (MA-6-B interview, 2009). Another businessman was more concerned about foreign competition, yearning for preliberalization conditions: "We are suffering from competition coming from countries like Egypt, Tunisia, or Turkey. Coming from an international company, emphasis on improving your product and productivity is crucial. I will compare myself to ten or fifteen years ago, and I prefer fifteen years ago. There was less competition, well protected by the government with duties and the like. You could do your business very easily." He also added that the liberalization policy might have been a "bad choice" for Morocco. In particular, privatization policy seemed to offer little to the Moroccan society other than increasing the level of "competitiveness" of the privatized companies, according to this businessman. The outflow of profits is deemed unfavorable for the country as a whole (MA-9-B interview, 2009).

Government Performance in the Economy

The opinions voiced by business owners regarding the Moroccan government's performance and the many problems experienced by the Moroccan economy serve well to outline their views and perceptions on economic liberalization. The state in Morocco, according to some business owners, has a "positive approach" to economic globalization (MA-8-B interview, 2009), and they recognize government efforts to establish a business-friendly environment in an open economy. Business owners recounted steps taken by the Moroccan government to enhance infrastructure, steps to improve the legal framework, social security, and taxes, to name a few. These improvements will eventually offer a "good climate" for economic competition (MA-14-B and MA-8-B interviews, 2009). This is despite the fact that subsidies offered by the Moroccan government are virtually nonexistent or are provisional on myriad conditions, according to business owners (MA-13-B interview, 2009).

A leading figure in the Textile and Apparel Manufacturers' Association (AMITH), which represents the textile sector in Morocco, expresses the responsiveness of the government to their concerns in the following way: "Before 2004, we were just complaining [about our problems]. In 2004, we started to change our way of communication with the government and tried always to propose solutions to our problems and be more constructive. I think government officials are trying their best to address these problems" (MA-6-B interview, 2009). Echoing these sentiments closely, another business owner proclaims, "The state has always been with the companies, [offering] technical help. Now, it is offering financial help, commercial help, and also training. Now, we are working on taxes" (MA-3-B interview, 2009).

Nonetheless, business owners pointed out multiple problems in the economy that begged for a solution. When analyzed more closely, however, it is striking that most of the problems identified by the business owners were strictly related to specific economic policies, not fundamentally political problems such as state-business marriage and corruption, as in the case of Egypt. Some business owners in exports were specifically concerned with their international competitiveness and complained about what they perceived as unfair conditions at home in Morocco. A textile company owner in Casablanca complains about the "laws and regulations from twenty to thirty years ago" and calls for modernization of "the duties, the [customs] administration, and the rules," and fixes for "the problems of the workers" (MA-13-B interview, 2009). Another business owner, in a similar spirit, states, "We ask not for money; we ask for facilitation, administration, transportation, logistics, communication.... This is fair competition" (MA-14-B interview, 2009). Another takes issue with the financial system, the most illiberal aspect of the Moroccan economy, which, if reformed, would complete the liberalization of the Moroccan economy (MA-1-B interview, 2009). An exporter alludes to yet another problem, one unique to those working in exports:

> In textiles, if we are exporting to Europe, this is mainly thanks to proximity. Our customers in Europe are expecting us to be able to ship their orders in two weeks. This is a big challenge because the garment factory has to plan its raw materials, accessories, try to create everything two weeks later. Sometimes you have buttons missing, and you cannot ship on time. If you buy this from Turkey, and your supplier ships it to you by DHL, it is blocked at the airport because of customs problems or something like that, and you will lose your business. If you do everything and ship on time, your shipment is blocked in Tangier for customs control; then you lose your customer satisfaction. So, logistics should be fluid. This is an issue the government has not been active in yet. (MA-6-B interview, 2009)

Although many find flaws in the legal system to be the most troublesome issue faced by Morocco, some business owners deem the judiciary responsible for Morocco's difficulties. One asserts, "Justice, we still consider justice—not enough action has been taken in this field. Give your money, and you can get different decisions from justices; that's not enough. They have to make a big effort to establish rule of law. The law is there; they just have to practice it. In this country, I think we have good laws. The problem is with the judiciary" (MA-8-B interview, 2009).

As is the case with exporters in the rest of the world, Moroccan exporters complained about the "high" Moroccan currency (dirham) (MA-13-B interview, 2009), social security costs (MA-2-B and MA-13-B interviews, 2009), energy costs (MA-6-B interview, 2009), ISO (i.e. international standardization) costs, and taxes (MA-4-B and MA-2-B interviews, 2009). For example, one manager in an export firm voices his concerns regarding the taxes they were paying for management staff: "We ask for decreases of tax for employees. Two years ago, we were paying 44 percent for all the management staff. If you hire engineers, you have to pay 44 percent taxes. We were asking them [the government] to decrease taxes in order to encourage companies to have good middle management. Today, we are paying 40 percent, and we have promises for 2010 we'll pay 38 percent."

The lower management costs will lead to more qualified personnel, and thus higher-quality products, according to this manager (MA-6-B interview, 2009).

Economic Conflict

The Moroccan economy displays three nonexclusive kinds of conflict: formal versus informal sectors, export versus import-competing sectors, and big business versus SMEs. All three conflicts have cross-cutting elements and hence are difficult to disentangle to identify the fine picture. Big businesses, for example, engage in both exports and production for the domestic market, a characteristic similar to SMEs, despite the fact that a sizeable portion of exporting companies are SMEs. Many informal companies target the domestic market, but at the same time many also engage in subcontracting business for European companies and are short-lived by their nature (MA-6-B interview, 2009).[34] I will discuss each conflict in turn.

The Moroccan informal sector drew the ire of some business owners as a major source of problems because of their perception that informality offers an unwarranted advantage for informal business. Specifically, it is an issue that concerns the domestic market. One business owner states, "In Morocco, [the] informal economy is the biggest issue in [the] business world. Moroccan companies have many taxes to pay, but the informal businesses can evade [these taxes]" (MA-4-B interview, 2009). Another business owner calls for government action on the same issue: "In the local market, we have a lot of informal businesses, people who are not paying any tax. These companies make it very difficult for normal companies to do business. So, we ask the government to do something against these informal companies to bring them to the formal sector" (MA-7-B interview, 2009). A business owner with seventy-five employees and $3 million in annual sales opposes the informal sector when he says, "I don't want to see small companies working in nonlegal ways" (MA-8-B interview, 2009).

Another conflict is between exporters and import-competing businesses. In big business associations like CGEM (Moroccan Confederation of Businesses) and AMITH (Textile and Apparel Manufacturers' Association), a visible and major source of conflict is in regard to the level of protection the association will demand from the government. One businessman notes, "If we are two members of CGEM as exporters and importers, I want the currency to decrease as an exporter, for example. The other wants the currency to increase, and eventually CGEM does not know what to do or what to say to the government. Another example: I am an exporter and I get advantage from a program created by the government; they [the government] will pay me back a part of the social [security] expenses. But other companies, which are not exporters, they will certainly be displaced" (MA-5-B interview, 2009).

The conflict between exporters and import-competing companies is most visible in AMITH, the sectoral business association in textiles (MA-2-B and MA-14-B interviews, 2009). Within AMITH, historically the textile producers mainly produced for the domestic economy. Hence these businesses are mostly older and are politically well connected. The garment producers, on the other hand, overwhelmingly produce for foreign markets, and most are newer companies established in the post-1983 period following the liberalization of the Moroccan economy. In the words of an exporting business owner, "The conflict is about protection. The textile [sector] asks for protection, and the garment [sector] asks for no protection and no duties because it facilitates the business with Europe. Because we import and we should make [the products] fast, the time is more important because if the duties are high, the customs will block it to control anything. If there are no duties, they will not control, and it will facilitate business. We win time. If we win two or three days, it is in our interest" (MA-13-B interview, 2009). Another aspect of the conflict between the two sides, that is, garment and textile producers, is more forward looking and based on the changing behavior of the European customers:

> The garment industry used to sell minutes—the garment companies don't buy the raw materials, they don't buy the accessories, the customer gives them everything and they will sell only minutes, just assembling. Now, their customers [abroad] are changing their buying behaviors; they don't want to do that [providing all material for production] for them anymore. They ask the Moroccan companies to propose the product. These garment companies say "How can we propose if we don't have the material? We should decrease the customs in order to be able to buy, import our own material from abroad." So the few companies who are producing the raw materials are not happy with that. (MA-6-B interview, 2009)

The source of dissatisfaction on the part of the domestic raw material producers is that the exporting companies are not satisfied with the quality and price of domestic production. The exporting companies can find the same raw material abroad with higher quality and for a better price. The other side of the problem is that Moroccan producers do not want to change their production behaviors, that is, quality and price, because of the captive market they enjoy in Morocco: "These companies who are in textiles have [a] good market in Morocco; they have good business. Why should they work with some exporters who are demanding in quality? They would ask for [a] small quantity; maybe, they will pay in 90 days or 120 days. They do not care about all this. This is the real problem, the conflict of interest" (MA-7-B interview, 2009). But according to another business owner, the endgame for the import-competing firms is drawing closer as customs duties decrease gradually:

Morocco signed many free trade agreements. If you import yarn in Morocco, you pay 10 percent customs. In 2010, we'll pay 5 percent. If you import some fabrics, you will pay 10 to 17.5 percent for fabrics. And these garment factories are asking the government to decrease from 17.5 percent to 2.5 percent. In 2012, it will be 2.5 percent. So companies in textiles that are not competitive today, they won't be competitive tomorrow if they don't do something. They want to be competitive in basic products only. There is no way. They can only be competitive if they compete on other bases, like the quality and creativity. The big players are old and not able to adapt [to competition]. (MA-6-B interview, 2009)

The final conflict is one between big businesses and smaller businesses. Big businesses are usually older, of Fassi origin and politically well connected, as I discussed earlier in this chapter. One businessman was clear in how he perceived the socioeconomic conflict in Morocco: "King, big businessmen, army, security, and police are all powers.... They are one in terms of their interests" (MA-8-B interview, 2009). As a result of this interconnected structure, big business owners try to use their influence to affect decision-making mechanisms in a liberal economic setting: "Those [big] businessmen are connected with some government or army officials in order to get decisions.... This is making some people richer and richer, and making things more expensive for normal people. This is a bad thing, businessmen related to politics and trying to take easy opportunities in this country.... Old powers are trying to hold on to their interests using their connections" (MA-9-B interview, 2009).

However, other business owners partly contradicted this sharp picture. More specifically, there is an important distinction between the king as a big businessman and other big business owners. Even though the king continues to use his power and influence in implicit ways as the country's biggest businessman, opportunities for other big business owners to use political connections to tilt the balance in their favor in an ever-liberalizing Moroccan economy are becoming extinct. For example, a business owner in Casablanca was defiant of big businesses in his own sector in the face of their opposition to decreasing barriers to free trade. However, when the discussion shifted to the king as a big businessman in the industry, the reaction was, "The king, we don't touch that" (MA-2-B interview, 2009). Another business owner in Rabat made a similar observation with a specific example: "The liberalization reforms, of course, do not affect big groups like ONA [which belongs to the king]. Recently, a big supermarket chain was about to enter the local market here in Morocco. You always act carefully. Why? Because the competition is Marjane. Who owns Marjane? The king. Therefore, you try not to step on some toes in the process. No one will ever come and question you about your business, yet you feel it all the time" (MA-1-B interview, 2009). Overall, this businessman summarizes his observation of the Moroccan economy as follows: "The big businesses continue to dominate Moroccan economy, but the SMEs make important headways in the business world" (MA-1-B interview, 2009).

Party Support Levels

Both AWI and the PJD remain significant political actors, even though their magnitude has been questioned in recent research.[35] Although there are no formal statistics of how strong the Islamist AWI is in Morocco, based on various accounts and interviews, it is fair to say that the movement enjoys broad support in Moroccan society (Glennie and Mepham 2007; Kausch 2007; Cavatorta 2007; Amara interview, 2009; El-Khalfi interview, 2009). Observers call AWI the "most popular Islamist group in Morocco" (Layachi 1998, 98), "the country's largest Islamist movement" (Spiegel 2015), and "very strong and organized" (Tlaidi interview, 2009) and note that AWI has a "greater rallying capacity" (Desrues and Moyano 2001) and a "larger support base than the PJD" (Willis 2004, 57). AWI officials echoed such observations. Nadia Yassine stated quite simply, "Al-Adl wal-Ihsan is the major Islamic group in Morocco" (Yassine interview, 2009). Similarly, AbdelWahed Al-Mutawakkil noted, "According to many people, Al-Adl wal-Ihsan is the largest movement in Morocco. It is well organized, and despite continuous harassment, despite continuous repression; and we have no newspapers, we cannot apply to do any public activities, yet every year people are coming to Al-Adl wal-Ihsan. This is not just an impression; this is according to statistics. We keep our own statistics. In every town, city you go, you will find Al-Adl wal-Ihsan" (Al-Mutawakkil interview, 2009).[36]

AWI's support base consists largely of the poor and marginalized in the society in line with the expectations based on AWI's extensive network of social services (Al-Mutawakkil interview, 2009). The reactionary and nonconformist stance of the group represents the exclusion of the peripheral groups from centers of economic and political power. Just as in the case of the MB in Egypt, AWI has a "growing number of followers among the educated young people unable to find work" (H. Munson 1993, 173). In other words, losers in the liberalization process identify more with AWI. Also reinforcing this conviction is the fact that the group views the well-educated and economically better off segments of society, inclusive of the members and representatives of the peripheral groups such as the PJD, as part of the "system," that is, the compromised power structure of Moroccan society that they so heavily criticize. Alex Glennie and David Mepham provide an estimate of the membership of AWI, claiming the group has 30,000 registered members (Glennie and Mepham 2007, 9), while Bekkaoui and Larémont note that AWI's membership is estimated to be around "100,000, according to a list of adepts contained within the association databases and confiscated by the police during a raid on the association's Oujda headquarters in 2006" (2011, 40).

Francesco Cavatorta offers a wider spectrum, suggesting that the membership of AWI is estimated between 50,000 and 600,000 (Cavatorta 2006, 213). Despite its abstention from formal politics, the movement is recognized as an Islamist force to be reckoned with.

Another indicator of the group's influence in Moroccan politics is its clout over the peripheral, that is, Islamic, constituency. A crucial test of this influence was the 2007 elections. The PJD was projected to win the 2007 legislative elections with a slight chance of an absolute majority of the votes. For example, Wegner and Pellicer state that prior to the elections, projections showed that the PJD "would gain up to 40% of the vote" (Wegner and Pellicer 2009, 168–69). Even the PJD officials claimed that "seventy to eighty seats were within reach and that the party would be the strongest bloc in the parliament" (Hamzawy 2008, 18). AWI called for a boycott of the elections on the grounds that the elections were illegitimate. Despite the preelection projections, the PJD obtained only 10.9 percent of the votes as the plurality winner and forty-six seats, making it the second-largest party in the legislature (five seats less than the winning Istiqlal Party). Some claim that the failure of the PJD to meet preelection projections was due to AWI's calls for a boycott (McFaul and Wittes 2008). PJD officials attributed their relatively poor performance in the elections to the slanted nature of the electoral system and gerrymandering (El-Khalfi interview, 2009).[37] For example, Bilal Tlaidi argues, "In 2007, they [the government] decided to make another political map in Morocco because they saw that the PJD is a strong party. If we have the real results of the elections, you will find that the PJD had a higher vote percentage. Many analysts stated that more than ten seats of the PJD were stolen" (Tlaidi interview, 2009).[38] Wegner and Pellicer observe that the poor performance of the PJD was due to the measures taken by the Moroccan state to ensure a divided legislature (and opposition). In a political context where governments are made up of multiple parties, a party winning a sizeable percentage of the votes, that is, 40 percent, would enable the party "to assert the prerogatives" of the party vis-à-vis the *makhzen*: "If an elected government is assertive and defends its prerogatives, it is uncomfortable for the regime, irrespective of the policies pursued by any particular party. However moderate the PJD might have been in office, for the regime, a party with such strength would have hampered the pursuit of divide-and-rule politics, an important pillar of regime stability in Morocco" (Wegner and Pellicer 2009, 169).[39]

The outcome of the 2007 election meant that the PJD was able to increase its electoral support by only a slight margin compared with the 2002 elections when it received 13 percent of the votes and forty-two seats in the parliament. Considering the highly fragmented and "profoundly atomized" nature of the Moroccan political system, these percentages are significant (Desrues and Moyano 2001, 30). According to the 2007 election outcomes, the top four parties obtained between 9.3 and 10.9 percent of the vote, and between 12 and 16 percent of the seats.

In 2011, the PJD made its most impressive electoral showing. In the parliamentary elections, the PJD obtained 22.8 percent of the votes, which translated into 27 percent of the parliamentary seats. This was a significant electoral victory for the PJD in the fragmented electoral system of Morocco. The PJD doubled both its vote and seat share. Just as important, the PJD performed much better than other parties in the elections. The closest party was the Istiqlal Party, which obtained 11.9 percent of the votes and 15.2 percent of the seats.

With regard to the PJD's societal support, the preceding numbers are only partially helpful. Self-censoring on the part of the PJD in elections is also necessary to consider when interpreting these data. In recent parliamentary and local elections, the PJD did not field candidates in all districts due to concerns over state reprisal for an overly successful performance.[40] For example, in the 2002 parliamentary elections, the PJD fielded candidates in fifty-five of the ninety-one electoral districts, roughly 60 percent of the seats. Even though some claim that the decision was imposed by the Ministry of Interior, party officials declared that the decision for limited participation was taken long ago "within the party" (Willis 2004, 63). The party's statement, however, contradicted with later statements from the party. Referring to the increased vigilance against Islamic activism in the post–September 11 world, the party recognized on an informal basis that "massive gains, or even victory, for the PJD in the elections was not in its own interest" (Willis 2004, 60). Similarly, following the terrorist attacks in 2003 in Morocco, in the face of increased pressure from secularist circles, the PJD contested only 15 percent of the districts in local elections, winning 700 seats nationwide (Tlaidi interview, 2009).[41] Specific figures on AWI's and the PJD's levels of popularity, therefore, should be taken with caution; they are far from being exact measurements. The main goal of the discussion here is to present rough approximations for each political actor's level of popularity. The overall picture I present clearly shows that both groups enjoy wide popularity in Morocco, and both are able to find an audience for themselves. For the analysis in this book, it is sufficient to have a reasonable conceptualization of the relative standings of the MDP and the conservative Islamist party, which the discussion earlier in this chapter offers.

Post–Arab Spring

Morocco and monarchy went through the Arab Spring relatively unscathed in comparison with countries such as Egypt, Tunisia, and Syria. The limits of the Arab Spring's effect over Morocco (and several other Arab countries) is attributed to its monarchical regime (Bulliet 2011). The fact that the source of legitimacy in monarchical regimes (hereditary and independent of actual performance in governance) differs from military-republican regimes (predominantly formed around performance of leaders) offered monarchical regimes of the Arab world an advantage in weathering the force of the protests in their societies with limited concessions. Morocco is no exception.

Shortly after the initial protests erupted in Tunisia and Egypt, various opposition groups took the initiative to organize protests in Morocco, largely formed around the February 20 Movement, which is named after the largest protests in Morocco during the Arab Spring. The PJD and AWI have opted to pursue different routes in their response to the protests in Morocco. Although sympathetic to the cause of the demonstrations, the PJD decided against taking part in protests due to the party's concern that such a move would "disrupt their own long ingrained path to power" (Spiegel 2015, 4) and that reform could be achieved via "political institutions" (Buehler 2013, 150). The move by the PJD as well as the pressure to undertake constitutional changes appears to have made an impact on the king; the new constitution adopted on July 1, 2011, paved the way for the winner of parliamentary elections to assume the premiership, eliminating the previous practice of arbitrary selection by the king (El Sherif 2012). Indeed, the PJD won the first elections following the constitutional change to ultimately being tasked with forming the government.

As for AWI, its participation in the protests was noticeable right from the beginning. Unlike the PJD, however, AWI's fundamentally antiregime stance gave it the initial push in joining the protests. AWI's participation in the protests that took the regime head-on made sense in this regard. Yet after several months the group decided to distance itself from the protests, at the end of 2011. Spiegel explains that the group's decision to withdraw deals with its strategic thinking:

> The major motivating factor to Al Adl leaving the February 20 movement related to its main Islamist foe [the PJD] and the long-term fears over losing its own base. It is no coincidence that Al Adl returned to the shadows only weeks after PJD's dramatic election victory. The ascent of PJD to the prime ministership, to the highest seats of government, placed Al Adl in a difficult position. Benkirane [the PJD leader] was personally popular with many young Islamists. And the fear among Al Adl was that it could be seen as a "spoil sport," as getting in the way of the most momentous moment for Islamists in the region. (Spiegel 2015, 10)

As far as the theoretical perspective developed in this book is concerned, it is the PJD's participation in Moroccan government for the first time in its history that interests us. In terms of its ideological stance, it is very interesting to observe that the PJD did not promote a more conservative agenda in the post-2011 period; rather, it held onto its nonconfrontational political disposition, emphasizing compromise, governance, and democratic rules. In this regard, the PJD's response to the Egyptian MB's removal from power and later suppression is noteworthy: "It [the PJD] responded not by defending the Muslim Brotherhood against the excesses of the Egyptian state—not by reasserting its own Islamist identity—but rather by faulting the Brotherhood for mismanagement, for poor performance. The PJD maintained that it was different from the Brotherhood, a better version of it, Islamism 2.0. It pointed out that it had done a better job of working with other parties, of taking its time in government, and of working side by side with existing state structures, rather than upsetting them" (Spiegel 2015, 7).

Hence it is not clear whether and how taking part in the government has changed the PJD's ideological outlook. Both the PJD and AWI have indicated in the post-2011 period that their actions as political actors are largely shaped by their desire to gain greater popular support and enhance their political standing. While doing this, both groups maintained the other's actions and the overall context in view.

Conclusion

THE ARGUMENT PRESENTED in this book rests on the basic assumption that Islamists, at both the individual and the party levels, are rational actors who respond to the changing political, social, and economic conditions in their environments. The major social and economic transformations that many Middle Eastern societies experienced in recent decades prompted the research question that motivates the analysis in this book: what factors underlie Islamist moderation toward a Muslim democratic discourse, and under which conditions do such parties become electorally successful?

In answering this pivotal question, I focused on processes of economic liberalization and their disparate impacts on societal dynamics. In particular, I drew attention to the role of politics in economic liberalization by demonstrating that the center-periphery cleavage that exists between the secular and Islamic constituencies interacts with the process of liberalization in creating the support base for Muslim democratic parties (MDPs) in some cases, but not in others. In presenting this argument, I introduced a new conceptual framework to distinguish between two different types of economic liberalizations: competitive liberalization and crony liberalization. When the Islamic social groups, largely on the periphery, benefit from a competitive liberalization process, the chances of the emergence of a successful MDP are high. We observed this in cases such as Turkey and Morocco, where we also observed a simultaneous fundamental shift in terms of where Islamic groups view their self-interest. Democracy (political openness), economic openness, and a much less politicized role for Islam constitute the core of the Islamic periphery's preferences. In cases where crony liberalization is sustained, a successful case of Islamist moderation toward an MDP is highly unlikely, as Egypt's Wasat Party illustrates particularly well. It is not a matter of whether a Muslim democratic platform would emerge; rather, the fundamental issue is the viability of such an ideology. Ideas such as an open economy, a social conception of Islam, and pluralism and transparency do not correspond to the preferences of the Islamic constituency that constitutes the core support base for Islamic parties in the region.

The analysis in this book carries with it several implications. First, despite the numerous criticisms that are leveled against economic globalization, and oftentimes rightly so, the very process of economic globalization may nonetheless introduce a new, independent, and powerful socioeconomic actor to the Middle

East if the conditions are ripe for such a development. This new group fuses a preference for a liberal political and economic order with a conservative outlook as far as the social values it heralds. Put differently, this conservative, or Islamic, constituency makes a deliberate choice in favor of a democratic and liberal system not because of the liberal values it upholds, but rather because of the material interests a democratic regime is likely to sustain. At a time when idealist supporters of democracy are far and few between, the fact that some groups have emerged with a material interest in democratic governance bodes well for the democratic future of these countries. Much like in many other contexts worldwide, the advent of societal actors with a vested interest in democracy greatly elevates the odds in favor of democratization.

The future course of party systems in the region will be shaped by the lasting impact of economic liberalization models adopted, contingent on the resulting social cleavages in each country. Socioeconomic divisions emanating from various economic liberalization policies as well as various conceptions of Islamic identity are two key elements of such cleavages, as I demonstrated in earlier chapters. In this regard, peripheral businesses and the moderation of Islamist parties into MDPs can pave the democratic path in the Middle East. The real issue facing democratization, then, is not the fear of "one man, one vote, one time" should Islamists be allowed to contest free and fair elections; rather, as Shadi Hamid argues, Islamists are comfortable working in a democratic system to promote their ideological discourse; they do not need to uproot democracy to achieve their goals. Islamists have a conviction that the "popular will" favors an "Islamic" state. Instead, what can sustain democratization ultimately is the creation of socioeconomic conditions that may weaken the societal demand for such conservative policies. As such, the "popular will" will have shifted away from favoring an Islamic state, placing Islamists into a lesser position.

Egypt post-2011 offers a striking case. Despite countless positive indicators early on, including the Muslim Brotherhood's (MB) inclination to play down its hand, the military's political quietism, and the euphoria surrounding the removal of an authoritarian leader, the political opening between 2011 and 2013 yielded a rather conservative outcome. Mohamed Morsi of the MB won the presidency, while Salafis and the MB captured 70 percent of the parliamentary seats between them. A remarkable electoral achievement by any standard, it nonetheless demonstrates the potency of societal conservatism. Explanations for Islamist moderation that strictly rely on state strategy or inclusion or exclusion of political actors simply fail in the face of such social conservatism.

What does my theory tell us about the future of democracy in the Middle East? Should we write off a future Egyptian democracy simply because Anwar Sadat's political motivations determined the course of Egyptian economic liberalization for the rest of history, a sort of path dependency? Certainly not. The

Egyptian revolution of 2011 offered a great opportunity to set things right as far as the excessive levels of socioeconomic inequality is concerned. This was in fact one of the earliest and most forceful demands of the protestors in Tahrir Square.

Islamist parties constitute the most viable and organized political group in an overwhelming majority of the regional countries. Any genuine long-term democratization movement must find a way to incorporate these actors into the democratic process. The crux of the problem, however, is not necessarily the Islamist ideology of these political actors in and of itself but rather the constituencies on which these parties rely for their electoral power. As long as the societal demand for conservative political discourse exists, political actors of various stripes will cater to it, be it through mainstream Islamist parties or newly emerging, unapologetically fundamentalist Salafi parties. Favorable conditions for democratization, as I have shown, are nurtured by the strengthening of hitherto peripheral groups under competitive economic liberalization. The economic empowerment of the politically, socially, and economically marginalized Islamic periphery offers the most viable path to democratization. Economic empowerment does not only mean economic prosperity; it underlies a fundamental shift in individual political preferences. Antisystem discourse characterized by a demand for a wholesale change of the political economic structure merely undermines the material interests of this Islamic constituency. A crucial implication of this analysis thus is that leaving Islamists and their social base out of democratization efforts would only be self-defeating.

My argument, however, is not foolproof; I do not, for example, naively believe that I have developed a miracle democratization drug and can now prescribe this perfect path to democratization to various Middle Eastern countries. Yet, even so, I have two goals in mind with this book. First, I underscore the significance of societal dynamics in Islamist politics and how political change that neglects to incorporate society, in particular the Islamic constituency, is likely to fail. Second, my emphasis on the societal aspect of Islamist moderation allows us a better opportunity to observe under which conditions arguments that focus on state strategy and institutional inclusion or exclusion to explain moderation might hold.

The current state of Turkish politics is a case in point. Turkey offers arguably the best-case scenario for how economic liberalization can lead to moderation of Islamist discourse and greater democratization of a Muslim-majority country. Yet recent developments toward greater authoritarianism since 2011 raise a vital question: in a country that liberalized well and has sizeable Muslim democratic support base, how can we ensure that democratization does not fall victim to the kind of leadership displayed by Erdogan? The answer lies in the strengthening of the institutional structure to increase accountability, decentralize governance, and encourage compromise rather than majoritarianism. In other words, shortcomings in institutional structure have allowed such circumstances to arise.

Future research on the topic may proceed in a number of different directions. First, building on the theoretical framework presented in this book, a region-wide analysis of economic liberalization policies and their impact on Islamist parties may broaden the conclusions reached here. In particular, this avenue of research is likely to carry key implications for those eyeing a wave of democratization in the aftermath of the Arab Spring. The findings of a region-wide analysis likewise are critical to better understanding the dynamic relationship between liberalization policies and democratization, ultimately underscoring the inseparable relationship between politics and the economy. This is particularly critical at a juncture when most analyses focus on a political solution to democratization at the detriment of economic woes soaring in the region.

Second, the cross-class coalition behind MDPs consists of two groups: peripheral businesses and masses. The support of the second group, that is, the peripheral masses, for a Muslim democratic platform should be the subject of further analysis. Although extant research has been conducted on the religious bases of masses' support for an Islamist platform, the economic foundation of their support remains largely an uncharted territory for research, and thus is a fertile subject for future research as well. Needless to say, this is another area for further analyzing the economic dynamics of political change.

Finally, an area that remains yet unexplored in this book that nonetheless demands an extensive analysis as it relates to Islamist moderation is the relationship between Islamist parties and the movements from which they hail. Islamist parties that can break away from their social organizations can obtain greater freedom in their dealings with other political actors and feel less obligation to cater to an exclusively religious base. By contrast, Islamist parties that are subdued by their religious organizations fail to display independence and an ability to compromise on policy issues, which is a necessary step for moderation to take root.

Appendix: List of Interviews

Egypt

Ibrahim Al-Bayyoumi Ghanim, professor, Cairo University; Cairo, October 27, 2008.
Khalil Al-Anani, scholar on Islamist movements, Al-Ahram Center; Cairo, October 27, 2008.
Husain Mohamed Ibrahim, former deputy chairman of parliamentary bloc, Muslim Brotherhood (MB); Cairo, October 28, 2008.
Rafik Habib, Egyptian writer and thinker; Cairo, October 28, 2008.
Hamdy Hassan, former MB parliamentarian; Cairo, October 28, 2008.
Hosam Tammam, journalist, Islamonline.net; Cairo, October 29, 2008.
Aboul Ela Mady, Wasat Party chairman; Cairo, October 29, 2008.
Muhammed Habib, former deputy Supreme Guide, MB; Cairo, October 30, 2008.
Abdul Moneim Aboul Fotouh, former member of Guidance Council, MB; Cairo, October 30, 2008.
Ahmed Hamid, youth director, Wasat Party; Cairo, October 31, 2008.
Mohamed Gamal Heshmat, former MB parliamentarian; Cairo, November 1, 2008.
Abdelmonem Mahmoud, MB blogger; Cairo, November 2, 2008.
Ahmed Diab, former MB parliamentarian; Cairo, November 3, 2008.
Mostafa Alnagar, MB blogger; Cairo, November 3, 2008.
Fahmy Howeidy, Islamist journalist; Cairo, November 4, 2008.
Cihan Al-Halafavi, former candidate for parliament, MB; Alexandria, November 8, 2008.
Ibrahim Zaafarani, member of Consultative Council, MB; Alexandria, November 8, 2008.
AbdelHamed Al-Ghazali, MB advisor, and professor, Cairo University; Cairo, November 11, 2008.
Osama Farid, Islamist intellectual; Cairo, November 11, 2008.
Amal Wahab, journalist; Cairo, November 12, 2008.
Tarek El-Bishri, Islamist intellectual; Cairo, November 14, 2008.
Fareed Abd Al-Khaleek, former member of the Guidance Council, MB; Cairo, November 16, 2008.
Hazem Farouk Mansour, former MB parliamentarian; Cairo, November 16, 2008.
Issam Al-Aryan, former member of the Guidance Council, MB; Cairo, November 17, 2008.
Ali Fath Al-Bab, former MB parliamentarian; Cairo, November 17, 2008.
Nahed Eizzeddeen Abd Al-Hamed, professor, Cairo University; Cairo, November 19, 2008.
Diaa Rashwan, scholar on Islamist movements, Al-Ahram Center; Cairo, November 19, 2008.

Mustapha Kamel Al Sayyid, director of the Center for the Study of Developing Countries at Cairo University; Cairo, November 20, 2008.
Eman Kandil, founding member, Wasat Party; Cairo, November 22, 2008.
Amani Aboul Fadl Farag, MB member; Cairo, November 23, 2008.
Ekmeleddin Ihsanoglu, former secretary general, OIC (Organization of Islamic Conference); Cairo, November 28, 2008.
Cumali Onal, journalist; Cairo, November 30, 2008.
EG-1-B, Businessman; Cairo, November 11, 2008.
EG-2-B, Businessman; Cairo, November 11, 2008.
EG-3-B, Businessman; Cairo, November 12, 2008.
EG-4-B, Businessman; Cairo, November 23, 2008.
EG-5-B, Businessman; Cairo, November 23, 2008.
EG-6-B, Businessman; Cairo, November 25, 2008.
EG-7-B, Businessman; Cairo, November 26, 2008.
EG-9-B, Businessman; Cairo, November 26, 2008.
EG-8-B, Businessman; Cairo, November 27, 2008.
EG-10-B, Businessman; Cairo, November 28, 2008.
EG-11-B, Businessman; Cairo, November 30, 2008.
EG-12-B, Businessman; Cairo, November 31, 2008.

Morocco

Mustapha El-Khalfi, Party for Justice and Development (PJD) official and editor of *Al-Tajdid* newspaper; Rabat, December 8, 2009.
Saad Eddin Uthmani, former secretary general, PJD; Rabat, December 8, 2009.
Dr. Driss Bouanou, youth leader and member of Committee on Foreign Relations, PJD; Rabat, December 10, 2009.
Abdulkader Amara, PJD parliamentarian and member of PJD General Secretariat; Rabat, December 17, 2009.
Bilal Tlaidi, independent researcher, and reporter for *Al-Tajdid* newspaper; Rabat, December 17, 2009.
Nadia Yassine, Al-Adl wal-Ihsan (AWI) spokesperson; Rabat, December 17, 2009.
Lahcen Daoudi, PJD parliamentarian; Rabat, December 18, 2009.
AbdelWahed Al-Mutawakkil, head of AWI political bureau; Rabat, December 21, 2009.
Nezha El-Ouafi, PJD parliamentarian and academician; Rabat, December 23, 2009.
Noureddine Karbal, PJD parliamentarian; Rabat, December 23, 2009.
Rida Bin Khaldun, PJD parliamentarian and member of PJD Committee on Foreign Relations; Rabat, December 24, 2009.
MA-1-B, Businessman; Rabat, December 8, 2009.
MA-2-B, Businessman; Fes, December 11, 2009.
MA-3-B, Businessman; Fes, December 11, 2009.
MA-4-B, Businessman; Fes, December 11, 2009.
MA-5-B, Businessman; Fes, December 12, 2009.
MA-6-B, Businessman; Casablanca, December 14, 2009.
MA-7-B, Businessman; Casablanca, December 14, 2009.

MA-8-B, Businessman; Casablanca, December 14, 2009.
MA-9-B, Businessman; Casablanca, December 14, 2009.
MA-10-B, Businessman; Casablanca, December 15, 2009.
MA-11-B, Businessman; Casablanca, December 15, 2009.
MA-12-B, Businessman; Casablanca, December 15, 2009.
MA-13-B, Businessman; Casablanca, December 16, 2009.
MA-14-B, Businessman; Casablanca, December 16, 2009.
MA-15-B, Businessman; Casablanca, December 22, 2009.
MA-16-B, Businessman; Casablanca, December 24, 2009.

Turkey

Yasar Yakis, former AKP parliamentarian; Ankara, August 29, 2008.
Nevzat Pakdil, former AKP parliamentarian; Ankara, September 2, 2008.
Dengir Mir Mehmet Firat, former AKP parliamentarian, and former deputy chairman, AKP; Ankara, September 3, 2008.
Reha Denemeç, former deputy chairman, AKP; Ankara, September 3, 2008.
Ali Riza Alaboyun, former AKP parliamentarian; Ankara, September 5, 2008.
Nursuna Memecan, former AKP parliamentarian; Istanbul, September 8, 2008.
Ibrahim Ozturk, Independent Industrialists and Businessmen's Association (MUSIAD) advisor; Istanbul, September 10, 2008.
Aziz Babuscu, Istanbul province chairman, AKP; Istanbul, September 11, 2008.
Feyzullah Kiyiklik, AKP parliamentarian; Istanbul, September 11, 2008.
Mustafa Atas, AKP parliamentarian; Istanbul, September 11, 2008.
Halide Incekara, former AKP parliamentarian; Istanbul, September 11, 2008.
Aysenur Bilgi Solak, former Istanbul province chairman, AKP; Istanbul, September 12, 2008.
Yusuf Tulun, former Sariyer-Istanbul mayor, AKP; Istanbul, September 12, 2008.
Omer Can, former Sahinbey-Gaziantep mayor, AKP; Gaziantep, September 17, 2008.
Adil Tekin, Gaziantep local official, AKP; Gaziantep, September 17, 2008.
Numan Kurtulmus, former FP chairman and current AKP parliamentarian; Ankara, October 12, 2008.
Mehmet Dulger, former AKP parliamentarian; Ankara, October 13, 2008.
Mustafa Ozbayrak, former AKP parliamentarian; Ankara, October 14, 2008.
Ersonmez Yarbay, former AKP parliamentarian; Ankara, October 14, 2008.
Edibe Sozen, former deputy chairman, AKP; Ankara, October 14, 2008.
Recai Kutan, former FP chairman; Ankara, October 15, 2008.
TR-1-B, Businessman; Kayseri, September 4, 2008.
TR-2-B, Businessman; Kayseri, September 4, 2008.
TR-3-B Businessman; Kayseri, September 4, 2008.
TR-4-B Businessman; Ankara, September 5, 2008.
TR-5-B, Businessman; Istanbul, September 9, 2008.
TR-6-B, Businessman; Istanbul, September 9, 2008.
TR-7-B, Businessman; Istanbul, September 10, 2008.
TR-8-B, Businessman; Gaziantep, September 16, 2008.

TR-9-B, Businessman; Gaziantep, September 16, 2008.
TR-10-B, Businessman; Gaziantep, September 16, 2008.
TR-11-B, Businessman; Gaziantep, September 17, 2008.
TR-12-B, Businessman; Gaziantep, September 17, 2008.
TR-13-B, Businessman; Izmir, September 23, 2008.
TR-14-B, Businessman; Izmir, September 23, 2008.
TR-15-B, Businessman; Izmir, September 24, 2008.
TR-16-B, Businessman; Izmir, September 24, 2008.
TR-17-B, Businessman; Izmir, September 26, 2008.
TR-18-B, Businessman; Izmir, September 27, 2008.
TR-19-B, Businessman; Ankara, October 10, 2008.

Notes

Introduction

1. The absence of a consensus is most clearly demonstrated by the use of a multiplicity of terms to define these parties such as Islamist, Islamic, post-Islamist, and Muslim reformist. The Justice and Development Party in Turkey, for example, does not accept the title "Muslim democratic party" partly due to the religious connotations of the name. Instead, the party calls itself a conservative democratic party (Akdoğan 2004; Karakaya and Yildirim (2013).

2. On the AKP's economic policy, see AKP Program 2001, sections 2 and 3.1; AKP Program 2007, section 3.1. On the Egyptian Wasat Party's economic policies, WP Political Program 2004, 10–11, 15–23; Mady interview, 2008. Finally, on Moroccan PJD's economic policy, see PJD 2007 Electoral Program. See Demiralp (2009).

3. Even though the policy positions of MDPs seem in conflict with each other, there are two similar cases in Europe that might make this case of MDPs more conceivable. The first one is the Third Way of Tony Blair in Europe, combining liberal and social economic ideas as well other cases of social market economies in Northern Europe. The second one is the Christian democratic parties in Europe, which have policy positions similar to those of MDPs as described above. For a detailed discussion, see Öniş and Keyman (2003).

4. Following the coup in Egypt in the summer of 2013, some Muslim Brotherhood members' take on violence and radicalization has begun to shift under extreme repression by the Sisi regime. It remains to be seen how long the youth within the Muslim Brotherhood in Egypt can sustain their tendency to violence. See Brown and Dunne (2015) and Fahmi (2015) for detailed discussion.

5. Notable exceptions to single case studies include Cesari (2014) and Driessen (2014).

6. Egypt's (−2) score in the Polity IV dataset comes on the heels of the Arab Spring and was short-lived, reverting (−4) after a year.

1. A Social Theory of Muslim Democratic Parties

1. Randall (2001) presents a well-thought discussion of social cleavages in the developing world, and how the original framework presented by Lipset and Rokkan (1967) might be inadequate for accurate analyses in a developing world context.

2. See Farah (2009) and Kuru (2007) for examples of analyses building on social cleavages to explain economic policies and secularism, respectively. Ergun Özbudun's account of state-society relations highlights the most important legacy of the Ottoman Empire on post-Ottoman countries; see Özbudun (1996). Ali Çarkoğlu provides empirical evidence for the division between center and periphery based on survey data. See Çarkoğlu (2006).

3. Unlike in the West, there was no industrial revolution and the associated economic structure nor landed elite until the late nineteenth and the early twentieth centuries. See Özbudun (1996), 137.

4. Steven Cook also points out the similarities between Turkey and Egypt and how Ataturk's model was replicated in other regional countries (2007, 9).

5. The use of "center" and "periphery" as concepts in sociopolitical analysis can also be found in Mardin (1989, 2006) and Yavuz (2003). Ali Çarkoğlu (2006) provides empirical evidence for the division between center and periphery based on survey data.

6. On democratization, see Milner and Kubota (2005). On government spending, see Rodrik (1998). On partisan politics, see Garrett (1998). On social policies, see Cameron (1978); Bates, Brock, and Tiefenthaler (1991); Katzenstein (1995); Rodrik (1997); Rudra (2002).

7. Erik Wibbels's (2006) discussion of "patterns of integration to the global markets" deals with the distinction mainly between developed and developing countries with respect to access to capital markets. Ben Ross Schneider's conceptual distinction between different elements of economic reform seems a step in the right direction, yet Schneider falls short of detailing his approach and its implications. See Schneider (2004a).

8. One factor facilitating the survival of peripheral SMEs in the open economy is their focus on the exports sector rather than the domestic market initially. Through subcontracting and other subsidiary mechanisms, peripheral businesses were able to remain in the market despite the threat of cheaper imports. See Gülalp (2001).

9. The concept of crony liberalization is based on the more familiar term "crony capitalism," usually applied within the context of East Asian economies in the post-1997 Asian crisis analyses. For detailed discussion of crony capitalism, see Enderwick (2005); Haber (2002). A more recent analysis by Amr Ismail Adly applies the concept of cronyism in a liberal economy context as "politically-embedded cronyism." See Adly (2009) for a detailed discussion.

10. Some of the differences between the two models include the level of export-orientation in the economy, depth of Import Substitution Industrialization (ISI) policies, and the role of partisan politics. See Kurtz and Brooks (2008) for a detailed discussion of "embedded neoliberalism."

11. For a thorough discussion of how rule of law and secure property rights relate to regime type, see Alexander (2002) and Jayasuriya (1996).

12. For Bellin (2000), the level of support that different social groups such as capitalists and labor give to democracy is contingent on several factors such as state dependency, fear, and aristocratic position. Though my analysis differs from Bellin's on the role of such factors, the basic intuition that material interest drives the preference on democracy is the same. Also see Amaney Jamal (2007) for discussion of how distinct political settings interact differently with social capital to result in varying preferences for democracy.

13. The argument I develop here does not envision fixed regime preferences for businessmen. Rather, businessmen's preference for a regime type will largely depend on the socioeconomic conditions they face in their own society. For a similar analysis of regime preference of business, see Schneider (2004b) on business-state relations in Latin America.

14. See Kenneth Shadlen's (1999, 2002) discussions of small industries in Latin America and Mexico. Shadlen conducts a thorough analysis of how, when, and why SMEs organize.

15. The interest in stability depends on changing stakes for all actors. Stability in a closed economy, by the very fact that it perpetuates current socioeconomic relations, conflicts with the interests of peripheral groups, whereas stability in a competitive liberal economy enables the same group to utilize the resources openness affords in order to protect its interests.

2. Modeling Economic Liberalization in a Comparative Perspective

1. Dillman argues that petroleum-related industries make up about 35 percent of the industrial production. See Dillman (2001).

2. For a thorough discussion of the use of trade-weighted tariff rates in comparison to other methods, see Anderson and Neary (1994) and Pritchett and Sethi (1994).

3. The WEF's competitiveness index is created based on two principal sources. Two-thirds of the indicators in the index are based on expert opinions through the Executive Opinion Survey the Forum conducts on a regular basis with more than 10,000 respondents in more than 100 countries worldwide. The remaining one-third rests on publicly available data sources. The survey responses range between a low of one and a high of seven.

4. See Rodrik (1990) for a critique of the economic programs implemented during the period.

5. Note that the exporting sector does not necessarily include the entire bourgeoisie and business class before 1980. In this era, we observe the emergence of a new group of entrepreneurs who find opportunities in the export sector. See Hansen (1991) for a detailed discussion of the policy export promotion in Turkey during that period.

6. Erol Katircioglu, "Neler Oluyor?," *Radikal*, June 7, 2008.

7. Others have taken a different view by dividing Turkish liberalization into phases between 1980 and 1983, 1983 and 1987, and post-1987. See Altinkemer and Ekinci (1992).

8. Data from the IMF *Government Finance Statistics Yearbook*, various years.

9. See *Delegation of the European Union to Turkey* website for a detailed historical account of the Turkey-EU relationship: http://www.avrupa.info.tr/AB_ve_Turkiye/Gumruk_Birligi.html.

10. Law 65 from 1971 is an early example of such attempts. Law 65 established free zones that enjoyed benefits such as tax exemption and various incentives to attract foreign investment. See Farah (2009) and Rivlin (1985).

11. The law stipulated that in order to qualify as a private enterprise and benefit from the incentives the state offered, joint ventures of limited extent would also count as private enterprise (Farah 2009, 38).

12. Although I do not theorize about the causes of competitive or crony liberalization and treat them as exogenous, it is an important question nonetheless. Two of the most important political economic explanations to that end come from Carles Boix (2003) and Daron Acemoglu and James Robinson (2005). By recourse to a rational choice model and various variables such as income inequality, capital mobility, economic crisis, and repressive capacities, they analyze the conditions that facilitate the emergence of a democratic system. Although such models might seem plausible for Egypt and Morocco due to the overlap between cronyism and the absence of democracy, in other cases they may fail to explain the persistence of cronyism in democratic settings. In the Turkish case, for example, the existence of democracy did not eliminate the entrenched crony relationship between the state and big business, particularly between 1950 and the 1990s. Hence the causal direction of the relationship between democracy and cronyism does not necessarily have to run from the former to the latter.

13. These six ministries were agriculture, foreign trade and industry, housing, health, social welfare, and transportation. See Farah (2009), 49.

14. Data from the World Bank's World Development Indicators.

15. See Farah's detailed discussion of several privatized companies in this period (2009, 45–46).

16. According to Atul Kohli's categorization, Morocco would fall under "fragmented-multiclass states" where economic development and industrialization are only two among many goals of the political elite. See Kohli (2004).

17. Although CGEM was only representing the big businesses prior to liberalization, with the integration of the newly emerging businesses throughout the Moroccan economy, it obtained a dual character in terms of the interests it intended to represent.

18. The study was conducted by the Moroccan Ministry of Planning in 1990 and 1991, and called *National Survey of Standards of Living, 1990–91*. The study is quoted in Denoeux and Maghraoui (1998).

19. Data from World Development Indicators and the International Labor Organization.

20. The decision to increase the level of relations with the European Union to the level of partnership rose due to a conflict between Morocco and the European Union over the comments of the European parliament on Moroccan human rights violations, on which the European Union blocked the financial assistance to Morocco. See Gregory White (1996) for a detailed discussion. Also see Gregory White (2001) for an exhaustive analysis of the EU-Morocco relations since 1960s.

21. Even though the European Union has been trying to implement a similar cooperation agreement with Egypt, such a complete agreement is not expected for several years. See Dillman (2001).

3. From the Periphery to the Center

1. For an extensive discussion on the origins of the divide between secular and conservative groups, see Feroz Ahmad's (1969) insightful analysis of the Young Turks and their influence over the course of the late Ottoman Empire and the early Turkish Republic.

2. Zafer Toprak's (1982) exhaustive analysis on the application of statist economic policies in the late Ottoman Empire is informative on the subject. According to Toprak, capital-holders or labor never was an integral part of decision making. All decision making pertaining to the economy was strictly controlled by the state.

3. See Ayse Bugra's (1994) thorough analysis of several businessmen from both the Ottoman and the Republican periods does an excellent job in documenting the relationship between businessmen and the state until economic liberalization begins in Turkey. Also see Charles Issawi's (1982) discussion in a comparative perspective.

4. An interesting fact relating to this period is the rationale of how such protectionist policies are implemented. The discussions from that period reveal the early forms of an Import Substitution Industrialization (ISI) rationale as the main dynamic behind protectionism rather than simply avoiding foreign competition. See the comments of Celal Bayar, the then minister of economy, on import substitution policies during that period in Tekeli and Ilkin (1982, 186–187).

5. See Hansen (1991) for a detailed discussion of Turkish statist economic policies during this period.

6. The early nation formation period saw the Kurds, the Alawites, and non-Muslim citizens (Orthodox Greeks, Armenians, and Jews) of the new state as potential threats to the unity of the Turkish and Sunni-Muslim Turkish Republic.

7. Sabrina Tavernise, "In Turkey, Bitter Feud Has Roots in History," *New York Times*, June 22, 2008.

8. National Outlook Movement (NOM; Milli Gorus Hareketi) has been the name of the universal political Islamist movement in Turkey with the following successive political parties: Milli Nizam Partisi (MNP), Milli Selamet Partisi (MSP), Refah Partisi (RP), Fazilet Partisi (FP), and Saadet Partisi (SP).

9. Reha Denemeç argues the following: "When you look at the founders, the founders of both parties are the selected elite of Turkey, the elite coming from inside the CHP, but the social base is distinct" (Denemeç interview, 2008).

10. The prime minister of the period, Suleyman Demirel, opposed Erbakan's election on the grounds that a person who is the general secretary of TOBB could not be the president simultaneously. Erbakan was removed from the office by police escort, and the issue was taken to the court, ending in Erbakan's dislike. Recently, Erbakan was invited to attend the Advisory Council Meeting of TOBB among the former presidents of TOBB, an implicit recognition of Erbakan's legitimate claim to the office back in 1969. "Erbakan, TOBB Yuksek Istisare Kurulu'na Katildi," *Milli Gazete*, February 16, 2010.

11. Erbakan's goal was to replace bank interests with a model of banking based on "investment and profit sharing," an idea almost identical to contemporary Islamic banking systems. See Erbakan (1975), Sarıbay (1985, 111, 125, and 199), and Şen (1995).

12. The emphasis on Anatolia is critical to distinguish the NOM's focus from that of Istanbul-based big businesses.

13. Erik Meyersson also shows that during the 1990s the WP empowered the poor and the marginalized in the society via its policies in party-controlled municipalities (2014).

14. See Bianchi (1984) for a discussion of TOBB-like business associations and the role of the state in trying to create a corporatist structure in Turkey.

15. For example, Mehmet Sonmez, the CEO of Eurobank Tekfen, stated in a recent interview, "In Turkey, SMEs with $2.5-$10 million [annual turnover] are a significant potential. To give an example, the economic potential in Umraniye, Istanbul, is the same as the Bologna region of Italy. SMEs constitute the backbone of economic development for a country. It is impossible to ignore the economic value of Turkish SMEs. You cannot reach anywhere with big holdings. It is the push of SMEs that have undergirded our country's economic growth in recent years." See "Sadece Buyuk Holdingler ile Olmaz, Turkiye KOBI'ler Sayesinde Buyudu," *Zaman*, June 18, 2009.

16. In 2010, MUSIAD membership stood at 4,720.

17. See various MUSIAD reports (www.musiad.org.tr) and Bolat 2007.

18. The support of MUSIAD for EU membership is another facet of the organization's support for democratic development, as discussed by the group's former president, Omer Bolat. See Bolat (2007), 22.

19. For example, for the video presentation prepared to celebrate the fifteenth year of the association, the theme chosen was "High Morals—High Technology." See Bolat (2007).

20. See Suleyman Yasar, "TUSIAD'a Ihtiyacimiz Yok," *Taraf*, March 24, 2009.

21. See Umit Boyner's (TUSIAD president) interview: "Anadolu Sermayesi, Demokratiklesmenin Gostergesi," *Zaman*, March 21, 2009.

22. See "Eski Isvec Buyukelcisi'nden TUSIAD'a Agir Suclama," *Zaman*, June 3, 2008.

23. Erbakan was not able to contest in the election because he was banned from actively taking part in politics.

24. In the elections, Abdullah Gul received 521 votes representing the reformist wing, whereas Recai Kutan won the election with 633 on behalf of Necmettin Erbakan.

25. See Akdoğan (2004) for a discussion of conservative democracy and Muslim democracy.

26. See Sabrina Tavernise, "Newfound Riches Come with Spiritual Costs for Turkey's Religious Merchants," *New York Times*, December 25, 2008.

27. See Sabrina Tavernise, "Turkish City Counters Fear of Islam's Reach," *New York Times*, May 15, 2007.

28. The AKP rejected all the evidence in this case, including that against the headscarf legislation, on the basis that none of the evidence in the indictment technically amounted to being evidence according to law. The AKP argued that all evidence was collected from newspaper

clips and articles, information that does not reflect the party's official position in any way. See the AKP's response to the indictment: *AK Parti'nin Esas Hakkindaki Cevaplari* (2008).

29. Sabrina Tavernise, "For Many Turks, Head Scarf's Return Aids Religion and Democracy," *New York Times*, January 30, 2008.

30. Ibid.

31. Ismet Berkan, "Laikler Akilli Olmazsa Laiklik Korunamaz," *Radikal*, January 30, 2008.

32. See Emre Akoz, "Su Sihirli Kelime," *Sabah*, April 3, 2008.

33. On various occasions and by different party officials, the party criticized the application of secularism in Turkey. For example, Bulent Arinc, the former speaker of the parliament, made the following statement: "Neither me nor anyone else can have a serious objection against secularism. But you need to clearly put forward what it is that you mean by secularism. An understanding that would turn people's social lives into jails with an application of rigid secularism is quite dangerous." See "Kati Laiklik Sosyal Cezaevi Yaratir," *Aksam*, April 26, 2006. In addition, the AKP continued its critique even in its defense against the indictment. The party argued that it adhered to secularism as a "political and legal principle" but not as a "life style." For the AKP, the prosecutor's interpretation of democracy and secularism was not up to the universal conception of the concepts. See *AK Parti'nin Esas Hakkindaki Cevaplari* (2008).

34. See "Turkiye'de Somurge Modeli Laiklik Uygulaniyor," *Zaman*, March 14, 2008.

35. See "Beyond the Veil," *Economist*, June 14, 2008. A *Financial Times* editorial also criticized the case against the AKP by pointing out the failures of the AKP government in pursuing more reforms and democratization. See "Upturning Turkey," *Financial Times*, March 21, 2008.

36. According to Emre Akoz, the bureaucratic elite consists of those high-level bureaucrats who are at a decision-making position such as generals, high-level judiciary, and university presidents. See Emre Akoz, "Ser Sebekesi," *Sabah*, June 11, 2008.

37. Ozbayrak argues that the kind of secularism applied in Turkey is very similar to a "Stalinist interpretation" where secularism is framed more as atheism (Ozbayrak interview, 2008).

38. Some secularists claim that certain types of headscarf styles (mostly the more modern and stylish veiling options) entail political symbolism. Specifically, they represent political Islam, which they argue violates the principle of secularism understood as the separation of religion and politics altogether. For a thorough discussion, see Islam (2010).

39. The big businessman making the statement is Rahmi Koc, the owner of the holding who is viewed as the personification of the state-business relationship par excellence throughout the statist period. The reference to the beard and mustache is perceived to be to the form of Islamic facial hair rather than any beard or mustache.

40. See the interview with Ayse Botan Berker of Fitch Turkey: "Darbe Rafa Kalkti Turkiye'nin Notu Artti," *Yeni Safak*, December 4, 2009.

41. The specific reference was to a bombing in Istanbul carried out by the PKK (Kurdistan Workers' Party). The concurrence of the bombing with increased political instability was the main reason for the canceled order.

42. The military published an electronic statement on its website on the night of the presidential election in the parliament, directly aimed at the AKP and its candidate, Abdullah Gul. See Mustafa Gurbuz, "Iletisim Cagini e-Bildiri ile Yakalamak," *Zaman*, May 22, 2007.

43. For a detailed discussion of the economic impact of recent political instability, see Seref Oguz, "30 Milyar Dolarlik Fatura," *Sabah*, March 18, 2008.

44. The reference with legal means is to the CHP's taking most legislation to the Constitutional Court following passage in the parliament. Many economic and social reform legislation packages were overturned by the court.

45. The reference to "a resource" is to economic privileges that the secular elite enjoyed throughout the closed economy period in Turkey. It is not a specific resource, but opportunities in the form of incentives, subsidies, and access to the market and credit.

46. The use of the term "majoritarian" in this context is distinct from the use of the term in Westminster-style democracies where the connotation of the term "majority" is to the rule of the majority as a method. In contrast, I use the term to denote the idea that the majority's decision is the rule regardless of its potential implications for the rights of the minority, which is in direct contrast to the use of the term in Westminster-style democracies. See Lijphart (1999).

47. Various international reports on human rights point to these issues in their reports on Turkey. For example, see the US Department of State's *2009 Human Rights Report: Turkey* (US Department of State 2009) or the European Parliament's *Turkey Progress Report 2009* (European Parliament 2009).

48. See the booklet prepared by the party, "Sorulari ve Cevaplariyla Demokratik Acilim Sureci: Milli Birlik ve Kardeslik Projesi" (2010), available at www.akparti.org.tr/acilim220110.pdf.

49. *Alevi Calistaylari Nihai Rapor* [hereafter, Alevi Workshops Final Report], February 4, 2010.

50. Traditionally, Alevis in Turkey have been associated with secular and socialist political discourse along the lines of the CHP. The level of tension between the conservative peripheral constituency and the Alevis are the most between any two social groups in Turkey.

51. Sahin Alpay, "Aleviligin Resmen Taninmasina Dogru Bir Adim," *Zaman*, February 16, 2010.

52. A point also mentioned by a local AKP official in Gaziantep. Adil Tekin, personal interview, September 17, 2008, Gaziantep.

53. Alevi Workshops Preliminary Report 2010; Talha Kose, 2010, *Alevi Opening and the Democratization Initiative in Turkey*, SETA Policy Report.

54. "'Alevilik' Ders Kitaplarina Girdi," *Radikal*, September 8, 2011.

55. See Erdogan interview: "We Are not Rooted in Religion," *Newsweek*, May 12, 2008.

56. EU progress reports 2004, 2005, 2008.

57. See "Ermeni Cemaati Ak Parti'ye Egilimli," *Ntvmsnbc*, June 11, 2007. Others in the AKP have reiterated the same idea: Ozbayrak interview, 2008; Yakis interview, 2008.

58. Sabrina Tavernise, "Turkey to Alter Speech Law," *New York Times*, January 25, 2008.

59. In interviews and other public statements, AKP officials did oppose the banning of all parties (Denemeç, Yakis interviews, 2008). However, the AKP did not invest the same level of opposition against the banning of political parties when the Constitutional Court decided on the DTP case as opposed to how it dealt with the move to ban itself.

60. A. Turan Alkan, "Timsahlarla Dans da Kural Gerektirir," *Zaman*, February 22, 2010.

61. The reference here is to the republican rallies prior to the presidential elections in 2007. When, according to surveys, the AKP candidate Abdullah Gul had the support of a majority both in the parliament and among the electorate, a secular group vehemently opposed Gul's candidacy on the grounds that he was antisecular. The CHP was one of the key actors in these rallies.

62. In addition to approval of the progress toward more transparency, another businessman also claimed that significant favoritism continues especially on local bids (TR-19-B interview, 2008).

63. Omer Bolat, the former president of MUSIAD, draws attention to the same point. See Bolat (2007).

64. Welfare Party Fourth National Congress Opening Speech by Necmettin Erbakan, quoted in Şen (2004, 106). The idea of the "Just Economic Order" lays out a relatively equitable

socioeconomic system that would help lower classes and smaller businesses, that is, the disadvantaged, through redistribution. It became a popular term, winning the Welfare Party significant support among lower classes.

65. See "Erbakan AK Parti'yi Elestirdi," *Sabah*, October 29, 2009.

66. AKP Fifty-Ninth Government Program, March 18, 2003, available at www.akparti.org.tr/tbmm/tbmmgrup/59hükümet%20programı.doc.

67. Data from the Turkish Statistical Institute, available at http://www.turkstat.gov.tr/SagMenu/gunceleng/guncel.xml (accessed March 23, 2009).

68. For Numan Kurtulmus's statement, see "Saadet Partisi'nden 'Komunist' Cikis," *Radikal*, January 23, 2010.

69. For Mehmet Bekaroglu's statement, see "Bekaroglu: Basortululer Jip Kullanamaz," *Haber 7*, February 12, 2009.

70. "Obama Says U.S., Turkey Can Be Model for World," *CNN*, April 6, 2009, available at http://www.edition.cnn.com/2009/POLITICS/04/06/obama.turkey/index.html; "Turkish Democracy: A Model for Other Countries?," *NPR*, April 14, 2011, available at http://www.npr.org/2011/04/14/135407687/turkish-democracy-a-model-for-other-countries.

71. "Hopes Fade for New Charter as Commission Dissolved," *Today's Zaman*, November 19, 2013; Yavuz Baydar, "Turkey's Draft Constitution Appears Dead," *Al-Monitor*, November 20, 2013, available at http://www.al-monitor.com/pulse/originals/2013/11/turkey-constitution-parliament-polarization-democratization.html.

72. Can Dundar of the daily *Cumhuriyet* put together a thorough report of the corruption, particularly as it relates to Erdogan. For the first day of the reporting, see Can Dundar, "'Tak Tak Cuvalla Gelir Insallah,'" *Cumhuriyet*, August 6, 2014. A misconception about the December 17–25 process is that it has been cast as a conflict of two Islamic groups, that is, the AKP and the Gulen Movement. This framing works perfectly with the image that the AKP and Erdogan want to create; by creating an imagined enemy, the AKP aims to solidify its support base and close the ranks. In the period leading up to critical elections, such polarization is being utilized as a valuable political tactic. In contrast to Prime Minister Erdogan's suggestions, the Gulen Movement has been critical of many AKP policies since the late 2000s, despite its expressed support for the party until very recently.

73. Ceylan Yeginsu, "Turkey Lifts Twitter Ban after Court Calls It Illegal," *New York Times*, April 3, 2014.

74. For detailed discussion of electoral fraud and statistical analyses on such fraud, see Erik Meyersson's analysis at http://erikmeyersson.com/2014/04/11/capital-fraud-in-turkey-evidence-from-citizen-initiatives (accessed August 25, 2015).

75. "Power Blackouts Mar Counting Votes," *Hurriyet Daily News*, March 30, 2014, retrieved from http://www.hurriyetdailynews.com/power-blackouts-mar-counting-votes.aspx?pageID=238&nID=64322&NewsCatID=338.

76. For statements about cats, poor weather conditions, and elections, see "Turkish Elections Power Blackout Culprit Found: A Cat," *Hurriyet Daily News*, April 1, 2014.

77. See Erik Meyersson's analysis at http://erikmeyersson.com/2014/04/06/trouble-in-turkeys-elections/ (accessed August 25, 2015).

78. "Cihan News Agency Web Page under Cyber Attack," *Dunya Times*, March 30, 2014, retrieved from http://en.dunyatimes.com/article/cihan-news-agency-web-page-under-cyber-attack-28305.html.

79. "Erdogan Targets Enemies after Poll Triumph," *Reuters*, March 31, 2014, retrieved from http://www.reuters.com/article/2014/03/31/us-turkey-election-idUSBREA2R12X20140331?feedType=RSS&feedName=topNews&utm_source=dlvr.it&utm_medium=twitter&dlvrit=992637.

80. Ahmet Kuru, "Corruption, Islamism, and Twitter in Turkey," *openDemocracy*, March 14, 2014, retrieved from http://www.opendemocracy.net/arab-awakening/ahmet-t-kuru/corruption-islamism-and-twitter-in-turkey.

81. Anup Shah, "Democracy" *Global Issues*, January 28, 2012, retrieved from http://www.globalissues.org/article/761/democracy.

82. Sergei Guriev and Daniel Treisman, "The New Dictators Rule by Velvet Fist," *New York Times*, May 24, 2015.

83. "Erdogan's Rise to Power through the Media," *Econoscale*, February 15, 2014, retrieved from http://econoscale.com/2014/02/15/erdogans-rise-to-power-through-the-media/.

84. For example, according to a survey conducted by the International Transparency Organization in Turkey, fewer than a quarter of AKP voters believe that corruption allegations will lead them to reconsider their vote choice (Uluslararasi Seffaflik Dernegi 2015, 20). Likewise, according to a different public opinion survey by KONDA, three-quarters of AKP voters view the allegations as a conspiracy against Erdogan, while 20 percent think corruption is happening at its usual levels in Turkey. Among respondents who think corruption is as much as at any other time in Turkey, about 40 percent are AKP voters (KONDA 2014, 34–35).

85. Kristin Fabbe, "Turkey's Secularization in Reverse?," *Washington Post*, February 9, 2015; Joseph Loconte, "Turkey, Islamism, and the West," *Weekly Standard*, June 22, 2015; Joost Lagendijk, "AKP: From Post-Islamist Back to Soft-Islamist?," *Today's Zaman*, December 26, 2014.

86. "Erdogan Meets Abbas with Military Dress Show," *Hurriyet Daily News*, January 12, 2015.

87. "Ottomans Enter Turkish Elections Race, Stoking Social Media," *Hurriyet Daily News*, February 26, 2015.

88. In an interesting episode that showcases the AKP's instrumental (rather than policy) approach to religion, former minister Egemen Bagis's mocking of the Qur'an is tolerated by party leadership despite a well-publicized surfacing of the audiotapes of Bagis. Taking action against Bagis would simply undermine the AKP's political legitimacy.

89. Tim Arango, "Turkish Leader, Using Conflicts, Cements Power," *New York Times*, October 31, 2014.

90. "Erdogan: 400 Milletvekilini Verin ve Bu Is Huzur Icinde Cozulsun," *T24*, March 7, 2015, available at http://t24.com.tr/haber/cumhurbaskani-erdogan-gaziantespte-konusuyor,289627.

4. Stuck in the Periphery

1. See Cooper (1982) for a detailed discussion of class structures in Egypt until 1970.

2. The reforms were initiated by Nasser with the March 30 Program in 1968. The program laid down stipulations to increase the share of the private sector by (1) increasing freedom of movement of goods and capital, (2) expanding the activity area of the private sector, and (3) ensuring private property rights. The program also included provisions on the public sector to "depoliticize" it (Cooper 1982, 44).

3. See Tamir Moustafa's innovative discussion on the origins of the Supreme Constitutional Court and a new constitution in Egypt, where Moustafa argues that the principal reason for Sadat to introduce a new constitution and increase the independence of the court was to provide a secure environment for the business sector (Moustafa 2007).

4. Cook notes, "The military establishment sought to capitalize on Sadat's much-vaunted infitah, particularly the benefits associated with foreign direct investment and the potential rent streams it produced. Besides financing for projects like Field Marshal Abu Ghazala's foray

into domestic car manufacturing—an initiative his partner, General Motors, initially considered less than prudent—there were lucrative opportunities to become consultants to, and representatives of, foreign corporations" (2007, 80–81).

5. Bread riots in Egypt erupted due to government plans to decrease subsidies on basic food items including bread. A sizeable portion of the Egyptian population depended on these subsidies for their daily livelihoods. The government backtracked on its decision to cut the subsidies following the violent conflict between the people and the Egyptian security forces leaving as many as 800 people dead.

6. Although Islamic investment companies also benefited from the open door policy throughout the 1980s, as Beinin (2005) notes, most of these companies were not associated with the MB or other Islamist groups.

7. Also see Beinin (2005) for a discussion on the rise of political Islam in Egypt and the role of economic developments.

8. Although Ziad Munson (2001) claims that the MB was "an explicitly apolitical religious reform and mutual aid society," interviews with various MB officials indicate that the group had political goals right from the beginning such as securing complete independence of Egypt and support for the Palestinian cause (Ibrahim Al-Bayyoumi Ghanim, personal interview, October 27, 2008). See Simms (2002) for the central role of Islamist groups on fostering anti-British activism in Egypt.

9. See the discussion of the MB's organizational structure and its ideology by Ziad Munson (2001).

10. It is also in this period until 1970 that we observe the MB underwent an ideological transformation whereby the group gave clear signals of moderation within the Islamist ideology, dismantling Sayyid Qutb's interpretation of the group's mission for most of the period between the 1950s and the 1960s. For example, the second general guide of the MB, Hasan al-Hudaybi, rejected Qutb's ideas by writing a "riposte" called "Preachers, not Judges" (Beinin 2005, 120).

11. Jason Brownlee (2007), recognizing the unofficial nature of the MB as a political organization, referred to the group as a "de facto" political party.

12. The regime's party, the National Democratic Party, has won every election in Egypt since Mubarak decided to hold elections, partly as a response to demands for political liberalization. In turn, Mubarak anticipated increased legitimacy to his rule. In 1987, the MB had thirty-eight out of the sixty seats that the Islamic Alliance won in parliamentary elections. The Islamic Alliance consisted of the MB, the Labor Party, and the Liberal Party.

13. The organizational structure of the MB consists of the following parts: (1) the general guide (al-Murshid al-'Amm), the leader of the MB; (2) the Guidance Bureau (Maktab al-Irshaad), the executive body of the MB elected by the group's Consultative Council, which has sixteen members; (3) the Consultative Council (Majlis al-Shura), which the legislative body of the MB, forming general policies of the group, a body that has between seventy-five and ninety members representing the twenty-two governorates of Egypt; (4) the Administrative Bureaus (al-Makaatib al-Idariyyah), the executive bodies at the level of governorate.

14. The emphasis on popular consent is critical to understanding variations among Islamist groups. Although the contention that Islamist groups and parties are predisposed to use force or violence in order to implement their societal and political vision in the face of social discontent is widely accepted, most Islamist groups do not uphold such a vision. As discussed in Chapter One (Table 1), this view finds resonance only among radical Islamist groups. Nonetheless, most moderate Islamist groups fail to clearly demonstrate how they would reconcile an Islamist program with a public opinion unfavorable to the program should Islamist groups

win power. See Anthony Shadid and David Kirkpatrick's discussion of the issue: "Activists in the Arab World View to Define Islamic State," *New York Times*, September 29, 2011.

15. See Roy's (1994) critique of political Islam's failure to come up with a clear-cut political program and his discussion of how different Islamist groups would deal with various social, economic, and political problems of their own societies.

16. See Wickham (2002) for a detailed discussion on how university students, graduates, and professionals made up the backbone of the MB in its ascendant public profile throughout the 1980s and the 1990s. Al-Awadi (2005) also explains how university students benefited from their association with the Brotherhood: "In addition to their religious appeal, the Ikhwan were able to address the basic concerns of students, which included the provision of affordable textbooks, study aid materials and free revision classes."

17. Ziad Munson offers an excellent analysis of the rise of the MB to prominence until the 1960s. In that, he emphasized the unique way that the MB's "three-tier membership structure" and ideology interacted to appeal to different socioeconomic groups. See Ziad Munson (2001).

18. Bayat notes that the regime utilized Law 100/1993 in its effort to curtail the power of the MB in professional associations, which laid out that "a syndicate election would be legitimate if at least 50 percent of the total membership cast votes" (1998, 165).

19. The extent of the government's harassment of the opposition was such that the government imprisoned more than 200, mostly young, members of the MB on the pretext that the government "claims to have found a 'paper trail' linking the Brotherhood with the outlawed Islamic militant groups Jihad and Gama'a Islamiya" over the foiled assassination attempt on Mubarak (Sullivan 1997, 69).

20. Various waves of government crackdowns on the MB occurred throughout the 1990s and 2000s. Each of these crackdowns against the group saw tens or even hundreds of group members being detained by Egyptian security forces. Such crackdowns include those in 1995, 1996, 2000, 2004, and 2006.

21. Figures on the number of seats contested by the MB vary in different sources. According to Hamzawy and Brown (2010), the number of MB candidates in 2005 was 150, whereas Noha Antar (2006) states that only 161 candidates were fielded. Muhammad Habib, former deputy general guide of the MB, also stated that the group fielded 161 candidates and approximately forty MB candidates were prevented from winning their districts due to NDP meddling in the elections (M. Habib interview, 2008).

22. Antar, along with some observers, claims that the MB could win a much larger share of the seats—up to 250 seats—in 2005 legislative elections, but chose not to do so. This particular strategy was chosen in order not to threaten the two-thirds majority of the NDP. Indeed, an International Crisis Group report on the MB states that an implicit accord was reached between the regime and the officials from the MB on districts particularly where leading figures from the ruling NDP ran for a seat. Similarly, the MB did not contest those districts where the MB engaged in "limited coordination" with certain leading figures from other opposition parties such as the Wafd and the Karama Parties. See "Egypt's Muslim Brothers: Confrontation or Integration?," International Crisis Group Middle East/North Africa Report No. 76 (June 18, 2008). Other opposition parties won only limited seats. The Wafd Party won six seats; the Tagammu Party and the Ghad Party won two seats and one seat, respectively. In a personal interview, former deputy general guide of the MB Muhammad Habib, confirming Noha Antar's observation, stated that the group did not want "to get into conflict with the regime" (M. Habib interview, 2008).

23. On the suppression of secular opposition groups by Arab regimes, see Ayoob (2005).

24. The Egyptian political system is categorized as semiliberal or semiauthoritarian due to the fact that procedural democracy was applied in a haphazard way with no real turn of power in major public offices. See Ottaway (2003).

25. The group made several applications in 1996, 1998, and 2004 for a license from the Political Parties Committee in the parliament—a committee formed by the members of the regime's National Democratic Party. All applications were rejected on the basis that the party platform failed to add anything new to the current line of parties until the 2011 Revolution. For a discussion of the Political Parties Law in Egypt and how it was manipulated by the NDP to block potential challengers, see Human Rights Watch (2007).

26. The Wasatiyya movement, or the "Islamic centrism," refers to the intellectual current among some of the Islamic intellectuals of Egypt. It represents the rise of "liberal" and "modern" Islam, for Wickham. According to Joshua Stacher, the movement is "not politically organized and do[es] not belong to any Islamist group." Among the leading figures of the movement are Yusuf al-Qaradawi, Tariq al-Bishri, Muhammad Imara, and Muhammad Salim al-Awwa, some of whom are closely associated with the WP. See Stacher (2002) and Wickham (2004) for a detailed discussion.

27. Muslim Brotherhood Supreme Guide's Reform Initiative (March 3, 2004) in Antar (2006).

28. There are different estimates on the number of the Copts in Egypt. But most figures claim that Copts make up at least 10 percent of Egypt's total population.

29. The MB, however, backtracked on this clause in their draft party program, recognizing the potential problems associated with it. See MB Draft Party Program (2007). The group raised the same issue in its 2004 Reform Initiative. See Antar (2006).

30. Osama Farid, a former member of the WP, underscored the "pragmatism" of the party in dealing with other groups and parties (Farid interview, 2008).

31. Two prominent members of the MB, AbdelHamid Al-Ghazali and Amani Aboul Fadl Farag, have used the exact same phrase during personal interviews (personal interviews, 2008).

32. See also Wickham (2004) for a detailed discussion of popular sovereignty in the WP platform.

33. WP leader Mady explains in great length the compatibility of Islam, that is, sharia, and democracy and argues that the fundamental problem in the discussions about the compatibility between Islam and democracy is due to incorrect interpretations. There are many interpretations of Islam and sharia that are affected by people's culture and environment. Instead, Islam, in its essence, is perfectly compatible with a democratic model. See Mady (2005).

34. Hamzawy, Ottaway, and Brown (2007) outline six "ambiguities" in the "Islamists' universe" that resemble the issues that the WP tries to tackle: application of the sharia, violence, political pluralism, individual freedoms, minorities, and women's rights.

35. Also see Antar (2006) for a general review of the parliamentary performance of the MB.

36. *Haram*, in Islamic terminology, refers to those actions strictly prohibited in Islam by God. *Halal* refers to those actions that are permissible for an individual to do.

37. See Abdel-Latif (2008) for an excellent discussion of the role of women within the MB, and its broader implications for Egyptian society.

38. Muslim Brotherhood Supreme Guide's Reform Initiative (March 3, 2004) in Antar (2006); Howeidy and Al-Ghazali interviews (2008).

39. The Greater Arab Free Trade Agreement is an initiative by the Arab League countries to establish a common market among Arab states. It was originally signed in 1998; however, it is unclear when the ultimate goal of establishing an Arab Common Market will materialize.

40. The MB opposes the use of interest in banking based on Islamic doctrines on this issue. More recently, MB leaders said that the "international financial crisis [in 2008] is basically because of the rate of interest, because of *riba* [interest]" (Al-Ghazali and M. Habib interviews, 2008).

41. In a personal interview (2008), AbdelHamid Al-Ghazali underscored a similar point when he was discussing the MB's economic perspective as aiming at "a self-sustaining economic development."

42. Indeed, Olivier Roy (1994) highlights this as one of the fundamental conundrums of Islamist ideology.

43. *Zakat* refers to the compulsory almsgiving in Islam equaling 2.5 percent of a person's annual disposable income. *Sadaqat* (pl.) is the voluntary donation a person makes, usually with an Islamic motivation.

44. Muslim Brotherhood Supreme Guide's Reform Initiative (March 3, 2004) in Antar (2006).

45. Some business owners underscored the stability effect of democracy in explaining how democracy is favorable for business (EG-9-B, EG-6-B interviews, 2008).

46. A leading Islamist intellectual and journalist, Fahmy Howeidy, saw the issue in the same light and argued that "economic liberalization is tied to the political liberalization" (Howeidy interview, 2008).

47. For a discussion of an important model on this point and its criticism, see Meltzer and Richard (1981) and Przeworski (1991).

48. Recently, cement industry was opened to competition, and seven to eight new firms were approved by the government to enter the market (EG-4-B and EG-8-B interviews, 2008).

49. Kareem Fahim, Michael Slackman, and David Rohde, "Egypt's Ire Turns to Confidant of Mubarak's Son," *New York Times*, February 6, 2011.

50. Emad Gad, "Political Participation for Egyptians," *Ahram Online*, April 27, 2011, available at http://english.ahram.org.eg/NewsContentPrint/4/0/10904/Opinion/0/Political-participationfor-Egyptians.aspx.

51. Article 2 of the 1971 constitution (which remained the same in the 2012 constitution) is as follows: "Islam is the religion of the state and Arabic its official language. Principles of Islamic law [sharia] are the principal source of legislation."

52. Mirette Mabrouk, "Round One of the Elections Over. Now What?," *Egypt Independent*, December 8, 2011.

53. When Hosni Mubarak was ousted from power in February 2011 in what became one of the defining moments of the Arab Spring, a furious public discussion ensued about the character of the soon-to-be-drafted Egyptian constitution. For many, the new constitution needed to guarantee the privileges of democracy to all societal groups involved. As part of these discussions, a popular idea, especially among secular opposition groups and those close to the military, was whether the "Turkish model" should define the parameters of the Egyptian path to democracy. The "Turkish model" was shorthand for the "guiding" role that the Turkish military assumed since 1923. In this role, the military would, in principle, stay out of politics, yet when the fundamental values and principles of the state were threatened (as determined by the military elite themselves), the military would undertake its constitutional sanction to intervene to set things "right." The Turkish military has utilized this power on numerous occasions since the 1950s.

54. Ahmet T. Kuru, "Egypt's Transition Two Years Later: A Turkish Perspective," *Foreign Policy Trip Reports*, no. 47 (January 29, 2013), retrieved from http://www.brookings.edu/blogs/up-front/posts/2013/01/29-egypt-turkey-kuru.

55. Shadi Hamid, "The Brotherhood Will Be Back," *New York Times*, May 23, 2015.
56. Ibid.
57. Bassem Sabry, "22 Key Points in Egypt's New Draft Constitution," *Al-Monitor*, August 23, 2013, available at http://www.al-monitor.com/pulse/originals/2013/08/egypt-draft-constitution-guide.html.
58. For example, only five ministries out of thirty-six (with relatively unimportant portfolios) were under FJP control, largely preventing the MB from implementing its program (Pioppi 2013, 59).
59. Hamid, "Brotherhood Will Be Back."
60. Bradley Hope, "Egypt in Peril of International Isolation," *National*, December 20, 2012; Juan Cole, "Morsi and Brotherhood Isolated vs. Military, Courts, Secularists," *Informed Comment*, July 10, 2012, available at http://www.juancole.com/2012/07/morsi-and-brotherhood-isolated-vs-military-courts-secularists.html.
61. "Friday Protests against Morsy, Poor Economy Sweep Nation," *Egypt Independent*, March 15, 2013, available at http://www.egyptindependent.com/news/friday-protests-against-morsy-poor-economy-sweep-nation; Stephen Glain, "Egypt's Muslim Brotherhood Adopting Caution on Economic Matters," *Washington Post*, January 24, 2012.
62. Suzy Hansen, "The Economic Vision of Egypt's Muslim Brotherhood Millionaires," *Bloomberg Business*, April 19, 2012, available at http://www.bloomberg.com/bw/articles/2012-04-19/the-economic-vision-of-egypts-muslim-brotherhood-millionaires#p4.
63. MB Statement, "Muslim Brotherhood Statement on Islamic Law and National Identity," available at http://www.ikhwanweb.com/article.php?id=30353.
64. Shaimaa Fayed, "Factbox: Policies of Egypt's Muslim Brotherhood's Party," *Reuters*, December 4, 2011, available at http://uk.reuters.com/article/2011/12/04/uk-egypt-election-brotherhood-idUKTRE7B30RM20111204.

5. Pathways from the Periphery

1. *Makhzen* is a term referring to the traditional seat of central government in Morocco dating back to precolonial times. Following independence, the term is used to refer to the Alaui royal power in Morocco. Azzedine Layachi (1998, 92) describes *makhzen* as follows: "In contemporary Morocco, *makhzen* refers to the central power that, on the basis of religious claims, requested allegiance from territorial and religious communities throughout Morocco." John Waterbury presents a thorough discussion of the concept of *makhzen* in great detail. See Waterbury (1970), 15–33.
2. Waterbury goes on to present a typology of Fassi families such as the *makhzen* families, the *sharifian* families, and the commercial families (Waterbury 1970, 94–95). Mark Tessler, in a similar way, identifies "a series of concentric circles" to describe the elite structure of Moroccan society (Tessler 1982).
3. The Istiqlal Party was established in 1943 and owes its legitimacy to its leading role in the national struggle for independence. In particular, the party proved to be instrumental in reinstalling the king following his exile by colonial authorities.
4. The royal family claims to be descendants of Prophet Muhammad, *sharifian* lineage. Based on this claim, one of the titles of the king is Amir al-Mu'minin, Commander of the Faithful.
5. Two such laws were I-73 210 dated March 2, 1973, and the investment code from August 1973. See Cammett (2007, 94–95).

6. Unemployment is the most important exception (Denoeux and Maghraoui 1998, 57; Cohen 2004, 76). The major societal discontent with the onset of reforms was due to price increases in basic commodities and educational fees, which resulted in violent rioting and the deaths of 150 to 200 people. In the aftermath of the rioting, price increases were rescinded (L. Anderson 1990).

7. For a detailed discussion of this question, see Henry Munson (1993).

8. This was indeed a rare combination. Elsewhere in the Muslim world, Islamists usually feel a strong antipathy toward Sufis, whereas Sufis virtually avoid political activism. The Budshishi order, indeed, viewed Islamism as fundamentally wrong (Shahin 1997, 55). Also see Henry Munson's discussion of the issue (1993, 163).

9. Yassine's first book, *Al-Islam Bayna al-Dawa wa al-Dawla* [Islam between Dawa and State], published in 1971, revolves around the idea that Islam is not only a personal religion, but it is both a religion and a state. In 1973, Yassine published his second book, *Al-Islam Ghadan* [Islam Tomorrow], where he compared and contrasted Islamist ideology with other ideological currents of his time such as Marxism, Maoism, and Liberalism.

10. This theme is a familiar one both among Islamists in general and in the case of AWI in particular. For example, Nadia Yassine's book *Full Sails Ahead* sets aside a whole section where Yassine discusses the political structure during the time of the Prophet and its immediate aftermath in an effort to demonstrate current political problems in the Muslim world and Morocco. See Nadia Yassine (2006).

11. Munson, and Bourgat and Dowell also report that Yassine was aware of potential consequences and "prepared his burial shroud." See Henry Munson (1993, 163) and Burgat and Dowell (1997, 167).

12. Indeed, others echo this observation: "Again, repression by the state seems to be breeding support for Islamic parties instead of eroding their influence. In fact, many researchers have put forward the idea that state repression, the lack of respect for human rights and similar factors may have had an important role in the growth of Islamic parties in the MENA region. In this article, we prove this empirically" (Garcia-Rivero and Kotzé 2007, 625).

13. Nadia Yassine presented more evidence to her claim that AWI was a legal entity: "Some members of the movement were arrested for possessing books of the movement [in the late 1980s]. When they went before the judge, he [the judge] said 'This movement is legal; why should I put them in jail?' Maybe that was an accident [on the part of the regime]; they did not have time to brief him [the judge]. Maybe the judge did not know the political dimension. But for us, it was very important because we have another proof that we are legal" (Yassine interview, 2009).

14. Indeed, Nadia Yassine emphasized the idea of "constructing bridges with all the people" to bring solutions to Morocco's problems (Yassine interview, 2009).

15. Despite the implications, Muti' rejected any part in the killing of Benjelloun. See Bourgat and Dowell (1997, 172).

16. Even though the group was formally outlawed in 1975, members continued its activities for several years (Shahin 1997, 188).

17. Shahin puts the official establishment of the association in 1983 (Shahin 1997, 189).

18. The account of "the Paper of Political Participation" rests on Bilal Tlaidi's reading and analysis of the report.

19. Although members of the group contested the local elections in 1997 as independents and won 100 seats in local city councils nationwide, it is the 1997 parliamentary elections that are generally accepted as the group's first official political participation (Tlaidi interview, 2009).

20. Samir Amghar notes that the union brought together around 200 different groups (Amghar 2007, 2).

21. Other officials from the PJD also confirmed El-Khalfi's account on this point: Noureddine Karbal, El-Ouafi, Driss Bouanou interviews, 2009.

22. Nadia Yassine and AbdelWahed al-Mutawakkil criticized the PJD for being part of the system and trying to change it from within (Al-Mutawakkil and Yassine interviews, 2009).

23. A similar observation is made by Wegner and Pellicer: "Rather, they feared a decrease in future electoral strength caused by being part of a government that was unlikely to improve the socio-economic grievances of those new voters whose support it had gained in the elections. Along the same lines, party leaders were aware that cabinet participation would make it more difficult to maintain its image as non-corrupt challengers of the Moroccan elite" (Wegner and Pellicer 2009, 165–66).

24. These five issues discussed in the "Towards a Better Morocco" program are authenticity (Islam), sovereignty, democracy, justice, and development. For a similar discussion, see Willis (2004).

25. Another PJD parliamentarian, Lahcen Daoudi, made a statement to the same effect (Lahcen Daoudi interview, 2009).

26. The Moroccan daily *Al-Tajdid*, a part of the MUR network, reported explicitly on the separation of the movement and the party. Similarly, the newspaper reported on the functions of the PJD and the MUR as distinct organizations. For example, see the extensive report in the newspaper on the MUR's position on various Islamic issues that differ from that of the party such as the caliphate. "Al-Tamayuz Bayna al-Haraka wal-Hizb Masar La Raja'ah Fihi" [The Separation between the Movement and the Party Now Irreversible], *Al-Tajdid*, August 28–29, 2007.

27. For a detailed discussion of the separation of the party and the movement, see Wegner and Pellicer (2009).

28. Former leader of the party Uthmani made a similar statement when he was asked about the PJD's Islamic reference: "We would compare it to Christian Democratic parties in Europe that base their platforms on the principles of Christian faith although their platforms may be civil in nature. These parties make decisions according to civil political realities, but viewed through a Christian lens. It is the same with the PJD, which is a civil, Moroccan nationalist political party" (quoted in *Arab Reform Bulletin* 3 [10], December 2005).

29. *Al-Tajdid*, October 13, 2003. Also see Hamzawy's discussion (2008, 9). Saad Eddin Uthmani contends that the PJD gave its support to the bill only after its views were incorporated into the legislation (Uthmani 2005).

30. Amghar also notes that AWI's support for democracy is a demonstration of opposition to the regime and for "tactical reasons" (Amghar 2007).

31. On various occasions, AWI expressed the impossibility of imposition in Islam with respect to both religion and individual preferences (Al-Mutawakkil and Yassine interviews, 2009). Moreover, the Sufi origins of the movement make it least likely to opt for imposition compared to other interpretations of Islam such as Salafism.

32. *Velayat-e faqih* (guardianship of the jurist) is the religio-political position created in the aftermath of the Islamic revolution in 1979. The position represents the highest post in the new Iranian state, held by a clergyman elected by a council of Islamic scholars. The position is regarded as the guarantee of the Islamic nature of the regime in Iran.

33. It is interesting to note that not only constituencies but also parties themselves see the similarities between them. See Perekli's (2012) discussion of the PJD's emulation of the "Turkish model" on the transitioning from an identity-based party to a policy-oriented party.

34. Melani Cammett's (2007) analysis of the Moroccan businesses in a historical perspective is one of the most authoritative analyses on the subject. In particular, Cammett's analysis of the conflict between old businesses and new businesses thoroughly discusses the conflict between "fat-cats and self-made men" of the Moroccan business world.

35. See Maghraoui (2002) for an account downplaying the political significance of both groups.

36. Despite my request, Al-Mutawakkil stated that the statistics were for internal use and not available for the public.

37. Amr Hamzawy states that the current electoral system makes it almost impossible for any single party to win a majority of the votes. In addition, he observes that the current districting favors rural areas at the expense of urban areas. This is an important problem, as the PJD views itself as an overwhelmingly urban party (Hamzawy 2008, 5). Other observers concur with the statements of PJD officials (Wegner and Pellicer 2009, 168; Willis 2004, 68).

38. A similar point is also raised by Willis (2004, 69).

39. Also see Lust-Okar's (2004) and Shahin's (1997) analyses on the monarchy's ruling tactic in Morocco. Waterbury presents the tactic of segmentation of elite factions and controlling the competition in a historical perspective (Waterbury 1970, 268).

40. McFaul and Wittes (2008); Amghar (2007).

41. Wegner and Pellicer (2009) also discuss the same dynamics prior to the 2003 elections.

Bibliography

Abdel-Khalek, Gouda, and Robert Tignor, eds. 1982. *The Political Economy of Income Distribution in Egypt*. New York: Holmes & Meier.
Abdellatif, Lobna M., and Ahmed Farouk Ghoneim. 2008. "Competition, Competition Policy and Economic Efficiency in Egypt." In *Competition and Efficiency in the Arab World*, edited by Khalid Sekkat, 21–67. New York: Palgrave Macmillan.
Abdel-Latif, Omayma. 2008. "In the Shadow of the Brothers: The Women of the Egyptian Muslim Brotherhood." *Carnegie Papers*, no. 13 (October).
Aboul Futouh, Abdoul Monem. Comments on "Islamist Movements and the Democratic Process in the Arab World: Exploring the Gray Zones" by Nathan Brown, Amr Hamzawy, and Marina Ottaway (*Carnegie Papers*, no. 67, March 2006). n.d.
Acemoglu, Daron, and James Robinson. 2005. *Economic Origins of Dictatorship and Democracy*. New York: Cambridge University Press.
Achy, Lahcen, and Khalid Sekkat. 2008. "Competition, Efficiency and Competition Policy in Morocco." In *Competition and Efficiency in the Arab World*, edited by Khalid Sekkat, 123–58. New York: Palgrave Macmillan.
Adly, Amr Ismail. 2009. "Politically-Embedded Cronyism: The Case of Post-Liberalization Egypt." *Business and Politics* 11 (4): 1–26.
Adsera, Alicia, and Carles Boix. 2002. "Trade, Democracy, and the Size of the Public Sector: The Political Underpinnings of Openness." *International Organization* 56 (2): 229–62.
Ahmad, Feroz. 1969. *The Young Turks: The Committee of Union and Profess in Turkish Politics 1908–1914*. Oxford: Clarendon.
Akdoğan, Yalçın. 2004. *AK Parti ve Muhafazakar Demokrasi*. [AK Party and Conservative Democracy.] Istanbul: Alfa.
Al-Anani, Khalil. 2012. "Islamist Parties Post-Arab Spring." *Mediterranean Politics* 17 (3): 466–72. doi:10.1080/13629395.2012.725309.
Al-Awadi, Hesham. 2005. "Mubarak and the Islamists: Why Did the 'Honeymoon' End?" *Middle East Journal* 59 (1): 62–80.
———. 2013. "Islamists in Power: The Case of the Muslim Brotherhood in Egypt." *Contemporary Arab Affairs* 6 (4): 539–51.
Albrecht, Holger. 2013. "Egypt's 2012 Constitution: Devil in the Details, Not in Religion." *United States Institute of Peace Brief* 139 (January 25).
Albrecht, Holger, and Eva Wegner. 2006. "Autocrats and Islamists: Contenders and Containment in Egypt and Morocco." *Journal of North African Studies* 11 (2): 123–41.
Alevi Workshops Preliminary Report. 2010. Ankara: T.C. Basbakanlik.
Alexander, Gerard. 2002. "Institutionalized Uncertainty, the Rule of Law, and the Sources of Democratic Stability." *Comparative Political Studies* 35 (10): 1145–70.
Alissa, Sufyan. 2007. "The Political Economy of Reform in Egypt: Understanding the Role of Institutions." *Carnegie Papers*, no. 5 (October).

Altinkemer, Melike, and Nazim Ekinci. 1992. "Capital Account Liberalization: The Case of Turkey." *Central Bank of Turkey Research Department Discussion Papers*, no. 9210.

Altinordu, A. 2010. "The Politicization of Religion: Political Catholicism and Political Islam in Comparative Perspective." *Politics & Society* 38 (4): 517–51.

Altunisik, Meliha Benli. 2005. "The Turkish Model and Democratization in the Middle East." *Arab Studies Quarterly* 27 (1–2): 45–63.

Amghar, Samir. 2007. "Political Islam in Morocco." *CEPS Working Document*, no. 269.

Anckar, Carsten. 2008. "On the Applicability of the Most Similar Systems Design and the Most Different Systems Design in Comparative Research." *International Journal of Social Research Methodology* 11 (5): 389–401.

Anderson, James E., and J. Peter Neary. 1994. "Measuring the Restrictiveness of Trade Policy." *World Bank Economic Review* 8 (2): 151–69.

Anderson, Lisa. 1990. "Liberalism in Northern Africa." *Current History* 89 (546): 145–75.

Anderson, Robert E., and Albert Martinez. 1998. "Supporting Private Sector Development in the Middle East and North Africa." In *Prospects for Middle Eastern and North African Economies: From Boom to Bust and Back?*, edited by Nemat Shafik, chap. 7. New York: St. Martin's.

Annuaire Statistique du Maroc. Various Years. Rabat, Morocco: Le Haut Commissariat au Plan.

Antar, Noha. 2006. "The Muslim Brotherhood's Success in the Legislative Elections in Egypt 2005: Reasons and Implications." *EuroMesco Paper*, no. 51.

Arat, Yesim. 1991. "Politics and Big Business in Turkey: Janus Faced Link to the State." In *Strong State and Economic Interest Groups: The Post-1980 Turkish Experience*, edited by Metin Heper, 135–48. Berlin, NY: Walter de Gruyter.

———. 2013. "Violence, Resistance, and Gezi Park." *International Journal of Middle East Studies* 45 (4): 807–9.

Ashour, Omar. 2012. "Egypt's Revolution: A Year After Mubarak." Brookings (February 7). Available at http://www.brookings.edu/research/opinions/2012/02/07-egypt-ashouro.

Atacan, Fulya. 2006. "Explaining Religious Politics at the Crossroad: AKP-SP." In *Religion Politics in Turkey*, edited by Ali Carkoglu and Barry Rubin, 45–58. New York: Routledge.

Ateş, Davut. 2005. "Economic Liberalization and Changes in Fundamentalism: The Case of Egypt." *Middle East Policy* 12 (4): 133–44.

Aydogan, Abdullah, and Jonathan B. Slapin. 2013. "Left-Right Reversed: Parties and Ideology in Modern Turkey." *Party Politics* 21 (4): 615–25.

Ayoob, Mohammed. 2005. "The Future of Political Islam: The Importance of External Variables." *International Affairs* 81 (5): 951–61.

———. 2008. *The Many Faces of Political Islam*. Ann Arbor: University of Michigan Press.

Baker, Andy. 2003. "Why Is Trade Reform So Popular in Latin America? A Consumption-Based Theory of Trade Policy Preferences." *World Politics* 55 (3): 423–55.

Barkey, Henri. 1995. "Can the Middle East Compete?" *Journal of Democracy* 6 (2): 113–27.

Bates, Robert H. 1981. *Markets and States in Tropical Africa: The Political Basis of Agricultural Policies*. Berkeley: University of California Press.

Bates, Robert H., Philip Brock, and Jill Tiefenthaler. 1991. "Risk and Trade Regimes: Another Exploration." *International Organization* 45 (1): 1–18.

Bayat, Asef. 1998. "Revolution without Movement, Movement without Revolution: Comparing Islamic Activism in Iran and Egypt." *Comparative Studies in Society and History* 40 (1): 136–69.

Beinin, Joel. 2005. "Political Islam and the New Global Economy: The Political Economy of an Egyptian Social Movement." *New Centennial Review* 5 (1): 111–39.

Bekkaoui, Khalid, and Ricardo René Larémont. 2011. "Moroccan Youth Go Sufi." *Journal of the Middle East and Africa* 2 (1): 31–46.

Bellin, Eva. 2000. "Contingent Democrats: Industrialists, Labor, and Democratization in Late-Developing Countries." *World Politics* 52 (2): 175–205.

Bendourou, Omar. 1996. "Power and Opposition in Morocco." *Journal of Democracy* 7 (3): 108–22.

Berger, Peter. 1967. *The Sacred Canopy: Elements of a Sociological: Theory of Religion*. Garden City: Doubleday.

Berkes, Niyazi. 1964. *The Development of Secularism in Turkey*. Montreal: McGill University Press.

Berman, Sheri. 2008. "Taming Extremist Parties: Lessons from Europe." *Journal of Democracy* 19 (1): 5–18.

Bianchi, Robert. 1984. *Interest Groups and Political Development in Turkey*. Princeton, NJ: Princeton University Press.

Bilgin, Fevzi. 2014. "Turkey Brief: Corruption Scandal and Ensuing Political Crisis." Rethink Institute. http://www.rethinkinstitute.org/turkey-brief-corruption-scandal-and-ensuing-political-crisis/.

Blaydes, Lisa. 2010. *Elections and Distributive Politics in Mubarak's Egypt*. Cambridge: Cambridge University Press.

Boix, Carles. 2003. *Democracy and Redistribution*. New York: Cambridge University Press.

Bolat, Omer. 2007. *Medeniyet Ideali*. [Civilization Ideal.] Istanbul: Kure.

Brooke, Steven. 2015. "The Muslim Brotherhood's Social Outreach after the Egyptian Coup." Brookings Institution. http://www.brookings.edu/~/media/Research/Files/Reports/2015/07/rethinking-political-islam/Egypt_Brooke-FINAL.pdf?la=en.

Brooks, Risa A. 2002. "Liberalization and Militancy in the Arab World." *Orbis* 46 (4): 611–21.

Brooks, Sarah. 2004. "Explaining Capital Account Liberalization in Latin America: A Transitional Cost Approach." *World Politics* 56 (3): 389–430.

Brown, Nathan J. 2012a. "When Victory Becomes an Option: Egypt's Muslim Brotherhood Confronts Success." Carnegie Endowment (January).

———. 2012b. "Contention in Religion and State in Postrevolutionary Egypt." *Social Research: An International Quarterly* 79 (2): 531–50.

———. 2013. "Egypt: A Constitutional Court in an Unconstitutional Setting." Working paper (prepared for the Constitutional Transitions and Global Comparative Law Colloquium, New York University School of Law, October).

Brown, Nathan J., and Michele Dunne. 2015. "Unprecedented Pressures, Uncharted Course for Egypt's Muslim Brotherhood." Carnegie Endowment (July). http://carnegieendowment.org/2015/07/29/unprecedented-pressures-uncharted-course-for-egypt-s-muslim-brotherhood/ie2g.

Brown, Nathan J., Amr Hamzawy, and Marina Ottaway. 2006. "Islamist Movements and the Democratic Process in the Arab World: Exploring the Gray Zone." *Carnegie Papers Middle East Series*, no. 67 (March).
Brownlee, Jason. 2002. "Democratization in the Arab World: The Decline of Pluralism in Mubarak's Egypt." *Journal of Democracy* 13 (4): 6–14.
———. 2007. *Authoritarianism in an Age of Democracy*. New York: Cambridge University Press.
Buehler, Matt. 2013. "Safety-Valve Elections and the Arab Spring: The Weakening (and Resurgence) of Morocco's Islamist Opposition Party." *Terrorism and Political Violence* 25 (1): 137–56.
Bugra, Ayse. 1994. *State and Business in Modern Turkey: A Comparative Study*. New York: State University of New York Press.
———. 2002. "Political Islam in Turkey in Historical Context: Strengths and Weaknesses." In *The Politics of Permanent Crisis: Class, Ideology and State in Turkey*, edited by Neşecan Balkan and Sungur Savran, 107–44. New York: Nova Science.
Bugra, Ayse, and Osman Savaskan. 2012. "Politics and Class: The Turkish Business Environment in the Neoliberal Age." *New Perspectives on Turkey* 46 (March): 27–63.
Bulliet, Richard. 2011. "Neo-Mamluk Legitimacy and the Arab Spring." *Middle East Law and Governance* 3 (1–2). Brill: 60–67.
Burgat, Francois, and William Dowell. 1997. *The Islamic Movement in North Africa*. Austin: University of Texas Press.
Byman, Daniel. 2013. "Explaining the Western Response to the Arab Spring." *Journal of Strategic Studies* 36 (2): 289–320.
Cameron, David. 1978. "The Expansion of the Public Sector: A Comparative Analysis." *American Political Science Review* 72 (4): 1243–61.
Cammett, Melani C. 2007. *Globalization and Business Politics in North Africa: A Comparative Perspective*. Cambridge: Cambridge University Press.
Campagna, Joel. 1996. "From Accommodation to Confrontation: The Muslim Brotherhood in the Mubarak Years." *Journal of International Affairs* 50 (1): 278–304.
Çarkoğlu, Ali. 2006. "The New Generation Pro-Islamists in Turkey: Bases of the Justice and Development Party in Changing Electoral Space." In *The Emergence of a New Turkey: Democracy and the AK Parti*, edited by Hakan Yavuz, 160–84. Salt Lake City: University of Utah Press.
Casper, Jayson. 2013. "Islamist Tendencies in the Constituent Assembly." In *The Development of Egypt's Constitution: Analysis, Assessment, and Sorting through the Rhetoric*, edited by Cornelis Hulsman, Diana Serôdio, and Jayson Casper, 40–45. Cairo: Arab-West Report.
Cavatorta, Francesco. 2006. "Civil Society, Islamism and Democratisation: The Case of Morocco." *Journal of Modern African Studies* 44 (2): 203–22.
———. 2007. "Neither Participation nor Revolution: The Strategy of the Moroccan Jamiat al-Adl wal-Ihsan." *Mediterranean Politics* 12 (3): 381–97.
Cavatorta, Francesco, and Fabio Merone. 2013. "Moderation through Exclusion? The Journey of the Tunisian Ennahda from Fundamentalist to Conservative Party." *Democratization* 20 (5): 857–75.
Cayhan, Esra. 1997. *Dunden Bugune ve Turkiye ve Avrupa Birligi Iliskileri*. Istanbul: Boyut Yayınları.

Cecen, A. Aydin, A. Suut Dogruel, and Fatma Dogruel. 1994. "Economic Growth and Structural Change in Turkey 1960–88." *International Journal of Middle East Studies* 26 (1): 37–56.
Cesari, Jocelyne. 2014. *The Awakening of Muslim Democracy: Religion, Modernity, and the State.* New York: Cambridge University Press.
Chaudhry, Kiren Aziz. 1994. "Economic Liberalization and the Lineages of Rentier State." *Comparative Politics* 27 (1): 1–25.
Chhibber, Pradeep K. 1996. "State Policy, Rent Seeking, and the Electoral Success of a Religious Party in Algeria." *Journal of Politics* 58 (1): 126–48.
Cizre, Ümit, ed. 2009. *Secular and Islamic Politics in Turkey: The Making of the Justice and Development Party.* New York: Routledge.
Clark, Janine. 2004a. *Islam, Charity, and Activism: Middle-Class Networks and Social Welfare in Egypt, Jordan, and Yemen.* Indianapolis: Indiana University Press.
———. 2004b. "Social Movement Theory and Patron-Clientelism: Islamic Social Institutions and the Middle Class in Egypt, Jordan, and Yemen." *Comparative Political Studies* 37 (8): 941–68.
Cohen, Shana. 2004. *Searching for a Different Future: The Rise of a Global Middle Class in Morocco.* Durham, NC: Duke University Press.
Collier, Ruth Berins, and David Collier. 1991. *Shaping the Political Arena: Critical Junctures, the Labor Movement, and Regime Dynamics in Latin America.* Princeton, NJ: Princeton University Press.
Cook, Steven. 2007. *Ruling but Not Governing: The Military and Political Development in Egypt, Algeria, and Turkey.* Baltimore: Johns Hopkins University.
Cooper, Mark N. 1982. *The Transformation of Egypt.* London: Croom Helm.
Dagi, Ihsan D. 2005. "Transformation of Islamic Political Identity in Turkey: Rethinking the West and Westernization." *Turkish Studies* 6 (1): 21–37.
———. 2006. "The Justice and Development Party: Identity, Politics, and Human Rights Discourse in the Search for Security and Legitimacy." In *The Emergence of a New Turkey: Democracy and the AK Parti,* edited by Hakan Yavuz, 88–106. Salt Lake City: University of Utah Press.
Danielson, Michael N., and Rusen Keles. 1985. *The Politics of Rapid Urbanization: Government and Growth in Modern Turkey.* New York: Holmes & Meier.
Davison, Roderic H. 1954. "Turkish Attitudes Concerning Christian-Muslim Equality in the Nineteenth Century." *American Historical Review* 59 (4): 844–64.
Demiralp, Seda. 2009. "The Rise of Islamist Entrepreneurs and the Decline of Islamic Radicalism in Turkey." *Comparative Politics* 41 (3): 315–36.
Denoeux, Guilain P., and Abdeslam Maghraoui. 1998. "The Political Economy of Structural Adjustment in Morocco." In *Economic Crisis and Political Change in North Africa,* edited by Azzedine Layachi, 55–88. Westport, CT: Praeger.
Desrues, Thierry, and Eduardo Moyano. 2001. "Social Change and Political Transition in Morocco." *Mediterranean Politics* 6 (1): 21–47.
Dessouki, Ali E. Hillal. 1982. "The Politics of Income Distribution in Egypt." In *The Political Economy of Income Distribution in Egypt,* edited by Gouda Abdel-Khalek and Robert Tignor. New York: Holmes & Meier.
Deutsch, Karl. 1961. "Social Mobilization and Political Development." *American Political Science Review* 55 (3): 493–514.

Devarajan, Shantayanan, and Dani Rodrik. 1989. "Trade Liberalization in Developing Countries: Do Imperfect Competition and Scale Economies Matter?" *American Economic Review* 79 (2): 283–87.

Dilipak, Abdurrahman. 1989. *Turkiye Nereye Gidiyor.* [Where Is Turkey Going?] Istanbul: Risale.

Dillman, Bradford. 2001. "Facing the Market in North Africa." *Middle East Journal* 55 (2): 198–215.

Driessen, Michael D. 2014. *Religion and Democratization: Framing Religious and Political Identities in Muslim and Catholic Societies.* New York: Oxford University Press.

El Amrani, Issandr. 2005. "Controlled Reform in Egypt: Neither Reformist nor Controlled." *Middle East Report Online* (December 15). Available at http://www.merip.org/mero/mero121505.

El-Ghazali, AbdelHamid H. 2001. *The Way to the Revival of the Muslim Ummah: A Study of the Thinking of Imam al-Banna.* Cairo: Al-Falah Foundation.

El-Ghobashy, Mona. 2005. "The Metamorphosis of the Egyptian Muslim Brothers." *International Journal of Middle East Studies* 37 (3): 373–95.

El Sherif, Ashraf. 2011. "Islamism after the Arab Spring." *Current History* 110 (740): 358–63.

———. 2012. "Institutional and Ideological Re-Construction of the Justice and Development Party (PJD): The Question of Democratic Islamism in Morocco." *Middle East Journal* 66 (4): 660–82.

Enderwick, Peter. 2005. "What's Bad about Crony Capitalism." *Asian Business and Management* 4 (2): 117–32.

Erbakan, Necmettin. 1975. *Milli Gorus.* [National Outlook.] Istanbul: Dergah.

———. 1991. *Adil Ekonomik Duzen.* [Just Economic Order.] S.n.

EU Turkey Progress Report 2004. Available at http://ec.europa.eu/enlargement/archives/pdf/key_documents/2004/rr_tr_2004_en.pdf.

EU Turkey Progress Report 2005. Available at http://ec.europa.eu/enlargement/archives/pdf/key_documents/2005/package/sec_1426_final_progress_report_tr_en.pdf.

EU Turkey Progress Report 2008. Available at http://ec.europa.eu/enlargement/pdf/press_corner/key-documents/reports_nov_2008/turkey_progress_report_en.pdf.

EU Turkey Progress Report 2009. Available at http://www.europarl.europa.eu/sides/getDoc.do?language=EN&reference=B7-0068/2010.

Evans, Peter. 1995. *Embedded Autonomy: States and Industrial Transformation.* Princeton, NJ: Princeton University Press.

Fahmi, Georges. 2015. "The Struggle for the Leadership of Egypt's Muslim Brotherhood." Carnegie Endowment. http://carnegie-mec.org/2015/07/14/struggle-for-leadership-of-egypt-s-muslim-brotherhood/idbr.

Farag, Mona. 2012. "Egypt's Muslim Brotherhood and the January 25 Revolution: New Political Party, New Circumstances." *Contemporary Arab Affairs* 5 (2): 214–29.

Farah, Nadia Ramsis. 2009. *Egypt's Political Economy: Power Relations in Development.* Cairo: American University in Cairo Press.

Feldman, Noah. 2008. *The Fall and Rise of the Islamic State.* Princeton, NJ: Princeton University Press.

Findley, Carter Vaughn. 1996. "The Ottoman Administrative Legacy and the Modern Middle East." In *Imperial Legacy: The Ottoman Imprint on the Balkans and the*

Middle East, edited by L. Carl Brown, 158–73. New York: Columbia University Press.
Garcia-Rivero, Carlos, and Hennie Kotzé. 2007. "Electoral Support for Islamic Parties in the Middle East and North Africa." *Party Politics* 13 (5): 611–36.
Garrett, Geoffrey. 1998. *Partisan Politics in the Global Economy*. Cambridge: Cambridge University Press.
Geddes, Barbara. 1990. "How the Cases You Choose Affect the Answers You Get: Selection Bias in Comparative Politics." *Political Analysis* 2 (1): 131–50.
Geertz, Clifford. 1968. *Islam Observed: Religious Development in Morocco and Indonesia*. Chicago: University of Chicago Press.
Gerges, Fawaz. 1999. "The Decline of Revolutionary Islam in Algeria and Egypt." *Survival* 41 (1): 113–25.
Gidengil, Elisabeth, and Ekrem Karakoc. 2016. "Which Matters More in the Electoral Success of Islamist (Successor) Parties—Religion or Performance? The Turkish Case." *Party Politics* 22 (3): 325–38 (published online September 15, 2014).
Gisselquist, Rachel M. 2014. "Paired Comparison and Theory Development: Considerations for Case Selection." *PS: Political Science & Politics* 47 (2): 477–84.
Glennie, Alex, and David Mepham. 2007. "Reform in Morocco: The Role of Political Islamists." London: Institute for Public Policy Research. Available at http://www.ippr.org/files/images/media/files/publication/2011/05/reform_in_morocco_1593.pdf?noredirect=1.
Gülalp, Haldun. 2001. "Globalization and Political Islam: The Social Bases of Turkey's Welfare Party." *International Journal of Middle East Studies* 33 (3): 433–48.
Gümüşçü, Şebnem. 2005. "No Bourgeois, No Moderation: Change in Political Islam in Turkey, Egypt and Algeria." Paper delivered at the 2005 Annual Graduate Student Conference, University of Virginia.
———. 2010. "Class, Status, and Party: The Changing Face of Political Islam in Turkey and Egypt." *Comparative Political Studies* 43 (7): 835–61.
Gunes-Ayata, Ayse. 2003. "From Euro-Scepticism to Turkey-Scepticism: Changing Political Attitudes on the European Union in Turkey." *Journal of Southern Europe and the Balkans* 5 (2): 205–23.
Gurcan, Efe Can, and Efe Peker. 2014. "Turkey's Gezi Park Demonstrations of 2013: A Marxian Analysis of the Political Moment." *Socialism and Democracy* 28 (1): 70–89.
Haber, Stephen. 2002. *Crony Capitalism and Economic Growth in Latin America*. Stanford, CA: Hoover Institution.
Haddad, Mona. 1993. "How Trade Liberalization Affected Productivity in Morocco." *The World Bank Policy Research Paper* WPS 1096.
Haklai, Oded. 2009. "Authoritarianism and Islamic Movements in the Middle East: Research and Theorybuilding in the Twenty-First Century." *International Studies Review* 11: 27–45.
Hallaq, Wael. 2012. *The Impossible State: Islam, Politics, and Modernity's Moral Predicament*. New York: Columbia University Press.
Hamid, Shadi. 2011. "The Rise of the Islamists: How Islamists Will Change Politics, and Vice Versa." *Foreign Affairs* 90 (3). Available at https://www.foreignaffairs.com/articles/north-africa/2011-04-03/rise-islamists.

———. 2014. *Temptations of Power: Islamists and Illiberal Democracy in a New Middle East*. Oxford: Oxford University Press.
Hamzawy, Amr. 2008. "Party for Justice and Development in Morocco: Participation and Its Discontents." *Carnegie Papers*, no. 93 (July).
Hamzawy, Amr, and Nathan J. Brown. 2010. "The Egyptian Muslim Brotherhood: Islamist Participation in a Closing Political Environment." *Carnegie Papers*, no. 19 (March).
Hamzawy, Amr, Marina Ottaway, and Nathan J. Brown. 2007. "What Islamists Need to Be Clear About: The Case of the Egyptian Muslim Brotherhood." *Carnegie Policy Outlook* (February).
Hansen, Bent. 1991. *The Political Economy of Poverty, Equity, and Growth: Egypt and Turkey*. New York: Oxford University Press.
Hellman, Joel S. 1998. "Winners Take All: The Politics of Partial Reform in Postcommunist Transitions." *World Politics* 50 (2): 203–34.
Henry, Clement M., and Robert Springborg. 2001. *Globalization and the Politics of Development in the Middle East*. New York: Cambridge University Press.
Heper, Metin. 2009. "Does Secularism Face a Serious Threat in Turkey?" *Comparative Studies of South Asia, Africa and the Middle East* 29 (3): 413–22.
Herzog, Michael. 2006. "Can Hamas Be Tamed?" *Foreign Affairs* 85 (2): 83–94.
Heydemann, Seteven. 2004. *Networks of Privilege in the Middle East*. New York: Palgrave Macmillan.
Hiscox, Michael J. 2002. *International Trade and Political Conflict: Commerce, Coalitions, and Mobility*. Princeton, NJ: Princeton University Press.
Human Rights Watch. 2007. "Monopolizing Power: Egypt's Political Parties Law." January 4, 2007. Available at http://www.unhcr.org/refworld/docid/45a4e0a92.html.
Huntington, Samuel. 1993. *The Third Wave: Democratization in the Late Twentieth Century*. Norman: University of Oklahoma Press.
Ibrahim, Saad Eddin. 1994. "Egypt's Landed Bourgeoisie." In *Developmentalism and Beyond: Society and Politics in Egypt and Turkey*, edited by Ayse Oncu, Caglar Keyder, and Saad Eddin Ibrahim. Cairo: American University in Cairo Press.
Inalcik, Halil. 1991. "The Status of the Greek Orthodox Patriarch under the Ottomans." *Turcica* 21–23: 407–36.
Inkeles, Alex, and David Smith. 1976. *Becoming Modern: Individual Change in Six Developing Countries*. Cambridge: Harvard University Press.
International Crisis Group. 2008. "Egypt's Muslim Brothers: Confrontation or Integration?" *Middle East/North Africa Report*, no. 76.
Islam, Merve Kavakci. 2010. *Headscarf Politics in Turkey: A Postcolonial Reading*. New York: Palgrave Macmillan.
Ismail, Salwa. 2001. "The Paradox of Islamist Politics." *Middle East Report* 221 (Winter): 34–39.
Issawi, Charles. 1982. *An Economic History of the Middle East and North Africa*. New York: Columbia University Press.
———. 1996. "The Economic Legacy." In *Imperial Legacy: The Ottoman Imprint on the Balkans and the Middle East*, edited by L. Carl Brown, 227–45. New York: Columbia University Press.

Jamal, Amaney. 2007. *Barriers to Democracy: The Other Side of Social Capital in Palestine and the Arab World.* Princeton, NJ: Princeton University Press.
Jayasuriya, Kanishka. 1996. "The Rule of Law and Capitalism in East Asia." *Pacific Review* 9 (3): 367–88.
Jenkins, Gareth. 2004. "Non-Muslim Minorities in Turkey: Progress and Challenges on the Road to EU Accession." *Turkish Policy Quarterly* 3 (1).
Justice and Development Party. 2001. Party Program. Available at www.akparti.org.tr.
——. 2002a. Electoral Manifesto. Available at http://www.akparti.org.tr/tbmm/tbmmgrup/SE%C3%87%C4%B0M%20beyanname-KISALTILMI%C5%9E.doc.
——. 2002b. *59th Government Program.* Available at www.akparti.org.tr/tbmm/tbmmgrup/59hükümet%20programı.doc.
——. 2007. *Party Program.* Available at http://eng.akparti.org.tr/english/partyprogramme.html.
——. 2008. *AK Parti'nin Esas Hakkindaki Cevaplari.* [The JDP's Response to the Indictment.] Ankara: Elips Books.
——. 2010. "Sorulari ve Cevaplariyla Demokratik Acilim Sureci: Milli Birlik ve Kardeslik Projesi." [The Democratic Opening Process in Questions and Answers: National Unity and Brotherhood Project.] Available at www.akparti.org.tr/acilim220110.pdf.
Kalyvas, Stathis. 1996. *The Rise of Christian Democracy in Europe.* Ithaca, NY: Cornell University Press.
Kandil, Amani. 1994. "Socioeconomic Policies and Interest Groups in Egypt." In *Developmentalism and Beyond: Society and Politics in Egypt and Turkey,* edited by Caglar Keyder and Saad Eddin Ibrahim. Cairo: American University in Cairo Press.
Karakaya, Suveyda, and A. Kadir Yildirim. 2013. "Islamist Moderation in Perspective: Comparative Analysis of the Moderation of Islamist and Western Communist Parties." *Democratization* 20 (7): 1322–49.
Katzenstein, Peter. 1985. *Small States in World Markets.* Ithaca, NY: Cornell University Press.
Kaufman, Robert, and Alex Segura-Ubiergo. 2001. "Globalization, Domestic Politics, and Social Spending in Latin America: A Time-Series Cross-Section Analysis, 1973–97." *World Politics* 53 (4): 553–87.
Kausch, Kristina. 2007. "An Islamist Government in Morocco?" *Democracy Backgrounder* 11. Available at http://fride.org/download/BGR_GovMorocc_ENG_jul07.pdf.
Keiswetter, Allen L. 2012. "The Arab Spring: Implications for US Policy and Interests." *Middle East Institute.* http://www.mei.edu/content/arab-spring-implications-us-policy-and-interests.
Kienle, Eberhard. 2001. *A Grand Delusion: Democracy and Economic Reform in Egypt.* New York: I. B. Tauris.
King, Gary, Robert Keohane, and Sidney Verba. 1994. *Designing Social Inquiry: Scientific Inference in Qualitative Research.* Princeton, NJ: Princeton University Press.
Kitschelt, Herbert. 1992. "The Formation of Party Systems in East Central Europe." *Politics and Society* 20 (1): 7–50.
Kohli, Atul. 2004. *State-Directed Development: Political Power and Industrialization in the Global Periphery.* New York: Cambridge University Press.

Konda. 2014. "30 Mart Yerel Secimler Sonrasi Sandik ve Secmen Analizi." Available at http://www.konda.com.tr/tr/raporlar/KONDA_30Mart2014_YerelSecimAnalizi.pdf.
Kosebalaban, Hasan. 2005. "The Impact of Globalization on Islamic Political Identity: The Case of Turkey." *World Affairs* 168 (1): 27–37.
Kurtz, Marcus J., and Sarah M. Brooks. 2008. "Embedding Neoliberal Reform in Latin America." *World Politics* 60 (2): 231–80.
Kuru, Ahmet. 2006. "Reinterpretation of Secularism in Turkey: The Case of the Justice and Development Party." In *The Emergence of a New Turkey: Democracy and the AK Parti*, edited by Hakan Yavuz, 136–59. Salt Lake City: University of Utah Press.
———. 2007. "Passive and Assertive Secularism: Historical Conditions, Ideological Struggles, and State Policies toward Religion." *World Politics* 59 (4): 568–94.
———. 2009. *Secularism and State Policies toward Religion: The United States, France, and Turkey*. New York: Cambridge University Press.
Kurzman, Charles, and Ijlal Naqvi. 2010. "Do Muslims Vote Islamic?" *Journal of Democracy* 21 (2): 50–63.
Lancaster, C. M. 2004. "The Iron Law of Erdogan: The Decay from Intra-Party Democracy to Personalistic Rule." *Third World Quarterly* 35 (9): 1672–90.
Langohr, Vickie. 2001. "Of Islamists and Ballot Boxes: Rethinking the Relationship between Islamisms and Electoral Politics." *International Journal of Middle East Studies* 33 (4): 591–610.
———. 2002. "An Exit from Arab Autocracy." *Journal of Democracy* 13 (3): 117–22.
Layachi, Azzedine. 1998. "State-Society Relations and Change in Morocco." In *Economic Crisis and Political Change in North Africa*, edited by Azzedine Layachi, 89–106. Westport, CT: Praeger.
Lerner, Daniel. 1958. *The Passing of Traditional Society*. New York: Free.
Lewis, Bernard. 2002. "What Went Wrong?" *Atlantic Monthly* (January). Available at http://www.theatlantic.com/magazine/archive/2002/01/what-went-wrong/302387/.
Lijphart, Arend. 1971. "Comparative Politics and the Comparative Method." *American Political Science Review* 65 (3): 682–93.
———. 1975. "The Comparable-Cases Strategy in Comparative Research." *Comparative Political Studies* 8 (2): 158–77.
———. 1999. *Patterns of Democracy: Government Forms and Performance in Thirty-Six Countries*. New Haven, CT: Yale University Press.
Lipset, Seymour Martin. 1994. "The Social Requisites of Democracy Revisited." *American Sociological Review* 59 (1): 1–22.
Lipset, Seymour Martin, and Stein Rokkan. 1967. *Party Systems and Voter Alignments: Cross-National Perspectives*. Toronto: Free Press.
Luebbert, Gregory M. 1987. "Social Foundations of Political Order in Interwar Europe." *World Politics* 39 (4): 449–78.
Lust, Ellen, Gamal Soltan, and Jakob Wichmann. 2012. "After the Arab Spring: Islamism, Secularism, and Democracy." *Current History*, December: 362–64.
Lust-Okar, Ellen. 2004. "Divided They Rule: The Management and Manipulation of Political Opposition." *Comparative Politics* 36 (2): 159–80.
Lynch, Marc. 2013. "Arab Uprisings: The Battle for Egypt's Constitution." POMEPS. http://pomeps.org/wp-content/uploads/2013/01/POMEPS_BriefBooklet17_Egypt_web.pdf.

Mady, Aboul Ela. 2005. *Raiyya al-Wasat fi al-Siyasiyya wa al-Majtama'*. [Al-Wassat Vision in Politics and Society.] Cairo: Maktaba al-Shorook al-Dawliyya.
———. 2008. "The Wasat Party and Egyptian Politics." Lecture delivered in Sophia University, Tokyo, Japan. February 23.
Maghraoui, Abdeslam M. 2002. "Democratization in the Arab World? Depoliticization in Morocco." *Journal of Democracy* 13 (4): 24–32.
Mahdavi, Saeid. 2004. "Shifts in the Composition of the Government Spending in Response to External Debt Burden." *World Development* 32 (7): 1139–57.
Manin, Bernard, Adam Przeworski, and Susan Stokes. 1999. "Elections and Representation." In *Democracy, Accountability, and Representation*, edited by Adam Przeworski, Susan C. Stokes, and Bernard Manin, 29–54. New York: Cambridge University Press.
March, Andrew. 2010. "Taking People as They Are: Islam as a "Realistic Utopia" in the Political Theory of Sayyid Qutb." *American Political Science Review* 104 (1): 189–207.
Mardin, Şerif. 1973. "Center-Periphery Relations: A Key to Turkish Politics?" *Daedalus* 102 (1): 169–90.
———. 1989. *Religion and Social Change in Modern Turkey: The Case of Bediuzzaman Said Nursi*. Albany: State University of New York Press.
———. 2006. *Religion, Society, and Modernity in Turkey*. Syracuse, NY: Syracuse University Press.
Mares, Isabela. 2005. "Social Protection around the World: External Insecurity, State Capacity, and Domestic Political Cleavages." *Comparative Political Studies* 38 (6): 623–51.
Masoud, Tarek. 2011. "Liberty, Democracy, and Discord in Egypt." *Washington Quarterly* 34 (4): 117–29.
———. 2014. *Counting Islam: Religion, Class, and Elections in Egypt*. New York: Cambridge University Press.
Maxfield, Sylvia. 1998. "Understanding the Political Implications of Financial Internationalization in Emerging Market Countries." *World Development* 26 (7): 1201–19.
McFaul, Michael, and Tamara Cofman Wittes. 2008. "The Limits of Limited Reforms." *Journal of Democracy* 19 (1): 19–33.
Meltzer, Allan H., and Scott F. Richard. 1981. "A Rational Theory of the Size of Government." *Journal of Political Economy* 89: 914–27.
Metawe, Mohamed. 2013. "How and Why the West Reacted to the Arab Spring: An Arab Perspective." *Insight Turkey* 15 (3): 141–55.
Meyersson, Erik. 2014. "Islamic Rule and the Empowerment of the Poor and Pious." *Econometrica* 82 (1): 229–69.
Milli Nizam Partisi [National Order Party]. 1970. *Party Program*. Ankara, n.p.
Milli Selamet Partisi [National Salvation Party]. 1972. *Party Program*. Ankara, n.p.
Milner, Helen, and Keiko Kubota. 2005. "Why the Move to Free Trade? Democracy and Trade Policy in the Developing Countries." *International Organization* 59 (1): 107–43.
Moore, Barrington. 1966. *Social Origins of Dictatorship and Democracy*. Boston: Beacon.
Morrison, Christian. 1991. *Adjustment and Equity in Morocco*. Paris: OECD Development Studies Center.

Moussalli, Ahmad S. 1993. "Hassan Al-Banna's Islamist Discourse on Constitutional Rule and Islamic State." *Journal of Islamic Studies* 4 (2): 161–74.
Moustafa, Tamir. 2007. *The Struggle for Constitutional Power: Law, Politics, and Economic Development in Egypt.* New York: Cambridge University Press.
Munson, Jr., Henry. 1993. *Religion and Power in Morocco.* New Haven, CT: Yale University Press.
Munson, Ziad. 2001. "Islamic Mobilization: Social Movement Theory and the Egyptian Muslim Brotherhood." *Sociological Quarterly* 42 (4): 487–510.
Muslim Brotherhood. 2005. *Electoral Program.* [English version as translated by the Muslim Brotherhood; available at ikhwanweb.com. Accessed November 6, 2008.]
———. 2007. *Barnamaj Hizb al-Ikhwan al-Muslimin, al-Isdar al-Awwal.* [Party Program of Muslim Brothers, First Draft.] N.p.
Nasr, Vali. 2005. "The Rise of Muslim Democracy." *Journal of Democracy* 16 (2): 13–27.
———. 2009. *The Rise of Islamic Capitalism: Why the New Middle Class Is the Key to Defeating Extremism.* New York: Free Press.
Norton, Augustus Richard. 2012. "Arab Revolts Upend Old Assumptions." *Current History* 111 (741): 14–18.
Oded, Haklai. 2009. "Authoritarianism and Islamic Movements in the Middle East: Research and Theory-Building in the Twenty-First Century." *International Studies Review* 11: 27–45.
OECD Observer. 2000. "Small and Medium-Sized Enterprises: Local Strength, Global Reach." *Policy Brief.* Available at http://www.oecd.org/cfe/leed/1918307.pdf.
Olson, Mancur. 1971. *The Logic of Collective Action: Public Goods and the Theory of Groups.* Cambridge, MA: Harvard University Press.
Öniş, Ziya. 2001. "Political Islam at the Crossroads: From Hegemony to Co-existence." *Contemporary Politics* 7 (4): 281–98.
———. 2006a. "The Political Economy of Turkey's Justice and Development Party." In *The Emergence of a New Turkey: Democracy and the AK Parti,* edited by Hakan Yavuz, 207–34. Salt Lake City: University of Utah Press.
———. 2006b. "Globalization and Party Transformation: Turkey's Justice and Development Party in Perspective." In *Globalising Democracy: Party Politics in Emerging Democracies,* edited by Peter Burnell. London: Routledge, Warwick Studies on Globalization.
Öniş, Ziya, and E. Fuat Keyman. 2003. "Turkey at the Polls: A New Path Emerges." *Journal of Democracy* 14 (2): 95–107.
Öniş, Ziya, and Umut Turem. 2001. "Business, Globalization and Democracy: A Comparative Analysis of Turkish Business Associations." *Turkish Studies* 2 (2): 94–120.
Ottaway, Marina. 2003. *Democracy Challenged: The Rise of Semi-Authoritarianism.* Washington, DC: Carnegie Endowment.
Özbudun, Ergun. 1996. "The Ottoman Legacy and the Middle East State Tradition." In *Imperial Legacy: The Ottoman Imprint on the Balkans and the Middle East,* edited by L. Carl Brown, 133–57. New York: Columbia University Press.
———. 2006. "From Political Islam to Conservative Democracy: The Case of the Justice and Development Party in Turkey." *South European Society and Politics* 11 (3–4): 543–57.

———. 2014. "AKP at the Crossroads: Erdoğan's Majoritarian Drift." *South European Society and Politics* 19 (2): 155–67.
Özbudun, Ergun, and Fuat Keyman. 2002. "Cultural Globalization in Turkey." In *Many Globalizations: Cultural Diversity in the Contemporary World*, edited by Peter L. Berger and Samuel Huntington, 296–320. New York: Oxford University Press.
Ozcan, Gul Berna, and Hasan Turunc. 2011. "Economic Liberalization and Class Dynamics in Turkey: New Business Groups and Islamic Mobilization." *Insight Turkey* 13 (3): 63–86.
Özel, Soli. 2003. "After Tsunami." *Journal of Democracy* 14 (2): 80–94.
Ozzano, Luca. 2013. "The Many Faces of the Political God: A Typology of Religiously Oriented Parties." *Democratization* 20 (5): 807–30.
Pamuk, Sevket. 1981. "Political Economy of Industrialization in Turkey." *MERIP Reports* 93: 26–32.
Pant, Manoj, and Manoranjan Pattanayak. 2005. "Does Openness Promote Competition? A Case Study of Indian Manufacturing." *Economic and Political Weekly* 40 (39): 4226–231.
Party for Justice and Development. 2002. *Al-Barnamaj al-Intikhabi: Nahwa Maghrib Afdal*. [Electoral Program: Toward a Better Morocco.] Rabat.
———. 2007. *Al-Barnamaj al-Intikhabi: Jamian Nabni al-Maghrib al-'Adala*. [Electoral Program: Together to Build a Just Morocco.] Rabat.
Pecastaing, Camille. 2012. "The Many Faces of Islamist Politicking." *Policy Review* (173): 45.
Perekli, Feriha. 2012. "The Applicability of the 'Turkish Model' to Morocco: The Case of the Parti de La Justice et Du Developpement (PJD)." *Insight Turkey* 14 (3): 85–108.
Pfeifer, Karen. 1996. "Between Rocks and Hard Choices: International Finance and Economic Adjustment in North Africa." In *North Africa: Development and Reform in a Changing Global Economy*, edited by Dirk Vandewalle. New York: St. Martin's.
Phillips, James. 2012. "The Arab Spring Descends into Islamist Winter: Implications for U.S. Policy." The Heritage Foundation. Available here http://www.heritage.org/research/reports/2012/12/the-arab-spring-descends-into-islamist-winter-implications-for-us-policy.
Pioppi, Daniela. 2013. "Playing with Fire: The Muslim Brotherhood and the Egyptian Leviathan." *International Spectator* 48 (4): 51–68.
Pritchett, Lant, and Geeta Sethi. 1994. "Tariff Rates, Tariff Revenue, and Tariff Reform: Some New Facts." *World Bank Economic Review* 8 (1): 1–16.
Przeworski, Adam. 1991. *Democracy and the Market: Political and Economic Reforms in Eastern Europe and Latin America*. New York: Cambridge University Press.
Przeworski, Adam, and Henry Teune. 1970. *The Logic of Comparative Social Inquiry*. New York: Wiley-Interscience.
Putnam, Robert D. 1988. "Diplomacy and Domestic Politics: The Logic of Two-Level Games." *International Organization* 42 (3): 427–60.
Qutb, Sayyid. 2007. *Milestones*. Dar al-Ilm.
Randall, Vicky. 2001. "Party Systems and Voter Alignments in the New Democracies of the Third World." In *Party Systems and Voter Alignment Revisited*, edited by Lauri Karvonen and Stein Kuhnle, 10–23. New York: Routledge.

Rethink Institute. 2015. "Turkey's 2015 Election Prospects." *Rethink Paper*, no 23 (April).
Reuveny, Rafael, and Quan Li. 2003. "Economic Openness, Democracy, and Income Inequality." *Comparative Political Studies* 36 (5): 575–601.
Richards, Alan, and John Waterbury. 1996. *A Political Economy of the Middle East*. 2nd ed. Boulder, CO: Westview.
Rivlin, Paul. 1985. *Dynamics of Economic Policy Making in Egypt*. New York: Praeger.
———. 2001. *Economic Policy and Performance in the Arab World*. Boulder, CO: Lynne Rienner.
———. 2009. *Arab Economies in the Twenty-First Century*. New York: Cambridge University Press.
Rodrik, Dani. 1990. "Premature Liberalization, Incomplete Stabilization: The Ozal Decade in Turkey." *CEPR Discussion Papers* 402.
———. 1997. *Has Globalization Gone Too Far?* Washington, DC: Institute for International Economics.
———. 1998. "Why Do More Open Economies Have Bigger Governments?" *Journal of Political Economy* 106 (5): 997–1032.
Roe, Alan. 1999. "The Egyptian Banking System: Liberalization, Competition and Privatization." In *Financial Development in Emerging Markets: The Egyptian Experience*, edited by M. El-Erian and M. Mohieldin. Cairo: Egyptian Center for Economic Studies.
Roy, Olivier. 1994. *Failure of Political Islam*. Cambridge, MA: Harvard University Press.
———. 2012. "The Transformation of the Arab World." *Journal of Democracy* 23 (3): 5–18.
Rudra, Nita. 2002. "Globalization and the Decline of the Welfare State in Less Developed Countries." *International Organization* 56 (2): 411–45.
———. 2005. "Globalization and Strengthening of Democracy in the Developing World." American *Journal of Political Science* 49 (4): 704–30.
———. 2008. *Globalization and the Race to the Bottom in Developing Countries: Who Really Gets Hurt?* Cambridge: Cambridge University Press.
Rueschemeyer, Dietrich, Evelyne Huber Stephens, and John D. Stephens. 1992. *Capitalist Development and Democracy*. Chicago: University of Chicago Press.
Rutherford, Thomas, E. E. Rutstrom, and David Tarr. 1993. "Morocco's Free Trade Agreement with the European Community." *World Bank Policy Research Paper* WPS 1173.
Salame, Ghassan. 1994. *Democracy Without Democrats? The Renewal of Politics in the Muslim World*. New York: I. B. Tauris.
Sarıbay, Ali Yaşar. 1985. *Türkiye'de Modernleşme, Din ve Parti Politikası: Milli Selamet Partisi Örnek Olayı*. [Modernization, Religion and Party Politics In Turkey: The Case Study of National Salvation Party.] Istanbul: Alan Yayıncılık.
Schmitter, Philippe. 1992. "The Consolidation of Democracy and Representation of Social Groups." *American Behavioral Scientist* 35 (4–5): 422–49.
Schneider, Ben Ross. 2004a. "Organizing Interests and Coalitions in the Politics of Market Reform in Latin America." *World Politics* 56 (3): 456–79.
———. 2004b. *Business Politics and the State in Twentieth-Century Latin America*. New York: Cambridge University Press.
Schwedler, Jillian. 1998. "A Paradox of Democracy? Islamist Participation in Elections." *Middle East Report* 209 (Winter): 25–29.

---. 2006. *Faith in Moderation: Islamist Parties in Jordan and Yemen.* New York: Cambridge University Press.

Scott, Rachel M. 2012. "What Might the Muslim Brotherhood Do with Al-Azhar? Religious Authority in Egypt." *Die Welt Des Islams* 52 (2): 131–65.

Şen, Serdar. 1995. *Refah Partisi'nin Teori ve Pratiği: Refah Partisi, Adil Düzen ve Kapitalizm.* [The Theory and Practice of the Welfare Party: Just Order and Capitalism.] Istanbul: Sarmal.

---. 2004. *AKP Milli Görüşçü mü? Parti Programlarında Milli Görüş.* [Is AKP National Outlook Movementist? National Outlook in Party Programs.] Istanbul: Net Books.

Senses, Fikret. 1991. "Turkey's Stabilization and Structural Adjustment Program in Retrospect and Prospect." *Developing Economies* 29 (3): 210–34.

Shadid, Anthony. 2001. *Legacy of the Prophet: Despots, Democrats, and the New Politics of Islam.* Boulder, CO: Westview.

Shadlen, Kenneth. 1999. *Small Industry in Postwar Latin America: Economic Internationalization and the Institutional Bases of Business Activism in Argentina, Brazil and Mexico.* Storrs: Center for Latin American and Caribbean Studies, University of Connecticut.

---. 2002. "Orphaned by Democracy: Small Industry in Mexico." *Comparative Politics* 35 (1): 43–62.

Shahin, Emad Eldin. 1997. *Political Ascent: Contemporary Islamic Movements in North Africa.* Boulder, CO: Westview.

Shehata, Samer, and Joshua Stacher. 2006. "The Brotherhood Goes to Parliament." *Middle East Report* 36 (240): 32–37.

Simms, Rupe. 2002. "'Islam Is Our Politics': A Gramscian Analysis of the Muslim Brotherhood (1928–1953)." *Social Compass* 49 (4): 563–82.

Snowden, P. N. 1996. "Financial Reform in Turkey Since 1980: Liberalization without Stabilization." In *The Economy of Turkey Since Liberalization*, edited by S. Togan and V. N. Balasubramanyam. New York: St. Martin's.

Sokhey, Sarah and A. Kadir Yildirim. 2012. "Economic Liberalization and Political Moderation: The Case of Anti-System Parties." *Party Politics* 19(2): 230–55.

Soliman, Samer. 2011. *The Autumn of Dictatorship: Fiscal Crisis and Political Change in Egypt Under Mubarak.* Stanford, CA: Stanford University Press.

Somer, Murat. 2007. "Moderate Islam and Secularist Opposition in Turkey: Implications for the World, Muslims and Secular Democracy." *Third World Quarterly* 28 (7): 1271–89.

Somer, Murat, and Glupker-Kesebir. 2015. "Is Islam the Solution? Comparing Turkish Islamic and Secular Thinking toward Ethnic and Religious Minorities." *Journal of Church and State*, 1–27.

Sonmez, Mustafa. 1988. *Kirk Haramiler: Turkiye'de Holdingler.* [Forty Thieves: Holdings in Turkey.] Istanbul: Ozlem.

Spiegel, Avi. 2015. "Succeeding by Surviving: Examining the Durability of Political Islam in Morocco." Brookings Institution.

Stacher, Joshua A. 2002. "Post-Islamist Rumblings in Egypt: The Emergence of the Wasat Party." *Middle East Journal* 56 (3): 415–32.

Stepan, Alfred. 1990. "On the Tasks of a Democratic Opposition." *Journal of Democracy* 1 (2): 41–49.

Stevens, Paul. 1993. "The Practical Record and Prospects of Privatization Programmes in the Arab World." In *Economic and Political Liberalization in the Middle East*, edited by Tim Niblock and Emma Murphy. London: British Academic Press.

Stiglitz, Joseph. 1998. "More Instruments and Broader Goals: Moving toward the Post-Washington Consensus." The 1998 WIDER Annual Lecture (Helsinki, Finland). http://time.dufe.edu.cn/wencong/washingtonconsensus/instrumentsbroadergoals.pdf. Accessed February 20, 2009.

Strom, Kaare. 1990. "A Behavioral Theory of Competitive Political Parties." *American Journal of Political Science* 34 (2): 565–98.

Sullivan, Denis J. 1997. "State and Civil Society in Conflict in Egypt." *Middle East Affairs* 3 (1–2): 67–86.

Tadros, Samuel. 2015. "The Brotherhood Divided." Hudson Institute. http://www.hudson.org/research/11530-the-brotherhood-divided.

Takayuki, Yokota. 2007. "Democratization and Islamic Politics: A Study on the Wasat Party in Egypt." *Kyoto Bulletin of Islamic Area Studies* 1–2: 148–64.

Taş, Hakkı. 2015. "Turkey—from Tutelary to Delegative Democracy." *Third World Quarterly* 36 (4): 776–91.

Taşkin, Fatma, and A. Erinç Yeldan. 1996. "Export Expansion, Capital Accumulation and Distribution in Turkish Manufacturing, 1980–9." In *The Economy of Turkey since Liberalization*, edited by S. Togan and V. N. Balasubramanyam. New York: St. Martin's.

Tekeli, Ilhan, and Rasit Gokceli. 1977. *1973 ve 1975 Secimlerinde Secim Cografyasi Uzerine Bir Deneme*. [An Essay on Electoral Geography in 1973 and 1975 Elections.] Istanbul: Milliyet.

Tekeli, Ilhan, and Selim Ilkin. 1982. *Uygulamaya Geçerken Türkiye'de Devletçiliğin Oluşumu*. [The Formation of Statism on the Road to Practice in Turkey.] Ankara: ODTÜ İdari İlimler Fakültesi.

Tesche, Jean, and Sahar Tohamy. 1994. "Economic Liberalization and Privatization in Hungary and Egypt." *Economic Research Forum Working Paper*, no. 9410.

Tessler, Mark. 1982. "Morocco: Institutional Pluralism and Monarchical Dominance." In *Political Elites in Arab North Africa: Morocco, Algeria, Tunisia, Libya, and Egypt*, edited by William Zartman. New York: Longman.

Togan, S. 1996. "Trade Liberalization and Competitive Structure in Turkey during the 1980s." In *The Economy of Turkey since Liberalization*, edited by S. Togan and V. N. Balasubramanyam. New York: St. Martin's.

Toprak, Zafer. 1982. *Turkiye'de "Milli Iktisat" (1908–1918)*. ["National Economy" in Turkey (1908–1918).] Ankara: Yurt.

Uluslararasi Seffaflik Dernegi. 2015. "Turkiye'de Yolsuzluk: Neden, Nasil, Nerede?"

Unver, H. Akin. 2009. "Turkey's 'Deep-State' and the Ergenekon Conundrum." Middle East Institute. http://www.mei.edu/content/turkeys-deep-state-and-ergenekon-conundrum.

US Department of State. 2009. *Human Rights Report: Turkey*. Available at http://www.state.gov/g/drl/rls/hrrpt/2009/eur/136062.htm.

US Department of State. 2010. Report on International Religious Freedom. Available at http://www.state.gov/j/drl/rls/irf/2010/.

Uthmani, Saad Eddin. 2005. Interview. *Arab Reform Bulletin* 3 (10).
Virtue Party. 1999. *Party Program*. Ankara, n.p.
Walsh, John. 2003. "Egypt's Muslim Brotherhood: Understanding Centrist Islam." *Harvard International Review* 24 (4): 32–36.
Wasat Party. 2004. *Political Program* (3rd Version). Heliopolis, Cairo: Al-Azzazy.
Waterbury, John. 1970. *The Commander of the Faithful: The Moroccan Political Elite*. New York: Columbia University Press.
———. 1991. "Twilight of the State Bourgeoisie?" *International Journal of Middle East Studies* 23 (1): 1–17.
———. 1992. "Export-Led Growth and the Center-Right Coalition in Turkey." *Comparative Politics* 24 (2): 127–45.
———. 1993. *Exposed to Innumerable Delusions: Public Enterprise and State Power in Egypt, India, Mexico, and Turkey*. New York: Cambridge University Press.
Wegner, Eva. 2011. *Islamist Opposition in Authoritarian Regimes: The Party of Justice and Development in Morocco*. Syracuse, NY: Syracuse University Press.
Wegner, Eva, and Miquel Pellicer. 2009. "Islamist Moderation without Democratization: The Coming of Age of the Moroccan Party of Justice and Development." *Democratization* 16 (1): 157–75.
Welfare Party. 1983. *Party Program*. Ankara, n.p.
White, Gregory. 1996. "The Mexico of Europe? Morocco's Partnership with the European Union." In *North Africa: Development and Reform in a Changing Global Economy*, edited by Dirk Vandewalle. New York: St. Martin's.
———. 2001. *A Comparative Political Economy of Tunisia and Morocco: On the Outside of Europe Looking In*. Albany: State University of New York Press.
White, Jenny. 2003. *Islamist Mobilization in Turkey: A Study in Vernacular Politics*. Seattle: University of Washington Press.
Wibbels, Erik. 2006. "Dependency Revisited: International Markets, Business Cycles, Social Spending in the Developing World." *International Organization* 60 (2): 433–68.
Wickham, Carrie Rosefsky. 2002. *Mobilizing Islam: Religion, Activism, and Political Change in Egypt*. New York: Columbia University Press.
———. 2004. "The Path to Moderation: Strategy and Learning in the Formation of Egypt's Wasat Party." *Comparative Politics* 36 (2): 205–28.
Willis, Michael J. 2004. "Morocco's Islamists and the Legislative Elections of 2002: The Strange Case of the Party That Did Not Want to Win." *Mediterranean Politics* 9 (1): 53–81.
Yakis, Yasar. 2002. "Ak Parti'nin Kimligi." [The Identity of the JDP.] Unpublished intraparty document.
Yassine, Abdeslam. 1971. *Al-Islam Bayna al-Dawa wa al-Dawla*. [Islam between Dawa and State.] Casablanca.
———. 1973. *Al-Islam Ghadan*. [Islam Tomorrow.] Casablanca: Matbaat al-Najah.
Yassine, Nadia. 2006. *Full Sails Ahead*. New Britain, PA: Justice and Spirituality.
Yavuz, Hakan. 2003. *Islamic Political Identity in Turkey*. New York: Oxford University Press.
———, ed. 2006. *The Emergence of a New Turkey: Democracy and the AK Parti*. Salt Lake City: University of Utah Press.

———. 2009. *Secularism and Muslim Democracy in Turkey.* New York: Cambridge University Press.
Yeldan, Erinc, Kivilcim Metin-Ozcan, and Ebru Voyvoda. 2000. "On the Patterns of Trade Liberalization, Oligopolistic Concentration and Profitability: Reflections from Post-1980 Turkish Manufacturing." Paper presented at the Annual Conference of the Economic Research FORUM, Amman.
Yildirim, A. Kadir. 2013. "New Democrats: Religious Actors, Social Change and Democratic Consolidation in Turkey." *Contemporary Islam* 7(3): 311–31.
———. 2015a. "Turkiye Demokrasi Denetim On Raporu." Available at http://demokrasidenetcileri.org/wp-content/uploads/2015/05/Türkiye-Demokrasi-Denetim-Ön-Raporu_2015.pdf.
———. 2015b. "Globalization, Political Islam, and Moderation: The Case of Muslim Democratic Parties." *Sociology of Islam* 3(1–2): 76–106.
Yokota, Takayuki. 2007. "Democratization and Islamic Politics: A Study on the Wasat Party in Egypt." *Kyoto Bulletin of Islamic Area Studies* 1-2: 148–64.
Yousef, Tarik M. 2004. "Development, Growth and Policy Reform in the Middle East and North Africa since 1950." *Journal of Economic Perspectives* 18 (3): 91–116.
Zakaria, Fareed. 2004. "Islam, Democracy, and Constitutional Liberalism." *Political Science Quarterly* 119 (1): 1–20.
Zeghal, Malika. 2008. *Islamism in Morocco: Religion, Authoritarianism, and Electoral Politics.* Princeton, NJ: Marcus Wiener.
Zielinski, Jacub. 2002. "Translating Social Cleavages into Party Systems: The Significance of New Democracies." *World Politics* 54 (2): 184–211.
Zubaida, Sami. 1992. "Islam, the State and Democracy: Contrasting Conceptions of Society in Egypt." *Middle East Report* 22 (179) 2–10.
———. 2000. "Trajectories of Political Islam: Egypt, Iran and Turkey." *Political Quarterly* 71 (1): 60–78.

Index

Page numbers in italics refer to figures and tables.

adil duzen. *See* "just order"
al-Adl wal-Ihsan (AWI), 18, 183, 193–98, 206–7, 209–10, 213–15, 225–28
AKP. *See* Justice and Development Party (Adalet ve Kalkinma Partisi)
Alevis, 99–101
AMITH. *See* Textile and Apparel Manufacturers' Association
Anatolia, 54, 77, 80, 84, 112, 114
antisystemic: discourse, 10, 26, 35–36, 232; parties, 3, 142, 197
anti-Westernism, 80
Arab socialism, 56–57, 63, 66, 130–32
Arab Spring, 139, 164, 173–77, 203, 227–33
Arinc, Bulent, 86, 244n33
Armenians, 99, 101, 103
al-Aryan, Issam, 134, 139, 141, 143, 145, 149, 151
Ataturk, Mustafa Kemal, 23, 24, 74–76, 90, 92, 102, 131, 193
austerity measures, 58–59, 67
authoritarian regimes and authoritarianism, 3, 13, 16, 32, 69, 120–21, 123, 125–26, 150, 231–32
al-Azhar University, 178, 193

balance of payments crisis, 31, 52, 58, 67
big business, 25–27, 29–31, 34; in Egypt, 15, 17, 47, 62, 65–66, 128–32, 138, 156, 158–78; in Morocco, 48, 69, 213, 222, 224; performance, 36–38; in Turkey, 53–56, 77–84, 96, 110, 114
Bourguiba, Habib, 23
business associations, 33–34, 54, 96, 129, 192. *See also* Egyptian Businessmen's Association; Independent Industrialists' and Businessmen's Association; Moroccan Confederation of Businesses; Textile and Apparel Manufacturers' Association; Turkish Industrialists' and Businessmen's Association
business concentration, 10, 29, 41

cemevis, 100
CGEM. *See* Moroccan Confederation of Businesses (Confederation Generale des Entreprises Du Maroc)
CHP. *See* Republican People's Party (Cumhuriyet Halk Partisi)
Christian democratic parties, 1–2, 4–5, 88, 146–47, 208
civil political party, 144, 254n28
civil society, 55, 82, 93, 157, 195, 213
CMPE. *See* Moroccan Export Promotion Center
competitive liberalization, 3, 12, 15–16, 20–21, 29–33, 36, 38–39, 41–42, 47, 50–51, 71, 118, 230
concentration, 47–48, 50, 212
conservative democratic party. *See* Muslim democratic party
Copenhagen Criteria, 102, 103
Coptic Christians, 145, 180
crony liberalization, 3, 10, 12, 15–17, 20–21, 29–32, 34, 36–39, 41, 47, 50–51, 71, 128, 173, 230
cross-class coalition, 3, 29, 36, 233
current account, 37, 58
current account deficit, 52, 67

dawa, 133, 141, 146, 199–201, 205–6
Demirel, Suleyman, 52
democratization, 13, 85, 233
Democrat Party (DP), 76, 78
Demokratik Toplum Partisi (DTP), 104
deregulation, 60
devlet baba, 75

early republican period, 74–82
Economic Reform and Structural Adjustment Program (Egypt) (ERSAP), 58, 63
economic risk, 10–11, 32–34, 76
effective protection. *See* globalization
Egyptian Businessmen's Association (EBA), 14–15
Egyptian independence, 17, 128, 139
Egyptian revolution, 172–81, 232. *See also* Arab Spring

275

electoral support, 9, 11, 27, 39, 87, 176, 226
embedded autonomy, 26
Employment, 34, 50, 63, 70, 87, 94, 109, 131
Ennahda, 8
Erbakan, Necmettin, 77–81, 86, 110–11, 243n10
Erdogan, Recep Tayyip, 86, 90, 101, 121–23, 125–27, 232
Ergenekon process, 124
etatisme. *See* statism
European Community (EC). *See* European Union
European Economic Community (EEC). *See* European Union
European Union (EU): customs union with, 56, 111–12; free trade agreement with, 70, 211, 219; integration into, 46, 50; membership, 56, 80, 87, 93, 99–104, 120, 126
export-led economy, 52
export-oriented strategy, 37, 67, 155, 219
exports, 42, 44–46, 51–53, 68, 81, 85, 109, 112–14, 164, 190–91, 221–23

Fassi: Hassan II and, 190–91; origins, 184–85; relationship to political elite, 186–89, 224
FDI. *See* foreign investment: direct
February 28. *See* military coup: of Turkey
Felicity Party (Saadet Partisi, FP), 11–13, 17, 87, 110–12, 117, 120
financial liberalization, 54, 112
First Gulf War, 58, 68, 198
foreign debt, 58, 65, 67, 190
foreign investment: direct, 61–62, 85, 97, 107, 108, 171; encouragement of, 30, 57–58, 60, 67, 161, 217
free capital movement, 52, 113
Freedom and Justice Party (FJP), 174–75, 179–82
free market economy, 4, 5, 16, 26, 28, 34, 53, 99, 110, 132, 155, 157, 162, 170, 213
Free Officers, 129–30
free trade agreements (FTAs), 46, 71, 116, 153, 211, 219, 224

General Agreement on Tariffs and Trade (GATT), 67
Gezi Park protests, 121, 124
global integration. *See* globalization
globalization, 9, 21, 46, 83, 156, 210, 220, 230
graft allegations, 121–22
Great Depression, 75
green capital, 84

gross domestic product (GDP), 44, 58, 61, 212; ratio of debt to, 66–67, 190; trade as percentage of, 27, 42
Gul, Abdullah, 86, 245n61
Gulen Movement, 121, 246n72

headscarf legislation, 74, 90, 95, 97, 243n28
Imam Hatip schools, 79, 91–92, 99, 104
Import Substitution Industrialization (ISI), 51–54, 66–67, 78, 187, 190
inclusion-moderation hypothesis, 6–7, 180–81
Independent Industrialists' and Businessmen's Association (MUSIAD), 14, 82–86, 96, 192
individual liberties, 4, 6, 17, 89, 92, 98, 103, 120, 152, 207–10
industrialization, 80, 114, 118, 129, 132, 188. *See also* Import Substitution Industrialization
Industrial Revolution, 22
infitah, 17, 56, 58, 128, 131–32, 135, 154, 166
inflation rate, 54, 56, 116
Inonu, Ismet, 75
instability, 33, 52, 95–98, 124, 170
Interest representation, 23
International Monetary Fund (IMF), 52–54, 58, 65, 67
Islam: and democracy, 2, 159–62, 209; as identity, 25, 92; role of, 4, 6, 15, 21, 33, 35, 79, 88–90, 95, 130, 140, 144–48, 159, 178, 201, 204–7, 215–17, 230; as a solution, 134, 149; speaking on behalf of, 26, 193
Islamic civilization, 145–46
Islamic constituency, 3, 8–10, 12, 15, 24, 71, 78, 166, 181–82, 226, 230–32. *See also* peripheral groups
Islamic state, 4, 35, 126, 134, 145, 148, 152, 178, 198, 231
Islamic values, 17, 33, 36, 120, 146, 202–3, 208, 210, 216–17. *See also* Muslim values
Islamic Youth Association, 198–99
Islamism, 6, 137, 140, 173, 229
Islamization, 5, 6, 7, 26, 37, 79, 83, 88–89, 91, 95, 148, 180, 201
Istiqlal Party, 26, 200, 226–27

Justice and Charity. *See* al-Adl wal-Ihsan (AWI)
Justice and Development Party (Adalet ve Kalkinma Partisi, AKP): banning case, 95–97; ideology, 17, 88–90, 101, 146; origins, 85–86; policy positions, 102–4, 108–12, 117–18;

success of, 1, 10, 16, 87, 121–24; support base, 73
"just order," 80

Kalyvas, Stathis, 1, 4
Kemalists, 74, 76, 77, 121, 124
al-Khatib, Abdelkarim, 200
King Farouk, 129–30
King Hassan II, 67, 165, 185–90, 193–96, 200, 213–14
Kurdish issue, 99–102, 126–27
Kurds, 99–101, 104, 124

laicite. *See* secularism
landed elite, 22, 57, 129–30, 132, 188
land redistribution, 57
level of competition, 29, 31, 41, 46, 49, 190, 219
liberal market economy. *See* free market economy
Lipset, Martin and Stein Rokkan, 8, 22

makhzen, 69, 184, 186, 226, 252n1
manufacturing exports, 44–46, 51
Mardin, Serif, 25, 74, 76–77
masses. *See* peripheral groups
merchandise exports, 44–46
middle class, 8, 9, 117, 134, 135, 139, 156, 188, 203, 215, 218
military, 24, 52, 54–56, 58, 74, 84, 87, 95, 102, 121, 129, 131, 174–76, 189. *See also* military coup
military coup: of Turkey, 52–55, 84, 96; of Egypt, 152, 174, 177, 181
minorities, 98–99, 101–2, 120, 145. *See also* Alevis; Armenians; Coptic Christians; Kurdish issue; Kurds
minority rights, 6, 98, 152, 210
modernization, 23–25, 76, 92, 94, 121, 170, 185–86, 189, 214, 221
Mohammad V, 184–86
Mohammad VI, 194, 196
monopolization, state, 29–30, 36, 62–63, 163; antimonopoly policies, 46, 49–50, 109–10, 154
Moore, Barrington, 8, 21
Moroccan Confederation of Businesses (Confederation Generale des Entreprises Du Maroc, CGEM), 14, 15, 69, 222
Moroccan Export Promotion Center (CMPE), 67, 191
Moroccanization, 188
Moroccanization Law, 190
Morsi, Mohamad, 175–76, 179–80, 231

most similar systems design, 11
Movement for Reform and Renewal (Hizb al-Tajdid al-Watani), 200–201
Movement of Unity and Reform (Harakat al-Tawhid wal-Islah), 193, 201
Mouvement Populaire Democratique et Constitutionnel (Constitutional and Democratic Popular Movement, MPDC), 200–201
MSP. *See* National Salvation Party (Milli Selamet Partisi)
Mubarak, Hosni, 2, 58, 129, 134, 136–39, 163, 165, 174–77
MUSIAD. *See* Independent Industrialists' and Businessmen's Association
Muslim Brotherhood (Ikkwan al-Muslimin, MB): ideology, 141, 151–56, 158, 176–77, 179–80; members, 142; programs, 137, 140; success, 139, 174; support base, 133–36, 172–73; and Wasat Party, 144–49
Muslim democratic party (MDP): definition of, 1, 4–6; preferences of, 38–39, 147–48, 158, 207, 216; socioeconomic theory of, 10–11, 15–19, 30–36; success of, 12, 42, 183, 198, 218, 230
Muslim reformist party. *See* Muslim democratic party
Muslim values, 6, 84, 89, 92, 215. *See also* Islamic values

Nasr, Vali, 1, 3, 4, 8
Nasser, Gamal Abdel, 23, 24, 56–57, 129–33, 135, 137, 141, 177
National Democratic Party (NDP), 137, 138, 155
nationalism and nationalist discourse, 6, 17, 26, 36, 39, 80, 100, 110–11, 120, 155, 184–85, 189
nationalization, 57, 60–61, 130–31, 167
National Outlook Movement (Milli Gorus Hareketi, NOM), 14, 73, 75
National Revolution, 22
National Salvation Party (Milli Selamet Partisi, MSP), 79
Nazif, Ahmed, 60–61, 164, 168, 170
al-Nour Party, 128, 175, 176–77

October Paper, 56–57
Omnium Nord Africain (ONA), 69, 187
one man, one vote, one time, 2, 231
1991 Invasion of Kuwait. *See* First Gulf War
open door policy. *See* infitah
Ottoman Empire, 23, 25, 73, 74, 125
Ozal, Turgut, 16, 52–54, 112, 114, 118, 165

parallel state. *See* Gulen Movement
partial reform equilibrium model, 28
Party for Justice and Development (Hizb al-Adalah wa Tanmiyya, PJD), 1, 6, 10, 11, 18, 183, 193, 196–98, 200–217, 225–29
patronage and patronage networks, 69, 82, 109, 185–86
patron-client relationship, 75. *See also* patronage and patronage networks
People's Assembly (Egyptian parliament), 134, 138–39, 152, 155, 173
Peoples' Democratic Party (HDP), 124
peripheral groups: businesses, 86, 112, 114–15, 166; economic preferences of, 29, 32–33, 80, 82, 162–64, 168; political preferences of, 16–17, 87, 92–96, 104, 154–56, 159, 217. *See also* small and medium enterprises
polarization, 3, 17, 33, 89, 97–98, 180
political Islam, 2, 4, 17, 35, 77–82, 88–89, 120, 128–29, 133–34, 137, 160–61, 183, 192, 201, 217
political stability, 9–10, 33, 85, 95, 106, 113, 217
populism, 77, 81
postliberalization, 15, 17, 30–31, 38, 69, 82, 98, 111, 114, 187
preliberalization, 3, 10, 15, 20, 28–29, 32, 34, 36, 38, 42, 73–74, 114, 159, 219
privatization, 16–17, 27, 29–31, 41, 50, 58–61, 63, 67–68, 71, 96, 108–10, 115, 118, 128, 154–55, 162, 166–68, 220
property rights, 31, 33, 57
protectionism, 5, 17, 26, 39, 71, 76, 110–11, 120, 155, 191
proto-cleavage, 24

Qutb, Sayyid, 140, 181, 198–99

radicalization, 7
redistribution, 57
religiously oriented party, 6, 125
renationalization, 60–61
Republican People's Party (Cumhuriyet Halk Partisi, CHP), 26, 74–76, 78, 87, 91, 97–98, 104, 124
rule of law, 17, 31, 33, 74, 107–8, 115, 120, 159, 218, 221

Sadat, Anwar, 56, 58, 129, 131–33, 135, 137, 163, 165, 231
Salafis, 128, 175–82, 231–32
secular center, 17, 73, 74, 82, 85, 94, 128, 204. *See also* social cleavages

secular ideologies, 24, 78, 132
secularism, 21, 24–25, 27, 82, 88–95, 97–98, 104, 216
secularism-religion divide. *See* social cleavages
semicompetitive liberalization, 12, 16, 18, 41, 50–51, 71, 183, 210
sharia, 89, 91, 134, 146, 148, 150–51, 177–80, 199, 204, 206–7
al-Sisi, Abdel Fattah, 176, 177, 181
six arrows, 75–76
Six-Day War, 131–32
small and medium businesses. *See* small and medium enterprises
small and medium enterprises (SMEs): owners, 53, 86, 191–92, 203; preferences of, 4, 17, 21, 32–35, 74, 83, 92–93, 105–6, 114–15, 216–17
social classes, 76, 110, 132
social cleavages, 3–4, 11, 15, 20, 21–29, 38, 73, 76–77, 82, 89, 128, 162, 188, 230–31
social conflict. *See* social cleavages
social Islam, 35, 96, 120
social learning, 8
social policies, 4–5, 27, 76, 118, 158
social protection, 5, 17, 55, 64–66, 69, 109, 117–18, 157–58. *See also* social policies
societal support, 3, 11–12, 18, 39, 138, 183, 192, 198, 227
Stabilization and Structural Adjustment Program, 52
state autonomy, 23, 26
state-business relationship, 10, 28, 30, 32, 38, 220
state-owned enterprises (SOEs), 59–60, 62–63, 75–76, 81, 109, 118, 168
state-society relations, 23, 25, 74, 126
state strategy, 6–7, 60, 232–33
statism, 28, 38, 59, 62, 75–78, 81, 98, 100, 104, 109, 118
structural adjustment, 17, 52, 67
Supreme Constitutional Court, 138, 178
Supreme Council of the Armed Forces (SCAF), 174–75

tariffs: rates and levels, 63–64, 77, 81, 153, 186; weighted, 46, 53, 56
technocracy, 60, 132
Textile and Apparel Manufacturers' Association (AMITH), 14, 15, 210, 222–23

trade liberalization, 16, 17, 37, 41, 53, 67, 69, 128, 191
transparency, 31, 145, 167, 207, 230
Turkish Industrialists and Businessmen's Association (TUSIAD), 55, 77, 81–85
Turkish lira, 54

uncertainty, 33, 74, 95–96, 106, 120, 178, 180, 203, 210
unemployment, 118, 132, 136, 157–58, 179, 189, 191, 214
Union of Chambers and Commodity Exchanges of Turkey (TOBB), 79, 81

vested interest, 9, 31–32, 231
violence, 5, 7, 127, 181
Virtue Party (VP), 85–87, 110–11, 117

Wafd Party, 129, 133–34
War of Independence (Turkey), 74
Wasat Party (Hizb al-Wasat, WP): ideology, 148–49; origins, 141–44; policy positions, 152–58; success, 181; support base, 172–73
Welfare Party (WP), 7, 84, 87, 110–11
Western Sahara, 189
White Turks, 88
Wickham, Carrie, 1, 6–8, 131–36, 142–43, 172
World Bank, 52–53, 58, 67
World Economic Forum, 49, 153

Yassine, Abdeslam, 193–94, 196, 206, 209, 215
Yassine, Nadia, 194–96, 206–7, 209, 214–15, 225

zakat and sadaqat, 157–58

A.KADIR YILDIRIM is a research scholar at Rice University's Baker Institute for Public Policy.

www.ingramcontent.com/pod-product-compliance
Lightning Source LLC
Chambersburg PA
CBHW030337240426
43661CB00052B/1659